Brian Ó Cianaigh
Ceannródaí Ildánach Gaeilge as Ard an Rátha
Beathaisnéis agus Rogha Saothair

Tá an leabhar seo á thoirbhirt do Brendan O'Keeney,
na Cealla Beaga

Séamus Ó Cinnéide
Nollaig Mac Congáil
eagarthóirí

Brian Ó Cianaigh
Ceannródaí Ildánach Gaeilge as Ard an Rátha
Beathaisnéis agus Rogha Saothair

Brian Ó Cianaigh
Ceannródaí Ildánach Gaeilge as Ard an Rátha
Beathaisnéis agus Rogha Saothair

Foilsithe in 2021 ag
ARLEN HOUSE
42 Grange Abbey Road
Baldoyle, D13 A0F3
Éire
Fón: 00 353 86 8360236
Ríomhphost: arlenhouse@gmail.com

978–1–85132–266–4, bog

Dáileoirí idirnáisiúnta
SYRACUSE UNIVERSITY PRESS
621 Skytop Road, Suite 110
Syracuse
New York 13244–5290
Fón: 315–443–5534
Ríomhphost: supress@syr.edu

Clóchur ¦ Arlen House

Grianghraif an chlúdaigh: Séamus Ó Cinnéide

Tá Arlen House buíoch de
Chlár na Leabhar Gaeilge
agus d'Fhoras na Gaeilge

Clár

SAOTHAR CRUTHAITHEACH: SCÉALTA AGUS DRÁMA

SCÉALTA GEARRA

Sceílíní

NÓTA BUÍOCHAIS

Nuair a bhí an taighde idir lámha againn fá choinne an leabhair seo thug roinnt daoine lámh chuidithe dúinn agus táimid faoi chomaoin mhór acu. Orthu siúd a bhfuil buíochas speisialta ag gabháil dóibh tá:

Vincie Shíle Bhilly Ó Domhnaill, Inbhear Náile agus Rann na Feirste 1945–2021, comharsa agus cara le Séamus thar chaoga bliain agus meantóir lena chois sin. Caill mhór é fosta dóibh siúd go léir ar spéis leo stair agus teanga na Gaeilge i dTír Chonaill.

An Dr. Síobhra Aiken a d'aimsigh ábhar i nuachtáin Mheiriceá a rann sí go fial linn.

An Dr. Ciarán Ó Duibhín a rann a chuid saineolais linn ar scríbhneoirí agus scríbhneoireacht Uladh.

Ar na daoine eile a chuidigh linn tá: Justin Furlong, Leabharlann Náisiúnta na hÉireann, Andrew Martin agus Michael Levy, Irish Newspaper Archives, Mari Hughes, Raphoe Catholic Archives, Bart Whelan, Ard an Rátha, Sharon Herron, Baile Dhún na nGall agus Seán Murray, Nua-Eabhrac.

Tá an foilsitheoir Alan Hayes le moladh go hard fosta as an chúram a ghlac sé leis an leabhar agus as an tslacht a chuir sé air.

Brian Ó Cianaigh
Fear Litríochta, Fear Teanga, Fear Cúise

Chuir buíon bheag daoine Conradh na Gaeilge ar bun sa bhliain 1893 agus tá an Conradh céanna ar cheann de na heagraíochtaí náisiúnta is buaine agus is tábhachtaí in Éirinn, ar bhealaí éagsúla, ó shin i leith. Tá stair fhada, chasta ag baint leis an Chonradh chéanna agus, nuair a reáchtáladh comóradh céad bliain in 1993, bhí deis ann breathnú siar ar a stair, ar bhuanna agus laigí na heagraíochta agus ar a thionchar ar chinniúint na hÉireann le corradh is céad bliain. Thapaigh lucht taighde an deis agus rinne siad mionchíoradh ar ghnéithe éagsúla den Chonradh ó shin i leith. Rud eile a rinneadh, beathaisnéisí idir chuimsitheach agus ghearr a scríobh ar chuid mhór de na daoine a raibh dlúthbhaint acu leis an Athbheochan go háirid sna blianta luatha. Ach, gan amhras, tá cuid mhaith daoine ann a fágadh i leaba an dearmaid, rud nárbh airí orthu, óir rinne a leithéidí a gcion féin – agus níos mó ná a gcion féin uaireanta – le fís an Chonartha a chur i gcrích. Is mithid, más mall, aitheantas a thabhairt dá macasamhail.

Ag deireadh an naoú haois déag agus sa chéad cheathrú den aois seo caite bhí Conallaigh ann, ar chainteoirí dúchais iad a mbunús, a chuir comaoin mhór ar Athbheochan na Gaeilge ach atá imithe as maíomh le fada an lá amach ó thagairtí fánacha thall is abhus dá gcuid saothar is dá gcuid oibre ar son na Gaeilge. Ar dhuine de na daoine gan iomrá sin a dhíreofar anseo le cuid den aoine sin i stair na hAthbheochana a líonadh. Brian Ó Cianaigh (Brendan O'Keeney) as Ard an Rátha atá i gceist.[1]

Brian Ó Cianaigh, c. 1900

Rugadh Brian Ó Cianaigh nó Bernard Keeney (Barney a thugtaí air ina cheantar dúchais féin) i nGleann Domhain in iardheisceart Dhún na nGall sa bhliain 1877. Charles A. (1833–1919), feirmeoir, agus Catherine/Kitty (*née* Cannon ó Altaveagh) (1858–1931) a bhí ar a thuismitheoirí. Pósadh iad ar 29/1/1874 ag Killaghtee (Dunkineely). Bhí Charles ina bhaintreabhach[2] agus é dhá bhliain is dhá scór nuair a pósadh é agus a bhean tríocha bliain d'aois. Dáta breithe na clainne: Bernard (1877), Ann (1878), Catherine Agnes (1881), Joe Daniel (1882) agus Patrick (1884). Fuair Brian a chuid bunscolaíochta i Scoil Náisiúnta Mhín Tine Dé atá tuairim is trí mhíle taobh amuigh de bhaile Ard an Rátha.[3] Is é an múinteoir a bhí aige ar an bhunscoil Mr. James/John O'Gallagher. Bhí an Gallchóireach ina mhúinteoir sa scoil sin ó 1876 go dtí gur éirigh sé as sa bhliain 1914. Ba chol ceathar í a bhean, Mary O'Donnell as Kilraine, le hEaspag Ráth Bhoth, Pádraig Ó Dónaill, a rinne an oiread sin ar son na Gaeilge i rith a shaoil.[4] Fear a bhí sa Ghallchóireach a raibh spéis mhór aige i gcúrsaí Gaeilge agus cultúrtha agus chuaigh sé i gcion go mór ar Bhrian.

Bhí Brian ina chainteoir dúchais mar a bhí an teaghlach ar fad agus is léir ó Dhaonáireamh 1901 go raibh idir léamh agus scríobh an Bhéarla agus na Gaeilge acu, rud a bhí annamh go maith sa Ghaeltacht san am sin. Is léir fosta go raibh traidisiún láidir scéalaíochta ina cheantar dúchais, a chruthú sin an corpas mór de scéalta béaloidis a d'fhoilsigh Brian sna 1930idí ar an *Derry People and Tirconaill News*.[5] Mhaígh Brian go raibh stór mór scéalta ag a athair agus gur fhoghlaim sé féin óna athair cuid mhór acu agus gur chuimhnigh sé go maith orthu go dtí deireadh a shaoil. Ó tharla gur rugadh Brian chomh fada sin ó shin agus nár fhág sé aon cháipéisíocht de chineál ar bith ina dhiaidh, go bhfuair sé bás sa bhliain 1943 agus go bhfuil a gharchlann chóir a bheith dall ar fad ar chuid na Gaeilge dá shaol, is tearc ar fad an t-eolas atá againn faoi ná faoina chúlra roimh thús na haoise seo caite. Is fiú breathnú ar a bhfuil ar eolas againn dá laghad é, áfach, ó tharla go bhfuil sé *ad rem* agus oiliúint Bhriain á scrúdú againn. Bhí an imirce go Meiriceá go mór i muintir Uí Chianaigh ó lár an naoú haois déag ar aghaidh. Bhí athair Bhriain páirteach sa Chogadh Chathartha i Meiriceá. Bhí uncailí agus deartháir Bhriain ag obair thall i Meiriceá roimh thús na haoise seo caite agus is orthu a thriall Brian nuair a chuaigh sé anonn sa bhliain 1903.

Bhí cáil ar uncal amháin le Brian, Niall, mar agóidí náisiúnaíoch agus is léir a thionchar ar Bhrian ón taobh sin de agus ar bhealaí eile fosta. Is fiú éisteacht leis an chuntas seo faoi Niall (1841–1935), agus d'aithneofá Brian air lena linn sin.

It would be difficult to equal Mr. Neal Keeney's impromptu address on the Decay of Ireland's National Customs.[6]

Is minic do chualaidh mé daoine léigheanta ag déanamh comhrádh ins an Bhéarla, & is minic do chualaidh mé comhrádh maith i nGaedhilg, acht do bhuaidhfeadh Niall Ó Cionaigh orra go léir. Ní fhaca is ní chualaidh mé riamh éin-nídh do b'fhearr ná é. Tháinig an chaint chuige ina tonntaibh móra meara gan stad ná comhnuidhe acht mar bheadh sruthán ag rith de thaobh Bheárnais Mhóir lá báistighe. Bhí brigh & fuinneamh ann, faghairt 'na shúilibh, gach uile bhall dá chorp ar oll-chrith. Dob' fhuirist aithne gur shíl sé féin gur bh'í an fhírinne do bhí dá rádh aige, & dar ndóigh is í leis. Tá súil le Dia agam go gcloisfidh mé arís é. Fear oibre gan tabhairt suas é.[7]

Thug Anna Johnston, Alice Milligan, Tomás Ó Concheanainn agus baill eile de Chonradh na Gaeilge cuairt ar áiteacha éagsúla i nDún na nGall le craobhacha a chur ar bun i mí Mheán Fómhair 1898. Nuair a shroich siad na Gleanntaí leis an aidhm sin a chur i gcrích, reáchtáil siad feis bheag agus bhain Niall bonn airgid as a óráid Ghaeilge i gcomórtas.[8]

The death of Neil Keeney, Stormhill, removes the last survivor of the Fenian band whose names were household words throughout Donegal in the dark days of '67 and during the scarcely less troubled days of the Land League. Deceased who was in his 97th year was in many ways a remarkable man ... From boyhood days he was a fearless champion of his country's rights, a patriot in everything that the term implies. When the remarkable 'split' occurred in the ranks of the Irish Party he stood unflinchingly by Charles Stewart Parnell. The advent of Sinn Féin found him an ardent and enthusiastic supporter ... At festive and social gatherings he was the life of every party he attended. His native wit and cheerful disposition made him a general favourite with young and old.[9]

Rud eile a dúradh faoi Niall: *'He was a veritable treasure-chest of Irish folklore.'*[10]

Bhí rud eile a bhain le cúlra Bhriain a chuaigh i gcion go mór air nárbh ionann agus an traidisiún dúchais cois teallaigh, mar atá, a chumas i gcúrsaí ceoil agus drámaíochta a léirigh sé go poiblí i rith a shaoil. Tá cuntas ar *The Derry Journal* faoi choirm cheoil a reáchtáladh i Mín Tine Dé ar oíche na Féile Pádraig 1886:

A few evenings ago a concert under the patronage of Mr. Arthur Brooke, Killybegs, was held in the schoolhouse, at Meentinadea, for the purpose of supplying some needed apparatus to the school, and although only a few days' notice had been given, at eight o'clock, the hour at which the concert was announced to begin, there were over two hundred persons assembled. Mr. Brooke contributed largely to the success of the evening by the interest he manifested in sending his men from Killybegs some days previous to execute a number of repairs to the school, which added much to the good appearance of the schoolroom. A number of young ladies and gentlemen selected from those present by Mr. O'Gallagher, principal of the school, having volunteered their vocal services in addition to those who had previously promised to attend for that purpose, a very respectable orchestra had been formed, and Mr. J.D. Cassidy opened the concert by his personation of the 'Quack Doctor'. In this Mr. Cassidy was extremely happy, as he brought the whole house with him in fits of laughter. Being encored, he sang the 'Hurdy-Gurdy Lad'. Mr. R. Evans' song, 'In the Gloaming', was rendered by this young gentleman in excellent style. Being loudly encored, he sang, 'They like it don't you know'. Mr. Sheerin's song, 'My mother's grave', was well received, and, being encored, he bowed and retired. A duet, 'My Erin O', by Miss Mary Ward and Miss Sarah Ward, was rendered in good taste, and much ability. Being loudly encored, they gave 'Blanche Alpin', with great effect. A serio-comic, by Mr. Cooke, gave very great satisfaction, and in response to an encore, he gave another comic. Dialogue, 'School-master', by Messrs. McCafferty and Brennan, elicited much laughter. Duet, 'Molly Darling', by Miss Gildea and Miss McGuire, had a very pleasing effect, and being encored, they bowed and retired. Song, 'Gathering Shells', by Mr. R. Evans, was

> *given with his usual ability and loudly encored, he gave 'Ella Lee', in good taste. Song, 'Things I don't like to see', by Mr. Breslin, created much merriment. Song, 'Ballyporeen' by Mr. Gavigan, was much applauded. This concluded the first part of the programme. The Christy Minstrel troupe, under the able guidance of Mr. J.J. Evans, Ardara, who was also master of ceremonies during the evening opened the second part of the programme. The performance of this troupe, as amateurs, could scarcely be excelled, and for upwards of an hour kept the house in one continuous roar of laughter, the merriment created arriving at its climax in that portion of the performance in which a ----- woman danced an Irish jig with her affectionate partner. Thus ended the evening's amusements, and all quietly dispersed and were highly pleased'...*

Tá cuid mhór ar shlí a ráite fán choirm cheoil seo. Mar rud amháin ní raibh aon rud dúchasach ná Gaelach ag baint leis an ócáid sin a bhí á reáchtáil sa Ghaeltacht. A athrach ar fad. Léiriú atá ann ar an dóigh a raibh an cultúr gallda i dtreis sa tír seo ar ócáidí poiblí siamsaíochta ag an am agus an chontúirt a bhí ann go ndíbreodh sé an cultúr Gaelach ar fad.[11] Cuimhnítear, áfach, gur stáitsíodh é seo sula raibh mórán iomrá ar Chonradh na Gaeilge ná Gluaiseacht Éire na nGael sa tír.[12] Bhain a leithéid seo le galldú na hÉireann, rud a spreag de hÍde lena óráid ar *de-anglicisation of Ireland* a thabhairt. Is fiú éisteacht le Yeats ar an téad seo.

> *Mr. W.B. Yeats said that a few years ago the cause of the Irish language seemed to be a lost cause. He had heard people singing London music hall songs of the vulgarest kind in a Connacht fishing village, 18 miles from any town. He was told that those who sang them thought it proved them to be better educated than their neighbours, who only sang the beautiful old Irish songs. But now, owing to the work of the Gaelic League, the pride was beginning to be all on the other side. Those that had the Irish were beginning to be proud of it, and to remember that the stories and songs it contained were their greatest possession, and those who had no Irish were beginning, like himself, to learn it ... If we allowed Irish to become forgotten or even debased, we would look foolish in the eyes of the world ... Every nation had its own duty in the world, its own message to deliver, and that message was to a considerable extent bound up with the language. The nations make a part with one*

harmony, just as the colours in the rainbow make a part of one harmony of beautiful colour. It is our duty to keep the message, the colour which God had committed to us, clear and pure and shining.[13]

Ní heol dúinn an raibh aon bhaint ag Brian leis an choirm cheoil áirithe sin ach is cinnte go raibh an cineál sin siamsaíochta faiseanta sa cheantar agus bhí Brian páirteach go minic ina leithéidí ina dhiaidh sin. Sa bhliain 1897, mar shampla: '*It was reported that he [Mr. B. Keeney] participated in the annual entertainment at Monargon (Co. Donegal) on Friday, 22 January, being one of the vocalists who rendered 'Let Erin Remember.' Recitations and songs etc. featured on the programme and the master of ceremonies was Patrick Keeney.*'[14]

I mí na Nollag an bhliain chéanna reáchtáil an *Ardara Emerald Football Club* coirm cheoil agus siamsaíocht na Nollag ar éirigh go maith léi. Ar chlár na hoíche sin tuairiscíodh gur léiríodh '*a dialogue, 'The Schoolmaster' which was performed in a very entertaining manner by Messrs. Brennan, B. Keeney, and Ward.*[15]

Bhí Brian (Bernard a tugadh air sa tuairisc nuachtáin) ina bhall den chór a ghlac páirt i gcoirm cheoil a reáchtáladh i Scoil Náisiúnta Mhín Tine Dé ar 7 Eanáir 1898.[16] Luaitear é arís an mhí dár gcionn '*at a concert and dramatic entertainment which took place at Croagh N.S. Dunkineely.*' Anseo arís is léir gur coirm cheoil d'ardchaighdeán a bhí i gceist '*at which excellent training was exhibited.*'[17] Dúradh sa tuairisc fosta: '*Mr. B. Keeney, Ardara, and Mr. Ward, Corker, gave a laughable dialogue, entitled 'The Master and the Pupil.' These two gentlemen are well known, and when they appear on the stage they always receive a hearty welcome.*'[18]

Is léir ó na tuairiscí sin go raibh cáil ar Bhrian i mblianta deireanacha an naoú haois déag mar cheoltóir agus mar aisteoir agus gur mhinic é ar an ardán i gcomharsanacht Ard an Rátha. Tharla dhá rud ansin a chuir cor i gcinniúint Bhriain. Mar rud amháin bhog an teaghlach isteach go baile Ard an Rátha[19] agus cheannaigh siopa grósaera[20] *cum* teach tábhairne ansin.[21] Bhí an t-athair agus Brian i mbun an tsiopa sin.

Baile Ard an Rátha ag tús an fichiú haois
(le caoinchead ó Mhúsaem Dhún na nGall)

Rud tábhachtach eile a tharla in 1900, bunaíodh craobh de Chonradh na Gaeilge ar an bhaile[22] bíodh is gur féachadh le spéis a mhúscailt i gcúis na Gaeilge roinnt míonna roimhe sin agus a raibh baint ag Niall Ó Cianaigh leis.

> *The Gaelic League Meeting in Ardara: The other evening a preliminary meeting was held in Ardara with the object of promoting a futherance of the Gaelic movement in the district. Mr. Neil Keeney was moved to the chair, and in the course of an eloquent address expressed his gratification in having an opportunity of conveying his feelings on the occasion, although he (Mr. Keeney) could not hope to inculcate the absolute advisability and necessity of a renewal of the mother tongue with half the strenuousness it deserved. Having before us the noble example of nearly every district in Ireland, he believed the men of Tyrconnell would scarcely consider it an impromptu movement, but rather would feel ashamed of not possessing and cherishing that priceless inheritance, the language of Columbkille.*[23]

Bhí toradh ar obair na ndaoine sin in Ard an Rátha a bhí ar mhaithe leis an Ghaeilge a chur chun cinn ar an bhaile.

The Ardara Feis: A most successful Feis, under the auspices of the local Gaelic Literary Association, was held at Ardara on Friday, 29th June, to encourage generally the cultivation of the Irish language, and to secure its continuance as the living language of the people. The Feis was held in the large national school in the village, but the gathering was so large that one half of the people were unable to obtain admittance. Consequently the windows had to be thrown open to enable the crowds outside to hear something of what was going on. The interest evinced in the proceedings from start to finish was admirable. Contingents arrived from the neighbouring parishes as well as from the branches of the Gaelic League established at Donegal, Killybegs, the Rosses and Londonderry.[24] *At the conclusion of the Feis a branch of the Gaelic League was established. Rev. H. McDwyer, C.C., was elected President, and Mr. A.J. McNelis, Secretary and Treasurer. From the enthusiasm shown by all present, and their great proficiency in Irish, it is confidently expected that the Ardara Branch will have a brilliant future, and that a new area in connection with the language movement has commenced in South Donegal.*[25]

Lean Brian dá chuid aisteoireachta sa bhliain 1900 óir luadh é sa chomhthéacs seo faoi ócáid siamsaíochta ar 26 Deireadh Fómhair:

a grand variety and dramatic entertainment which was held in the Town Hall under the auspices of the Ardara Lighting Committee. Part of the entertainment was 'a farce, in three acts, 'The Irish Tutor,' by the Ardara Dramatic Company, [which] did credit to those who took part therein, viz., Miss M. Fallon, Miss B. Gilbride, Messrs. Gildea, Keeney, Brennan and Mulreany.[26]

An chéad tagairt eile do Bhrian sna meáin chlóite, níor bhain an scéal lena chumas aisteoireachta ná ceoil an iarraidh seo ach bhain sé le cás cúirte a tugadh ina éadan mar dhíoltóir biotáilte. Ar bhealach, d'fhéadfaí a mhaíomh gur bhain sé úsáid as a scil mar aisteoir agus é á chosaint féin ar an ócáid. Bhí cuntas ar an *Derry Journal* faoin *Ardara Petty Sessions* ar 11 Nollaig:

A spirit grocer named Keeney was prosecuted by Constable Mahoney for having in his kitchen a townsman on the night of 14th November about 10.30 p.m. Evidence was given by the spirit grocer, his brother, and a lodger in the house that no drink was asked for, sold, or paid for. Constable Mahoney charged Keeney with having concocted his story.[27]

Fuarthas Brian ciontach gí gur chosain sé é féin go láidir, deisbhéalach, greannmhar ach, ar an drochuair, níor creideadh a leagan féin den scéal. Cháin sé ina dhiaidh sin cruinneas na tuairisce ar an chás a foilsíodh ar an nuachtán.[28]

Sa bhliain 1901 luaitear Brian i gcomhthéacs Athbheochan na Gaeilge den chéad uair go sonrach, in Ard an Rátha i dtús ama. Creideadh ag an tús nach raibh mórán á chur i gcrích ansin ó thaobh na Gaeilge de nuair a dúradh: '*The committee regretted that they observed no signs of activity ... in such Irish-speaking districts as Kilcar, Glencolumbkille and Ardara*'.[29] Níorbh fhíor sin go hiomlán óir admhaíodh: '*there was a class in Ardara where adults could learn to read and write Irish.*'[30]

Bhí cur is cúiteamh faoi chúrsaí Gaeilge ar an *Journal* ag tús na bliana ag daoine éagsúla, ina measc, Seamus Mac Manus a raibh baint aige le Conradh na Gaeilge i dTír Chonaill san am, agus spreag an comhfhreagras seo Brian le scríobh ionsar an nuachtán.

The Irish Language: To the Editor of The Derry Journal: Sir – There seems to be quite a controversy in the Journal lately under the above heading, and as you have always shown an unmistakable interest in the revival and cultivation of the language I trust you will permit me to trespass briefly on your valuable space. Anyone interested in the Gaelic Movement would naturally expect to find something important under such a heading, but, unfortunately, the productions that are appearing latterly are neither instructive nor amusing, and cannot fail to have a demoralising effect eventually. One person is anxious to inculcate his knowledge of the mother-tongue, and wishes to know the capabilities and qualifications of some other one. Another replies suggesting the propriety of purchasing a 'Boer' hat from John Wannamaker, of New York, and hears again that neither head gear nor leg gear has anything to do with the matter, and that it makes no difference whether a man is clothed in a Donegal home-made coat or a covering of British broadcloth. Is it from such silly and uncalled-for productions that we are to acquire an attachment to the old tongue?

Is this the means adopted to enkindle within us a living interest in the language? It is not for me, in observations merely meant to set aside such work, to attempt to lay down the limits within which a revival of the Irish language may be practicable, but I respectfully request them to dismiss the thought that an ambition to preserve our national language will arise from hurling volleys of sarcasm at one another. Thanking you in anticipation, yours truly, Bernard Keeney. Ardara, 21st February, 1901.

Thug comhfhreagraí darbh ainm *Go Ahead* freagra air ar 27 Feabhra agus thug Brian freagra air ar 1 Márta.

Ardara 27/2/1901: To the Editor of The Derry Journal: Sir – I notice in your issue of to-day (Wednesday) that somebody signing himself 'Go Ahead' has asked me to devise some plan by which many of the hindrances to the 'real success of the Gaedhilge' (as far as my native village is concerned) might be dispelled. I think I stated definitely that my observations were merely meant to set aside 'the thresh of personal controversy' (as you, Mr. Editor, term it), and did not pretend to anything more than a sort of tourist acquaintance with the 'Gaelic world.' I am not, however, prepared to rank myself with the 'almost invulnerable,' who are to be carried away with 'Go Ahead's' 'tide of popularity;' but my wonder is why one who is able to summarise and discern so many hindrances, restrictions, prohibitions, &c., could not suggest a remedy himself. Yours truly, Bernard Keeney.[31]

Is cosúil gurbh é seo an chéad uair do Bhrian a bheith i gcló agus cúrsaí Gaeilge faoi thrácht aige.

Tionóladh cruinniú de Chraobh Ard an Rátha le slacht cheart a chur ar obair na Craoibhe agus luadh go raibh Brian ina rúnaí ar an Chraobh. Dúradh fosta gur cheol sé féin agus cúpla duine eile amhráin Ghaeilge ag deireadh an chruinnithe.[32] Is cinnte gur imir Brian tionchar mór ar Chonradh na Gaeilge in Ard an Rátha fhad is a bhí sé ann agus d'fhág sé a lorg ar an áit fiú i ndiaidh dó imeacht.

Ardara Concert: A Suggestion: Adara, in the County Donegal, has had its Irish concert. The posters, the tickets, the programmes, the music, and with a few healthy Anglo-Irish exceptions, the songs and recitations were also Irish. There was also an Irish play. What gives this concert such special significance is the fact that it was held in the heart of Irish-speaking Donegal. The Ardara Branch of the Gaelic

League was established a little more than twelve months ago and this is its first fruit. Financially, as well as in all other respects, it was very successful, but its greatest value is the example it gives to the rest of Donegal to go and do likewise ... Ardara is on a fair way to become the rival of Ballyvourney ... The people of Ardara have made it (Irish), as is natural, the language of their public entertainments.[33]

D'fhág Brian Ard an Rátha an bhliain chéanna sin agus thug a aghaidh ar an tSrath Bán le dul ag obair mar mhúinteoir Gaeilge. D'fhéadfaí an cheist a chur cén oiliúint a bhí faighte aige i gceird na múinteoireachta ach seans maith gur leor dó a bheith ina chainteoir dúchais Gaeilge mar cháilíocht agus go raibh idir léamh agus scríobh na Gaeilge aige. Cuireann Aindrias Ó Muimhneacháin síos ar stair na múinteoirí taistil seo i dtúsré an Chonartha:

Ag an dara Ard-Fheis sa bhliain 1897 is ea cinneadh ar 'Gaeilgeoir nó breis a sholáthar mar mhúinteoirí nó mar thimirí don Ghaeltacht.' Ceapadh Tomás Ó Concheanainn ina thimire sa bhliain 1898, agus laistigh de dheich mbliana eile bhí beagnach fiche timire agus tuairim 150 múinteoir taistil fé sheirbhís lán-aimsire ag an gCoiste Gnótha, agus ní sa Ghaeltacht amháin a bhíodar ach ar fuaid na tíre go léir ... Mhúineadh na múinteoirí agus na timirí seo an Ghaeilge in áiteanna iomadúla i bhfad óna chéile istoíche agus ins na scoileanna ... Chraolaidís agus léirídís mór-shoiscéal an Chonartha, leis, de shíor agus do chách i ngach aon sórt áite dá mbídís ... Ba bheag duine de na soiscéalaithe tosaigh seo a raibh aon tsain-oiliúint dá laghad fachta acu dá gcúram: tiomantacht a dtír-ghrá agus a dhearfa a bhíodar ná mairfeadh beo náisiún na hÉireann d'uireasa na Gaeilge a bheir dóibh pé éifeacht a bhí iontu, agus thugadar suas iad féin agus a raibh ar chumas dóibh ar son na cúise sin.[34]

Fuair Brian a chéad phost mar mhúinteoir Gaeilge i dTír Eoghain. Is léir gurbh é a bhí i gceist sa chuntas seo a leanas gí nár luadh a ainm go sonrach:

Strabane Gaelic League: A special meeting of above was held in their classroom, Church Street, the other evening. The usual varied and instructive programme of this flourishing class, which includes conversational phraseology and songs in Gaelic, having been disposed of, the members decided to affiliate the class with the Gaelic League ... The success attained by the class in Strabane has been chiefly due to the valuable work by Messrs. O'Keeney, McGeehan, O'Boyle and O'Callaghan, whose familiarity with our language enables them to teach it in poetry and prose to their less favoured associates with the best results. The active interest taken in the class by all concerned augurs well for the future of our Irish revival in Strabane ...[35]

Gaelic in Strabane: Scarcely a week passes without practical proof being given of the benefits conferred on the people of Strabane – young and old alike – through the medium of the Catholic Association ... During the past week a Gaelic class has been started, and as evidence of the earnestness which the association have entered into the movement, they have at considerable expense secured the services, as teacher, of Mr Brian O'Keeney, Ardara, a gentleman who has a thorough knowledge of the Irish language. There are two classes, one for males and one for females. On Monday night the first lesson was given in the Barrack Street Hall, and though notice of the establishment of the class had only been given the evening previous, fully one hundred persons turned up at the hour appointed. Mr. O'Keeney had as he thought sufficient numbers of O'Growney's but in a very short time the supply was exhausted. Father McElhatton was present at the lessons and he pointed out the value of the Irish language, and the benefits which knowledge of it would confer. On Tuesday evening the second lesson was given and the attendance was very large, fully seventy females were present at the 7 o'clock class, and there could not have been less than 100 males at the 9 o'clock class ... Mr. O'Keeney on both evenings favoured his pupils with a number of songs in Irish. We are requested by Mr. O'Keeney to state that a most unwarrantable liberty was taken with his name in connection with a report which appeared in Wednesday's Journal. He wishes it to be distinctly understood that he is not connected with any other class in Strabane but that of the Catholic Association.[36]

Tugadh poiblíocht mhór sna nuachtáin áitiúla don dul chun cinn mór a bhí á dhéanamh ó thaobh na Gaeilge de sa cheantar.[37]

Taobh amuigh dá chuid teagaisc ag an am seo, títhear Brian agus aidhm eile de chuid an Chonartha á cur chun cinn aige go láidir, aidhm ar chreid sé go láidir inti agus ar thrácht sé uirthi i rith a shaoil, mar atá, an gá le tionscail agus déantúsaíocht[38] a bhunú in Éirinn le deireadh a chur leis an imirce. Port a bhí anseo aige ar dhírigh sé air arís agus arís eile in óráidí agus i litreacha i nuachtáin i rith a shaoil.

An Srath Bán, 1902 (Grianghraf: E.R. Gray & Sons)

Irish Industries: To the Editor of the Derry Journal:[39] *Sir – I have read with satisfaction and interest Mr. P.T. McGinley's letter under above heading in your issue of to-day. The development of Irish Industries is certainly worth of strict and careful attention. It may indeed be regarded as the only means of lessening the flow of Irish emigrant tide, and the safest remedy to secure the permanent advancement of the material prosperity of our peasantry. The whole-hearted and genuine interest with which the Gaelic League has coupled the development of Irish industry with the revival of the Irish language is worthy of more than passing observation.*[40] *It is not necessary to add that the most gratifying results are already perceptible, but much remains to be done, and the co-operation of public bodies would prove a stalwart factor in the industrial movement. Then, on the other hand, if Irish tweeds found a more prominent place in our drapery establishments, there would be less room for improvement in the patronage in that department, and English and Scotch manufactured goods would eventually find themselves in the background.*[41] *The increased demand for 'homespuns' has occasioned a fair amount of competition amongst the manufacturers, and although the samples latterly produced were superior in quality and design, the prices realised were scarcely sufficient to cover the extra cost and trouble, all for a want of a better market to sell them in. Local depots might be successfully established in better centres, and the better patterns offered for sale, and I am confident this suggestion has utility enough to recommend it. I regret, however, to state that I am credibly informed that Irish-made boots and shoes cannot be sold at similar prices to those of English and Scotch manufacture. This is easy of solution when we consider that they are much superior in quality and finish, and although the wearer will readily admit that they are better, he is tempted by the lower prices and buys the inferior article. One dealer has told me that the difference in the ordinary prices was something about 1s 6d per pair, and he was prepared to state that the Irish boot would wear twice as long and give greater satisfaction. Yet he could not sell as many Irish-made boots and shoes as would warrant the stocking of them. Again, a large quantity of English and Scotch manufactured goods is often bought at clearance sales in Liverpool and Manchester, much below manufactured prices, and hence the difficulty in competing with them. Still we should consider that an inferior article is dear at any price and the sooner Irishmen and Irishwomen can bring home to themselves the fact that they can get genuine value in Irish goods the better for themselves. When Irish people speak their native language and support their native industries, the objects of the Gaelic League will be fulfilled, and Ireland will be as Irish as she was in the days of old, 'ere her faithful sons betrayed her.' – I am, sir, yours faithfully, Bernard Keeney*[42]

Irish Industries: To the editor of The Derry Journal: Sir – Having already permitted me on several occasions to offer my remarks on the above subject, I again seek your kind indulgence to trespass on your valuable space. I notice in your issue today (Friday) a letter from Mr. C.H. Ward, chairman of Donegal Board of Guardians, in which he takes exception to Mr. P.T. McGinley's remarks in Monday's issue of the Journal *in reference to the contracts for supplies to the Donegal Workhouse. Notwithstanding the fact that I have neither the intention nor the presumption to lay down practical rules relative to the development of public Boards or Institutions in Donegal or elsewhere, I find the chairman's remarks are applicable to me as one of the 'individuals here and there who heaps insults upon public Boards,' and consequently I deem it incumbent on me to reply thereto. In my letter, which appeared in Wednesday's issue, I simply said 'that the co-operation of the public bodies would prove a stalwart factor in the industrial movement,' and I now repeat it. This suggestion would require to be scanned in a most equivocal fashion to give the flavour of an insult, or render it more applicable to the Donegal Board of Guardians than to any other public institution in*

Ireland. Whilst I readily admit that the Board of Guardians are justified in soliciting tenders for the supplies and making their selections whenever they please, I would, however, remind them that justification to retard or prevent public criticism does not follow. Mr. Ward's explanation as to why the Donegal Board of Guardians have given to two Derry houses contracts for their supplies is certainly definite (there being no tenders from county Donegal), but we do not hear from Mr. Ward that it was a condition of the contract that the goods should be of Irish manufacture – that being the least which might be expected from a board of Guardians with 90 per cent of Gaelic Leaguers. 'If Irish industries are only to be developed thus (Mr. Ward further adds) I fear the mode of procedure will not tend to promote the object in view.' In this I agree with Mr. Ward, as words may certainly be regarded as volatile and inefficacious, but many national grievances have been remedied by the suggestiveness of a straightforward controversy, which would be effective in rousing public opinion to action. Being absolutely acquainted with the workings of the public Boards I am not to be considered as either decrying their actions or heaping insults upon them, but I am emphatically expressing my intention of exercising my humble influence towards the advancement and development of Irish industry as one who has little fear of censure or praise. Apologising for trespassing so far, and thanking you in anticipation – I am, dear sir, faithfully yours, Brian O'Keeney, Strabane, July 12th, 1901.[43]

Fuarthas samplaí eile de chumas Bhriain agus é i mbun bolscaireachta ar son na Gaeilge an bhliain sin. Luaitear é ar ócáid eile ag tabhairt óráide as Gaeilge agus as Béarla, nós a chleacht sé i rith a shaoil, in Inis Eoghain. Tá an óráid i gcló ar *The Derry Journal*.[44] Is sampla maith atá ann dá chumas óráidíochta. Is léir nár leasc leis a chuid tuairimí a chur os comhair an tsaoil mhóir i rith a shaoil.

Is léir fosta gur mhúinteoir éifeachtach a bhí i mBrian ón tús, rud a aithníodh.

A branch of the League has been started in Strabane under promising circumstances. Over one hundred pupils attend the classes, and when the summer is over a large increase is expected. The services of a capable paid teacher have been secured. We trust that Strabane may be a strong link between the flourishing Tyrone branches and the Irish-speaking districts of Tirconnaill.[45]

Rinne Brian soiléiriú ar a cheapachán ar an tSrath Bán agus ar a chúraimí múinteoireachta i litir a chuir sé chuig *An Claidheamh Soluis*.

> *The Teaching of Irish in Convent Schools: To the editor of* An Claidheamh Soluis & Fáinne an Lae. *Dear Sir, I have been asked by Father McElhatton, President of the Strabane Gaelic League Branch, to request you to make a slight correction relative to the following in your next issue of* An Claidheamh Soluis. *It has been stated in several leading papers, and in the* Claidheamh Soluis, *that the pupils attending the Convent of Mercy, Strabane, were asked to ascertain from their parents when at home on vacation whether they would wish to have Irish taught them when the schools would open again, and that a teacher would be accordingly procured.*[46] *This is not true. My services as Irish teacher in the Convent Schools had been secured before vacation, irrespective of the opinions of the parents of such pupils, and the nuns deserve great credit for it. I am teaching for the Strabane Catholic Men's Association, by whom the branch of the League was established, and I am instructed to be prepared for the teaching of Irish in the Mercy Convent Schools as soon as the vacation is over, namely on the 19th August. Please make a slight correction to this effect, and oblige. Yours faithfully, Bernard Keeney, Irish Teacher, Strabane. August 3rd, 1901 P.S. Classes here are doing very well.*[47]

Is léir faoin am seo go bhfuil Brian ag tacú go láidir le hidé-eolaíocht Chonradh na Gaeilge[48] agus nach bhfuil scáth ná eagla air a thuairimí a chur os comhair an tsaoil go tréamanta, deisbhéalach, mar is léir, mar shampla, i litir fhada leis faoin chúrsaí oideachais *'Irish Language Movement and National Board'* in *The Derry Journal* (13/9/1901, 3).[49]

Is ag an am seo fosta a thoisigh Brian a chumadh filíochta leis an dán 'Gleann Domhain' faoina cheantar dúchais féin Gleann Domhain.[50] Thairg Brian duais ar leagan Béarla den dán sin mar is léir ón litir seo a sheol sé ionsar an *Derry Journal*.

> *Sir: Having offered a prize for the best translation into English, or, an essay embodying the substance of above poem, which recently appeared in your columns, I shall, with your kind permission, deal*

briefly with the result. The competition was confined to Strabane Gaelic League classes, and, although the papers were handed in to me the day before I left Strabane, it was only to-day that I found time for a perusal thereof. I promised to publish the results in your valuable paper, and I, therefore, take advantage of this opportunity of recording my signal recognition of the talent and energy which so laudably distinguishes the youth of Strabane. This is abundantly evidenced by the fact that seven out of nine pieces in this competition are so equally meritorious that I cannot conscientiously undertake to give any one of them preference. They are clearly written; rich in the beauties of ornamental language; singularly illustrative of the original subject, and deeply descriptive of the burning love of the country which must be intensified by the desire to renew the acquaintances of youth. I am therefore, obliged to have recourse to some other remedy, and consequently I have decided to award the prize for the best essay on 'The Utility of the Irish Language,' and also to give a second and third prize according to the order of merit, open only to those who have entered the poem competition. This will not only afford them another opportunity of displaying their intellectual superiority, but will further enhance their unquestionable love for the language of their forefathers. I remain, dear sir, your obedient servant, B. O'Keeney, Gaelic Organiser. Newry, 9th October, 1901.[51]

Gí gur éirigh go hiontach maith le Brian mar mhúinteoir i dTír Eoghain, níor fhan sé rófhada ansin gur bhog sé go dtí an taobh eile den chúige.

Mr. B. Keeney, Irish Teacher, Strabane: We are pleased to learn from an official source that Mr. B. Keeney, who has so successfully conducted the Irish class in Strabane during the past four months,[52] *has been appointed to the important position of Gaelic organiser for the district of Newry, Omeath and Dundalk. Perhaps in no town in the North of Ireland has the Gaelic Revival movement taken such a firm hold as in Strabane, as was made abundantly clear to anyone who attended the entertainment in the Town Hall on Friday evening; and to the bringing about of this pleasing state of affairs, Mr. Keeney, by the zealous and energetic manner in which he entered into the good work, contributed in no small degree.*[53]

Fógraíodh post mar mhúinteoir taistil in oirdheisceart Uladh:

Situations Vacant: A couple of young, energetic teachers required by the Newry, Dundalk and Districts Organising Committee to organise and teach Gaelic classes in the district. Must possess a good literary knowledge of the language and speak it fluently. Speakers of Northern Irish preferred. Age from 20 to 40. Salary £80 a year; if found satisfactory, will rise by annual increments to £120. Applications stating qualifications to be sent immediately to P. Ward, Hon. Sec., Omeath, Co. Louth.[54]

Chuir Brian isteach ar an phost agus ceapadh é.

At a meeting of the Dundalk and Newry joint committee yesterday, two Donegal men – Patrick McGeehan of Fintown, and Bernard O'Keeney of Ardara, were appointed teachers for the district formerly worked by Mr. Nugent.[55] *After carefully examining all the applications, Mr. Bernard O'Keeney and Mr. Padraig McGeehin were considered most suitable. Mr. McGeehin is a nephew of Mr. P.T. McGinley, and Mr. O'Keeney is a native of Ardara, Co. Donegal.*[56] *The appointment of teachers was then proceeded with. The two teachers selected, Messrs. B. O'Keeney and Mr. P. MacGeehin, came before the meeting and were tested in reading and translating at sight, and ultimately on the motion of Mr. Bowen, seconded by Rev. M.J. Quinn, C.C., Dundalk, Mr. O'Keeney was appointed senior teacher and organizer, and Mr. MacGeehin assistant teacher.*

Gaelic League: The classes under the Dundalk branch will be open on Tuesday evening next at the Christian Schools. Ladies' class at 6 p.m. and men's at 7.30. Mr. Keeney has been appointed to conduct the classes.[57]

Tugann na tuairiscí ar na nuachtáin logánta sa taobh sin tíre léargas dúinn ar an obair a bhí ar siúl ag Brian, na dualgais a bhí air, na ceantair a bhí faoina chúram, a fheabhas a d'éirigh leis mar mhúinteoir agus a dheisbhéalaí a bhí sé mar chainteoir agus agóidí ar son na Gaeilge.

Mr. O'Keeney will conduct classes in Newry on Mondays and Thursdays; in Dundalk on Tuesdays; in Armagh on Wednesday and Friday, and class for National Teachers in Newry every Saturday ... Mr. Mac Geehin will assist Mr. O'Keeney with the Teachers' class. Now that two able energetic young teachers have been employed who will give their whole time and attention to teaching Irish in this district, it is expected that great work will be done during the coming year. Both teachers are from Donegal, and know Irish from the cradle. It was the first language they learned to lisp from their mothers' knee. The senior teacher has considerable experience of teaching Irish as he was employed teaching classes in Strabane for some time past, where, according to reports from local papers, great work has been done in a short space of time, and great regret is felt at the departure from amongst them of their teacher, Mr. O'Keeney.[58]

An tIúr ag tús an fichiú haois

Cuireadh síos sna nuachtáin ar chlár oibre Bhriain agus é i mbun a phoist.

Brian O'Keeney will conduct classes in Newry every Monday; in Dundalk every Tuesday and Wednesday; in Armagh every Thursday and Friday; the National Teachers' class in Newry every Saturday; the Carlingford class on Saturday evenings and the Grange class every Sunday.[59] *On Tuesday evening last the Irish class in the Christian Brothers' Schools was resumed. The teacher on Tuesday evening was Mr. Bernard O'Keeney who has been recently appointed by the Dundalk and Newry District Committee of the Gaelic League. He is a fluent Irish speaker and a sound scholar. He is also a proficient teacher of Irish music. On each Tuesday evening he will teach two classes of juniors: the first class for women will commence at 6 o'clock, and will continue till 7.30; the second class, a mixed class for men and women who cannot attend the earlier class, will commence at 7.30 and will continue till 9 o'clock.*[60] *A public meeting will be held at Mullabawn on Sunday evening at 4 o'clock, p.m., to establish a branch of the Gaelic League. Messrs. Green, Brown, Keeney, Nugent, and several other distinguished members of the Gaelic League will address the meeting.*[61]

Is dócha go bhféadfaí a mhaíomh faoin óráid a thug Brian ar an Mhullach Bhán faoin Ghaeilge go bhfuil sé ar cheann d'óráidí móra na hAthbheochana agus go bhféadfaí í a chur ar an iomaire chéanna le hóráidí cáiliúla eile na hAthbheochana a bhfuil eolas forleathan orthu.[62]

Fuair Brian ceapachán eile i gCo. Ard Mhacha ansin.

St. Patrick's Seminary, Armagh: His Eminence Cardinal Logue ... has made arrangements to have Irish taught in the Seminary. We understand that Mr. B. O'Keeney has been accordingly appointed. He will devote his spare time to this work, and give the number of lessons which will be required weekly, and simultaneously carry on the duties of co-teacher and organiser in the district.[63]

Rud eile de, níor thráigh spéis Bhriain i gcúrsaí litríochta i rith an ama seo. D'aistrigh sé 'Slievenamon' go Gaeilge agus foilsíodh é ar an *Dundalk Democrat* (23/11/1901, 5) agus ar an *Irish Emerald* (7/12/1901). *'The above translation of 'Slievenamon' is from the pen of Mr. B. O'Keeney, and will soon be published to the music of that charming Munster air'*.[64]

Lean Brian lena chuid oibre gan stad agus tugadh cuntas ar a raibh ar siúl aige sna nuachtáin logánta.[65] Cuireadh béim sna cuntais ar a éifeacht mar mhúinteoir agus mar chainteoir ar son na hAthbheochana.[66] Leis an dlaoi mhullaigh a chur ar an bhliain, chum Brian dhá shaothar ag deireadh na bliana, mar atá, dán 'Solas ar an Bhealach' agus leagan Béarla de '*A Light on the Way*',[67] agus scéal, '*A Donegal Fireside Tale*'.[68]

Chuir Brian iris dhátheangach ar bun ag tús 1902 agus *Éire go Bragh* an teideal a bhí air.

A New Irish Magazine: The Language Movement is showing on every hand such forcible signs of vigour and progress that a new development, or the introduction of some new feature into its working, is a matter of no surprise, and creates but a momentary interest. A work, however, is being initiated, which must affect the movement in Ulster to such an extent as to arouse more than passing attention. A great difficulty with Northern students has been the want of a sufficient supply of reading matter in easy Ulster Irish. It is partly to meet this difficulty that the Newry, Dundalk and Armagh Executive of the Gaelic League have decided to publish a monthly magazine, which will contain easy Ulster Irish, with English translations. We are sure this will be welcome news to Northern students. The news will be more welcome when we mention that the arrangements have been entrusted to Mr. Bernard O'Keeney, the organiser for the Newry, Dundalk and Armagh District. Mr. O'Keeney is well known to our readers, especially in North Tyrone, Derry and Donegal, and his friends in Strabane, where he displayed such great enthusiasm and ability in the movement, will be glad to hear that the new magazine will be edited by him, and that through its pages they will have the means of keeping up the acquaintance, and of benefitting by his knowledge, and his teaching ability. The magazine will also contain branch reports, and as it is expected to be published early in February, reports should be sent not later than the end of January. Mr. O'Keeney's present address is Frontier Hotel, Newry. We give a hearty welcome to the new magazine and we are sure that Mr. O'Keeney will spare no pains to make it a success. Its title will not easily be forgotten; it is Erin go Bragh.[69]

Tugadh cuntas ar an iris ar na nuachtáin logánta agus ar *An Claidheamh Soluis*.

Eire go Bragh: This is the title of a new Magazine devoted to the interests of the Gaelic language movement, published by Mr. B. O'Keeney, Gaelic teacher at Dundalk, Newry and Armagh. The first number contains a good deal of interesting matters in both Irish and English, and gives promise of better things in the future.[70]

*The Cuchullin Saga: Under the title, 'A King's Treasure,' in the first number of the Eire go Bragh is a very interesting article on the Cuchullin Saga from Bodhbh Dearg. We extract a few paragraphs ... [*tugtar sliocht ansin*].*[71]

Review: Éire go Bráth: This is a monthly bilingual magazine published in Newry at twopence, and one which we hope will do good work in Ulster for the movement. Its policy is, in its own words, 'Advocacy of the principles so strenuously inculcated by the Gaelic League will be to us a labour of love; the bringing back of the

> *old traditions and associations of our race, the preservation and cultivation of our national language, the development of Irish industries, music, art, and literature are all indispensable factors, if we are to preserve our nationality, our individuality, and put an end to emigration.' The first number contains comments and news, branch reports, two pages of Irish, a lecture by Mr. B. O'Keeney, and an article by Bodhbh Dearg 'About the Cucullin Saga' and some illustrations. Céad fáilte romhat, a* Éire go Bráth *& go mbadh suairc é do shaoghal.*[72]

Is trua nár foilsíodh aon eagrán eile den iris seo.[73] Lean Brian air ag teagasc thar thrí chontae i rith 1902 agus is léir go raibh ualach trom teagaisc agus taistil air. *Mr. O'Keeney will conduct classes in Newry every Monday; in Dundalk, every Tuesday and Wednesday; in Armagh, every Thursday and Friday, the National Teachers' class in Newry, every Saturday; the Carlingford class on Saturday evenings and the Grange class every Sunday.*[74]

Is cinnte go raibh an t-ualach oibre a bhí air róthrom agus buaileadh tinn é, rud a tharla do mhúinteoirí taistil eile thar na blianta.

> *Illness of a Gaelic Teacher: The numerous friends of the energetic teacher of the Gaelic League classes in Newry, Dundalk and Armagh etc. – Mr. B. O'Keeney – will regret to learn of that gentleman's serious illness. Mr. O'Keeney was taken suddenly ill on Saturday night last at his lodgings in Canal Street, and early on Sunday morning Dr. Crossle was summoned, found Mr. O'Keeney was suffering from inflamation of the membrane of the stomach and described (sic!) accordingly. Rev. Fr. O'Hare was also summoned, so that Mr. O'Keeney's illness was grave. However, under the skilful treatment of Dr. Crossle the patient is regaining some strength, but for some time the Gaelic League classes will have to be conducted by some of the more advanced students at various centres. Mr. O'Keeney has worked with unexampled energy and enthusiasm since his appointment as Irish teacher in this district organising branches, teaching classes, writing articles to Press, courting the Muses in hours of relaxation, or when travelling by rail from town to town in pursuit of a vocation and that it is not surprising his health gave way in the great strain of physical and mental hardship and worry to*

which he exposed his constitution during the past few months – Newry Telegraph.[75]

Mar a tharla, fuair múinteoir taistil eile bás agus é i mbun a chuid oibre sa cheantar chéanna ag an am[76] agus chum Alice Milligan dán faoi.[77]

Ba cheoltóir breá é Brian riamh agus ba mhór a spéis agus a chur amach ar chúrsaí ceoil. Labhair sé go minic faoin ábhar seo agus scríobh sé faoi go rialta ina shaol agus ba mhinic é ag gabháil cheoil ina chuid ranganna, ag ócáidí poiblí agus ag coirmeacha ceoil. Tá a chuid smaointe maidir leis an ábhar seo le fáil i litir fhada leis a foilsíodh ar an *Derry Journal* i mí Aibreáin:[78] *The National Music and Ballad Poetry of Ireland.*

Bhí fáilte roimh Bhrian achan áit a ndeachaigh sé, ní mar mhúinteoir éifeachtach amháin, mar chainteoir agus mar óráidí, ach mar cheoltóir agus aisteoir chomh maith, mar is léir ó na tagairtí dó ar na nuachtáin.

Sgoraidheacht in Moy: Moy Irish class held a fine Sgoraidheacht on Friday night last in the Courthouse ... Mr. John McMenamy, teacher of Moy Irish class, introduced to the audience Mr. Brian O'Keeney, who addressed them in Irish, complemented them on the truly patriotic spirit manifested in their endeavours to resuscitate the language of their forefathers, and expressing his pleasure at being in their midst to encourage their perseverance. Mr. O'Keeney sang 'Óglaoch na Rann' and 'An tSean-Bhean Bhocht,' for which he was vociferously cheered. He also sang a couple of comic songs, to the immense enjoyment of the audience, who taxed his endurance by repeated calls ... and 'The West's asleep,' by Mr. O'Keeney, brought ringing rounds of applause, which were renewed again and again as each of them concluded his response with respectively 'Let Erin remember,' 'Robert Emmet,' and 'The low-backed car.' ... The singing of 'God Save Ireland' by Mr. O'Keeney brought the proceedings to a close.[79]

Rinne Brian gaisce sa bhliain 1902 óir bhain sé duais ag an Oireachtas, nuaíocht mhór do Chonallach.

1902 Winner of First Prize (All Ireland) at the Oireachtas in Dublin, for best original poem dealing with the 'Battle of Benburb,'

> *was Mr. Brian O'Keeney, Ardara, County Donegal, who is well-known throughout Ulster as a writer of pure Gaelic.*[80]

Tionóladh an chéad fheis riamh i nDún Dealgan in 1902 agus bhí baint ag Brian leis mar mholtóir agus mar bhronntóir duaise.

> *Dundalk Feis unique and historic event. Large attendances in the Christian Brothers Schools: On Sunday the genuinely Irish people of Dundalk and neighbouring districts attended at the Christian Brothers Schools, to participate in the first FEIS, or similar gathering, held in this historic old town for generations. Examiners: H. Morris, Thomas Concannon, B. O'Keeney, James Bryne, P. Johnston, &c! In our opinion the Central Committee of the Dundalk Branch of the Gaelic League are to be heartily congratulated on the success of their first effort in the direction of holding a Feis in the town. Of course there were hitches and mistakes inseparable from a first effort, but they were hardly noticed by the general public whereas they were keenly felt by many of those deeply interested in the Feis. The programme contained several competitions divided into three grades, namely – one for juniors and two for seniors – the senior classes being reckoned by the date at which candidates commenced the study of Irish, whether before or since August last. The subjects for competition included Irish reading, translation, writing and conversation, with, in the case of the seniors, composition to be written in Irish. In the senior grades recitation also formed one of the subjects, the highest measure of praise for the wholehearted manner in which they entered into the movement. The committee are indebted to the following for donations of books and other prizes: ... Mr O'Keeney, (teacher) – a silver bangle.*[81]

Is minic a bhí trácht i rith na bliana ar an obair a bhí ar siúl ag Brian thall is abhus. Tugann sin léargas dúinn ar an obair mhór, ilghnéitheach a bhí ar siúl aige agus é ag imeacht ó áit go háit.[82]

Tharla sé ag an am seo fosta gur reáchtáladh coirm cheoil sa '*Brigade Hall, Castle Street, as the initiative step in the formation of a Gaelic class in connection with St Colman's Boys' Brigade.*' Ar na daoine a bhí i láthair, bhí '*Father McGrath ... in the chair, and several leading local members of the Gaelic League.*' Spiorad Gaelach a bhí san ócáid ach go raibh tromlach na n-amhrán as Béarla, agus Brian i measc na gceoltóirí. Ag deireadh na hoíche chláraigh cuid mhaith de na buachaillí fá choinne na ranganna Gaeilge. An rud is spéisiúla fán choirm cheoil gur reáchtáladh é ag *'Lieutenant Hughes and Lieutenant Murphy. Lieutenant McCann presided at the piano, with ability.'*[83]

Sampla atá ansin den fháilte a chuir Conradh na Gaeilge ag an am roimh chuile dhuine ba chuma cén creideamh, cén pholaitíocht nó cén aicme lenar bhain siad. Is fiú éisteacht le Hannay ar an téad seo:

> *Not only is the League by its constitution non-political and non-sectarian; the general sentiment of the rank and file is absolutely true to the constitution in these respects. Protestant and Roman Catholic, Unionist and Home Ruler, are friends when the Irish language is on their lips though they were never friends before. That is the general spirit of the League ... The great mass of Gaelic Leaguers, and all those who are most enthusiastic for its work, are perfectly determined that the League shall remain what it has been in the past – a national body. They will not let it be dressed in the uniform of a political party or put into a cap and apron to serve as handmaid to the Roman Catholic Church.*[84]

Tá sampla d'oscailteacht na hAthbheochana i leith chuile dhuine san eachtra seo a leanas fosta a raibh baint lárnach ag Brian leis.

> *The British Association: Excursion to Rostrevor and Carlingford: On Saturday last a large excursion party of the members of the British Association, whose annual meetings are at present being held in Belfast, visited Rostrevor and Carlingford ... In the afternoon inside the walls of this old fortress a delightful entertainment was organised in honour of the visit of the British Association, through the kindness of Mrs. Gartlan, of Newry. It consisted of Irish songs, music, and dances, which were particularly appropriate in a town that is so steeped in the traditions of the past. Mr. Markay played a fine selection of Irish airs on the pipes, and Miss O'Hanlon sang a song in Irish with great feeling and expression. Mr. O'Hegarty also sang, and a number of school children, who took part in the Irish chorus, were loudly applauded. One of the most noticeable features*

was the Irish jig, danced by the Misses Campbell of Warrenpoint, in costume. Mr. O'Keeney acted as master of ceremonies ...[85]

Ní dhearnadh dearmad ar Bhrian ar an tSrath Bán le linn dó a bheith sa taobh eile den chúige.

Language Movement in Strabane: Feis in the Home Industries Hall: The Feis which took place in the Home Industries Hall on Monday last, and which was followed in the evening by a concert of purely Irish character is, as we have stated last week, an epoch in the advance of the work of the Gaelic League in the district, and is bound to create in Strabane a great public interest in the movement. This is only as it should be, and to Father McElhatton, a lot of credit is due for bringing Strabane into line with the rest of the country. Without his aid and powerful influence it would have been utterly impossible to have carried on the work to such a successful issue. Barely twelve months have elapsed since, through his efforts, the services of a very competent and capable Irish teacher, Mr. Brian O'Keeney, were secured, and since that time classes have been conducted nightly in the Barrack-street Hall. These classes were remarkably well attended, and what progress the pupils have made in the study of the language was evidenced in a striking degree at last Monday's Feis.[86]

Fiú amháin agus é ar laetha saoire sa bhaile in Ard an Rátha an bhliain sin, ní raibh Brian ina thost.

Killybegs: The annual combined excursion of the Strabane Catholic Association and the Clonleigh Temperance Society was held on Wednesday, 2nd July ... Irish songs and recitations were abundantly contributed ... Speeches were delivered by ... Mr. B. O'Keeney.[87]

Faoin am seo aithníodh go raibh Brian ina shaineolaí maidir le cúrsaí Gaeilge agus níor leasc leis a shaineolas a chur in iúl, mar is léir ón litir seo a leanas uaidh.

Irish Idiom: To the Editor of Dundalk Examiner: *Sir, It may appear to some that by advocating strenuously the spoken language of to-day, a tendency to belittle the works of our best writers might follow as a matter of consequence. I think on the contrary that it is only in perfect keeping with the unmistakeable object of such writers which was and is 'modernisation.' It must be admitted that every Irish-speaking district has its own peculiar corruptions, but Irish writers are careful to omit such corruptions, and there is, therefore, ample reason to believe that the Irish language will be daily increasing in*

> *purity of idiom and construction. Many of our students have now advanced so far as to be able to collect songs, stories, proverbs, &c. from the peasantry in Irish-speaking districts, but they should be more anxious to add to their knowledge something they had not known hitherto, than to cast aside what they have learned and substitute something which is, in their opinion, better. I have known several students who have swallowed the grossest corruptions from peasantry, who gave them these so-called 'idiomatic constructions,' etc., on the authority of an illiterate grandfather or grandmother, and adopted them in preference to the faultless usage found in the writing of An Craoibhín Aoibhinn. Whilst I admire the idea of collecting from the old people many things which are in danger of being lost, I would respectfully remind the collectors that they should be prepared to meet some 'thorns among the roses.' Trusting I am not trespassing too far on your valuable space. Faithfully yours, Brian O'Keeney.*[88]

Thart ar an am seo fosta thoisigh Brian ar scéalta beaga a chur i gcló ar *An Claidheamh Soluis* agus bhí cúpla cúis aige leis sin. Mar rud amháin bhí fonn air píosaí gearra, éadroma a sholáthar do lucht foghlama na Gaeilge agus, lena chois sin, bhí fonn air samplaí de Ghaeilge Chúige Uladh a chur i láthair léitheoirí *ACS* óir mhaígh sé féin agus Ultaigh eile nach raibh cothrom na Féinne á fháil ag canúint Uladh ar leathanaigh *ACS* thar na blianta.[89] D'fhéach sé féin, Séamus Mac a' Bháird agus P.T. MacGinley leis an scéal sin a leigheas.[90]

Chreid Brian go láidir i rith a shaoil go raibh slánú na Gaeilge ag brath ar na páistí óga agus gur cheart iad a mhealladh agus a bhroslú i gceann na Gaeilge. Seans maith go raibh Brian ina bhall den *Fireside Club*[91] nuair a bhí sé óg agus go ndeachaigh idé-eolaíocht agus cur chuige an chumainn sin i bhfeidhm air, mar a chuaigh i gcás daoine ar nós Thomáis Uí Choncheanainn, Éamoin de Valera, Úna Ní Fhaircheallaigh, Eoin Uí Shearcaigh, Énrí Uí Mhuirgheasa, Louis Walsh srl. Ag tacú leis an tuairim sin, bhí baint aige le *Crann Eithne*[92] ina dhiaidh sin agus leis an *Fireside Club* thall i Meiriceá. Seo a leanas litir leis chuig *ACS* ar an téad áirithe seo.

*The Children's League: To the editor of An Claidheamh Soluis: A Chara, The holiday season is speedily passing away, and Gaelic Leaguers should consider the best means of conducting the Irish classes for the coming season. Permit me to suggest the formation of what might be termed 'The Children's League' in connection with each Craobh. The teaching of Irish has not been adopted as yet in many of our so-called National Schools, and the children are consequently neglected. No effort should be spared in offering every facility to the children for the study of their national language. A meeting of the children themselves might be held at the time of opening the classes, and a Craobh of the 'Children's League' established, the President, Secretary, etc. to be elected by the children. The local Craobh should supply them with membership cards (*is forus páisde a shásadh*), have classes held at a suitable hour, say, three times a week, and make an earnest appeal to the parents to ensure the most regular attendance. Common salutations, phrases, etc., should be taught them, and prizes offered to those who would acquire and cultivate the best spoken knowledge of Irish during the season, the voting in this case to be by the children also. A purely Irish concert might be organised for them during winter, the proceeds of which would be well spent in an annual excursion, at which nothing but Irish would be spoken during the entire day. Mise do chara sa chúis,* Brian Ó Cianaigh[93]

Agus Brian sa bhaile ar a laetha saoire chum sé agallamh beag '*Beirt Fhear ag Tarraingt ar an Fheis in Ard an Rátha Lá Fhéile Muire*' a foilsíodh ar *ACS*.[94] Píosa beag gan mórán tábhachta atá ann ach bhain sé leas as cur chuige an chomhrá nó an agallaimh ní ba dheireanaí ina shaol nuair a chuir sé an tsraith as Gaeilge agus Béarla i gcló ar an *Derry Journal*.[95]

Phill Brian ar a chuid oibre i ndiaidh laetha saoire an tsamhraidh agus chuaigh i mbun oibre ar ais.[96] Ghlac sé an deis le cur síos ar an dóigh a raibh ag éirí le Gluaiseacht na Gaeilge ina chontae féin. Ní raibh sé róshásta go raibh cúrsaí polaitíochta ag cur isteach ar an scéal ansin ná go raibh gnéithe den chultúr ghallda róláidir i gcónaí i measc na gConallach. Litir bhroslaitheach atá sa litir seo a leanas.

Irish language movement in Donegal: A few observations to the Editor of the Derry Journal: Sir – Having just returned to my native county for a brief holiday I have been tempted to enquire, 'How is old Donegal, or how does she stand?' As one who is not altogether unacquainted with the towns and villages of Donegal I think I may be permitted to say that the general spread of the language movement throughout the county is by no means of a satisfactory character, and while hostility to the movement is – I am glad to say – practically unknown, enthusiasm is pre-eminently conspicuous by its absence. Besides, it would seem that there is some misconception existing in Donegal with regard to the aims of the Gaelic League, and that political differences are to a certain extent interfering with the harmony which must exist amongst us if we wish to raise our National language to its proper position and combat the nation-killing influence of foreignism once and forever. The Gaelic League must never become the appendage of any political party, but its members are free to hold and propound their own political feelings whatever they may be. Neither political opinions nor religious convictions must be necessarily discarded in order to become a member of the Gaelic League, but the League will nevertheless remain a non-political and non-sectarian society.[97] *It is indeed somewhat difficult to understand how a spiritual and patriotic people – at least according to the newspapers – can display so much indifference towards a movement which goes at once to the very foundation of nationhood. Are we entirely regardless of the inroads made by English smut and corruption, or does our patriotism mean nothing more than hatred towards the English and contempt of her laws? Would such patriotism (if we may call it by that name) be effective in raising our people from the servility of toadyism and shoneenism? Does it not seem rather contradictory and inconsistent to applaud the fiery patriots who curse and condemn 'England's rotten army,' and sing 'Dolly Gray' at our social entertainments? This, by the way, reminds me of the fact – and anyone who knows Donegal will agree with me in saying so – that our grand old county has lost, or is losing rapidly, whatever musical taste it once could boast of. There is not, perhaps, another county in Ireland posessing such a treasure of songs and airs as Donegal. Yet, what do we hear? The children at the breakfast table reciting 'Dolly Gray' by way of grace; the cartmen going along the road whistling this consoling strain. In many parts of Ireland, and even in parts of Donegal, the language movement has spread like a prairie fire. The thought and intellect of Ireland are unquestionably on its side – men who do not look upon a National language as unimportant and distinguishable, but a mighty living factor. And these men in endeavouring to save this sacred legacy of our ancestors naturally and hopefully need the backing and assistance from Irish-speaking districts. Therefore the eyes of Irish Ireland are placed upon Donegal. Hence the well-known lines:*

The Saxon chain our rights and tongues alike doth hold in thrall,
Save where, amid the Connaught wilds and hills of Donegal,
And by the shores of Munster, like the broad Atlantic blast,
The olden language lingers yet and binds us to the past.[98]

The Irish classes for the coming season are now about to open, and it is hoped that Donegal will (mindful of the fact that her children have written some of the most brilliant pages of Ireland's history) endeavour to cling to her noblest heritage and foster, develop, and encourage the aims of the Gaelic League. Thanking you in anticipation. Faithfully yours, B. O'Keeney.[99]

Lean Brian ar aghaidh lena chuid oibre in oirdheisceart Uladh.

Gaelic League: Annual General Meeting: The third annual general meeting of the Newry, Dundalk, and Districts Organising Committee was held in the Catholic Club, Mill Street, Newry, on Friday evening, the 19th inst ... In the three places public meetings were held, which were attended by Mr. Brian O'Keeney, organiser and teacher, and several members of the Coisde Ceanntair.[100]

Tá cuntas ag P.T. MacG. ar an obair mhór a bhí ar siúl ar an tSrath Bán ó thaobh na Gaeilge de agus Brian luaite mar an chéad mhúinteoir ansin.

A northern centre of Gaelic work: Strabane has become a vigorous centre of Gaelic activity. Like many other places that are doing good work, it was slow to move ... At last Father McElhatton moved on the matter, and his great personal influence prevailed where, perhaps, no other force could. A teacher was employed, and a number of local merchants and others subscribed the necessary funds to pay him. Mr. Brian O'Keeney was the first teacher, and on his taking up appointment under the Newry Committee, Mr. Gildea, from the same district in Donegal was retained as teacher. Not only in the town of Strabane, but at several points in the neighbourhood, classes were started, and progress made. I had recently occasion to see one of these classes at work, and nothing that I have witnessed in recent times was more inspiring.[101]

Tharla ag deireadh 1902 gur foilsíodh leabhar foghlama Gaeilge le Brian a raibh ráchairt mhór air agus a tharraing cliú ar Bhrian mar mhúinteoir agus mar shaineolaí Gaeilge i bhfad is i ngearr.

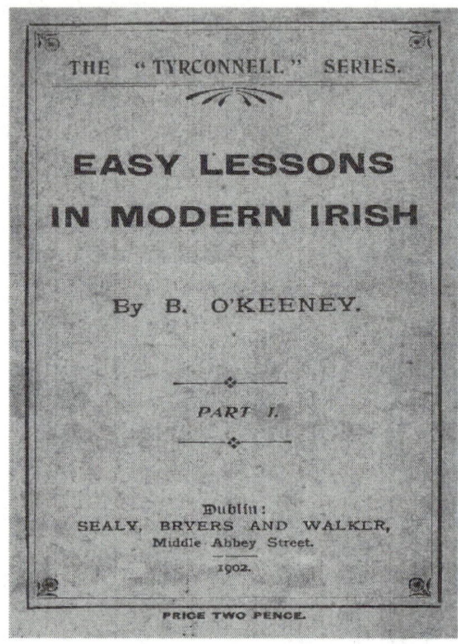

THE "TYRCONNELL" SERIES.

EASY LESSONS IN MODERN IRISH

By B. O'KEENEY.

PART I.

Dublin:
SEALY, BRYERS AND WALKER,
Middle Abbey Street.

1902.

PRICE TWO PENCE.

Easy Lessons in Modern Irish 1902

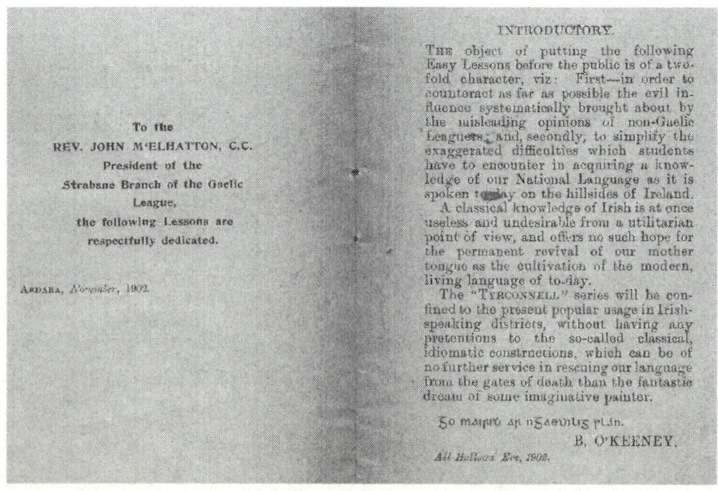

To the
REV. JOHN M'ELHATTON, C.C.
President of the
Strabane Branch of the Gaelic
League,
the following Lessons are
respectfully dedicated.

ARDARA, *November*, 1902.

INTRODUCTORY.

THE object of putting the following Easy Lessons before the public is of a two-fold character, viz: First—in order to counteract as far as possible the evil influence systematically brought about by the misleading opinions of non-Gaelic Leaguers; and, secondly, to simplify the exaggerated difficulties which students have to encounter in acquiring a knowledge of our National Language as it is spoken to-day on the hillsides of Ireland.

A classical knowledge of Irish is at once useless and undesirable from a utilitarian point of view, and offers no such hope for the permanent revival of our mother tongue as the cultivation of the modern, living language of to-day.

The "TYRCONNELL" series will be confined to the present popular usage in Irish-speaking districts, without having any pretentions to the so-called classical, idiomatic constructions, which can be of no further service in rescuing our language from the gates of death than the fantastic dream of some imaginative painter.

Go mairiḋ ar nGaeḋilg slán.

B. O'KEENEY.

All Hallows' Eve, 1902.

Réamhrá, Easy Lessons, *1902*

Reviews: The 'Tyrconnell' Series of Easy Lessons in Modern Irish[102] *I have just received a copy of Mr O'Keeney's latest effort, which I am sure will come upon the people of Ulster as a pleasant surprise. In the midst of so much Southern Literature which is just now inundating us, and certainly not improving out taste for the study of our mother tongue, it is refreshing to open Mr. O'Keeney's bright little treasure. The publishers are to be congratulated for the admirable manner in which they have turned out their work; the letterpress, especially, being remarkably clear and correct ... It is hoped, therefore, that Mr. O'Keeney's efforts to advance the study of Irish in Ulster will be warmly supported, and that he will continue the series of which he has made such a faithful beginning.*[103]

On the 14th March 1903, Derry City and Donegal got a new newspaper ... The advertisement from Brian O'Keeney's recently published Irish language book called 'Easy Lessons in Irish' appeared on the front page of the first ever publication of The Derry People and Donegal News *and inside the newspaper was a half-page of Gaelic lessons from Brian O'Keeney with the English translation. Also in the first ever edition was a Gaelic poem by Brian O'Keeney. Brian O'Keeney's lessons were also published in many other newspapers notably* The Ulster Herald and The Fermanagh Herald.[104]

Foilsíodh an t-amhrán 'A Bhuachaillín mo Chroí' (Fonn: 'Péarla an Bhrollaigh Bháin') leis ar *ACS*.[105]

Gaelic Leaguers and Gaelic Students, at the Request of a large number of our Readers, we have undertaken to publish in Book Form Part II of Mr. B. O'Keeney's 'Tyrconnell Series' of Easy Lessons in Irish which are at present appearing weekly in The Fermanagh Herald and have won such golden opinions on every side. The book will be ready on May 1st next. Price 3d.[106]

From the Irish Daily Independent: *We have just received a copy of Part II of the 'Tyrconnell' series of easy lessons in modern Irish, printed and published by the North-West of Ireland Printing and Publishing Company, Ltd., Omagh, price three pence. In a few introductory sentences the author explains that the speedy and rapidly-increasing sale of Part I will sufficiently explain its early appearance and modestly asks those who will derive any advantage from a perusal of the work to remember that his chief ambition was to meet at a seasonable and critical period the growing requirements of students of the Irish language. It is divided into two parts, the first being devoted to the more elementary lessons and exercises. The arrangement appears to be excellent throughout, and the explanations and vocabularies are so numerous and comprehensive that no intelligent and earnest learner can experience much difficulty in mastering the valuable information embodied in the forty-seven pages, of which the little book consists.*[107]

Donnyloop in the Loop ... On Friday evening, the 27th March, a meeting of the parishioners was held at Donnyloop to discuss the propriety of forming a Craobh. The Rev. John McElhatton was in attendance, accompanied by ... Mr. Brian O'Keeney, the very talented Irish teacher of the district. Mr. O'Keeney then pointed out the steps to be pursued towards the establishment and carrying out of a Craobh and his address enumerated the many difficulties to be encountered before becoming thoroughly acquainted with the Irish language, but as a consolation, he showed forth that these difficulties had been already overcome by thousands; and in a few years these thousands will become millions. And as an instance that all persons, both young and old, can succeed, he pointed out the fact that the late revered Father O'Growney was not only ignorant of the Irish language, but also of the very existence of such a language until he had reached the years of manhood. He impressed firmly on those present that the Gaelic League was strictly non-political, notwithstanding the fact that it had emblazoned on its banner the sentiment of 'Ireland a Nation.'[108]

Foilsíodh an dán 'Cill Airne' sa leabhrán seo.

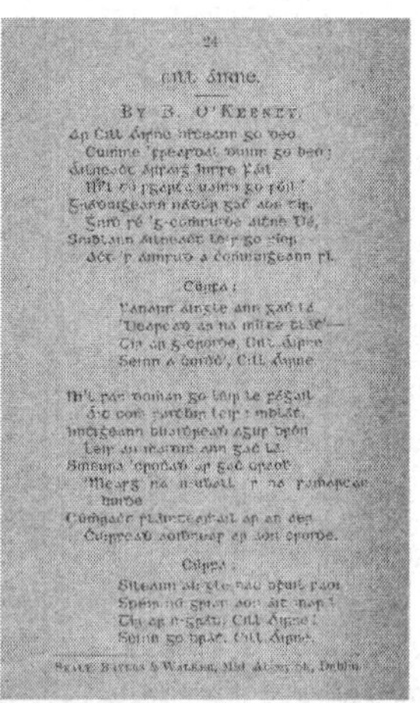
24

Cill Áirne.

By B. O'Keeney.

Dán in Easy Lessons, *1902*

Bhí Brian ar ais i dTír Eoghain i mí na Samhna arís agus é i mbun oibre.

The Gaelic League: Strabane and District Committee: The second meeting of the Strabane and District Committee was held in the Rooms, Barrack Street, on Monday evening 27th last ... On the motion of Father McElhatton, seconded by F. McLaughlin, Mr. B. O'Keeney, late teacher and organiser under the Newry District Committee, and who already did sterling work for the movement in Strabane, was again appointed.[109]

Opening of Strabane Gaelic Lessons: The opening of the Strabane Gaelic classes for the coming season took place in the Barrack-Street Hall on Thursday evening at eight o'clock under the most favourable and auspicious circumstances. No fewer than two hundred members were present, and highly interesting lessons were given by Mr. Concannon, Mr. O'Keeney, and Mr. Nolan ... Mr. O'Keeney read an interesting paper on the Gaelic Revival, and a number of Irish songs and recitations, &c., were afterwards contributed. A bright future seems in store for Strabane and the surrounding districts.[110]

Mar ba dhual dó, lean sé dá chuid ceoil agus aisteoireachta.

Clann na nGaodhal Hurling Club: Concert at Rabstown: On Friday night, 7th inst., a very enjoyable concert was given at Rabstown, near Sion Mills, by the Clann na nGaodhall Hurling Club ... The following contributed songs, recitations, dances, &c.: ... B. O'Keeney ... The most notable feature in the whole entertainment was the fact that every item on the programme was either Irish or Anglo-Irish, with the single exceptions of a sacred song and a Scotch song sung by a Scotch lady.[111]

Lean sé fosta dá bholscaireacht ar son na hAthbheochana agus é sáite go poiblí sna meáin sna ceisteanna a bhí á bplé agus á gcur chun cinn ag Conradh na Gaeilge, cúrsaí oideachais ina measc.

University Commission; Dr Salmon's Evidence; To the Editor of the Derry Journal; Sir – Dr. Salmon, Provost of Trinity College, in his evidence dealing with the Irish language before the University Commission,[112] *has given us another sample of that celestial humour for which this institution is so long remarkable. In the opening portion of his evidence he says: 'There is a current of misrepresentation that we in Trinity College are opposed to the study of that language. Quite the opposite is the truth; all the modern cultivation of the Irish language originated in Trinity College ... Nor has Trinity College's interest in the language ceased. The authority of one of our Professors (Atkinson) in this department stands very high ...' As to 'Trinity College's interest in the language, I would merely draw Dr. Salmon's attention to the following quotation from a leading article in the* Manchester Guardian *(Nonconformist) in 1899 – 'Not for the first, or the hundred and first time has that institution (Trinity College) exposed itself as a foreign, unassimilated body, differing only from great institutions abroad in its intense desire to belittle all things Irish. Three hundred years have passed even Trinity College, and it can boast that no one can lay to its charge that it ever gave the least encouragement to anyone who wished to know how the people of this country (Ireland) lived and thought.' The Rev. Richard Henebry, Ph.D., Professor of Celtic languages in the Catholic University of America says: 'Dr. Atkinson has edited certain easy texts and done some valuable index work. Strangely enough his edition of Dr. Keating's* Three Shafts of Death *(by the way, he should have translated the title* Three Stings of Death*), has contributed largely to making the present language revival possible. The technical work on that book was done by poor John Fleming, an old time neighbour of mine. He lived in a garret in Dublin on a pittance of 10s a week, contributed by Dr. Atkinson. In the preface to that book the name John Fleming does not occur. Perhaps the doctor thought his 10s a week entitled him to pick the brains of the old man without acknowledgment. Father O'Leary, writing in the* Freeman's Journal *of February 27th, 1889, says: 'I will ask any sane man whether a person can be relied on to translate a sentence correctly who calls the subject of it the predicate and the predicate the subject. The inevitable inference is that Dr. Atkinson cannot be relied on to translate correctly a single sentence of this text of Keating which he edited. I will ask your readers, therefore, to pay no attention whatever to the opinions of Dr. Atkinson regarding Irish.' Dr. Salmon believes, or at least pretends to believe, that the revival of the Irish Language would be an immense injury to the material prosperity of the country. 'Want of knowledge of English,' he adds (quoting from* Many Memories*), 'is the cause that principally keeps down the people of Wales. It excludes them from domestic service. It prevents their employment in the English towns. It indisposes them to emigrate; if they enter the army it prevents them from rising above the lowest rank. In short, it is a badge and a cause of inferiority.' Might this portion of Dr. Salmon's evidence be translated* *as follows, and take the shape of an advice to the Irish People? – 'Prepare for domestic service; seek employment in English towns; prepare for emigration; enter the English army and rise above the lower ranks – unless you are shot; speak not a language which is the hallmark of inferiority, but utilise and cultivate the language in which Cromwell prayed for the preservation of the Irish race before he was transported into heaven.' Dr. Salmon goes on to say: 'It is now too late to make Irish supercede the vernacular use of English, which has now become almost universal in this island. You cannot make men unlearn a language which they have been taught at their mother's knee and which all around them are speaking. Anyone who endeavours to effect such a revolution may be very clever, but must certainly be described as a goose.' Now, as two things that are equal to the same thing are equal to one another, Dr. Salmon will have no difficulty in finding his 'goose' amongst the Commissioners of National Education, who are diligently endeavouring to bring about such a 'revolution' in the National Schools in Irish-speaking districts. With the latter portion of Dr. Salmon's evidence I would gladly deal, but I feel I have already trespassed too far on your valuable space. Thanking you in anticipation. Faithfully yours, B. O'Keeney.*[113]

Tugann nuachtáin an ama sin cuntas dúinn ar a raibh ar siúl ag Brian agus cé chomh dícheallach, ildánach is a bhí sé i mbun a chuid oibre. Is fiú a rá go raibh sé mar pholasaí ag Conradh na Gaeilge an ama sin go mbeadh oiread tráchta sna nuachtáin Bhéarla logánta agus náisiúnta ar imeachtaí Gaeilge agus an Chonartha agus ab fhéidir. Gné thábhachtach eile dá mbolscaireacht a bhí ansin. Agus ó tharla go raibh Brian chomh dícheallach i gceann a chuid oibre, go raibh bua na cainte agus an cheoil aige, agus gurbh amhlaidh a bheireadh sé cuid mhór óráidí ar son Chonradh na Gaeilge agus a gcuspóirí, is iomaí tuairisc a foilsíodh faoina chuid imeachtaí agus cainte ar na nuachtáin áitiúla.[114]

Chuir Brian tús leis an bhliain 1903 le filíocht,[115] léachtaí[116] agus sraith de cheachtanna foghlama ar an *Ulster Herald*. Cuireadh tús le *The 'Tyrconnell' Series Easy Lessons in Modern Irish Part II* ar an *Ulster Herald* ar

17/1/1903, 6. Dúradh ansin go raibh ráchairt mhór ar *Part I*, rud a chuir dlús le foilsiú na sraithe seo.[117]

Foilsíodh an dán beag '*Sing, Birdie, Sing*' leis ar an *Ulster Herald* ar 17/1/1903, 6[118] agus lean sé dá chuid scéilíní ar *An Claidheamh Soluis*.[119]

Lean sé dá chuid oibre i rith an ama i dTír Eoghain.[120]

> *Strabane Coisde Ceanntair: Mr B. O'Keeney presented his report on the progress in the district since the last meeting. From this it appeared that upwards 1,300 are now learning Irish in the district worked by Coisde Ceanntair. Irish is taught in nearly all schools under Catholic management, and will be introduced into the others at the end of the month ... 'That we beg to draw the attention of the Publication Committee of the Coisde Gnótha to the fact that, with the exception of* Greann na Gaedhilge *there are not any easy texts in Northern Irish, suitable for readers who have finished the 3rd and 4th O'Growney; and that we think that, in justice to Northern students, a few texts of the kind should be published, provided with vocabularies, and based on the Northern usage; for we are convinced that it entails enormous waste of time and energy if the spoken language in a pupil's own neighbourhood is not made the basis of his or her studies, and that it is only by having a foundation laid in this way that he or she will be afterwards able to master the peculiarities of the other provinces with any degree of ease or rapidity.' Several of those present also complained that the* Claidheamh Soluis *appears week after week, with only an occasional scrap of Northern Irish, making it impossible to work up a good circulation for the paper in this district.*[121]

Foilsíodh dán leis 'Smaointe an Deoraí' ar an *Ulster Herald* (14/2/1903, 7). Bhain an dán seo an dara háit i gcomórtas de chuid an Oireachtais sa bhliain 1902. Leanadh i gcónaí leis na tagairtí d'obair Bhriain sna nuachtáin logánta.[122]

Bronnadh an chéad duais air san Oireachtas as a aiste '*The Cottage Industry*.'[123] Sin ábhar ba gheal lena chroí i rith a shaoil. Chum sé an óid 'Teangaidh na hÉireann' fosta.[124]

I mí na Bealtaine cuireadh tús le colún ar *ACS* darbh ainm GIOTAÍ a lean ar aghaidh go rialta ar feadh na bliana. Bhí trí mhír i gcló ag Brian ar an cholún sin (6/6/1903, 29/8/1903, 5/9/1903). Is píosaí gearra greannmhara seanchais iad óna cheantar féin. Tá éagsúlacht sa cholún ó thaobh na gcanúintí de agus Brian agus Seaghán Mhíchíl a sheas an fód do chanúint Dhún na nGall. An cuspóir a bhí leis an cholún, ábhar éadrom, soléite a chur ar fáil do lucht foghlama na Gaeilge. Dúradh ar *An Claidheamh Soluis:*

> *Since we started our Giotaí column, readers from every point of the compass have been discharging at us regular volleys of GIOTAÍ, good, bad and indifferent. Every post brings its complement. We would wish for more short ranns, riddles, charms and the like than we have hitherto got.*[125]

Bhí duais ann gach mí don ghiota ab fhearr.

Gabhadh buíochas le Brian as an chuidiú a thug sé do M. Mullen lena leabhar ar chanúint Uladh.[126] Foilsíodh alt leis 'Cranneolas' faoin ghá a bhí le tuilleadh crann a chur in Éirinn, port a bhí ag Conradh na Gaeilge san am.[127]

Cuireadh tús le colún úr don lucht foghlama ar *An Claidheamh Soluis* dar theideal *Oideachas* i mí an Mhárta 1903. *In this section we propose to cater for the wants of students who are not sufficiently advanced to grapple with the Irish of our news and literary columns ...*[128] As sin amach bhí scéal i gcló sa cholún. Ní raibh aon scéal scríofa i gcanúint Uladh go dtí 18/7/1903 nuair a foilsíodh an scéal 'An Scéal Bréagach' le Brian. Níor ainmníodh údair na scéalta éagsúla ach is féidir a bheith cinnte gurbh é Brian a scríobh ceithre scéal sa cholún seo a foilsíodh ansin ó lár mhí Iúil go deireadh mhí Mheán Fómhair.[129] Istigh le gach scéal tá *mionfhoclóir* (*glossary of words*) agus *tagra* (*a translation of particular words or idioms*). Níl aon aistriúchán ag gabháil leis an scéal.

Foilsíodh aiste le Brian, mar atá, 'Imeacht na nGael' ar *Irisleabhar na Gaedhilge* Vol. 13 September 1903, 388–9.[130] Foilsíodh na scéilíní 'I bPurgadóir ar an tSaol Seo' (6/6/1903), 'Dóigh Úr le Breith ar Ghadaí'(29/8/190) agus 'An Comhrá Deireanach' (5/9/1903, 3) in *ACS*.

Ainneoin a raibh ar siúl ag Brian in Éirinn ag teagasc agus ag eagrú agus ag scríobh, agus ainneoin ar chan sé faoi cheist na himirce, chroch sé a chuid seolta ag deireadh na bliana agus thug a aghaidh ar Mheiriceá áit a raibh leasdeartháireacha leis ina gcónaí le fada. D'fhan sé lena dheartháir Joe Daniel in Hoboken.

Ag cé Hoboken, c. 1900

We are sorry to learn that Mr. B. O'Keeney, whose work in the Gaelic movement is known through the length and breadth of Donegal, Ulster and the country, is leaving Ireland. It is hoped his absence will be but temporary. Mr. O'Keeney will help the movement wherever he goes, and we understand he intends giving bilingual lectures in America, where he will be staying with relatives.[131]

Scríobh Brian dán '*The Brothers Flynn*' i mí na Samhna agus é ar bhord an SS Astoria.[132] Is ar éigean a bhí Meiriceá bainte amach aige nuair a thoisigh sé ar a chuid oibre ar son na Gaeilge ansin mar a bhí ar siúl aige sa bhaile. Bhí aithne air thall cheana féin i measc Gaeilgeoirí de bharr a chuid scríbhneoireachta ar *ACS* ach go háirithe.

The Irish Language Revival: On Sunday evening, Nov. 29, Mr. B. O'Keeney, the popular Irish lecturer and novelist, will make his first public appearance in this country and deliver a bilingual lecture on the Irish language movement at Odd Fellows' Hall, Hoboken. The lecture will be followed by a concert consisting of Irish songs, Irish music and Irish dances. The services of several eminent artists have been secured for the occasion, and a genuine Irish entertainment may be expected. The dances will include the following: 'The Limerick Reel;' the 'Wavy Reel' danced by eight persons and the 'Fairy Reel' danced by six persons.[133]

Is léir ón chuntas seo a leanas nach féidir idirdhealú ar bith a dhéanamh idir a leithéid seo d'ócáid Ghaelach thall i Meiriceá agus sa bhaile in Éirinn. Is suntasach an rud é go bhfuil deartháir Bhriain gafa san obair chomh maith le seanchara leis as Ard an Rátha.

Irish Ireland: The Irish language movement in America: Mr. B. O'Keeney opens a promising campaign: On Sunday evening Mr. B. O'Keeney, whose name is so well known in Gaelic League circles, delivered the first of a series of lectures at Odd Fellows' Hall, Hoboken, New Jersey, taking his subject 'The Irish language – the revival movement.' The spacious building was packed to overcrowding and the chair was occupied by Mr. H. Gildea, who is also a native of Ardara. The lecturer dealt exhaustively with the language movement from the point of view of Irish Nationality, and seems to have touched an answering chord in the hearts of those who were present. Mr. O'Keeney has made arrangements for lectures in Brooklyn, Jersey City, New York and Weehawken during the month of December as also for the formation of a number of Branches of the Gaelic League. The following was the programme on Sunday evening, November 29th: Part First: Selection of Irish airs; introductory remarks by the chairman, Mr. H. Gildea; Lecture (in Irish and English) on 'The Irish language – The Revival Movement' by Mr. B. O'Keeney. Part Second: Selection of Irish airs, Messrs. McGinley and Fitzsimons; (chorus in Irish and English). 'The Harp' song, and 'The Gaelic of Old' Mr. Joe Daniel Keeney (brother of Brian O'Keeney); Dance, 'The Limerick Reel' danced by eight; Song, 'Old Ireland I love you,' Mrs. Keeney; Pianoforte selection, Mrs. H. Gorman; Song, 'An Maidrín Ruadh,' (an Irish hunting song), Mr. Brian O'Keeney; Dance 'The Fairy Reel,' danced by six; Song, 'My dear old Irish home,' Mr. M. Gorman; Recitation, 'The Felons of our Land,' Miss L. Palihnich; Song 'Killarney,' Mrs. Keeney; Pianoforte selections Mr. J. Conrad; Song, 'The Minstrel Boy,' Mr. Brian O'Keeney; Dance, 'The Wavy Reel,' danced by eight; Recitation, 'A rally for Ireland,' Miss Julia Keeney; Chorus, 'God Save Ireland.'[134]

Foilsíodh an scéal *'Larry Brogan on the Ocean'* ar an *Fermanagh Herald* (19/12/1903, 13).[135]

I rith na mblianta nuair a bhí Brian i Meiriceá bhí post tábhachtach aige le comhlacht árachais agus mórán sílte de sa phost chéanna mar is léir ón teistiméireacht seo a leanas ó uachtarán an chomhlachta.

I am much gratified to observe in analysing the returns of the recent canvass conducted in commemoration of my seventieth birthday anniversary, the remarkable showing of your assistancy contributory to what proved to be a world-breaking record. In extending my congratulations, I wish in this way to personally assure you of my profound appreciation of this striking demonstration of devotion on the part of yourself and staff to our great cause, and the high compliment to me personally. Trusting that in your future endeavours you may meet with all the good things which your splendid deeds encourage you to anticipate. Believe me, Dear Mr. O'Keeney, Yours very truly, John F. Dryden, President of the Prudential Insurance Company of America, Newark, N.J., 18 August, 1909.[136]

Scríobh Brian amhrán le haghaidh bhaill an *Young Ireland Club* agus é thall i Meiriceá. An raibh baint aige leis an eagraíocht sin ina óige? Is léir go raibh baint ag Brian le cuid mhaith eagraíochtaí Éireannacha de chineálacha éagsúla i rith a shaoil agus spéis ar leith aige in eagraíochtaí do pháistí ó thaobh na Gaeilge de.

Seanchus: My Dear Children: This week I publish for you 'A Song for St. Patrick's Day,' dedicated to the members of the Young Ireland Club, written by Mr. B. O'Keeney, formerly the Gaelic League teacher in Strabane, and sent by him all the way across from America. It is a rousing little song to the air of 'Shan Van Vocht' and as it is peculiarly appropriate to the objects and work upon which you are all engaged as Young Irelanders, I trust it will become a favourite amongst you. Kathleen Ni Houlihan.
A Song for St. Patrick's Day[137] *Air: 'An tSeanbhean bhocht'*
(Dedicated to the members of the Young Irelanders' Club)
B. O'Keeney, 22 Willow Terrace, Hoboken, N.J.[138]

Is nuair a bhí sé thall i Meiriceá a léiríodh an chéad dráma a scríobh Brian agus is léir go bhfaca an t-uafás daoine é.

'Gaelic America': Echoes from beyond the sea: Donegal, Derry, and Tyrone exiles to witness first production of The Rebel of Innishowen*: To say that extensive preparations are being made for the first grand production of Mr. B. O'Keeney's new Irish melodrama,* The Rebel of Innishowen, *at St. Mary's Hall, Hoboken, N. J., on Monday evening, October 24th, is putting it mildly. It is confidently estimated that the occasion will be marked by the coming together of at least 2,000 of the sons and daughters of Donegal, Derry and Tyrone. The new melodrama is beyond doubt one of the most brilliant and stirring productions ever offered to the public. The plots are conservatively consistent and afford prominent opportunities for every character in the cast. The play throughout is replete with the most pathetic scenes notwithstanding that it is teeming with Irish wit and humour. The various scenic effects will be strikingly realistic especially, Scene 2, 'Mass on the mountainside.'*[139]

Barney O'Keeney is author and actor: Will Play Leading Part in His Irish Drama The Rebel of Innishowen*: The above cut is a picture of Mr. Barney O'Keeney, the author of a new Irish play,* The Rebel of Innishowen, *which will be given in the Hall of Our Lady of Grace Monday and Tuesday evenings, October 21st and 23rd. The author's name, which has prominently figured in modern Irish Literature during the last few years is well known to many of his fellow countrymen who have made this their adopted home, and it is with great interest that they look forward to his new play, which promises to be a great success. The scene of* The Rebel of Innishowen *is laid in the north of Ireland, the birthplace of the author, and is dramatized from historical and traditional information. It deals in a forcible and* *interesting manner with the rebellion of 1798. The laws that were then in existence in Ireland had become so unbearable that the peasantry resolved to rebel against them, and the play centres around the leader, 'Michael O'Brien,' the part to be taken by Mr. O'Keeney ... Mr. J.D. Keeney, 'Col. Simmons,' who is in charge of the English soldiers ...*[140]

Tharla ag an am seo fosta, ag cur lena theist mar dhrámadóir, gur foilsíodh dráma eile leis ar ais in Éirinn, mar atá, *Seaghan Ruadh,* gearrdhráma Gaeilge in aon ghníomh ar *The Frontier Sentinel* ar 22/10/1904. Léiríodh an dráma céanna go minic thall i Meiriceá agus in Éirinn i gcaitheamh na mblianta ina dhiaidh sin.

Signal honour for Donegal man: America press refers to The Rebel of Inishowen *as 'The King of Irish Plays': The Irish-American Advocate in reviewing Mr. B. O'Keeney's new melodrama says: It is indeed with extreme pleasure that we welcome such a valuable addition to Irish Dramatic literature, and in doing so have little hesitation in predicting for what has been already termed 'The King of Irish Plays,' the most unprecedented success. The author's name is well known to many of our readers and while admitting in full the envied reputation which he enjoys as a gifted writer, whether in poetry or in prose, we feel that as a play-wright his talent commands even greater admiration. The scene of* The Rebel of Innishowen *is laid in County Donegal. The play is a clever and powerful dramatization of the rebellion of 1798 in the north of Ireland. The laws which were then in existence against Catholics became so unbearable that the peasantry resolved to rebel against them hence the term 'rebel' which was commonly used to signify 'leader' or promoter of this dangerous, though by no means unjustifiable, undertaking. Ever ready to play a foremost part in any movement which might be calculated to hasten the advent for freedom for their suffering country, the sturdy sons of Innishowen under the leadership of the hero of this play, displayed the most commendable courage and bravery in their efforts to cast off once and forever the yoke of the foreigner. The able manner in which these efforts are reproduced constitutes what we consider the most admirable feature of the new drama. It must not, however, be inferred from this observation that the production is lacking in Irish wit and humour. On the contrary, we have seldom seen any production of its character which, as a witty son of Erin once happily put it, contains such a 'skinful of laughs.' We wish it the success it deserves.*[141]

Is léir gur choinnigh Brian súil ar a raibh ag tarlú sa bhaile in Éirinn i rith an ama agus é thall i Meiriceá ó thaobh na Gaeilge de.

> *Hoboken New Jersey: A plea for Ulster Irish! Letter from Mr. B. O'Keeney: Dear Sir – At a time when the sturdy Gaelic Leaguers of the North-West are evidently nearing a satisfactory accomplishment of their aims in uniting and consolidating the hitherto scattered force of Gaeldom throughout the Counties of Donegal, Derry, and Tyrone, I feel it is a pleasure, as well as a duty, to offer my humble services in the promulgation of a project which means so much for the advancement of the Gaelic movement not only in Ulster but throughout Ireland, England, Scotland, and America.*[142] *As one who claims some acquaintance with the workings of the movement, I know that it is only the most persistent and untiring effort that will bring about an issue of such importance. Opposition, apathy, and a want of proper organisation must be met with and conquered. I am aware of the fact that there is at present no view of further encouragement, for as an old Donegal man remarked to me a few evenings ago at a Gaelic class in New York City: 'The Northerners are slow at first, but when they get a-going the devil couldn't stop them.' 'He that wrestles with us,' says Edmund Burke, 'strengthens our nerves and sharpens our skill. Our antagonist is our helper.' 'Again,' he adds, 'when bad men combine the good must associate, else they will fall one by one an impitied sacrifice in a contemptible struggle.' What we need, therefore, is work and organisation, and although I am far removed for the present from the scene of action, any assistance I can give will be cheerfully forthcoming. Without reflecting in any way upon what is usually termed 'Southern Irish,' I will briefly describe my first visit to one of the leading societies in New York, which took place soon after I landed in this country. Accompanied by a friend of mine who is a member of the Society referred to, I entered the classroom. There were fully 200 members in attendance, the fair sex being the majority. I took up my O'Growney, Part II, answering in turn the questions put by the teacher. By the time the classes had adjourned for the evening my friend had made known my identity to the president, and I was not only obliged to address the meeting in Irish, but also to sing 'An Spailpín Fánach,' 'Péarla an Bhrollaigh Bháin,' and 'An Madairín Ruadh.' As I was about to leave the hall, the old gentleman already spoken of in this letter treated me to a 'shake-hands' which was as Irish as the hills of Ireland. 'My buachaill,' said he, 'you have the same kind of Irish they*

have in Ireland.' A laugh from several of those who heard his remark followed. 'The Irish,' said I, 'which is being taught at these classes, is just the same, if we can overlook the fact that beginners cannot acquire the proper pronunciation at once.' 'I admit that,' he said, 'but when the mare is a horse now isn't that bad enough!' Knowing that he referred to the word 'capall' which is used to translate 'mare' in the north of Ireland, I could not help joining with the others in a hearty laugh. The paramount idea of the aforesaid campaign must be, however, to do what has been left undone, and not to undo what has been done. It is a case of getting even with ourselves rather than 'getting even' with our neighbours. Our own apathy has been our worst enemy. Let us then be up and doing. The time has come when we must do so if we wish to preserve and propagate the grand old 'gems' which are still living in the mountains and valleys of the north-west. God grant that we shall live to see the day when a purely English-speaking person will be looked upon in true light, viz:- ' A stranger in Ireland.' Wishing the movement abundant and continued success.[143]

Is féidir imeachtaí Bhriain ó thaobh na Gaeilge de a leanstan sna cuntais a foilsíodh ar na nuachtáin thall i Meiriceá. Bhí an obair chéanna ar siúl aige thall ansin is a bhí agus é sa bhaile. Bhí sé ag teagasc ach go háirithe ag *The St. Brendan Branch of the Gaelic League, 160, East Sixtieth street, corner Third Avenue, NYC* agus, mar a tharla, thug an Craoibhín cuairt orthu agus é ar a thuras thall i Meiriceá.

St. Brendan Branch, New York City: There was a large attendance of eager students at last Sunday's session of the St. Brendan Branch of the Gaelic League, 160 East Sixty-Fifth Street. There were five large classes under the tutelage of Messrs. Ferriter, O'Keeney, Sheehan, O'Sullivan and O'Reilly. It is expected that Dr. Douglas Hyde will pay his promised visit on next Sunday. A new play in Gaelic, written by Mr. Brian O'Keeney, will be produced early in February. The title of the play is Seaghan Ruadh. *The author, Mr. O'Keeney, is an Irish scholar of known ability. In the early days of the Gaelic League he did very useful work for the language in Donegal and Tyrone.*[144]

Dr. Douglas Hyde visits New York branches[145] *St. Brendan Branch: Douglas Hyde had a strenuous day last Sunday visiting branches of the Gaelic League. His experiences were like those of a political campaigner in the busy days immediately preceding an American election. He covered three meetings in New York in the afternoon and evening and wound up by attending another in Brooklyn. He first visited the Philo-Celtic Society, at 341 West Forty-Seventh Street, then went to the Gaelic Society at 47 West Forty-Second Street and then went to the St. Brendan Branch at Jenning's Hall Sixty-Fifth street and Third Avenue. The classes of the St. Brendan Branch were in full swing when An Craoibhin Aoibhinn, accompanied by several members of the Philo-Celtic Society, entered the room, and the sight evidently gladdened his eyes. The classes were of various grades and of all ages. There were grown men and women, many of whom were native Irish speakers, youths of both sexes in their teens and little boys and girls from six years of age upwards. The scene was like a school in Ireland, and it was this demonstration of practical work for the language which most pleased him. He was at once recognized, the classes were broken up and the branch was called to order for a regular meeting, at which the leader of Irish-Ireland was treated to an exhibition of Irish oratory in the purest and most idiomatic Gaelic, such as he could not hear perhaps anywhere else outside of the Irish-speaking districts of Ireland – and it could not be excelled even there. Mr. B. O'Keeney then gave 'An Maidrin Ruadh' in a fine tenor voice, and as an encore, 'Gradh Mo Chroidhe Mo Chailin Ban.'*[146]

THE "CEILIDH" SCENE ACT III.

BÓC ina shuí, an 5ú duine C-D, mar aisteoir i ndráma le Andrew O'Boyle, 1905

Luigh Brian amach ar a chuid drámaíochta agus é thall i Meiriceá, ag scríobh agus ag aisteoireacht, é ag tarraingt as a chleachtadh ar a raibh ar siúl aige roimhe sin sa bhaile..

St. Brendan Branch: The St. Brendan Branch of the Gaelic League, 160, East Sixtieth street, corner Third Avenue, is in a very flourishing condition and its membership is increasing by leaps and bounds. There is a special class for Irish speakers and the non-Irish speakers are graded according to proficiency. Perhaps the most interesting class in the school is the children's class. The youngsters are making marvellous progress in the Irish language and in Gaelic singing ... No efforts are being spared to make the production of Seaghan Ruadh, *the new Gaelic play, a success worthy of this branch, worthy of the Gaelic League and the Irish race. The play will be produced at the New York Turn Hall, Lexington Avenue and East Eighty-Sixth Street, on Thursday evening, March 1. The play is the production of the Gaelic poet and scholar, Mr. B. O'Keeney. Mr. O'Keeney will himself act the leading role of* Seaghan Ruadh. *There are frequent rehersals, and those who are to take part in it are doing their utmost to perfect themselves in their respective roles. The play is full of action and humorous incidents, the actions will suggest the words and those who have a slight knowledge of Gaelic will be able to follow with ease, while those who have no knowledge of Gaelic cannot fail to find interest in the play, as a synopsis of it in Irish and in English will appear in the programme.*[147]

New Gaelic Play: Seaghan Ruadh *to be given by St. Brendan Branch: A new Gaelic play which is to be produced under the auspices of the St. Brendan Branch of the Gaelic League is another indication of the vitality of the Gaelic revival. The play is entitled* Seaghan Ruadh *and is to be staged on Thursday evening March 1, at New York Turn Hall, Lexington avenue and East Eighty-Fifth street. Though the play is in the Irish language it is stated that it can be followed with interest by those who have no knowledge of Gaelic. A synopsis of the play in Irish, with English translation, will aid those who cannot understand it in the original.* Seaghan Ruadh *is a humorous play depicting Irish rural life. The author, Mr. B. O'Keeney is a prominent Gaelic Leaguer, and as a Gaelic League organizer in Donegal and Tyrone his work was invaluable in the early days of the language movement. He is also a Gaelic poet, and he will sing one of his own melodies in the play. A short concert will precede the production of the play. There will also be some rare exhibitions in Irish step and figure dances. A reception and dance will immediately follow the production of the play.*[148]

BÓC i lár báire i gcuideachta aisteoirí Seaghan Ruadh, *Nua-Eabhrac, 1906*

Brian O'Keeney, Playwright, Seaghan Ruadh[149]: Seaghan Ruadh, *an original Gaelic play, by B. O'Keeney was produced last Thursday evening at Turn Verein Hall, Lexington Avenue and Eighty-Fifth Street, under the auspices of St. Brendan Branch of the Gaelic League. More than one thousand persons were present. It was an intensely humorous play.* Seaghan Ruadh *ought to stand among the classics. The dialogue was good, the characterization excellent, and the way it was presented reflected credit upon those who were in the cast. The audience nearly all of whom understood Gaelic went into roars of laughter over the grotesque exhibitions of the hero. He was dressed in an eighteen century costume and carried a broom. It was good work and the audience was indebted to Mr. O'Keeney the author-actor. Miss Sheela O'Shea was almost a recollection of 'Dark Rosaleen.' Molly Roache, M.J. Mullarkey, James Brennan and two very clever children Margaret Quinn and Seamus O'Reilly made up the remainder of the cast. Mr. Michael O'Reilly, President of the St. Brendan Society made the opening address. It was in Gaelic and Mr.*

O'Reilly was at his best. He is one of the very best in this country, a native speaker of intellectual force – a poet whose songs are still unsung. Father Dennis O'Sullivan, of Valencia, Kerry, sang two songs of his own composition and made a very scholarly speech on the influence of the Gaelic movement. The St. Brendan's junior class, a combination of pretty girls arranged like a Cupid's bow, rendered two musical selections in Gaelic. The poetry in motion was illustrated by the splendid dancing of the Misses Geaney, whose jig and reel exhibition was a triumph of salutatorian art. Those who knew something about the old country didn't miss the flavour of the four-hand reel to the air of 'The Blackberry Blossom,' danced exquisitely by Misses A. Treacy, L. Jenkins, F. Jenkins and E. Treacy.

The story of the play: Nora and Peadar compare notes. The English pedlar arrives with his samples. Maura comes on the scene but not for the purpose of buying English-manufactured wares. Seaghan Ruadh as a housekeeper, sings his favourite song, 'My Girl from Killarney.' This song has been specially written for this drama and is couched in very simple language. Even those with an elementary knowledge of Irish should have little difficulty in following the words intelligibly. The words and music are by Mr. O'Keeney. Seaghan makes a discovery. Maura explains matters. 'Love's young Dream.' The clock meets with an accident. Donnchadh is sent for with a view of having the clock repaired before the arrival of Sheela, who is absent on a visit to the home of her mother. Seaghan sings another song. Donnchadh arrives but is more interested in story-telling than clock-repairing. The homecoming of Sheela, Seaghan proves himself an adept at excuse-making and finds his courage taxed to the fullest extent. Sheela admires the courageousness of her son and is ready to listen to his pleadings. She consents to his marriage. The pedlar arrives once more. So does Donnchadh. Neither one appreciates the reception tendered them by Seaghan. Sheela believes in supporting home industry and Seaghan becomes the owner of a new suit of clothes. Love in a cottage. Song, 'Maureen.' Seaghan Ruadh happy. 'All's well that ends well.'[150]

Bhí baint mhór ag Brian leis an *Fireside Club* agus é thall i Meiriceá, rud a bhéarfadh le fios go raibh sé ina bhall den eagraíocht nuair a bhí sé óg in Éirinn. Bhí craobhacha agus baill den *Fireside Club* le fáil ar fud na cruinne, áit ar bith a raibh imircigh as Éirinn lonnaithe sa cheathrú dheireanach den naoú haois déag agus sa chéad cheathrú den aois seo caite.

> *Irish American Fireside Club*[151]*: A special meeting of the Irish American Fireside club was held at Jennings Hall 65th St. and Third Avenue. Mr John S. O'Connor occupied the chair; Mr. J. D. Keeney acted as secretary in the absence of John D. Baxter, Feis secretary. Mr. B. O'Keeney, organiser of Feis, explained in detail the object of the club and the brilliant prospects that foreshadow the grand festival of Feb. 13. The chairman, Mr. O'Connor, referred to Mr. O'Keeney's ability and experience in matters of this kind and felt assured that an Irish Feis would be the means of bringing together the best talent in greater New York ... There is every prospect that the hopes of the promoters of the Feis will be realised.*

Rinne siad feis a reáchtáil, an chéad cheann riamh i Nua-Eabhrac.[152]

> *Irish-American Fireside Club's entertainment next Tuesday night: The Gaelic festival to be held at Tammany Hall next Tuesday evening, February 13th, will be an excellent criterion of the progress of the Gaelic movement in the City so far. Taking into consideration the fact the promoters of this promising entertainment are offering valuable prizes for Irish step-dancing, figure-dancing, singing, oratory and instrumental music, one would imagine that even the most haphazard enthusiast would expect a record-breaking Irish gathering on this occasion. The principal, and in fact the only, object for which this festival was inaugurated is the popularization of Irish songs, music and dances. Its promoters are Irishmen and Irish women who have long ago ceased to place their faith in a Parliamentary party who would wring from England the justice she so long withheld. They do not belong to the 'God Save the King' nationalist brigade, who believe in taking pseudo-loyalty on the 'floor of the British House of Commons,' but rather to that party which embraces the best intellect of Ireland, and aims at building up an Irish nation out of native material. 'Bring back,' says the organizer Mr. O'Keeney, a well-known writer, 'our ancient language, songs, dances and customs, and with them will come the pride of a race, and Ireland will flourish as a nation – not as now a shameful anomaly shrieking out her nationhood by tearing from her bosom its very badge, while at the same time her life-blood flows from wounds (many self-inflicted) which she is too lazy to staunch. It is not to be wondered at, however, that so many Irishmen have drifted with the*

tide of West Britonism which for years has deluged the country. It is questionable whether Irish nationality has suffered more from the Orange Saxons than it has from the Green Saxons – the latter more commonly known as the 'chosen representatives of the people.' And had not the Gaelic movement sprung into existence ten years ago, the doctrine of conciliating England would in all probability be preached to-day from every platform in Ireland. But thanks to the untiring efforts of the men like Dr. Hyde, the late Father O'Growney and numerous other self-sacrificing Irishmen, the scene is changed. The game of humbug is at last a failure not only in Ireland but in this country. Irish-Ireland entertainments are taking place of the so-called 'Irish' meetings – events characterized by nothing save 'emphatic resolutions, thrilling speeches and false promises.' Let us hope that every Irish organization in the city will join hands in celebrating in a becoming manner the festival to be held at Tammany Hall next Tuesday night.

Irish Fireside Club: Festival Report: The Gaelic festival held on Tuesday, February 13th, at Tammany Hall, was Gaelic in reality as well as in name. Nowhere outside of a provincial feis in Ireland or the National Oireachtas in Dublin has such an array of Irish talent been brought together. It would, indeed, be hard to convince those who were fortunate as to be present that the Irish language and the Irish manners and customs were dead or dying. There were competitions in solo singing, dancing and instrumental music. In the figure dances there was an interesting competition in which teams from the St. Brendan Branch, the Monaghan Men's Association and the Fermanagh Men's Association participated. The step dancing was particularly interesting. The majority of the competitions were not affiliated with any Irish organisations. The festival was under the auspices of the Irish-American Fireside Club, and this club deserves the thanks of Irish-Irelanders. The chairman was Mr. B. O'Keeney, an Irish speaker and scholar.

Gaelic festival in New York: To say that the Irish festival given under the auspices of the Irish American Fireside Club on Tuesday evening, March 20th has eclipsed anything of its kind ever held in this country, is, indeed, putting it mildly. Never, outside of the Oireachtas, which is held annually in Dublin, has such an array of Irish talent appeared together on a single platform. It was an intellectual treat such as the oldest resident of this city has never had an opportunity of enjoying. All of the competitions were keenly contested, and those who have secured the highest percentage of marks may feel justly proud. At 8.30 o'clock the chair was taken by Mr. B. O'Keeney, who conducted the proceedings throughout with his usual ability and tact ... Mr. O'Keeney, after a few appropriate remarks in Irish said – 'Ladies and gentlemen, we are about to celebrate the 'First Gaelic festival of the city of New York', a festival inaugurated for the purpose of stimulating an interest in the cultivation and preservation of the songs, music and dances of our country. It is hardly necessary to refer to the work the Gaelic League is accomplishing when addressing an audience such as this. The fact that you are here present is an indication in itself that you have cut yourselves adrift from English ideas, and have shed, or are rapidly shedding, the last scales of Anglicisation. It therefore only remains for me to extend to you all a cordial welcome and to express the hope that you will enjoy the treat which we have endeavoured to prepare for you.'[153]

Chum Brian an dán 'Teangaidh na hÉireann' agus foilsíodh é thall i Meiriceá.[154]

Ba léir fosta go raibh barúlacha láidre, náisiúnaíocha ag Brian i rith a shaoil agus nár leasc leis iad a nochtadh go poiblí.

The Same Old Story: To the Editor, Gaelic American: *Under the heading 'T.P. O'Connor on Ireland's Hope, the* World *of yesterday's date contained an article which, to say the least of it, is highly amusing. Mr. O'Connor, we are told, looks forward to an Irish Home Rule Bill at the coming session of Parliament. He held out the same hope when he was here, in a similar capacity, about seventeen years ago. Every Irish Parliamentarian who has visited the United States since then has followed this example; and if the Irish people will only continue to support this 'game of humbug,' Parliamentarians would be offering the same consolation seventeen years hence. Ireland's hope lies – as lay the hope of every other nation similarly circumstanced* – in the self-dependance of its people – *a doctrine to which Parliamentarianism by virtue of its very existence is diametrically opposed. B. O'Keeney.*[155]

Lean Brian lena chuid oibre ar son na Gaeilge gan stad thall i Meiriceá i gcaitheamh na mblianta.

The Springfield Feis: Two Days of Irish Song and Story. Literary Competitions Reach a Very High Standard. Springfield, Massachusetts, October 1: The enthusiasm and earnestness which characterized the opening of the second Feis of the Springfield Irish Language Society in the hall of the United Irish Societies on Worthington Street yesterday, augurs well for the revival of the Gaelic Language and customs. The hall was not large enough to accommodate the large number of visitors who came to participate in and witness the interesting programme, and standing room in the corridors in the rear of the hall was at a premium during most of the afternoon. The interest showed far exceeded the expectations of the most optimistic promoters of the Feis, and gives great encouragement for the continuation of these exercises on an even larger scale next year. The Feis brought together a body of people who are proud of their nationality and of their ancestry, who seek to preserve all that is best in the Irish race, and especially to cultivate those characteristics which have brought distinction to the sons of Erin ...

Literature: Best original poem in Gaelic, (one prize), Mr. B. O'Keeney, of Sag Harbor, Long Island. Thus far Springfield has been the only city in this country to hold a Gaelic Feis, it being difficult to arouse sufficient enthusiasm among the members of the League in other cities.[156]

St. Brendan Branch: The usual weekly meeting of the St. Brendan Branch, Gaelic league, was held at 160 East Sixty-Fifth Street, New York on Sunday afternoon last. An entertainment and dance will be held on Saturday evening, March 9. Mr. B. O'Keeney, Mr. J. Moylan and other Irish-speaking vocalists, will sing the choicest Irish melodies.[157]

The Sag Harbor Express Sag Harbor Express (Front page story) Sag Harbor, Suffolk County, N.Y. March 21 1907. Irish music and song: A paper by Barney O'Keeney of Sag Harbor before St. Brendan Gaelic Union, New York.

Bhí spéis ag Brian i ngnoithe Mheiriceá fosta mar is léir ón litir seo a leanas uaidh.

'The Star Spangled Banner.' To the Editor of the Express: Dear Sir: I was pleased to notice in last week's issue of the Express *that Baltimore intends to celebrate the centennial of 'The Star Spangled Banner.' The proposition is one that is sure to meet with approval of every true American, and the patriotic enthusiasm of such a celebration must needs be productive, will doubtless result in eliminating from the public schools for all time the "revised" version of the National Anthem. 'The power,' says a contemporary, 'which pillaged Washington, burned the Capitol and destroyed priceless records, has captured our public schools and a portion of the press.' In the public*

schools in New York City the children are taught more about English history than the history of their native land. The public school libraries are stuffed with books which tend to make England a veritable fairyland to the minds of American children. It would be expected, however, that those influences which are trying to Anglicize the minds of Americans would not have the hardihood to tamper with the National Anthem. The demasculation of 'The Star Spangled Banner' was commenced many years ago, and as the result of this vandalism a correct version of the song as originally written is difficult to find. The following is the original version of the third verse which has either been mutilated or entirely eliminated from the school reader:

'And where is that band who so vauntingly swore,
'Mid the havoc of war and the battle's confusion
A home and a country, they'd leave us no more?
Their blood has washed out their foul footsteps' pollution.
No refuge could save the hireling and slave,
From the terror of flight or the gloom of the grave,
And the star-spangled banner in triumph doth wave,
O'er the Land of the Free, and the Home of the Brave.

When the words of this song are better understood by the people of this country there will be a considerable falling off in the numbers of Anglo-maniacs who now hover around the British Ambassador at Washington. April 8, 1907. Brian O'Keeney.[158]

Is cosúil go raibh ceangal ag Brian le cumainn náisiúnaíocha Éireannacha agus é thall i Meiriceá.

Sinn Fein Entertainment: Among those who will assist in the annual entertainment of the New York Society, which will be held to-morrow night in the Nineteenth Ward Bank Building, Fifty-seven street and Third Avenue, are James Connor Roach, the playwright; Thomas P. Murphy, vocalist; Denis Murphy, in Irish step dances; Mrs. Edmund McKenna, vocalist, assisted by Miss Mollie Smith, of the Gaelic Society; Barney O'Keeney and George Potter, in Gaelic songs, and P.J. McNamara, violinist, in a selection of Irish airs. Patrick O'Meara, chairman of the Central Council of America Sinn Fein, will deliver an address.[159]

Luaitear fosta go raibh sé ina '*corresponding and financial secretary*' ar an *Donegal Men's Association* agus é thall i Meiriceá.[160]

Rinne an *Brooklyn Philo-Celtic Society* Oireachtas a reáchtáil sa bhliain 1910 agus cheol Brian amhráin as Gaeilge agus as Béarla ar an ócáid, rud a thaitin go mór leis an lucht éisteachta.[161]

Phill Brian ar Ard an Rátha sa tsamhradh sa bhliain 1911. Bhí na blianta caite aige ag obair i Meiriceá i gcúrsaí árachais agus ba léir gur chruthaigh sé go maith sa cheird sin, a chruthú sin an teistiméireacht bhreá a thug fear ceannais an chomhlachta dó. Cha ndearna sé neamart i gcúrsaí Gaeilge ansin ach oiread ach é ag plé le cúrsaí Gaeilge mar a bhí ar siúl aige roimhe sin in Éirinn: ag teagasc, ag tabhairt óráidí, ag cumadh dánta agus drámaí, ag eagrú craobhacha agus feiseanna srl. Is léir, áfach, ainneoin a fheabhas a chruthaigh sé thall i Meiriceá, nach raibh sé i gceist aige buanchónaí a dhéanamh ansin. Tháinig Margaret Roarty, a raibh cónaí uirthi in Philadelphia ach a rugadh sna Gleanntaí, go hÉirinn fosta agus bhí an bheirt le pósadh.

Bhí siopa grósaera agus biotáilte ag athair Bhriain i gcónaí in Ard an Rátha ach bhí fonn ar Bhrian a bheith ag obair le comhlacht árachais arís. Chónaigh sé ar phríomhshráid Ard an Rátha nuair a tháinig sé ar ais go hÉirinn. Níor thráigh a spéis i saothrú agus i gcur chun cinn na Gaeilge nuair a phill sé ar Éirinn.

Bhí litir ar an *Derry Journal* ag *Ratepayer* ag gearán go raibh na sráideanna in Ard an Rátha faoi uisce nuair a thit fearthainn throm ar an ábhar go raibh na draenacha stoptha agus ar lá aonaigh go raibh cac bó ar fud na háite.[162] Thug Brian freagra air, á cháineadh: '... *A little consideration for those who are endeavouring to keep the streets in repair would convince 'Ratepayer' that criticism of this kind is not only uncalled for, but is calculated to injure those who are doing their very best under existing conditions.*'[163] Chum '*Old Timer*' dán greannmhar, magúil faoin chonspóid seo ina dhiaidh sin.[164]

Pósadh Brian i mí Mheán Fómhair, 1911.

Popular young couple married: The wedding took place at Glenties on Wednesday morning of Mr. B. O'Keeney (whose name is familiar to most of our readers), and Miss Margaret Louise Roarty, late of Philadelphia, U.S.A. The very Rev. James Canon MacFadden, P.P., V.F., performed the ceremony. The bridegroom, whose contributions in prose and verse have frequently appeared in our columns, has also returned recently from the United States. He is an accomplished Gaelic scholar, and the author of the Tyrconnell Series of Easy Lessons in Irish. His dramatic productions include The Rebel of Innishowen, The Martyr's Prayer, In Dark '98, etc. all of which have been successfully staged in America. Miss Roarty, (now Mrs. O'Keeney), enjoys an extensive popularity in social circles on both sides of the Atlantic. The wedding breakfast was served at O'Donnell's Hotel, after which the happy couple left Glenties by the 10.5 train to visit several places of interest on the Northern sea-board.[165]

Ba ghairid gur phill Brian ar a chuid drámaíochta i ndiaidh dó teacht ar ais abhaile. Léiríodh *Rebel of Innishowen,* dráma leis a léiríodh cheana cúpla uair i Meiriceá, ina bhaile dúchais féin. Is léir, áit ar bith ar léiríodh a chuid drámaí, go raibh ráchairt mhór orthu.

Radharc as an dráma Rebel of Innishowen, *Ard an Rátha, 1915. Bata i lámh Tom Fisher (le caoinchead ó Michael Fisher)*

Rebel of Innishowen *in Ardara: One of the largest audiences seen in Ardara for several years witnessed the first production in Ireland of Mr. B. O'Keeney's popular melodrama* The Rebel of Innishowen, *on Friday evening. Many of those who formed the audience were not prepared for an intellectual treat this drama affords, having already heard of (or perhaps seen) the successful productions of* The Rebel of Innishowen *in the United States. To say, however, that their expectations on this occasion were fully realised, would, indeed, be putting it mildly, and the fact that the artists were obliged to yield to the general and imperative demand for a repetition of the play the following night is sufficient proof of meritorious work on their part, and high appreciation on the part of the audience. In short the production was such as is rarely seen in any provincial town, and reached a standard of perfection not always attained even by professional talent. The first production of his historical drama* The Rebel of Innishowen *took place in St. Mary's Hall, Hoboken. N.J. for the benefit of St. Mary's Orphanage and by special request of many of the Irish societies in New York City, the play was subsequently produced in the Murrayhill Lyceum Theatre in that city. The immense audience assembled on that occasion was fully represented of the 32 counties of Ireland.*[166]

Ó tharla gur éirigh chomh maith sin le Brian i gcúrsaí árachais, ní hiontas ar bith é gur ceapadh é i bpost den chineál chéanna agus é sa bhaile. Bhí sé fostaithe ag an *Pearl Life Assurance Company.*

Donegal Man's Promotion: One of the most popular appointments for many years in County Donegal is that of Mr. B. O'Keeney, of Ardara, who has been appointed ordinary branch inspector by the Pearl Life Assurance Company for the North-West of Ireland, on the recommendation of the local superintendent Mr. T. J. Conn. During this past ten years Mr. O'Keeney has been a prominent figure in the Life Insurance business in America, having held positions of trust and responsibility in two of the largest American companies. His records in both these institutions have been in many instances without parallel, and time after time drew forth the hearty congratulations of the directors. We congratulate the Pearl Life Assurance Company upon securing the services of such a brilliant advocate and enthusiastic worker as Mr. O'Keeney, whose successful career must appeal very strongly to the numerous staff of the agency over whom his inspectorship bears sway, and with whose co-

operation we feel sure Mr. O'Keeney will during 1913 – the Company's jubilee year – figure prominently amongst the leaders in that most important branch of the Company's business.[167]

Lean spéis Bhriain sa drámaíocht i rith na mblianta ina dhiaidh sin: ag scríobh, ag léiriú, ag ceol agus ag aisteoireacht.

Concert and dramatic performance at Castlederg: A high class concert and dramatic performance was given by the Castlederg Amateurs on Tuesday evening in St. Patrick's Hall, Castlederg. The dramatic portion of the entertainment included an excellent production of Mr. Brian O'Keeney's ever popular melodrama, 'The Rebel of Innishowen.' The commodious hall was packed to its utmost capacity, and the enthusiasm displayed throughout the entire performance was abundant evidence of the fact that the Castlederg Amateurs had on this occasion attained a standard of excellence which is seldom excelled, even on the professional stage. To say that the performance eclipsed anything hitherto attempted by the local thespians would indeed be putting it mildly ... A most enjoyable farce, entitled 'Barry's Vacation,' also by Brian O'Keeney, concluded one of the most successful entertainments ever held in Castlederg.[168]

BÓC, Cigire Árachais, Doire 1913

Is léir gur éirigh go hiontach maith le Brian ina phost leis an chomhlacht árachais agus tugadh creidiúint agus moladh dó dá réir.

> *Pearl Life Assurance Co. Ltd. District staff meeting: The Derry District of the Pearl Life Assurance Co. Ltd., under Mr. T. J. Conn, came out first in Ireland for ordinary and combined increased and sixth in the Kingdom for 1914. They were also the only Irish district to secure the 'Jubilee Certificate of Honour' offered by the directors in commemoration of the company's jubilee. These honours necessitated a calling together of the staff by the general Superintendent Mr. J. T. Hopkins, Belfast, to offer his congratulations. A large number from all parts of the country were present on Thursday evening last ... The toast of 'The Ordinary Branch' was left in the capable hands of Mr. B. O'Keeney, who, in a speech, masterly, eloquent, and brilliant, gave some reminiscences of his canvassing experiences in the States, and the ways and means of successfully carrying on the company's business. He was proud of the position Derry took for the year, but advised the men present to arrange for a special week this quarter, to be called 'Generals'' week, and to bind themselves there and then to complete a certain amount of business in the meantime ... The Chairman, responding, congratulated Mr. O'Keeney upon his eloquence, and also thanked him for his able and helpful address ... Songs were rendered during the evening by Mr. B. O'Keeney ... A vote of thanks was proposed by Mr. O'Keeney.*[169]

Radharc as Willy Riley

Radharc as Willy Riley, *1914 (le caoinchead ó Bart Whelan, Ard an Rátha)*

Léirigh an *Ardara Dramatic Company* dráma eile le Brian, mar atá, *Willy Reilly*, ag tús 1914 agus is léir gur thaitin sé go mór leis an lucht éisteachta. Bhí tóir mhór ar an dráma chéanna sna fichidí agus léiríodh leaganacha méadaithe agus forbartha den dráma in Ard an Rátha sa tréimhse 1935–1937.

BÓC mar abhcóide i lár báire: Willy Riley, Ard an Rátha, 1914

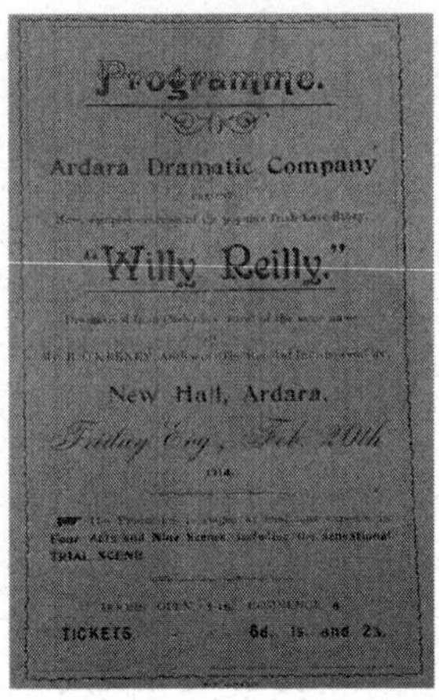

Programme.

Ardara Dramatic Company

"Willy Reilly."

New Hall, Ardara.

Friday Evg., Feb. 20th

1914

TICKETS 6d. 1s. and 2s.

Clár Willy Riley *(le caoinchead ó Celine Childs & Ann Lough, SAM)*

> *New Irish Drama Successfully staged in Ardara: A few evenings ago the Ardara Dramatic Company gave a most successful production of Mr. B. O'Keeney's latest contribution to Irish dramatic literature 'Willy Reilly' dramatized for this occasion from Carleton's novel of the same name. The local performers, who were ably supported by Messrs. E. McSorley and J. Sheridan, Castlederg, received well merited congratulations from a large and most appreciative audience, many of who journeyed 15 to 30 miles to attend the performance. It is scarcely necessary to say that very few 'first night' productions (even on the professional stage) attain such a high standard of excellence, and there can be little hesitation in predicting for such a delightful version of this ever popular love story a prominent place amongst the leading contributors of modern dramatists. The scenic effects, kindly lent by the Castlederg Dramatic Club, came in for a good deal of admiration, while the music supplied by McGinley's Orchestra added immensely to the success of the entertainment. The cast as follows: ... Sergeant Fox, K.C., B. O'Keeney.*[170]

Léiríodh dráma eile leis, *'Eileen Alanna,'* in Ard an Rátha i mí Dheireadh Fómhair, 1914, agus d'éirigh go hiontach maith leis an cheann sin fosta.

> *'Eileen Alanna': Tomorrow (Thursday) evening at 8 o'clock in the magnificent new hall, Ardara, the curtains will rise for the first time on Mr. B. O'Keeney's masterpiece production, 'Eileen Alanna.' A*

talented cast of 25 characters, enchanting music, brilliant display of costumes and scenery, realistic boating scene (showing real boats in action), are all features of what promises to be a musical and dramatic treat of rare excellence. The performance will be repeated on the Friday evening followed by a ball. Special arrangements for the conveyance of large contingents from the neighbouring towns are being made and seating accommodation for 2,000 persons has been provided.[171]

Bhí ráchairt ar dhrámaí Bhriain i gcaitheamh na mblianta agus is léir gur léirithe gairmiúla den chaighdeán ab airde a bhí iontu i gcónaí.

The National Festival: Irish Drama Successfully Staged in Ardara: The celebration in Ardara included an elaborate production of the popular melodrama 'The Rebel of Innishowen,' under the auspices of Division 107, A.O.H. The spacious building (known as the Mart) which accommodates 2,000 persons, was packed to overflowing, and many enthusiastic lovers of Irish drama were obliged to forgo the pleasure of witnessing this beautiful production owing to the crowded condition of the building. The local artistes, who already enjoy an enviable reputation, covered themselves with glory on this occasion, and many demonstrations of well-merited appreciation greeted the talented performers. In addition to the play a variety concert was given. Incidental to action of drama Mr. B. O'Keeney was heard to advantage in 'Savourneen Dheelish,' 'Kathleen Mavourneen,' and 'Nora McNamara.' The applause of the evening seemed however, to be especially reserved for the duet, 'Life's Dream is O'er,' in which Miss Molly Fisher and Mr. B. O'Keeney captivated the hearts of all present. Even in high class operatic productions a more pleasing item is rarely found. The following comprised the cast of characters: Messers: B. O'Keene ...[172]

Tharla go bhfuair bean Bhriain Margaret Louise O'Keeney bás i dtinneas clainne in 1915 agus gan í ach 38 mbliana d'aois. Fuair an leanbh, a gcéadghin, Mary, bás ansin fosta.[173]

Is cosúil go raibh páirt ghníomhach ag Brian san eagraíocht *Crann Eithne* a chuir an tEaspag Ó Dónáill ar bun sa bhliain 1909. Bhí an eagraíocht chéanna ar an eagraíocht Ghaeilge ba láidre sa chontae sa chéad trian den aois seo caite agus lántacaíocht aici ón chléir. Bhí Brian ina rúnaí ar an eagraíocht.[174]

> *Crann Eithne organisation* Ardara Craobh: *The regular quarterly meeting of the above branch was held on Sunday 6th January. The following were present; Rev. J. Byrne (chairman), Messrs. M.J. Sweeney, J. McNeilis (Brackey), J. McNeilis (Mennavalley), T. Gavigan, P. J. Braddon, J. Cassidy, M. Sweeney, P. McNeilis. B. O'Keeney (secretary). Reports of a highly satisfactory character were received from each of the school districts throughout the parish, and an interesting discussion followed. In conformity with a resolution adopted at last meeting a number of Gaelic story books were distributed, the object being the formation of Irish reading classes in each townland. (Books to be exchanged fortnightly) – Cor.*[175]

I rith a shaoil bhí baint lárnach agus ghníomhach ag Brian lena raibh ag tarlú ina cheantar dúchais féin taobh amuigh ar fad de chúrsaí Gaeilge. Ba bhall measúil den phobal é agus bhíodh ról tábhachtach aige i ngnoithe an phobail go minic. Mar shampla, nuair a d'éirigh an Dr. Charles H. Falvey as oifig in Ard an Rátha, i ndiaidh blianta fada seirbhíse a thabhairt ansin, is é Brian a d'eagraigh ócáid mhór scoir ina onóir, a rinne tromlach na hoibre fá choinne na hócáide agus, gan amhras, a labhair go deisbhéalach ar an oíche.[176]

Mar agóidí i rith a shaoil, char leasc leis deargadh ar dhaoine agus ar eagraíochtaí agus ar bheartais a bhí, ina thuairim, mícheart, mí-ionraic nó in aghaidh leas an phobail. Tharla sin, mar shampla, nuair a thug sé aghaidh a chraois ar lucht an *Irish Homestead, 'The Organ of Irish Agricultural and Industrial development.'* D'ionsaigh sé iad go fíochmhar as ionsaí a rinne an tréimhseachán sin ar an *Congested Districts Board* a bhí ag tacú le scéim in Ard an Rátha a bhí glan in éadan thoil mhuintir na háite. Char chuir sé fiacail ann. Is leor an sliocht seo a leanas óna litir ar an *Derry Journal* le blas a thabhairt dá fhearg.

> *The journal that would stoop to such shabby tactics would be more honourably employed in inaugurating a campaign for the destruction of cats that go about the country with microbe-laden*

whiskers. It is asserted that 'a general meeting of shareholders was held in September.' This refers in all probability to the famous outdoor assembly that was attended by at least seven farmers, three schoolboys, an itinerant fiddler, and a stray goat. Does the Irish Homestead *imagine that the C.D.B. is such fools as to hand over a valuable site to a few promoters of dissension, ignore the wishes of 90 per cent of the farmers of this district, and become advertising agents for the I.A.O.S.?*[177]

Pósadh Bernard O'Keeney (39) agus Josephine Maguire (18) ar 16/10/1917 agus bhí naonúr clainne acu: Bernard (1919), Kathleen (1920), Maureen (1922), Charles (1926), Bridget (1929), Vincent (1930), Stella (1933), Brendan (1935) agus Eileen (1937).

Cárta breithlae (3 bliana) ó BÓC chuig a níon Kathleen, 1923

Chan iontas ar bith é mar dhuine a raibh grá láidir dá thír aige go mbeadh Brian sáite in obair na nÓglach ina cheantar féin. Bhí sé ina chathaoirleach ar chlub Ard an Rátha de Shinn Féin agus ba mhinic é ag labhairt as Gaeilge agus as Béarla ag a gcuid cruinnithe poiblí m.sh. ar lá aonaigh in Ard an Rátha i mí Eanáir 1918 nuair a bhí c. 3,000 duine i láthair.[178] Ar ócáid eile labhair Brian (*President of Ardara Sinn Féin Club*) ag ócáid phoiblí in aghaidh an choinscríofa:

BÓC, a bhean Josephine, a mháthair Catherine agus cuid dá pháistí: Bernard, Kathleen & Maureen, Loughros Point, Ard an Rátha, 1924

Mr. B. O'Keeney (President of Ardara Sinn Fein Club) said that as free people the Irish nation not only denied the right, but they also defied the might, of any power on earth to conscript them. Never since the days of O'Connell did they so fully realise the significance of political truism: 'United we stand, divided we fall.' The democracy of America (Mr. O'Keeney continued) would never turn its back upon Ireland in her final struggle for sovereign independence.[179]

BÓC, a bhean, beirt mhac Bernard & Charles, triúr níonach Maureen (a fuair bás go hóg in 1940), Kathleen & Stella, c. 1934
Tá muintir McGinley sa ghrianghraf fosta.

Ar ndóigh, ag an am sin bhí na páirtithe náisiúnaíocha *Sinn Féin* agus an *Irish Party* in adharca a chéile fosta.

> *Rival meeting in Glenties: Sinn Fein and Irish Party supporters availed themselves of the fair in Glenties on Thursday to have a final rally in that town. The Irish Party meeting which was large, and was attended by the Hibernians of the outlying districts, was presided over by the Rev. C. Cunningham, P.P., Glenties who made a strong appeal on behalf of the Party candidate ... All the Party speakers were subject to incessant heckling from a large crowd of Sinn Feiners, who had collected hard by. Before the conclusion of the Party's meeting, the Sinn Fein meeting began. Mr. Daniel Mulhern, Glenties, presided, and the speakers included Messrs. Sean O'Murthuile, Jos. McDevitt, Seaghan McMenamin and Brian O'Keeney, Ardara, as well as Dr. McGinley, Letterkenny. Heckling was freely indulged in while the supporters of the two parties cheered and counter-cheered to their heart's content.*[180]

I rith na mblianta seo bhí Brian fostaithe ag comhlacht Árachais, *The Irish National Insurance Society*. Seo an ghairm a chleacht sé ar feadh na mblianta agus é thall i Meiriceá. Is léir gur éirigh leis chomh maith céanna ina chuid oibre in Éirinn agus fuair sé ardú céime de bharr a fheabhas a chruthaigh sé i gceann a chuid oibre.

Mr. B. O'Keeney who needs no introduction to most of our readers, has been promoted from the superintendence ranks, and has assumed the duties of divisional inspector for the North-West, where the society is making unprecedented progress. The directors are to be congratulated in securing for this important position the services of a representative who is not only a competent and courteous official, but also an accomplished Gaelic scholar and prominent Irish Irelander.[181]

Fuair athair Bhriain bás ar 30/1/1919.[182]

Bhí Sinn Féin iontach láidir fá Ard an Rátha sna blianta sin agus am corrach go maith a bhí ann. Bhí Brian ina uachtarán ar an chumann áitiúil agus ba mhinic tagairt dó sna nuachtáin nuair a bhíodh achrann ann. Mar shampla, bhí cruinniú mór poiblí ag na hÓglaigh in Ard an Rátha ar an 31 Lúnasa, rud a bhí toirmeasctha ag an arm, agus chuir na saighdiúirí an ruaig orthu le lámh láidir. Go hádhúil, níor loiteadh ach duine amháin. Tá cuntas iomlán ar an eachtra le fáil ar an *Derry Journal* (5/9/1919).

Bhí spéis i gcónaí ag Brian sa déantúsaíocht Éireannach agus is minic a labhair agus a scríobh sé faoin tábhacht a bhain léi le fostaíocht a chur ar fáil do mhuintir na Gaeltachta agus deireadh a chur leis an imirce lena linn. Tharla go bhfuair sé deis le fiontar áirithe, mar atá, *Donegal Homespun Industry*, a chur ar bun ina cheantar féin ag deireadh 1919. Bhí sé luaite sna nuachtáin go raibh Brian mar *Managing Director and Secretary* ar an tionscal seo.

Donegal Homespun Industry: New Mills to be Erected: Mr. B. O'Keeney, Ardara (on behalf of Donegal Homespun Manufacturing Company of which he is organising manager) has purchased the property known as Inchin Island, situated near Maghera, Ardara, with water-power which is perhaps second to none in the North of Ireland. It is estimated that the cost of new buildings and machinery will be approximately £9,000 and share certification for this amount will be issued.[183]

Tugtar cuntas níos iomláine ar a raibh i gceist leis an tionscal seo sna cuntais seo a leanas.

Donegal Homespuns Limited: A meeting of the directors of the above company was held in Craig's Hotel, Donegal on Monday last. The whole of the capital ten thousand pounds (10,000) is offered to the public, and the erection of the new woolen mills at the famous Assaranca Falls (near Ardara) will be proceeded with at once. (Mr. B.O'Keeney) reported that the project would receive generous support from every county in Ireland. The company capital is divided into ten thousand shares of £1 each.[184]

Support home industry: It is true to say Ireland is a country devoted predominantly to agriculture. All the greater necessity exists, therefore, for the establishment and extension of local industries appropriate to the nation's needs. In countries considerably smaller than Ireland such industries have vastly contributed to the comfort, the wealth and happiness of their people. It is with gratification, therefore, we direct our readers' attention to particulars of a flotation appearing in page one of this issue, which possesses several features that ought to rally to it the speedy and substantial support of Irishmen generally, and particularly of investors in the Northern Province. We refer to the Donegal Homespuns Limited, the capital of which is £10,000, divided into ten thousand shares of £1 each. A splendid site near Ardara the worth of which is enhanced by very valuable potentialities through the agency of water power has been secured. Moreover, this enterprise has several other associated advantages which afford solid grounds for the conclusion that, as it is thoroughly practical and patriotic in its aims, so also it is likely to establish for itself an enduring financial success. The excellent reputation of the textile products of Donegal is already firmly founded throughout a marketable area of worldwide extent. Manufacturing undertakings of a kindred character, though not possessed of the important facilities for obtaining water-power and skilled operatives which lie within reach of Donegal Homespuns, Limited, have done remarkably well, and the prospects of widely extending a profitable business connection such as this new Company contemplates, were never better than at present. The promoters are experienced gentlemen who are laying out plans with judgement and foresight so as to greatly enlarge present production and ensure proper deliveries of goods. Already a special motor transport has been established by the Company to deal with the development of their business in wool yarn and in finished webs of homespun. Thus promptitude of distribution at the homes of the workers and of collection therefrom will be assured, and a great saving of time and labour will be effected. The Managing Director and Secretary Mr. Brian O'Keeney, bringing to bear unflagging energy upon the furtherance of the Company's interests, has already secured the co-operation of reliable agents in all populous centres throughout Ulster and Connacht. This network of commercial connections should be of great assistance in capturing a big share of the trade of the home market, the Directors being entitled by the Memorandum of Association to 'buy, sell and deal in homespuns.' Today the subscription list opens, and as the merits of the appeal for public support are undoubted, it may be anticipated that the required capital will be forthcoming in a very short time.[185]

Ar an drochuair, theip ar an tionscnamh seo, rud a tharla do thionscnaimh eile a chuir Brian ar bun ina dhiaidh sin. Bhí an scéal céanna ann, mar shampla, i gcás *The Pearl Boot Polish Company* sa bhliain 1926.[186]

Stáitsíodh an dráma *Willie Riley* in Ard an Rátha ar 28 Deireadh Fómhair 1921 ag aisteoirí de chuid an cheantair agus d'éirigh go hiontach maith leis.[187] Foilsíodh leabhar foghlama Gaeilge eile le Brian in 1922.

Tús maith (A good beginning). Ár dTeanga Fhéin, aig cois na teineadh by Brian Ó Cianaigh: A complete course in simple Modern Irish, which (if carefully studied), will enable the learner to converse freely with any Irish speaker. Contains a number of songs and fireside stories carefully compiled, from the living speech of to-day. Dundalk: Dundalgan Press, 1922.[188]

Tugadh Brian agus fear eile os comhair na cúirte in Ard an Rátha in 1923 agus é curtha ina leith nár thug siad duais don fhear ar bhain a chapall an rás ag rásaí capaill Loughrosmore a raibh Brian agus a chara mar eagraithe orthu. Níor tugadh creidiúint ar bith don líomhain a rinneadh agus caitheadh amach an cás. Is spéisiúil gur cuireadh síos ar Bhrian mar *merchant* sa chás dlí seo.

Tháinig Brian os comhair an phobail arís sa bhliain 1929 le dráma úr dá chuid, *Under Three Flags*.

All roads will lead to Ardara on Friday next when the first performance of Mr. B. O'Keeney's dramatic masterpiece Under Three Flags *will be staged in Iona Hall. Fri. 11 and Sun. 13th.*[189]

Grand production of New Irish drama: Success, beyond their highest anticipations crowned the efforts of the Iona Dramatic Society, when Mr. B. O'Keeney's great masterpiece: Under Three Flags, *was staged in Iona Hall, Ardara, on Friday evening, and again on Sunday evening, before two of the largest audiences ever seen in the North-West. Never perhaps in the history of dramatic work in Donegal did any production give such admirable satisfaction and delight. Both gatherings were fully representative of the leading business and professional people of the county, many of whom expressed the hope that before the acting rights of this drama are transferred to Dublin, an opportunity will be given to lovers of Irish drama in Donegal, Derry and Tyrone to see this charming production ... But the great ovation of both nights seemed to be reserved for Mr. O'Keeney when he appeared before the curtain to return customary thanks. Speaking in his own delightful vein the author who by the way sustained the role of 'Father O'Reilly' in the new drama, referred amid cheers and laughter to the 'exemplary conduct of the congregation during the time he had been a parish priest.'*[190]

Foilsíodh an dán 'Machnamh an Deoraí ar a Bhaile Dúchais' ar an *Derry People and Tirconaill News* (28/9/1929, 9).

Rinneadh an dráma *Come Back to Erin* a léiriú in Ard an Rátha agus d'éirigh go hiontach maith leis.

Ardara notes: It has now been definitely decided to hold an advertising exhibition and fancy fair (the first of this kind held in the North-West) at Ardara towards the end of February ... There will be a number of novel attractions, particulars of which will appear by advertisement, but none perhaps is looked forward to with such joyous anticipation as the first production of Brian O'Keeney's romantic drama, Come Back to Erin. *'Danny's vision of the old home in Dungloe,' is the description of a novel experiment to be introduced into a New York drawing-room scene in act 2 of the new Irish Drama,* Come Back to Erin *which will shortly be staged. This novelty is regarded as the most artistic triumph ever staged in a provincial town. Rehearsals for the first part of the romantic love story from the Rosses are now in full swing. The production will synchronise with the Exhibition, and will be staged in the Iona Hall on Friday, 28th February, and on Saturday March 1st and Sunday March 2nd, at 8 p.m. No lover of genuine Irish drama should miss this exceptional dramatic treat. There will also be the first appearance in the North-West of the Ward family, Colum, Eileen, Kevin and Enda,*[191] *the nation's greatest exponents of Irish step and figure dancing.*[192]

Come back to Erin: The first annual North-West of Ireland Advertising Exhibition which opens at Ardara on Monday next ... The principal attraction of the week, however, will be the first grand production of the new romantic drama of the Rosses, Come Back to Erin *from the pen of the author Brian O'Keeney who also wrote highly acclaimed dramas such as* Under Three Flags, Seaghan Ruadh, The Rebel of Innishowen, Eileen Alanna, The Martyr's Prayer, In Dark '98 and Willy Reilly. Come Back to Erin, *the drama deals with the stirring days of the United Irishmen and the scenes are laid in Dungloe and the U.S.A. The first act depicts the departure of the hero, Danny O'Donnell, for America, and the parting scene with his mother. Presented in Irish and English this scene is described as a masterpiece, concluding with the song 'Mother Machree.' Danny is next seen at the home of his uncle in New York where he makes acquaintance of a wealthy Irish American (Peadar O'Reilly) and his daughter, Kathleen. The hero's object in going to New York was to seek financial aid from his uncle for the purchase of a farm near Dungloe, and the heiress on hearing his story, lays her fortune at his feet and accepts his offer of marriage on condition that he should turn his back upon the Rosses forever. Apart, however, from her wealth, Danny's love for the beautiful heiress is apparent from their first meeting, but a promise given to his mother at 'partin'' makes his acceptance of the offer impossible and with a broken heart he decides to return 'to the Rosses and Mother Machree.' The drama then takes a most unexpected turn and comes to a happy ending, the final scene being the Post Office, Dungloe, on Christmas Eve ... The Sona Saxaphone Band will be in attendance. Further particulars may be seen by advertisements in this issue.*[193]

Is fiú cuimhneamh go raibh tábhacht mhór ag baint leis an Ghaeilge ó bhunú an tSaorstáit sa chóras oideachais agus do phoist phoiblí éagsúla. Tapaíodh an deis le hábhar foghlama Gaeilge a sholáthar agus ghlac Brian, a raibh cleachtadh fada aige ar theagasc na Gaeilge cheana féin, leis an deis seo lena chuid ceachtanna Gaeilge féin a chur i láthair an phobail ar an nuachtán áitiúil.

The Irish Language: Good News for Students: Series of Lessons Commence next Week: We are pleased to announce that we have made arrangements for publication in this newspaper of a complete Course of Easy Lessons in Irish, from the pen of a well-known Gaelic scholar and native Irish speaker. The author, who has been employed for a number of years as Gaelic League organiser and teacher, is also an ex-professor of Irish in one of the leading Irish colleges, and a valued contributor to many Gaelic periodicals. He holds the unique distinction of having won two first prizes in Irish prose and poetry at the OIREACHTAS in Dublin in an All-Ireland competition. Few Irish writers can lay claim to having helped so many Irish boys and girls into lucrative positions where a knowledge of Irish was essential, and we have therefore much pleasure in recommending this Course to all who wish to acquire a speedy and accurate knowledge of the Mother Tongue. The first lesson will appear in our next issue.[194] *Attention is drawn to the first of a series of very helpful lessons in Irish appearing in this issue of the* Derry People. *This series will continue for some time ... The lessons are not only intended to supplement other studies, they are complete in themselves and will be found to be of valuable assistance to young and old.*[195]

Cuireadh tús ar an *Derry People and Tirconaill News* leis an tsraith alt le Brian *Easy Lessons in Irish (With Condensed Grammar Notes)* ar 5/10/1929 agus lean ar aghaidh go rialta go dtí 23/8/1930 (21st *Lesson*).

Seo a leanas an réamhrá a cuireadh leis an tsraith.

The following Course of Easy Lessons is written in accordance with the pure, living, Gaelic speech of today, as it is used by the fireside in the Gaeltacht. Its object is twofold: firstly, to enable those, whose time is limited, to acquire as speedily as possible a conversational knowledge of Irish, and secondly, for the benefit of hundreds who are studying the language in order to secure a certificate or a 'pass' in Intermediate or Matriculation examinations. The former should memorise phrases and sentences regardless of Grammar; the latter should study such Grammar as the Lessons contain. All should endeavour, in the absence of a competent teacher, to spend as much time as possible in getting the correct pronunciation from a native speaker.[196]

Cuireadh tús le *Part 2, Lesson 1* ar 30/8/1930.

We desire to draw the attention of students of the Irish language who are desirous of acquiring a fluency in conversation to a specially-prepared series of lessons dealing with the various moods and tenses of Irish verbs as used in pithy sentences in everyday use in the Gaeltacht. This method is regarded as a very desirable improvement on the stereotyped rule of learning conjugations by rote as the student almost unconsciously absorbs the different verbal changes and finds little difficulty in putting them into practice. The first lesson of this series appears in this issue.[197]

As sin amach lean an tsraith ó sheachtain go seachtain gan stad thar na blianta nuair a tháinig críoch gan choinne léi ar 23/3/1935 óir dúradh ag deireadh an phíosa sin '*to be continued*.' Lean an teideal ar aghaidh ina dhiaidh sin ach scéalta béaloidis a bhí i gceist feasta, chan ceachtanna gramadaí. Thar na blianta sin bhí éagsúlacht mhór ábhair ann gan amhras: ábhar gramadaí, ceachtanna, píosaí ceapadóireachta, agallaimh, ceisteanna, scéilíní srl. agus aistriúcháin leis na píosaí Gaeilge ar fad. I bhfolach, ar bhealach, i gcuid de na ceachtanna sin bhí roinnt scéalta gearra, greannmhara den chuid is mó a chuala sé ina óige, is dóiche, agus léiríonn siad acmhainn grinn Bhriain.[198] Rud eile de, seift mhaith foghlama a bhí iontu óir chuideodh ábhar éadrom léitheoireachta mar sin spéis a chothú i bhfoghlaim na Gaeilge.

Saothar cuimsitheach a bhí ann dáiríre agus caithfidh sé go raibh ráchairt air mar is léir ón phíosa seo a leanas.

Our Irish Lessons: An appreciation: 'Admirably Graduated and Clearly Exemplified.' Permit me to express my appreciation of the series of Irish lessons at present appearing in your paper. To those – such as I – who have always wished to acquire a working knowledge of the Irish language, but whose circumstances have hitherto prevented the realization of that ambition, these lessons present a unique opportunity. Many, I am sure, are already availing of the assistance they offer, and I pen these few words of appreciation in the hope that they may be of some effect in persuading more readers of your paper to seize the opportunity which these lessons present. The lessons – which teach the language according to modern Ulster usage – are admirably graduated and clearly exemplified.

Grammatical rules and exceptions are introduced so adroitly and judiciously that the student instead of being confused and disheartened by a wearisome catalogue of irregularities and exceptions finds himself unconsciously absorbing the language – both syntax and vocabulary. The vocabulary – augmented weekly – is eminently practical, and comprises words most likely to be of greatest use in writing and conversation.

Altogether, the system of these lessons is admirable and is, apparently, the fruit of careful consideration. The lessons are bound to be of immense assistance to those who wish to gain a mastery of the Gaelic tongue; and the author is to be congratulated upon the evolution of a system most likely to produce speedy and permanent results. Lughaidh Ó Murchadha.

The above letter is only one of many congratulations we have received from schoolteachers, private students and others on our 'Easy Lessons,' nor have the letters of appreciation been confined to Ireland, since several of them have come from America, England, Scotland, and one of the most encouraging from a well-known priest on the Chinese Mission. We publish the foregoing as it epitomises in an ideal way the merits of the lessons and as an incentive to those who would familiarise themselves with the national tongue to avail of the opportunities they provide. The Editor[199]

Lean Brian le léiriú a chuid drámaí agus is léir gur dhrámaí proifisiúnta a bhí iontu, rud a aithníodh agus a d'fhág go raibh tóir mhór orthu.

Fuair mac óg, Vincent Patrick, le Brian agus Josephine, bás i mí Aibreáin 1930.

Chuir an *Derry People* and *Tirconaill News* tús le *Irish Essay Competition Juniors Under 14* ar 26/4/1930, 8. Bronnadh Teastas orthu siúd ar éirigh leo sna comórtais. Bhí aistí, scéalta gearra agus ceapadóireacht i gceist sna comórtais agus d'fhoilsítí ainmneacha na bpáistí ar éirigh leo ar an nuachtán in aghaidh na míosa.[200] Thugtaí treoir mar chuidiú uaireanta. Arís seo sampla eile de chur chuige Bhriain, mar atá, páistí a spreagadh i gceann na Gaeilge, mar a tharla leis an *Irish Fireside Club* agus *Crann Eithne* roimhe sin. Ar an téad seo arís, scríobh Brian an cuntas seo a leanas ag broslú na dtuismitheoirí ó thaobh na Gaeilge de.

> *Irish-speaking parents: Their duty to the nation: In view of the extensive circulation of the* Derry People *throughout the Northern Gaeltacht we desire once again to impress upon Irish-speaking parents the duty and importance of speaking in Irish to their children – in fact to all children with whom they come in contact. This is a phase of the Gaelic movement which at the moment demands the attention of everyone who really believes that the revival of the 'grand old tongue' is at last a living reality and has long since ceased to be regarded as the dream of enthusiasts. No one can gainsay the fact that Irish speakers love their native language and are delighted when spoken to in Irish. That is the medium of their thoughts, and they and their thoughts have been so long despised that it comes as a relief to them to find strangers appreciating the language in which they are men and women instead of that in which they are less than children. They are at last getting rid of that unconscious feeling – the result of a false conviction, that one of the prime necessities for the success in life of their children is an English education. It is not sufficient, however, to realize the errors of the past. Something more is necessary, and surely the time is at hand when the importance of cultivating the habit of speaking in Irish whenever possible, is apparent to all. The habit of speaking in English has become engrafted even upon the best Irish speakers in the land, and as a habit is instructive, nothing but a strenuous effort will suffice to counteract it. The progress already made is gratifying, but much more remains to be done. All who know the Irish language have a sacred duty to perform, and should speak it in season and out of season as a help and an encouragement to those who are striving to acquire it. 'Progress' must be the watchword until the last barrier of foreignism goes down before the rushing tide of Gaelic culture and enlightenment.*[201]

Cuireadh tús le rang Gaeilge in Ard an Rátha agus Brian a bhí ina bhun.[202] Foilsíodh 'Éire Mo Ghrá' *Air*: '*Eibhlín a Rún*' (or 'Erin the Tear') leis.[203] Thoisigh sé a chumadh filíochta arís. Chum sé dán '*Be Sad in Your Deepest Mourning*' faoi Louis Gildea, cara leis, a fuair bás.[204] Chum sé '*Far from Ardara*'[205] agus 'Slán le Deoraíocht.'[206]

Is léir nár theip ar dheis a labhartha agus a chruthú sin an chaint a thug sé in Ard an Rátha ar Lá Fhéile Pádraig.[207]

I rith na mblianta seo bhí Brian ina oide Gaeilge ina cheantar dúchais féin faoi choiste gairmoideachais an chontae.

Loughros Point: Gaelic Classes: The members of the Loughros Point Irish classes were honoured on Friday evening by a surprise visit from a delegation representing the classes which are held in Ardara, and gave the visitors a cordial Irish reception. The Oide Gaedhilge Brian Ó Cianaigh in introducing and welcoming the members of the delegation gave, in the course of a lengthy Gaelic address, an interesting account of the revival movement from its inception. 'The intellectual awakening of the country,' he said, 'for which the Gaelic League was primarily responsible, did not take place a moment too soon. Half a century before the Gaelic League was founded, when the clarion call of Thomas Davis was ringing throughout the land for the preservation and cultivation of the national language, it would have been a simple matter to check the inroads of the Béarla *and foster and retain the vernacular speech of the vast majority of the Irish people. The task, however, was a much more difficult one when the pioneers of the revival movement began to preach the doctrine of self-reliance and the saving of the language which was the embodiment of the nation's soul. Nevertheless, the impassioned pleading of Arthur Griffith and his contemporaries found a responsive echo in the hearts of the descendants of those whom Davis failed to rouse to action and to-day, thank God, the Ireland of which Davis dreamed is fast becoming a living reality.'*[208]

Chum sé 'Tóg do Cheann, a Mháthair Éire' agus foilsíodh é ar an *Derry People and Tirconaill News* ar an 27/6/1931, 10.

Bhí Brian san iomaíocht arís ag Feis Thír Chonaill agus d'éirigh leis an bhuaidh a thabhairt leis in dhá chomórtas.

Feis Thír Chonaill 1931: Best original song in Irish to a popular air for Derry People *prize of 4 guineas. The winner was Brian O'Keeney of Loughros Point, Ardara, whose song 'Tóg do Cheann, a Mháthair Éire' was written to the air of 'The Wearing of the Green.'* Foilsíodh an dán ar 22/8/1931, 6. *Best original short story in Irish, dealing with Irish life. The same contributor won this test, with a prize of four guineas.*[209]

Fuair máthair Bhriain bás i mí na Samhna, 1931 agus aois mhór aici.[210]

Sa chuid deiridh dá shaol, teagasc na Gaeilge, soláthar ábhar foghlama don nuachtán, saothar cruthaitheach agus cúrsaí drámaíochta is mó a bhí idir lámha ag Brian.

Ardara Notes: Classes for the study of Irish language have been opened at Ardara and Loughros Point and the most commendable enthusiasm prevails amongst the students who have already enrolled for the session. The Ardara class meets in the Courthouse from seven to nine, Tuesdays and Wednesdays, and the Loughros Point class from seven thirty to nine thirty, Mondays and Thursdays. At the conclusion of the Ardara class on Tuesday evening Mr. Sean O'Caiside, N.T. (speaking in Irish) proposed a vote of sympathy with the Oide Gaedhilge in connection with the death of his mother. The vote was supported by Garda P. O'Halloran, Garda O'Sionnaith, Mr. J. Maguire, Mr. M. Mullin and several other members, and passed in silence. Replying (in Irish also) Mr. O'Keeney feelingly referred to the fact his first Irish lessons were learned at his late mother's knee ... Some idea of the progress made in the study of Irish in this area may be gleaned from the fact this year's course is conducted exclusively through the medium of Irish. In this way the members are rapidly acquiring a spoken knowledge of the language and are showing an absorbing interest in the new method. Practical demonstrations of a simplified character are skilfully introduced into every lesson, and with the result that even those whose knowledge of Irish is limited, cannot fail to be impressed and benefitted.[211]

Thug Brian óráid mhór ar Lá Fhéile Pádraig agus, mar is léir óna chuid cainte, é dílis don Ghaeilge agus ar a dhícheall ag iarraidh í a chur chun cinn. '*Gaeltacht League Launched at Ardara*' an teideal a bhí ar an chaint.[212]

D'éirigh le Brian ag Feis Thír Chonaill in 1932 arís.

Feis Thirchonaill: *Details of Literary Awards: No 1. – Best original song in Irish, to a popular air, for prize of four guineas, presented by* The Derry People. *There was a fine entry in the section for which the* Derry People *offered a prize of four guineas. The competition test was the writing of a poem to any of the airs: 'God Save Ireland,' 'Boyne Water' or 'The Foggy Dew.' The successful competitor was Brian O'Cianaigh, Loughros Point, Ardara, who gained 75 marks. His poem 'Brat na hÉireann' to the air of 'God Save Ireland' will appear in a later issue.*[213] *Prize awarded to Brian O'Keeney of Loughross Point, Ardara, with a rousing song entitled 'Brat na h-*

Eireann.' The runner-up was the well-known Donegal poet, Neil McBride,[214] *of Feymore, Creeslough, who was only a few marks behind the winner, with a song entitled, 'An Timeall Bréagach,' in denunciation of the border.*[215]

Níor leasc le Brian riamh a chuid barúlacha faoin Ghaeilge a chraobhscaoileadh go náisiúnta mar is léir ón litir seo a leanas uaidh.

To the Editor of the Irish Press: *Tír agus Teanga: A Chara – At a time when Mr. de Valera and the vast majority of the Irish race, at home and abroad, are engaging in what may well prove to be the final (and successful) struggle for national and economic independence, the silent enactment of an appalling tragedy is progressing within the 'four shores of Erin.' The native language (without which we can never attain to the full-fledged dignity of nationhood) is dying rapidly in the Gaeltacht areas. Is the timely suggestion, made by that eminent Gael, Mr. Cathal Ó Tuathail, during the past week, in an address delivered at the Ulster College of Irish – viz. the immediate appointment of a native-speaking organiser in every parish in the Gaeltacht, to meet with the same fate as all the other suggestions and recommendations advanced during the past decade in connection with the future of our country? Must the matter of a few paltry thousand pounds deprive us of a treasure which, when once lost, can never be restored?* Do chara i gcúis na teangan, *Brian Ó Cianaigh,* Oide Gaedhilge, *Loughros Point,* 22/8/1932.[216]

Bhí Brian ceangailte le Fianna Fáil sna tríochaidí agus is minic a labhair sé ar a son ag cruinnithe toghcháin.

Meeting at Ardara: Interesting speeches: One of the largest outdoor meetings seen in Ardara in recent years was held on Sunday after 11 o'clock Mass. The entire district is at the moment a hotbed of election activity and a vigorous campaign of house-to-house canvassing is in full swing. Sunday's meeting was largely attended and it was evident from the enthusiasm shown that Fianna Fáil can count upon a greater measure of support than ever before. Mr. Brian O'Cianaigh, who presided, said according to Mr. Cosgrove the people were to get back in three days a market that did not exist, for the merest schoolboy at this meeting can tell them that the difference between the price of cattle in the Six Counties and in the Free State was the difference between tweedledum and tweedledee. If they assumed that the tariffs were responsible for the downfall of their markets he would ask: who were responsible for the tariffs? Did they need to be told that the first man to suggest to England the imposition of these tariffs was Mr. Ernest Blythe? And the tariffs are being maintained today not because they were paying England, but in the forlorn hope that Cumann na nGaedheal would come back to power. There was one way, and one way only, by which they would get rid of tariffs, and get rid of British interference in their national and domestic affairs and that was by the return of Fianna Fáil at this election by an overwhelming majority.[217]

Bhí ócáid cheiliúrtha ag Fianna Fáil i lár Ard an Rátha i mí Feabhra 1933 agus, gan amhras, Brian i gceartlár an chruinnithe.

The chair was taken by Mr. Brian O'Cianaigh who in the course of a vigorous address outlined the relationships between Britain and Ireland. In the original draft of the Treaty, he said, the Land Annuities became the property of the Parliaments of Southern and Northern Ireland, and the Northern Government were never asked to pay a penny of these annuities to Britain from that day to this. In the Free State, however, a Government came into power and one of their first acts was to enter into a secret agreement for the payment to Britain of enormous sums that were neither legally nor morally due. And now they are wondering how the Irish people turned against them at the General Election.[218]

Níor chaill Brian a spéis i gcúrsaí tionsclaíochta, trádála agus fostaíochta i rith a shaoil.

Industrial development in Donegal: Enthusiastic meeting in Ardara: Lesson of collapse of British market: Creamery and handspun industry: A very enthusiastic public meeting was held in Ardara on St. Patrick's Day, after eleven o'clock Mass ... Mr. Brian O'Cianaigh, speaking first in Irish and subsequently in English, said: 'The collapse of the British market due to world-wide depression made it necessary for the farmers of Ireland to change their methods. The days were gone when British ships go into the ports of the world and dispose of their cargoes of merchandise at huge profit and then return back to England laden with the fruits of plunder. For over 700 years Britain has been pursuing this policy with regard to Ireland, and a British Commission in 1911 was obliged to admit that we had been robbed of 300 million pounds since the Act of Union.

And after the signing of a so-called Treaty, England continued for ten years to exact a tribute from the Irish people until she was at last confronted by a statesman who reminded her that in her relations with Ireland she was a debtor rather than a creditor nation. England's purchasing power has gone down and it was now the duty of the people, when the agricultural arm had become temporarily paralysed, to co-operate in every way with the Government in strengthening the industrial arm. Cows of good milking strain should be introduced into the country, as the present stocks were in many cases a liability rather than an asset. The establishment of a creamery at Ardara was, at the moment, a matter of pressing necessity. Taking the lowest possible estimate, a calf consumed new milk to the value of £6 10s in the first 13 weeks. The present price of such an animal was 20s to 30s. It is time such losses were stopped, and the farmer paid a reasonable price for his milk and butter.[219]

Ardara Notes: An outdoor meeting was held at Ardara on St. Patrick's Day ... Mr. Brian O'Cianaigh said there were many ways in which the people themselves could assist the Government in the solution of the unemployment problem. Every penny that was sent out of the country for goods that could, and should, be produced at home was an encouragement to the foreigner to strengthen his economic stranglehold upon the life of the nation. He was fully satisfied the Government would do their part in establishing industries suitable to the needs of the district, but the initiative rested with the people concerned, and the Government should not be approached for financial aid in any scheme that did not hold out a reasonable hope of being successful as well as necessary.[220]

Auxiliary creamery corn mill in Ardara: Proposals discussed at farmers' meeting: Decision to get project under way: At a meeting of the farmers of the parish of Ardara, held after late mass on Sunday, proposals were put forward and adopted for the immediate erection of an auxiliary creamery and cornmill combined. Arrangements were made to hold a further meeting on 25th inst. (Ascension Thursday) when a full report of the number of cows in the entire area will be submitted and the 'Ardara Dairy Society' brought into actual being. Outlining the proposals, Mr. Brian O'Cianaigh dealt at considerable length with the locality's need for such an undertaking ... They are now coming to realise, however, that the whole industrial and economic fabric of the nation is undergoing a complete and much needed change, and that to stand still while others are marching onwards is a neglect of duty for which the rising generation will hold them responsible ... A further meeting will be held on Saturday next at 8 p.m. to arrange for the general meeting on 25th inst.[221]

Lean Brian dá bhaint le cúrsaí polaitíochta i rith na mblianta seo fosta.[222]

Bhain sé an chéad duais as dráma dá chuid ag Feis Bhéal Feirste.

Ardara teacher as dramatist: Winner in All-Ireland competition: The prize offered by Belfast Feis Committee for best Irish drama was won by Mr. Brian O'Cianaigh, teacher of Irish under County Donegal Vocational Education Committee, by the narrow margin of one mark in the keenest contest of recent years. That a remarkably high standard has been attained is evident from the decision of the judges.[223]

Brian O'Keeney's Drama Gníomhartha Lae 'san nGaedhealtacht: 1st Prize at 1933 BELFAST FEIS: Literary Distinction for Irish Teacher: Donegal Man's Success, Belfast Feis Awards: In one of the most keenly-contested competitions of recent years, Mr. Brian O'Cianaigh, Ardara, secured first place for 'best original drama of Irish life,' at Belfast Feis. A very high standard was attained, second and third places taken by two eminent Irish authors. After an exhaustive scrutiny the judges awarded marks as follows: Brian O'Cianaigh, 92 marks, Maighread Ni Chanainn 91 marks; Michael Breathnach 90 marks. None of the other competitors secured more than 80 marks. The winning of this important literary event brings to Mr. O'Cianaigh a unique distinction. Apart from the latest (and perhaps his most notable success) Mr. O'Cianaigh has three other 'All-Ireland' successes to his credit. During his term as Professor of Irish in St. Patrick's College, Armagh, he won first place for Gaelic Poetry at the Gaelic League Oireachtas in Dublin. Two years later he secured first place (all Ireland) for an essay on 'Cottage Industries.' And a year later he was also winner of first prize (singing) 'Péarla an Bhrollaigh Bháin.' His successes at Tirconnail Feis in recent years include: Winner of Derry People *prize for best Gaelic song to the air of 'Wearing of the Green' (1931); Winner of* Derry Journal *prize for 'Best original story of Irish life' (1931); Winner of* Derry People *prize (1932) for 'Best song in Gaelic' to the air of 'God save Ireland.'*[224]

Léiríodh an dráma i mBéal Feirste in 1935.[225] Lean sé air ag cumadh filíochta: *'Speak to me in Irish.' Poem written by B. O'Keeney.*[226]

Cuireadh tús le sraith de scéalta béaloidis ó pheann Bhriain ar *The Derry People and Tirconaill News* ar an 30 Márta 1935 agus lean an tsraith ar aghaidh seachtain i ndiaidh seachtaine go dtí deireadh mhí Aibreáin 1937. Bhí aistriúchán leis na scéalta seo i gcónaí. Scéalta béaloidis is mó atá i gceist agus dúradh gur scríobhadh cuid acu mar a tháinig siad ó bhéal an tseanchaí. Ar an drochuair, ní luaitear cén uair a bailíodh an t-ábhar, ná cén áit, ná cé uaidh a bhfuarthas iad. Is eol dúinn, áfach, gur scéalaí breá a bhí in athair Bhriain agus gur ghnách leis bheith ag scéalaíocht sa teach nuair a bhí Brian óg. Fear mór béaloidis a bhí in uncal Bhriain, Niall, fosta. Thug Brian féin cuid mhór de bhuanna an tseanchaí leis, mar atá, cuimhne mhaith, deis a labhartha agus é ábalta caint chraicneach, shlachtmhar a thabhairt. Bhí bua eile aige, mar atá, spéis a chuid éisteoirí a mhealladh agus a chothú.

Gabhann leagan Béarla le gach scéal. Tá na scéalta le fáil sa cholún faoin teideal *EASY LESSONS IN IRISH with condensed grammar notes*. Sin an teideal a bhí ar cholún eile leis roimhe sin ach níl nótaí gramadaí ná eile i gceist sa tsraith seo.

Chreathnaigh Brian roimh an tuar cogaidh a bhí leitheadach an t-am sin sna tríochaidí. Níor chreid sé go raibh tairbhe ar bith i gcogadh.

> *War as an alternative: To the Editor of the Derry Journal: Brian O'Cianaigh: Sir – In various parts of the peaceful county of Donegal I have heard during this past month the expression: 'Another war would be the best thing that could happen. It would settle the world's economic troubles.' I am not going to conjecture how many of those who used the above and similar expressions were really in earnest. Some of them undoubtedly were. War as an alternative! What a ghastly picture to contemplate! Can it be possible that the mentality of our own people is becoming tarnished with the putridity of thought and intellect that characterises the unfortunate inhabitants*

of countries that have thrown God overboard, as far as lay in their power, and that we are drifting, unconsciously perhaps, into a mental attitude which may one day challenge the very existence of the remnants of our ancient civilisation? Let us hope that such is not the case, but 'coming events cast their shadows before.' The thought of war should make us shudder whether the venue is Abyssinia, Germany, France or Belfast. The general feeling of insecurity that was abroad in the world in 1914 is rampant to-day, despite the efforts (sincerely or otherwise) that have been made to stabilise civilisation. Add to this the maddening craze for pleasure for which the past decade is remarkable, and who can wonder that little advantage is being taken of the blessing of peace? How many will stop to think that, altogether apart from the appalling loss of life, from the money expended in the world war, a sum of £800 could have been paid to every family in Great Britain, Ireland, Germany, France, Russia, Belgium, Canada and Australia, and still leave a substantial balance in the Treasury of each of those countries? War talk may thrive where economic depression prevails but peace alone is the remedy, and it is only in a peaceful atmosphere that men may look for sane development, progress and prosperity.[227]

Lean Brian air ag scríobh faoi ábhair a bhain le stair, teanga nó cultúr na hÉireann.[228]

Ó tharla go raibh baint ag Brian leis an I.R.A. blianta roimhe sin, is léir go raibh amhras ar na húdaráis faoi i dtólamh agus uair amháin in 1935 chuartaigh na gardaí a theach cónaithe agus thug chun na beairice é. Níor cuireadh rud ar bith ina leith agus scaoileadh saor é an lá dár gcionn. Gí gur tuigeadh ag an am sin go raibh sé ina

respectable citizen of a quiet disposition, [he] was associated with the old I.R.A. and his house was the regular haunt of I.R.A. and volunteer troops of that time. He is at present one of the vice presidents of the Kilaghtee Fianna Fáil Cumann. The search on his premises ... was for arms.[229]

Dúradh gur atoghadh Brian ina leasuachtarán ar chumann Killaghtee, Fianna Fáil.[230]

Mhair Brian ag teagasc na Gaeilge ina cheantar féin agus ag caint agus ag scríobh fúithi.

Teaching through the medium of Irish: Views of an Irish Teacher: At the conclusion of the Loughros Point Irish class on Friday evening the local teacher, Mr. Brian O'Keeney, addressed the members in the English tongue in order to refer to the controversy regarding the teaching carried on for a considerable time in the Press. In the course of his remarks he said: 'I have purposely refrained from taking part in the recent discussion in view of the fact that the controversialists were much more qualified to deal with the subject of Irish teaching. Seeing that there are some persons present who would not understand my remarks if made in Irish I shall use the Béarla *in a short talk based on my own experience. When classes were opened here six years ago the members who enrolled did not understand a single word of Irish, consequently the course of instruction for the first two sessions were conducted largely in the English language. During the third session we were about to discard the* Béarla *to a considerable extent, and during the last three years it has disappeared completely. A visit to this class in recent years was akin to visiting an Irish-speaking family in the heart of the* Gaeltacht. *I am fully satisfied that if I began to teach the Loughros Point classes exclusively in Irish for the first two sessions, I would not have sufficient members to 'rake the fire,' and the classes would have gone out of existence long ago. I applied the same method in teaching junior pupils in such Convent Schools as Strabane, Newry, and Armagh etc. Some of the members who first enrolled in this class are here to-night, and are fluent Irish speakers, despite the fact that they only receive tuition for four hours weekly during the winter months. I am not in favour of teaching small children, whose home language is English, through Irish exclusively, until they have reached fourth standard. In a bilingual school they should then be fit subjects for instruction through the medium of Irish. I would regard this as rational as well as National education. I pity the teachers, however, who have to deal with pupils some of whom know Irish from the cradle and others who do not. In such cases they should have a free hand so that they might use that discretion to which their training, observation and experience entitles them.'*[231]

Is léir go raibh éadóchas ag teacht ar Bhrian i mblianta deiridh a shaoil maidir leis an chúis ar chaith sé dúthracht saoil léi, mar atá, athbheochan na Gaeilge. Níor leasc leis a chuid tuairimí faoin scéal a reic go logánta agus go náisiúnta.

Gaeltacht is Becoming English: Teacher's remarkable address: Irish as school medium: There is no use in hoodwinking facts – The Gaeltacht *areas are becoming English-speaking at an alarming rate. This was a statement of Mr. B. O'Cianaigh, a former Gaelic League organiser, speaking at the close of Loughros Point (Donegal), Irish classes, of which he was teacher. Referring to the controversy regarding Irish as a teaching medium, Mr. O'Cianaigh said that it was regrettable that the views of the National teachers – than whom no one was better qualified to speak – had not been more fully heard. He was afraid that a number of the controversialists were living in the regions of perpetual 'make-believe' and that their arguments, however plausible, were not in accordance with the facts. They did not care to admit that English was the home language of more than 95 per cent of the people, and bid fair to become the home language of the other 5 per cent within a few years, if the Government and the Nation refused to carry out the only conditions that would prevent that national calamity.*

Twenty years ago: He spoke, he continued, with an intimate knowledge of Donegal, the last Gaelic stronghold, and he would tell the experience of a returned American. That man left one of the most Irish-speaking centres in the county, less than 20 years ago. On the night before his departure the people of almost a dozen townlands came to his home to hold a 'convoy,' and not one word of English was spoken. His homecoming was welcomed last year by an even greater number from the same area, but he did not hear from them a single Irish phrase. Now, asked Mr. O'Cianaigh, in the view of facts such as these, what was to be gained by speeches and newspaper articles painting in glowing terms the progress of the revival movement? Would it not be better to find the truth and try to find a remedy? He had, he continued, no quarrel with those who contended that any subject could be taught through Irish. What he questioned was the advisability – from the language revival point of view – of such a course in districts where the home language was English. He held that such a child should be taught Irish gradually through the medium of English, until it had reached fourth standard. By then in a bilingual school the child was ready for instruction in all subjects through Irish until it had reached the end of the course. Children so taught would grow up with a love of Irish. On the other hand if the children of English-speaking parents were given a surfeit of Irish from the hour they entered school, was there not the danger that they would in many instances loathe the language?

After school days: Needless to say when the door of the school closed behind such pupils after the age of 14, they had finished with Irish. Proof of that was found in the fact that only 3 per cent of the children who had left school for the past two years joined an Irish class. The 3 per cent included those seeking Government positions. That was not the case in the early days of the Gaelic League when organisers and an army of teachers were at work throughout the country. Classes with a membership of from 100 to 200 were numerous and they had in those days a hostile Government. He was glad that Mr. J.J. O'Kelly (Sceilg) had given the official attitude of the Gaelic League of today in the Irish Press. *He had great respect for Mr. O'Kelly as an Irishman and scholar, but he was afraid he had not convinced Irish revivalists that the organisation he represented had retained its former virility. As remedies for the present language position, the speaker suggested pensions of 10/– weekly to Irish-speaking parents regardless of age, in rural areas. The £2 grants to children should be extended. A representative body of the National teachers should meet the education authorities and draw up a rational programme. The teachers should be given discretionary powers. Full cognisance should be taken of the fact that English was the bridge by which they were tempted to abandon the pure Gaelic streams, and that it was the bridge they must cross returning to those streams. The bridge might then be burned.*

Night classes: The school-leaving age should be raised to 15 and compensation paid to parents when the child attained 14. He suggests 4/– weekly for boys and 3/– for girls. A kitchen should be built in connection with each school. Bread and butter and coco should be provided for pupils whose homes were over a half mile distant. One hour from 12.30 to 1.30 should be allowed for lunch and play. Hours should be from 10 a.m. to 3 p.m. Subjects apparently useless should not be tolerated. Night classes should be held in every school three nights weekly for Irish, songs, music and dances. The attendance of persons between 15 and 17 should be obligatory, unless they were attending other classes. Teachers should be native speakers. These changes would cost a considerable sum, but it was not beyond their capacity, and was the price they must pay if they hope to retain their greatest national heritage.[232]

Mhair sé ag caint ar an téad seo go minic, mar shampla, ina phíosa '*Noted Gaelic Author on Language Revival.*'[233]

Ag deireadh 1936 thug Brian léacht dar theideal '*The Bilingual Aspect of the Irish Language*'[234] in Loughros Point. Bhí coirm cheoil ann ina diaidh a thug deis do Bhrian cuid dá shaothar chruthaitheach a chur i láthair an phobail.

> *The following well-known artists contributed – Mr. Brian O'Cianaigh, songs – 'Tóg do cheann, a mháthair Éire,' 'Tá an Taca Thart go Deo.' The above items are of Mr. O'Cianaigh's own authorship, to the air of 'The Wearing of the Green' and 'God Save Ireland,' the songs that have won the* Derry People *first prize at two successive Feiseanna at Letterkenny, also two songs in Irish and an Anglo-Irish song dealing with the revival movement, and entitled: 'The Gaelic of Old.'*[235]

I mí Eanáir 1937 reáchtáladh coirm cheoil agus caitheamh aimsire drámata san Iona Hall, Ard an Rátha. Léirigh an *Ardara Dramatic Club* an choiméide *Paid in his own Coin* ina raibh Brian mar aisteoir. Bhí páirt aige fosta sa sceitse *The Croppy Boy* ar an ócáid chéanna.[236] Is léir nár thráigh a spéis san aisteoireacht agus é ag dul anonn in aois.

Fógraíodh ar an *Derry Journal*[237] go mbeadh dráma Bhriain *Under Three Flags* á léiriú san Iona Hall ar an 3 Márta. Maíodh sa chuntas sin: '*Competent critics are unanimous in declaring it Mr. O'Keeney's masterpiece, and taking into account the fact that the cream of dramatic talent of the South-West will appear in this production it goes without saying that all roads will lead to Ardara on next Wednesday night.*'

Bhí Brian páirteach i bhFeis Thír Chonaill in 1937 arís agus bhain dhá dhuais ansin. Tapaíodh an deis ar an tuairisc nuachtáin le moladh a dhéanamh ar obair Bhriain ar son na Gaeilge i rith a shaoil.

> *Mr. Brian O'Keeney's unique record: Fresh laurels for Ardara author: The winning of the two principal first prizes in the literary section of* Feis Tirconaill *on 29th June, has added to Mr. Brian O'Keeney's already unique record as a Gaelic poet and story writer, and has brought him numerous congratulations from literary friends in many parts of Ulster. There are very few authors among the host of modern Gaelic writers who can pen a more fascinating or*

enchanting picture of everyday life of the Irish peasantry than Mr. O'Keeney, and few still who can match his incomparable style as an Irish-Ireland poet. As one who owes his knowledge of Irish to a study of the Ardara author's brilliant series of Irish lessons appearing in the Derry People *and the* Derry Journal *for many years I can visualize a veritable army of Gaelic students, who, thanks to Mr. O'Keeney and the newspapers mentioned, are like myself today in a position to converse freely in Gaelic with native Irish speakers. Due to the fact that the lessons covered (and are covering) every conceivable subject of conversation, and have been specially written in strict accordance with the living native speech of the purely Gaelic-speaking fireside, I am voicing the opinions of hundreds of earnest Gaels whom I have met in saying that a volume of Mr. O'Keeney's Gaelic lessons and poems would be a treasure in the hands of the rising generation, and would make the study of our native tongue a pleasure rather than toil. Running through all his writing there is a vein of delightful humour which grips the student from the beginning and makes him long for more. As a grammarian and a master of Irish idiom, Mr. O'Keeney has made a name for himself among the highest educational authorities in the land, and newspaper cuttings from his writings may be found in every county in Ireland and are known to be treasured by Irish missionary priests in far-off China and in South Africa. At a risk of displeasing the unassuming author I will mention a few of his outstanding successes in the field of Gaelic literature. These facts were obtained from one of Mr. O'Keeney's intimate friends.*[238] *'Rossanach.'*[239]

Seo a leanas smaoineamh ag Brian a chuireann inár gcuimhne *modus operandi Crann Eithne,* eagraíocht a raibh baint ag Brian léi blianta roimhe sin. Sampla eile atá anseo de thiomantas Bhriain don Ghaeilge go deireadh a shaoil.

Gaelic hour plea: Mr. Brian O'Cianaigh, Irish teacher, Loughros Point, who spoke in Irish and English, said that he believed that the only way the Irish Language could be popularized in the home was by the revival of the 'Gaelic Hour.' The method of making Irish a living language in the home was tried with much success years ago, Mr. O'Cianaigh continued, and if it is taken seriously today I am certain it would have beneficial influences. A suitable hour could be fixed when only Irish is spoken and the current events discussed in our native tongue. The schoolchildren would naturally welcome such an hour, Mr. O'Cianaigh continued, and they could play a big part in making it a huge success by going into the houses in their neighbourhood where the people had only a poor knowledge of the language and help them acquire knowledge by conversing with them. The schoolchildren, continued Mr. O'Cianaigh, have now a sound knowledge of Irish when they leave school but unless something is done to preserve and keep fresh that knowledge they may allow it to grow stale and all the good work done by the teachers and the years of sacrifices and effort on the children's part will have been in vain. If the Irish language never existed, continued Mr. O'Cianaigh amidst applause, we would have to invent a new language to show the world we are a distinct race. By preserving for us such a priceless heritage as a language our forefathers deserve from us our deepest gratitude and we can sense our spirit of appreciation in no better way than by preserving that heritage. The language is our greatest link with our glorious past; it has kept the spirit alive in dark and evil days. Let us do our part in making certain that the rising generation will inherit the great language which has been bequeathed to us, concluded Mr. O'Keeney amidst applause.[240]

Bhí scéal mór ann sa bhliain 1937 go rabhthar le scannán a dhéanamh de dhráma le Brian.

Under three flags: Donegal author's play to be filmed: *Negotiations are now in progress for the filming of Mr. Brian O'Cianaigh's well-known Anglo-Irish drama,* Under Three Flags, *which has been produced successfully in various centres in South-West Donegal during the past seven years. The drama deals with the stirring election period of 1918, when there was an avalanche in favour of Sinn Féin, and the setting is in Tandaragee, Co. Armagh. A romantic love story runs through the whole drama, which is interspersed with an abundance of healthy Irish humour. The 'Fair Day' scene at Tandragee, in which the election speeches by the three candidates, Sinn Féin, Parliamentary Party, and Unionist, are made, has captivated audiences at productions ... Mr. O'Cianaigh has received several messages of congratulations on the success of his drama, and in an interview he told our Ardara correspondent that he hopes to have it filmed at an early date, when the present negotiations are completed.*[241]

Is cosúil nach raibh aon toradh ar na cainteanna sin, áfach.

Mr. Brian O'Cianaigh, Cranogbois, the well-known Gaelic scholar, and author, has been appointed teacher to the Loughross Point Irish

> *Classes for the ninth successive time. Mr. O'Cianaigh is considered to be one of the finest Irish scholars in the county, and his articles on the native language are keenly sought by Gaelic students.*[242]

Níor thráigh spéis Bhriain sna comórtais liteartha i ndeireadh a shaoil.

> *Literary competitions:* Feis *poem: The following is the winning poem at Feis Tir Chonaill, held at Letterkenny in June last for the* Derry People *prize of £2 2s which was won by Mr. Brian O'Keeney, Ardara, the well-known Donegal Gaelic author and playwright. Several entries were submitted in the competition, which the judges declared to be the most interesting, and Mr. O'Keeney's composition was unanimously awarded the premier prize. Áilleacht Thír Chonaill.*[243]

Ó tharla go dtáinig deireadh le scéalta béaloidis Bhriain go luath sa bhliain 1937 mar shraith leanúnach a mhair thar chúpla bliain, is léir gur bhraith sé folús ina shaol. Chuir sé tús le sraith úr ar an *Derry Journal*, as Gaeilge agus Béarla, i mí Dheireadh Fómhair 1937 go dtí 1941. Comhráití gearra idir beirt seandaoine amuigh faoin tuath agus ábhar comhrá cois tine in aimsir an chogaidh atá i gceist. Tá na leaganacha Béarla den tsraith sin foilsithe ag Séamus Ó Cinnéide in *Pull Up a Chair* (U.S., 2018). Tá gnáthchomhrá faoi chúrsaí an lae i gceist sa tsraith ach tá barúlacha Bhriain faoin Ghaeilge, faoin Ghaeltacht, faoi Athbheochan na Gaeilge, faoin imirce, faoin déantúsaíocht, cúrsaí polaitíochta in Éirinn agus thar lear chomh maith le scéalta gearra béaloidis, seanchas srl. le fáil sa tsraith. Scáthán atá sa tsraith ar shaol Bhriain agus na rudaí is mó a raibh spéis aige iontu agus ar chaith sé dúthracht leo.

Chum sé an dán 'Fáilte don Uachtarán' in 1938 in ómós don Chraoibhín Aoibhinn a raibh ardmheas aige air i rith a shaoil.[244]

Chomh maith leis na duaiseanna liteartha a bhain Brian i mblianta deireanacha a shaoil, bhí gradam amháin eile ag fanacht air, gradam saoil ó chomhlacht árachais.

Donegal man's honour: Mr. Brian O'Keeney, Ardara, has been admitted to the Honour Roll of the Canadian Life Assurance Company in recognition of distinguished service, and has been presented with a beautiful certificate and embossed wallet by the London manager. Only a limited number of the company's representatives have shared this distinction.[245]

Foilsíodh a scéal 'Tarngaireacht an Bhacaigh Mhóir' ar an *Derry Journal* (26/8/1938 agus 2/9/1938). Léirigh na *Ardara Players* dráma Bhriain *Gníomhartha an Lae* i halla bhaile na nGleanntach i mí Feabhra 1939.[246]

Rinneadh Feis Thír Chonaill a reáchtáil an deireadh seachtaine deireanach i mí an Mheithimh, 1940 agus chuir Brian isteach ar dhá chomórtas agus bhain duais sa bheirt acu: *first prize for the best original unpublished Irish story and second prize for the best original Irish poem.*[247] Chuir sin an dlaoi mhullaigh ar a shaol liteartha. Is é an scéal atá i gceist 'Fógra na Mná Sí' a foilsíodh ar an *Derry Journal* (22/1/1941).

Radharc ón tseanscoil i bpáirc inar chónaigh BÓC i mblianta deireanacha a shaoil

Fuair Brian bás ar an 16/3/1943.

> *Death of Mr Brian O'Keeney, Ardara: In Gaelic circles in many parts of Ireland, the news will be learned with deep regret of the death of Mr. Brian O'Keeney, well known Gaelic writer which took place at his residence, Crannoboys, Ardara, after a brief illness. Identified with the Irish-Ireland movement since 1900, he was a protagonist in the language revival cause, and not merely in his native Donegal, but far beyond its confines, was his name known as a writer of pure Gaelic. He was a regular contributor to the newspapers circulating in the county. Although he had a varied career as a businessman in commerce and insurance, at home and in America, the great part of his active years were given over to the fostering of the native tongue. In his early life he held positions as teacher of the language in several parts of Ireland and latterly acted as tutor under the Co. Donegal Vocational Educational Committee. He was author of several plays in Irish. One of these took first place at the Belfast Feis some years ago. As all-rounder Irish-Irelander, he was from its inception a staunch supporter of Sinn Féin. He had the distinction of acting as chairman for Mr. de Valera at a meeting in Ardara in 1918 on the occasion of the Taoiseach's first visit to Donegal. He was an enthusiastic follower of the leader's policy and gave the party strong support in every election campaign, figuring several times as chairman at important public gatherings. He had been in failing health for some time past, but was active up to a few weeks ago. Widespread sympathy will be extended to his widow and family of three sons and four daughters.*[248]

Mar a tharla, foilsíodh an colún deireanach ó pheann Bhriain ar an *Derry Journal* an lá sula bhfuair sé bás. Má fuair sé bás féin, mhair a chuimhne agus lorg a phinn i gceann theagasc na Gaeilge ar an *Journal* ina dhiaidh sin mar is léir ón mholadh seo a leanas a rinneadh ar a shaothar.

> *'Are you Learning Irish?' With last Monday's instalment, Brian O'Keeney the noted Gaelic teacher, author, playwright and poet, completed ten years of this 'Students' Column.' The next day this great and distinguished Gael passed to his reward. No feature in the* Journal *was more popular or more deeply appreciated. Again and again have we received tributes to its value from both teachers and students. Very many of those who began their study of Gaelic with*

the first conversation lessons ten years ago are today fluent speakers and writers of the language. Teachers have used them in their classes with proved success. In order to ensure a continuance of this feature we were arranging for a successor to Brian O'Keeney, but we have had requests from language teachers in Donegal and Derry for a republication of the series. A new generation of Gaelic students, they say, has sprung up since the first conversation lesson appeared. They expect a fresh influx following Eamon de Valera's St. Patrick's Night broadcast appeal,[249] *and they feel that there could be no greater help to the students than these lessons by a Gael who was master of teaching method. In deference to these requests from teachers, all of weight and experience, we have decided to republish the ten years' conversations lessons. Mar. 1943.*

Tá Brian Ó Cianaigh ar dhuine de cheannródaithe na hAthbheochana a ndeachaigh idé-eolaíocht Chonradh na Gaeilge i gcion go mór air ón tús agus níor scar sé léi i rith a shaoil. Chreid sé go láidir go gcaithfí an Ghaeilge a shlánú má bhí sé i ndán don tír seo a bheith ina náisiún in athuair mar a bhí sa tsean-am. Rinne sé a chion féin leis an aidhm sin a bhaint amach: ag teagasc na Gaeilge, ag tabhairt eolas ar shaibhreas an chultúir Ghaelaigh, agus ag spreagadh idir óg agus aosta thall is abhus i gCúige Uladh agus thall i Meiriceá. Fear ildánach a bhí ann: ceoltóir agus cainteoir a raibh deis a labhartha aige agus pearsantacht bhreá a mheall daoine. D'fhág sé corpas scríbhneoireachta ina dhiaidh as Gaeilge agus as Béarla a thugann leid dúinn ar a phearsantacht, a chumas scríbhneoireachta agus a bhuanna liteartha. Tá dearmad déanta air le fada – is mithid an neamart a rinneadh ann le fada a leigheas anois. Más mall, is mithid.

Nótaí

1 Níl aon chuntas air in ainm.ie ach déanfar é sin a leigheas gan mhoill.

2 Hannah Gallagher a bhí ar a chéad bhean agus rugadh seisear clainne dóibh: Thomas, James, Margaret, Mary, Charles agus Neil. Chaith siad uilig cuid mhaith dá saol thall i Meiriceá. Féach an nóta báis seo a leanas faoi James: *The many friends of his youthful days have learned with deep regret of the death in United*

States of James Keeney, formerly of Glendoan, Ardara. Deceased was prominently identified with the business life of the city of Hoboken, New Jersey, for about forty years, and his home in Park Avenue was always open to the exiled sons and daughters of Donegal and other Irish counties. The funeral was one of the largest seen in Hoboken for many years. The members of the numerous organisations with which deceased was connected attended in a body. Derry People and Tirconaill News (8/9/1934, 1).

3 Cuireadh an Scoil Náisiúnta sin ar bun i lár an naoú haois déag agus thóg an tiarna talaimh teach do mháistir na scoile.

4 Pádraig S. Ó Baoighill, *Cardinal Patrick O'Donnell 1856–1927* (Foilseacháin Chró na mBothán, 2008).

5 Is fiú an chaint seo a leanas a luaitear in *Pull Up a Chair* a thabhairt anseo óir is féidir glacadh leis go mbíonn Séamus ag caint faoi féin sna comhráití seo. *'My father was the best storyteller in the parish, and when he was telling stories, you are certain that I was listening studiously.'* (Uimh. 119).

6 *ACS* (14/7/1900, 279).

7 *ACS* (21/7/1900, 290).

8 *Shan Van Vocht* Vol. III, No. 10 (3/10/1898, 183–4).

9 *Derry People and Tirconaill News* (23/2/1935, 10); *The Derry Journal* (22/2/1935, 9).

10 *The Donegal Democrat* (2/3/1935, 12).

11 Seo a leanas an léamh a níos John Moulden, saineolaí i gceol Béarla na tíre seo, ar chlár na ceolchoirme. *The songs listed ... seem to fall into two broad categories: parlour songs, for genteel family use, and more generally popular items, suitable for public houses or, as here, local concerts ... a surprising amount seems to have originated in America – hence the Minstrels Troupe ... Many of the songs will have circulated directly among the class of people that I assume took part, in sheet music, piano album or songster form as well as those on ballad sheets. I'd guess that the people concerned tended towards the 'West British' and that they themselves sourced the songs in print. There is little or no evidence of oral circulation in Ireland of any of these items. .. I'd be quite interested in a couple of things – that a concert party and audience of 200 could be summoned in only a few days, and that 'A number of young ladies and gentlemen selected from those present by Mr O'Gallagher ... having volunteered their vocal services in addition to those who had already promised to attend for that purpose, a very respectable orchestra had been formed ...' – which indicates that a number of those present had formal musical training. I think this is a middle-class affair,*

conducted entirely in English, in an area which, at the time must have been largely Irish speaking. As to the frequency of concerts of this kind, I think the success of this one, with a fair number of people and a Christy Minstrels Troupe taking part, argues that there was some demand.

12 Seo a leanas breithiúnas na nGael ar a leithéid de choirm cheoil ag tús an chéid seo caite:
Cumann Litiordha na Gaedhilge, Doire
The following resolution was unanimously adopted:
'That we strongly protest against the character of the concert and entertainment held in St. Columb's Minor Hall ... and we hope that all future entertainments will be free from objectionable features.' We have read a description of the entertainment referred to ... and found it to be an extremely vulgar, degrading and un-Irish 'show,' consisting of a mixture of Christy Minstrel jabbering, and music hall rubbish, the whole concluding with a screaming farce 'My Girl from Donegal.' It speaks well for Catholic Derry that 'so great was the sale of tickets ...' ACS (21/9/1901, 442). Agus arís: *'They are working in Strabane for the Gaelic revival. An appeal has reached us asking the people to leave off patronising foreign songs, drama, and entertainments in general, and patronise only, firstly, Irish songs, or, failing these, songs that are Irish in tone and sentiment. We say arís to this, arís! Arís!' ACS* (19/10/1901, 505).

13 *ACS* (29/7/1899, 314–5).

14 *The Derry Journal* (29/1/1897).

15 *The Derry Journal* (6/12/1897).

16 *The Derry Journal* (14/1/1898). Is léir ón chuntas ar an nuachtán gur siamsaíocht d'ardchaighdeán – agus gallda cuid mhaith – a bhí i gceist. *The opening chorus was everything that could be, apart from large theatrical performance, the song selected was one of T.D. Sullivan's –'Dear old Ireland' – with a fine chorus ... The second part of the entertainment was a farce, entitled 'The Young Widow.'*

17 Ag an choirm cheoil bhí *'orchestra ... songs, recitations, duets, dialogues, dancing* srl.' Dúradh roinnt amhrán Gaeilge ar an ócáid fosta.

18 *The Derry Journal* (17/2/1898).

19 Bhí tuairim is 500 duine ina gcónaí ansin sa bhliain 1900.

20 Luaitear B. Keeney mar ghrósaeir in Ard an Rátha sa bhliain 1900 de réir an *Towns' Directory* (1900) 206.

21 Is minic sa tsean-am i mbailte beaga faoin tuath go mbíodh an dá shiopa seo faoi aon díon amháin.

22 Tá cuntas cuimsitheach ar staid na Gaeilge in Ard an Rátha sa bhliain 1930 le fáil ar an *Derry People and Tirconaill News* (23/8/1930, 1).

23 *The Derry Journal* (16/10/1899, 6).

24 *ACS* (14/7/1900, 278).

25 *ACS* (14/7/1900, 278–9).

26 *The Derry Journal* (31/10/1900).

27 *The Derry Journal* (14/12/1900).

28 *The Derry Journal* (17/12/1900).

29 *ACS* (9/2/1901, 761).

30 *ACS* (9/2/1901, 761).

31 *The Derry Journal* (1/3/1901, 6). Tugtar fá dear go dtugann sé Bernard Keeney air féin anseo.

32 *The Derry Journal* (6/3/1901, 7). Dúradh sa tuairisc chéanna go raibh ranganna Gaeilge ar siúl oíche Dhomhnaigh agus oíche Chéadaoin. Ritheadh rún '*that the members undertake to speak Irish in their everyday business as far as possible.*'

33 *The United Irishman* (8/2/1902, 5).

34 Aindrias Ó Muimhneacháin, *An Claidheamh Soluis: Tríocha Bliain de Chonradh na Gaeilge* (Conradh na Gaeilge, 1966).

Tá cuntas níos iomláine ag Fionán Mac Coluim ar an mhúinteoir taistil a foilsíodh ar an *Cork Examiner* (26/7/1911) 10. Seo a leanas sliocht as:

No body of men in Ireland has a more strenuous or more exacting life than they. Indeed, a man whose constitution is not of the strongest cannot hope to be able to continue as a travelling teacher for a longer period than three or four years, so great and so constant is the strain upon his energy ...

In some districts a teacher is working every day in the week (Sunday included, on which day many a branch holds its meetings) and has schools to prepare Irish lessons for and to worry his brains over. The session is usually from September to the end of June, and all through the wild, wet winter months the travelling teacher is obliged to literally fly from one place to another on his bicycle because no other mode of convenience would suit him, cars being too expensive to be even thought of, and trains (where there is railway communication) being out of the question when schools and branches in places far apart have to be reached by a certain hour.

To be a teacher of the language itself is not the only qualification a man must possess in order to carry through successfully the work in which he is engaged. He must also be a singer, a dancer, a musician, a public speaker, a diplomat and an enthusiast, whose enthusiasm must always be at fever-heat, and be as real and intense as to magnetise all who come in contact with the personality of its possessor. *To bring a number of adults together (even though they have youth on their side) who have left school some years previously, and have left off study for the simple pursuits of country life, to bring them together, to fire them with zeal for a knowledge of the language; to be mild, and patient and persevering with them; to keep them together after the novelty of a beginning has worn off until they have gone so far into the work that its own mysterious charm is strong enough to hold them – to do all this a man must be ever on the alert, ever resourceful, ever watchful of himself and of others, and must have a real passion in his heart for the work that lies before him.*

35 *The Derry Journal* (12/6/1901, 6).

36 *The Strabane Chronicle* (15/6/1901, 2).

37 *THE GAELIC REVIVAL IN STRABANE*
FORMATION OF CLASSES
Amongst the many praiseworthy achievements accomplished by the Strabane Catholic Men's Association, not least is the formation of classes for learning and cultivation of the Irish Language. Rarely do we find a more brilliant or successful start than that made in the Barrack-street Hall during the past week. There were present at the classes on Tuesday evening no fewer than 170 members, and ever since a continued increase is noticeable. Father McElhatton, the worthy president of the association, delivered an eloquent address immediately before class work on Tuesday evening, and in the course of which he expatiated on the merits of the language and the many reasons why we should spare no effort to secure its permanent revival. The universal interest which young and old have taken in the movement in the district is gratifying in the extreme and is evidenced by the frequent use of such salutations as 'Go mbeannaí Dia dhuit', 'Dia is Muire dhuit' etc. Indeed, one would require no better proof of the success to which the movement is rapidly attaining in Strabane than to notice the amount of pride already displayed by the children in their being able to salute their respected teacher, Mr. O'Keeney, in the language of the Gael. We sincerely trust that our people will take pride in it and all do their part in the sustainment. – Communicated.
The Derry Journal (19/6/1901).

38 Féach, Regina Uí Chollatáin, *An Claidheamh Soluis agus Fáinne an Lae 1899–1932* (Cois Life, 2004) 84–86.

39 *The Derry Journal* (10/7/1901, 3).

40 Féach, Aindrias Ó Muimhneacháin, *An Claidheamh Soluis: Thirty Years of the Gaelic League* (Clólann Uí Mhathúna, 1955) 4.

41 Tugadh poiblíocht mhór do cheist na dtionscal teallaigh ag *Féile Ghartáin* in 1897 agus ag *Aonach Thír Chonaill* in 1898.

42 *The Derry Journal* (10/7/1901, 3).

43 *The Derry Journal* (15/7/1901, 6). Seo léiriú eile ar bhua agus ar chumas cainte Bhriain.

44 15/7/1901, 6 agus arís sa leabhar Béarla atá le foilsiú go luath. Gheofar sa leabhar Béarla samplaí dá chuid óráidí Béarla, dá chuid filíochta Béarla, de na scéalta béaloidis leis a d'aistrigh sé agus roinnt píosaí eile chomh maith le hachoimre ar a shaol as Béarla.

45 *ACS* (3/8/1901, 330).

46 3/8/1901, 328.

47 *An Claidheamh Soluis agus Fáinne an Lae* (10/8/1901, 343).

48 Féach, Proinsias Mac Aonghusa, *Ar Son na Gaeilge* (Conradh na Gaeilge, 1993) 72–98.

49 I gcló sa leabhar Béarla.

50 'Gleann Domhain' le Brian Ó Cianaigh, Strabane, 9th September 1901. I gcló ar *ACS* (21/9/1901, 439) agus *The Derry Journal* (13/9/1901, 2).

51 *The Derry Journal* (11/10/1901).

52 Tagairt eile do thuairimí agus do chumas cainte Bhriain agus é ar an tSrath Bán. *Mr. B. Keeney, after eloquently supporting the vote of thanks in Irish, said: ... 'Mr. Doyle in his able exposition of the Intermediate programme, and of the elementary system of education in Ireland, has sufficiently demonstrated the flagrant injustice that has been perpetrated against us for years by the Commissioners of National Education. Our demand for a proper system of bilingual education must be sustained, and every advantage taken of the scanty means already at our disposal. The National Board is either artificially constituted for the purpose of denationalising the country, or it is an utterly incompetent body. A child at one of our National Schools, for instance, who is entirely ignorant of Irish history, could give you an elaborate description of a Brahmin procession in the forests of India. The Irish language is the key to the history of our race, and let us cherish the hope that the rapid progress of the movement will soon enable us to remedy the present existing evils and secure the advancement of National, intellectual prosperity. The Ulster Herald* (5/10/1901, 7). Is trua nár fhoilsigh na nuachtáin Bhéarla óráidí Gaeilge Bhriain ach go hannamh. Bhí coirm cheoil Ghaelach ann i ndiaidh na n-óráidí agus cheol na páistí

ón rang Gaeilge amhrán Gaeilge ar dúradh faoi: '*The harmony and accuracy of pronunciation that characterised the singing reflected much credit on the ability of the children themselves as well as their teacher Mr. O'Keeney.*' Ag deireadh na hoíche dúirt Mr. O'Keeney '*The Minstrel Boy*' agus '*Donegal.*' Ar na hócáidí poiblí seo go léir baintear leas as a dhá bhua mhóra, cumas cainte agus cumas ceoil.

53 *The Ulster Herald* (5/10/1901, 5).

54 *ACS* (21/9/1901, 445).

55 *The Dundalk Democrat* (28/9/1901, 4).
Cuireadh in iúl don Choiste Ceantair [i mí Mheán Fómhair] gur mhian leis an Mháistir Mag Uinseannáin éirí as a phost ... Fógraíodh go raibh folúntas ann do mhúinteoir taistil. Ba Chonallaigh an bheirt a chuir iarratais isteach – Brian Ó Cianaigh (Ard an Rátha) agus Pádraig Mac Gaoithín (Baile na Finne). Tháinig an Coiste le chéile arís chun iad a chur faoi scrúdú – sa léitheoireacht agus san aistriú gan ullmhú! – agus d'éirigh chomh breá sin leo gur ceapadh an bheirt acu. Roinneadh Craobhacha an cheantair eatarthu. Bhí a sá oibre acu mar bunaíodh ranganna Sathairn do mhúinteoirí náisiúnta agus glacadh isteach faoi choimirce an Choiste cathair Ard Mhacha, áit a mbeadh ceachtanna ar siúl dhá oíche sa tseachtain. Socraíodh go mbeadh an Cianach ag teagasc i nDún Dealgan Dé Máirt. Séamas Céitinn, *Craobh den Chonradh: Dún Dealgan, 1899–1976* (Coiste Mhuirtheimhne, Dún Dealgan: 1980) 12.

56 *ACS* (5/10/1901, 6).

57 *The Dundalk Democrat* (5/10/1901, 5).

58 *The Dundalk Democrat* (12/10/1901, 2).

59 *The Dundalk Democrat* (12/10/1901).

60 *The Dundalk Democrat* (12/10/1901, 4).Tá cuntais eile ar a chuid oibre sa taobh sin tíre nach gá a chur isteach anseo. Is leor a bhfuil anseo. Mar ba dhual do mhúinteoirí taistil, bhí sé seasta ag taisteal thart ag bunú craobhacha, ag tabhairt óráidí, ag teagasc agus i mbun bolscaireachta ar son an Chonartha. Féach ar chuntas Thaidhg Uí Rabhartaigh ar shaol an mhúinteora taistil in Nollaig Mac Congáil (eag.), *Lorcán Ó Tuathail: Drámadóir Mhaigh Cuilinn* (Arlen House, 2018) 50–52.

61 *The Dundalk Democrat* (26/10/1901, 4). *Meeting held to establish a new branch at Mullabawn, district organiser Keeney attended and spoke. ACS* (9/11/1901, 557–8).

62 Tá an óráid le fáil sa leabhar Béarla.

63 *The Derry Journal* (11/11/1901).

64 *The Dundalk Democrat* (23/11/1901, 5).

65 *Meeting at Grange*

A large and representative meeting of the Grange Branch of the Gaelic League was held on Thursday for the purpose of establishing a new class for the study of the National language ...

Mr. Keeney, organiser for the district, who, on rising to speak, was enthusiastically greeted, delivered a spirited address in Irish, every word of which was followed with rapt attention. Continuing in English, he said the Irish people now saw that the revival and cultivation of their national language were essential factors if Ireland was ever again to occupy her rightful position among the nations of the earth. The principles enunciated by the Gaelic League commended themselves to every Irishman who had the interest of his country at heart and with the result that the language of the Gael was once more becoming a hopeful and universal power in Ireland. Who could look back upon the past history of Ireland and fail to perceive the noble achievements, deeds of valour and bravery which were successfully accomplished and cherished by the aoirí *of a native tongue. Thanks to the efforts of the Gaelic League, they were once more on the eve of a similar period. Once more they beheld in the new horizon a self-dependent and Irish Ireland, an Ireland that appealed to her sons and daughters to stay at home and extended a Céad Míle Fáilte to her exiles. Ireland's position upon the face of the earth admirably adapted her for universal intercourse – a position which would enable her to intercept the trade of the Western world from all other nations, if she only enjoyed the advantage of legislative independence and unrestricted commerce. Her unequivocal determination to claim her rightful privileges was again demonstrated in her national language; the energies and talents of her people were once more directed and churned (?) by its influence, and they chose no other course than to become enabled from the misfortunes of their country, or identified with its prosperity. The chief ambition, therefore, of every Irishman should be to do his own part towards the accomplishment of this work, for the independence of their race. They should endeavour as far as lay in their power to stem the tide of emigration, and impress upon public bodies the desirability of assisting them in the revival of their industries. That was the public policy of the Gaelic League – a policy which he was proud to say was meeting with the hearty cooperation and approval of every Irishman who entertained the proper love and devotion for the language and land of their forefathers. The Dundalk Democrat* (30/11/1901, 2).

66 *Two new classes were reported, one at Beleek and the other at Grange, both of which are in splendid working order. It was unanimously decided to increase Mr. O'Keeney's salary by £10 per annum. No more efficient or painstaking tutor could be found than Mr. O'Keeney, and this tribute to his usefulness will be universally recognised as being well deserved. If the future is to be judged by the past the Organising Committee will, in a year or two, represent a constituency having few rivals of its kind in Ireland in points of general prosperity and attainment. The Dundalk Democrat* (30/11/1901, 4), *ACS* (7/12/1901, 619) agus *The Irish News and Belfast Morning News* (29/11/1901).

GAELIC LEAGUE: NEW BRANCH AT MAYOBRIDGE

Enthusiastic Inception

On Tuesday evening one of the most enthusiastic gatherings that have ever been assembled in the cause of Ireland's national tongue took place at Mayobridge, when a branch of the Gaelic League was formed under very auspicious circumstances ...

Mr. B. O'Keeney, the district organiser, whose presence at a meeting is sufficient to ensure its success, ... after speaking fluently in Irish, said:

'Nothing could give me greater pleasure than to be with you this evening, to render my humble assistance in enabling you to establish a branch of the Gaelic League at Mayobridge. I am sure it would be extravagant on my part to delay you by demonstrating the various reasons why we should spare no effort to revive our national language. There is one thing to which I would like to draw you attention, and that is the general belief so prevalent in non-Irish speaking districts – viz. that the Irish language is very difficult to learn. This is by no means consistent with the fact that those who apply themselves diligently to the study of Irish can sustain a conversation in the mother tongue in less than twelve months. In such districts as I have referred to Irish must, of course, be learned through the medium of English. I cannot help contrasting this state of affairs, with our so-called system of National education, or what might be more appropriately termed 'the anti-National system of education.' In many Irish-speaking districts in my native county (Donegal), where the children speak Irish as the vernacular language, the National teachers are entirely ignorant of Irish, and consequently, the best results of education are cast aside by their incapacity to utilise Irish as the natural medium of instruction. Yet the Commissioners of National Education were practically indifferent,

while educational experts continue to assure them that this system was defective, irrational, and impractical.

The present movement for an Irish Ireland has already been effective in wringing some slight concessions from the National Board, but we must remain persistent in our demands until we are granted a proper system of bi-lingual education, and until the melodious voice of our native language will ring as of yore through every glen and valley in Ireland.

The Gaelic League does not fail to inculcate most strenuously the fact that 'when Ireland's renown was world-wide, when she was by the nations esteemed above others, Irish was the vernacular speech of her people.' The spirit which animated our ancestors in those days, thank Heaven, is not dead, but is to-day perceptible throughout the land. The love of country and freedom which filled their hearts and caused them to rally to the fierce war-cry 'O'Donnell Abu' seems to have taken possession of their descendants, who to-day rally round the standard of the Gaelic League – an organisation which, unquestionably, points the way to national prosperity and salvation.

'Already we feel that the light of liberty is beginning to dispel the darkness and ruin that for years have hung around us. Morning and evening we are greeted by our friends in the language of the Gael, and we need not fear that its stimulating influence will fail, sooner or later, to make 'Ireland a nation' in the truest sense of the word.' The Irish News and Belfast Morning News (5/12/1901).

Thug sé léacht bhreá eile '*Our National Grievances*' i gCo. Lú ar an Ghaeilge i mí na Nollag agus tá an téacs sa leabhar Béarla. Agus, ag deireadh na hóráide, chuir sé draíocht ar an lucht éisteachta lena chuid ceoil.

... Mr. O'Keeney sang 'Maureen,' 'The Wearing of the Green,' and 'Clare's Dragoons' in his usual exquisite style. ... A very pleasing item was a duet, 'Óg-Laoch na Rann,' by Messrs. O'Keeney and MacVerry. The Dundalk Democrat (11/12/1901).

Luaitear go raibh céilí ar siúl i nDún Dealgan i mí na Nollag agus go raibh Brian i bhfeighil cúrsaí. *The Derry Journal* (13/12/1901).

67 *Supplement to The Dundalk Democrat* (21/12/1901, 10). An dán a bhí i gceist 'Solas ar an Bhealach', agus leagan Béarla ag gabháil leis agus dúirt Brian go raibh sé '*suitable as a recitation for children.*'

68 *The Dundalk Democrat* (28/12/1901). I gcló sa leabhar Béarla.

69 *The Ulster Herald* (18/1/1902, 7). Féach, fosta, *The Newry Reporter* (8/2/1902, 3).

70 *The Dundalk Democrat* (8/2/1902, 4).

71 *The Dundalk Democrat* (15/2/1902, 3).

72 *ACS* (15/2/1902, 825).

73 Níor éirigh linn aon chóip den iris seo a aimsiú.

74 *The Dundalk Democrat* (25/1/1902, 3).

75 *The Dundalk Democrat* (25/1/1902, 3).

76 *Ó Méith: Great regret was felt by all at the sad death of our veteran teacher, whom all so much respected and loved for the many qualities which endeared him to Gaelic Leaguers. He died in harness, as he was accidentally drowned on this day week while returning from teaching an Irish class near Forkhill. ACS* (4/1/1902, 708).

77 *'The Man on the Wheel'* ag cur síos ar Phroinsias Mac Uinseannáin a báitheadh.

78 I gcló sa leabhar Béarla.

79 *The Irish News and Belfast Morning News* (30/4/1902).

80 Tá seo luaite ar chúpla ócáid ach níl aon eolas faoi le fáil in *ACS* (31/5/1902, 218–9) ná in *Scéal an Oireachtais* áit a liostaítear na buaiteoirí.

81 *Dundalk Examiner and Louth Advertiser* (31/5/1902).

82 *MADDEN*

A very enthusiastic and largely-attended meeting of the Gaelic League was held at Madden, county Armagh, ... Mr. B. O'Keeney who arrived from Dundalk at the appointed hour of meeting, was introduced by the Rev. Chairman, and met with a most cordial and enthusiastic reception.

In the course of an able and stirring address, Mr. O'Keeney dealt forcibly with the importance of the movement, which was speedily bringing about a modern Ireland – an Ireland which was Irish in every sense of the word. He heartily congratulated them on the genuineness of spirit so perceptible amongst them, and felt assured that their voices in future would continually blend with the rest of Ireland in reviving and sustaining the noblest and sweetest language on earth. The Derry Journal (2/6/1902).

GAELIC LEAGUE

NEWRY, DUNDALK, AND DISTRICTS ORGANIZING COMMITTEE

The quarterly meeting of the above committee was held in the Catholic Club, Mill Street, Newry, on Thursday evening last.

Reports were read from the Secretary, and also from Messrs. J. O'Hegarty and B. O'Keeney, the two teachers employed by the committee, and same were, after some discussions, adopted. Dundalk Examiner and Louth Advertiser (21/6/1902).

GAELIC SUMMER CLASSES
We understand that the Committee of the Dundalk and Newry Branch of the Gaelic League are making arrangements for holding a class for the teaching of Irish under the tutorship of Mr Brian O'Keeney in Warrenpoint and Blackrock (Dundalk) during the summer months. We are sure that the people of Blackrock will avail themselves of this opportunity of gaining knowledge of the sweetest of all languages, Ár dteanga féin. Dundalk Examiner and Louth Advertiser (28/6/1902).

83 *The Newry Reporter* (10/6/1902). Maraíodh na hoifigigh sin sa chéad chogadh Domhanda.

84 James O. Hannay, '*The Wonderful Growth of the Gaelic League*' in *The World's Work*, Chalmers Roberts (ed.), May 1907, 604–6.

85 *The Newry Reporter* (16/9/1902).

86 *The Strabane Chronicle* (5/7/1902).

87 *ACS* (12/7/1902, 312).

88 *Dundalk Examiner and Louth Advertiser* (12/7/1902).

89 Féach, mar shampla, *ACS* (7/2/1903): *The members of the Strabane Coisde Ceanntair complain that An Claidheamh does not contain enough of Irish in the Northern dialect. We have the same complaint to make. The Ulster-men do not send us their dialect, and, unless we get a decent supply of it, we are not likely to learn and take as our own many of the Northern idioms. One must be first accustomed to a dialect. You cannot appreciate the beauty of a phrase before you see and hear it several times. If the Ulster-men write their dialect and send it to us, they will no longer have the complaint made by the members of the Coisde Ceanntair.* Féach, fosta, *ACS* (14/2 srl., 1903).

90 Mar shampla, an scéal beag 'An tAsal' ar *ACS* (9/8/1902, 369), 'An Fhidil,' *ACS* (14/2/1903, 10), 'Dhá Sheanduine i dTír Chonaill: Comhrá ar Chúis na Talún,' *ACS* (30/5/1903, 1).

91 Ríona Nic Congáil, '*Fiction, Amusement, Instruction: the Irish Fireside Club and the Educational Ideology of the Gaelic League*' in *Éire-Ireland*, 44 (2009) 91–117.

92 Maidir le *Crann Eithne*, féach, *The Strabane Chronicle* (31/7/1909, 6 agus 21/8/1909, 8).

93 *An Claidheamh Soluis* (23/8/1902, 410).

94 *ACS* (6/9/1902, 440).

95 Féach, *Pull Up a Chair*.

96 *CRAOBH OMEITH (OMEATH BRANCH.) The Omeath Branch resumed its classes on Friday evening, the 29th August, after being adjourned for a month. There was a fairly large attendance, under the*

tutorship of Mr. O'Keeney. Everyone seemed highly pleased with the number of prizes gained at the recent Feis. Three first prizes, four seconds, and one third went to their credit. This is more creditable when it is considered that they were all gained in the Literary Competitions, and do not include the now famous Nelly O'Hanlon, who carried off the story-telling competition this year again. Dundalk Examiner and Louth Advertiser, (6/9/1902).

97 Féach, James O. Hannay, '*The Wonderful Growth of the Gaelic League*' in *The World's Work*, Chalmers Roberts (ed.), May 1907, 604–608.

98 '*The Celtic Tongue*' (gan ainm údair) atá le fáil in Edward Hayes, *The Ballads of Ireland* (1856) 251–253.

99 *The Derry Journal* (26/9/1902). Tugann 'Anxious' freagra ar litir Bhriain ar an 29/9/1902 agus tugann 'Gaelic Leaguer' freagra airsean ar 1/10/1903.

100 *Dundalk Examiner and Louth Adv*ertiser (27/9/1902).

101 P.T. MacGinley, in *ACS* (27/9/1902), *The Derry Journal* (3/10/1902), *ACS* (27/9/1902, 487).

102 Chuir Brian béim i rith a shaoil ar chaint bheo na Gaeltachta.

103 *The Ulster Herald* (13/3/1903).

104 *The Derry People and Donegal News* (14/3/1903, 6).

105 21/3/1903, 3.

106 *The Fermanagh Herald* (2/5/1903, 3).

107 *The Fermanagh Herald* (29/8/1903, 7).

108 *The Derry People and Donegal News* (4/4/1903).

109 *The Strabane Chronicle* (2/11/1902). '*A travelling teacher Mr. B. O'Keeney has been appointed by Strabane Coiste Ceantair.*' *ACS* (15/11/1902, 598).

110 *The Derry Journal* (2/11/1902).

111 *The Derry Journal* (12/11/1902).

112 Féach, '*University Commission: Evidence Taken re The Study of Irish. June 12th, 1902. Rev. Dr. Salmon's Evidence.*' *ACS* (8/11/1902, 6).

113 *The Derry Journal* (14/11/1902).

114 *THE GAELIC LEAGUE IN DONOUGHMORE*

Studies at the Donoughmore Teachers' Gaelic Classes were resumed on Saturday, 8th inst., at Crossroads. Mr. B. O'Keeney who has been recently appointed Gaelic instructor for Strabane again and surrounding districts was in attendance. This class was inaugurated last February, by Mr. Gildea. the then Gaelic instructor at Strabane, who attended two hours and a half once a week till the end of June, when studies were suspended until now. Mr. O'Keeney will also give similar attendance. The teachers in the parish, besides introducing Gaelic into the schools, have opened evening classes on two evenings each week for anyone anxious to learn the language ... Rev. M. Mullin, C.C., ... thanked the travelling teacher B. O'Keeney, he has been untiring in his exertions to bring about every opportunity for the spread of the dear old tongue in the district, and we hope to see his efforts crowned with success in the near future.

Thomas Concannon spent ten or twelve days in the Strabane district, working in conjunction with the Coisde Ceanntair there – with much success. The half-dozen branches, which are under the supervision of the Coisde Ceanntair, are all in fine form, and in good working order. Mr. Brian O'Keeney has been appointed travelling teacher. Undertaking the reclamation of the Scottisized districts of the Finn and the Mourne Valleys was a fairly large order for the Irishmen of Strabane to undertake in the first instance; but they put him into their work, and, thank goodness, they are, season by season, pushing further and further their little outposts of ardent workers. Let Strabane flourish! ACS (15/11/1902, 600).

Grand Concert in Strabane

BOC sang 'Maureen' and 'Shan Van Vocht.'[1] *The Strabane Chronicle* (15/11/1902).

BRANCH ESTABLISHED IN DONEMANA

Mr. B. O'Keeney next addressed the meeting, and in the course of a forcible speech, said – I need hardly say that it affords me very great pleasure to be in your midst this evening and to render my humble assistance in establishing a Branch of the Gaelic League in Donemana. I will therefore put before you as briefly as possible, a few of the many reasons why Irishmen should endeavour to farther by every means in their power the interests of this movement, which embraces at once the moral, social, intellectual, and industrial regeneration of Ireland. Such a movement cannot fail to commend itself to every Irishman worthy of the name, and who wishes to save his country from the fate which has befallen the many nations that have adopted a foreign language at the sacrifice of their own. Did not such nations adopt the lowness and vulgarity of those nations with which they became assimilated? Did they not become part and parcel of, or rather, should I say, the very footstools of the nations they were aping? And is not this unfortunate state into which Ireland has been drifting for years? We were becoming so much absorbed by English ideas, customs, and habits, that there was really some justification in the assertion that we became 'more English than the English themselves.' We were taught to believe our language was the hallmark of ignorance; that our Nationality merely existed in the minds of the sentimentalists; that the deeds of bravery accomplished by Irishmen for Ireland and for Irishmen were only the results of fiction, and that we ourselves were only the remnants of a barbarous race who looked to England for enlightenment and civilisation. From whence, might I ask, did England derive this civilisation and enlightenment she wishes to impart to Irishmen?

Does this not seem to be the case of the pupil teaching the master, for, when Irish was the vernacular speech of the people of Ireland – as it still is, thank God, in many parts of the country – our schools were crowded with English scholars, who came to draw from our treasure-house of knowledge the wisdom and enlightenment they could not find elsewhere.

However, through the untiring efforts and energy of the Gaelic League, the Irish people are now awakening to a sense of their duty to their country and to themselves. The lesson which history teaches us is now becoming understood, and we may confidently hope to save ourselves even yet from assimilation with a race, the most material on earth, but let us remember that 'the chief instrument for this purpose is our National language, which is not only our safeguard, but a part of our nationality.'

Again, if the study of Irish has proved so interesting to philologists, what must it be for Irishmen? Is it not true if we knew our own language the very names of the townlands we live in, the names of our rivers that flow by our doors, and of the mountains that look down upon our homesteads, could talk history with us?

Will we continue to deplore the social condition of Ireland and forget that our national songs, music, and customs are locked up in our language and stand idly by with key in our own hands?

Certainly not! Such neglect would not be in keeping with the spirit which should animate the sons and daughters of so noble a race. I am confident that no words of mine are necessary to commend to you the study and cultivation of your national language and the furtherance of the aims and objects of the Gaelic League. The Derry Journal (28/11/1902).

Sgoruidheacht at Murlog

On Wednesday evening the first Sgoruidheacht in the district was held at Murlog Branch ... Paper on Irish music, Mr. Brian O'Keeney. The paper was illustrated by the singing and playing of old Irish airs.

..

The last item was 'O'Donnell Abú' in Irish by Mr. Brian O'Keeney, the splendid and popular Irish teacher for the district, the members of the classes joining in. The Strabane Chronicle (29/11/1902).

Is maith is fiú cuntas a fháil ar an dóigh a raibh ag éirí le cúis na Gaeilge i dTír Eoghain agus Brian i mbun oibre ansin.

THE GAELIC LEAGUE IN THE NORTH-WEST

STRABANE AND DISTRICT COISDE CEANNTAIR

On Saturday, 13th December, the third regular meeting of the above committee was held in the rooms, Barrack-street Strabane ... The Chairman called on Mr. Brian O'Keeney, to read his reports of the work done since last meeting.

Mr. O'Keeney read his report ... on the state of the various Branches in this District, Strabane, Killygordon, Rabstown, Murlog, Newtownstewart, Victoria Bridge, Donemana.

... It will be seen from the foregoing that already there are fully 900 persons learning the language within the district. I consider it my duty to congratulate the members of the local committees on the flourishing state of their respective Branches. The various classes are regularly and punctually attended, and the most commendable enthusiasm prevails throughout. I may, however, be pardoned in making a few observations of a propagandist character, not, indeed, that they concern this district more intimately than any other part of Ireland. There are three great sources which can largely contribute to the success of the language movement, and these are: First, the National Schools; 2nd, the native speakers of the language; and lastly, the propagation of healthy, national amusement. Of course, as you are aware, the number of schools throughout the country into which the language has been introduced as yet is comparatively small. It is, however, encouraging to know that the vast majority of the National teachers are diligently acquiring knowledge of the language, and healthy indications are by no means wanting.

The second great factor, and one which should be more largely availed of, is the native speakers. The success of no class is so assured as the one that can boast of a number of native Irish speakers. It is contended that it takes a long time to acquire a spoken knowledge of Irish, but it should be remembered that this is due, in a marked degree, to insufficient intercourse with the living tongue. Again with regard to amusement, monthly sgoruidheachta should be held in connection with each Branch. These should be made as attractive and as interesting as possible. Local, instrumental, and vocal talent should be liberally encouraged, especially in the case of those who are members of the Gaelic classes. Besides, apart from their social value, these entertainments can be made invaluable from an educational point of view, as they afford special opportunities for the reading of interesting papers on Irish music, history, &c., or indeed for the reading of propagandist literature supplied by the publication committee of the League.

In conclusion, I would respectfully suggest that the industrial aspect of the movement be kept prominently before the members of each Branch. The support of home-manufactured goods demands attention on every possible occasion, and should go hand in hand with the revival of the language, although the latter must be always considered the foremost plank in the platform of the Gaelic League.

Correspondence was read from the Omagh branch, and after some discussions it was decided to send Mr. O'Keeney to Omagh for a few days to assist in organising the district. The Derry Journal (17/12/1902, 6).

Leis an chuntas seo a leanas ar Scoraíocht, aithnímid go bhfuil an cultúr Gaelach i dtreis go mór sna siamsaíochtaí a reáchtáladh faoi scáth an Chonartha ag an am sin.

SGORUIDHEACHT IN STRABANE

There can be no doubt that the sgoruidheacht has come to stay. On account of the fact that most of our pupils are not yet very far advanced in the study of our language, the greater part of the programme at our sgoruidheacht is at present made up of Anglo-Irish items; but as we go on this will be quickly changed. We should set it before us as our ideal to be able to hold a sgoruidheacht in which we shall not have a word of English; and in the meantime every new effort should be an improvement on the last in this respect; if at each succeeding sgoruidheacht we add one more item in Irish, it will not be long before our ideal shall be attained. Some may object that a tendency to crush out the Béarla may also tend to keep away some of the outside public who would support our entertainments if the items were mainly in English, but who would not be inclined to sit out a performance given mainly in a tongue which they could not understand. That answer to this objection is our sgoruidheacht are mainly for the members of the Branches; we must develop them on Irish lines as fast as the progress of our learners will admit, and considerations of the possible effect on outsiders can't be allowed to enter into the question at all. Besides, as the development must take place gradually it is questionable whether we shall lose any of the support of the outside public. A thoroughly Irish sgoruidheacht would be well worth seeing and hearing.

... The following were the items: ... Humorous reading, by Mr. B. O'Keeney; ..
The second part of the programme opened with a fine paper on, 'Irish Music,' by Mr. B. O'Keeney. In the paper the following songs were introduced: 'The Fairy Boy,' by Edward McIvor; 'O'Donnell Abu,' in Irish, by Miss Alice Kearney; 'Caitheamh an Ghlais,' by Miss Agnes Gormley and Miss Mary Ann McDevitt. And a number of Irish airs on the violin, which were played by Mr. James McCrossan. The other items of the second part were as follows: 'Songs of the Caman,' by Mr. John O'Doherty; Song, 'A nation once again,' by Mr. John P. O'Doherty; Song, 'The Croppy Boy,' by Miss O'Hagan; Song, 'The Irish Emigrant,' by Miss Mary Ann McDevitt; Song, 'Mavoureen,' by Miss Bridget Calvert; Song, 'Lay me on the hillside,' by Mr. Peter Dunleavy; Step-dancing by Mr. John Sweeny; Song, 'Go saoraidh Dia Eireann,' by Mr. B. O'Keeney. The accompaniments were played throughout by Mr. James McCrossan. The Strabane Chronicle (27/12/1902).

115 'A New Year's Song,' *The Derry Journal* (2/1/1903) & *The Ulster Herald* (3/1/1903, 4).

116 *Céide: A very interesting lecture was delivered on Sunday evening last by Mr. B. O'Keeney, Lifford, Co Donegal: subject 'Irish Music.' An Claidheamh Soluis* (3/1/1903, 23).

117 Léirigh 'Scoláire Bocht' a mhíshástacht le cuid de na rialacha gramadaí an mhí dár gcionn (24/1/1903, 5). Thug Brian freagra air ar (7/2/1903, 4) agus scríobh 'Scoláire Bocht' arís ar (14/2/1903, 8).

118 I gcló sa leabhar Béarla.

119 *An Claidheamh Soluis* (31/1/1903, 782).

120 *ENTERTAINMENT AT BALLYAROL, KILLYGORDON ... Mr. Brian O'Keeney, the very accomplished Irish teacher of the Killygordon district, also rendered two songs in Irish entitled 'The Dawning of the day' and 'Little Mary.' The Derry Journal* (11/2/1903).

121 *ACS* (7/2/1903, 22).

122 *A lecture will be given by BOK in Castlederg on Irish Music. The Derry People and Donegal News* (11/4/1903). *Sgoruidheacht in Castlederg, A lecture by BO'K in Castlederg on Irish Music and Song. The Derry People and Donegal News* (25/4/1903). *Sgoruidheacht. Dornat Branch of GL. Song in Irish and lecture on Gaelic revival by BO'K. The Strabane Chronicle* (9/5/1903).
Ceapadh é mar thoscaire ag an Oireachtas:
Delegate at Oireachtas

Duilleachán an Oireachtais (9/5/1903).
Publication in Book form of Tyrconnell Series of Lessons, The Derry People and Donegal News (6/6/1903, 1).
Concert in Dunamanagh:Miss McGovern and Mr. B. O'Keeney gave a vocal duet in a manner that left nothing to be desired, and to the entire delight of the audience, by way of an arís, Mr. O'Keeney sang 'An Spailpín Fánach' in excellent style ... The Derry People and Donegal News (6/6/1903, 1).
June Strabane Feis, The Derry People and Donegal News (13/6/1903).
He then introduced Mr. B. O'Keeney, who recited a stirring poem in honour of the Feis, which will appear in our next issue.
There are now numerous Branches in the district, and the services of Mr. Brian O'Keeney who has done yeoman work since his engagement, have been secured, and he has devoted himself heart and soul towards teaching of the different classes the past two years, and no better proof could be given of the success which he has attained than by the training and efficient answering of his pupils in the several competitions which came off at today's Feis. The reel dancing of the classes from the Convent of Mercy, and the Strabane, Murlog, and Rabstown Branches were items of much interest, and evoked all-round applause. In fact, it would be invidious to go into the detail of the several competitions; they were well and numerably filled and were more interesting and some gave rise to much enjoyment and merriment. The several officials connected with it, especially Mr. O'Nolan secretary and Mr. B. O'Keeney deserve the highest praise for the success it attained. There is no doubt, that the first Feis held in Strabane augurs favourably for the success of future festivals, and is an unprecedented record of the success of the Irish Language movement in the district and Ulster. The Strabane Chronicle (13/6/1903). *Donoughmore Parish Feis: Examiner BO'K. The Derry Journal* (3/7/1903).

123 *The Derry Journal* (15/5/1903). Féach, Donncha Ó Súilleabháin, *Scéal an Oireachtais 1897–1924* (An Clóchomhar, 1984) 159.

124 *The Derry People and Donegal News* (20/6/1903, 7).

125 *ACS* (27/6/1903, 7).

126 *The Derry People and Donegal News* (20/6/1903).

127 *ACS* (11/7/1903, 1).

128 *ACS* (14/3/1903, 3).

129 Tá na scéalta seo i gcló sa chnuasach béaloidis atá sa leabhar seo.

130 I gcló san Aguisín chuí.

131 *ACS* (3/10/1903, 5).
132 *The Ulster Herald* (20/11/1903). I gcló sa leabhar Béarla.
133 *Irish American* (21/11/1903).
134 *The Derry People and Donegal News* (19/12/1903, 1).
135 I gcló sa leabhar Béarla.
136 *The Strabane Chronicle* (1/2/1913).
137 Tá an t-amhrán seo sa leabhar Béarla.
138 *The Ulster Herald* (12/3/1904).
139 *The Derry People and Donegal News* (17/9/1904).
140 *The Evening Journal*, Jersey City (3/10/1904).
141 *The Derry People and Donegal News* (19/11/1904, 1).
142 *First Meeting of Ulster Union Gaelic League. The Ulster Herald* (31/12/1904, 8). Féach, fosta: *Derry People and Tirconaill News* (4/7/1931, 6).
143 *The Ulster Herald* (10/9/1904, 6).
144 *The Gaelic American* (23/12/1905).
145 Maidir le cuairt de hÍde ar Mheiriceá, féach, L. Mac Mathúna, B. Ó Conchubhair, N. Comer, C. Ó Seireadáin, M. Nic an Bhaird (eagarthóirí), *Douglas Hyde: My American Journey* (UCD Press, 2019).
146 *The Gaelic American* (30/12/1905).
147 *The Gaelic American* (10/2/1906).
148 *The Gaelic American* (17/2/1906).
149 Marc Shell (ed.), *American Babel: Literatures of the United States from Abnaki to Zuni.* (Harvard University Press, 2002). I gcomhthéacs dhrámaíocht luath na Gaeilge ag tús an chéid seo caite in Nua-Eabhrac, deirtear ansin: '*After the turn of the century, Irish language plays, including some written in this country, were performed in New York, right up to the late 1960s. Two early examples are* Ar Son Cháit, a Chéad Ghrádh, *written by Andrew O'Boyle, a native of Sligo who was active in the New York language movement in the first decade of this century, and* Seaghan Ruadh *performed in New York in 1906 and written by B. O'Keeney, a native of Donegal who was also a major figure in New York Irish-Language circles at this time.*'
150 *The Gaelic American* (10/3/1906) .
151 Ríona Nic Congáil, 'Fiction, Amusement, Instruction: the Irish Fireside Club and the Educational Ideology of the Gaelic League' in *Éire-Ireland*, 44 (2009) 91–117.
152 *The Gaelic American* (10/2/1906).
153 *The Derry Journal* (6/4/1906, 2).
154 *The Gaelic American* (14/4/1906).

155 *The Gaelic American* (13/10/1906).
156 *The Gaelic American* (13/10/1906).
157 *The Gaelic American* (16/2/1907).
158 *The Sag-Harbour Express* (11/4/1907).
159 *The Brooklyn Citizen* (27/10/1908).
160 *Irish American Advocate* (3/2/1910).
161 *The Weekly Freeman* (19/2/1910).
162 4/9/1911, 6.
163 6/9/1911.
164 *The Derry Journal* (11/9/1911).
165 *The Derry Journal* (22/9/1911).
166 *The Derry Journal* (12/1/1912).
THE KILCLOONEY PARISH HALL
Mr. O'Keeney's, attractive play, entitled, The Rebel of Innishowen *... attracted crowded houses on 29th and 30th ult., in Ardara town ... On the occasion of the play the scenery and fixtures being obtained from Ardara, and the hall lighted up, one might travel farther and fare worse for a genuine spectacular sight and a night's entertainment.*
Mr. O'Keeney, who in years not so long distant, spread the light in this and other counties of Ireland in the Gaelic movement, spent some years in the City of New York. Gifted as he is with musical and dramatic talents he has strung together this play, to which the above title alluded to. It may be described as 'Historic melodrama,' at the end of which the 'Rebel' is pardoned by the Government and marries the daughter of an Irish Chieftain. Mr. O'Keeney, himself acts the 'Rebel' and it is remarkable that in such a short time the various other characters, some twenty, fell into the places and parts so as to astonish play goers who have seen such in much more pretentious places.
In an interlude in the middle of the play a ceilidh is introduced, which is a concert in itself, and then comes the real plot of the play, the rescue of the child (abducted, so as to catch the Rebel) himself. A real battle ensues, shots exchanged, and crackling of musketry is heard for a considerable time. The costumes are of the times in which the plot is laid, and in a word, to describe it is a must see.
A ball followed, and the spacious comfortable hall was again packed to its upmost. Mr. Hamil's string band (Derry) discoursed very suitable music both during the concert and ball, a most enjoyable night, the memory of which will long be 'kept green' in old Kilclooney, was brought to a close.

Without taking away from any of the artists the credit to which they are justly entitled, too much cannot be said in praise of the part taken by little Miss McNelis (a child of seven years), who as Baby O'Neill was the subject of special mention in Father Gallagher's remarks. The Derry Journal (24/1/1912).

167 *The Strabane Chronicle* (1/2/1913). *Appointment for Donegal Man: Many of our readers will be pleased to hear that Mr. B. O'Keeney of Ardara has been appointed Insurance Inspector, with headquarters Londonderry, for the Pearl Life Assurance Company, one of the strongest and most progressive of our larger life offices, commencing operations on the 20th inst. Mr. O'Keeney has for many years past been an interesting figure in the insurance business in America, having represented offices of such magnitude as the Prudential and the Metropolitan. He is the possessor of a strong personality, full of energy and enthusiasm and is well known all over Ireland. We join with our readers in congratulating Mr. O'Keeney on his promotion and in wishing him a very prosperous New Year. The Derry Journal* (17/1/1913).

168 *The Derry Journal* (28/9/1913).

169 *The Strabane Chronicle* (31/1/1914, 7).

170 *The Derry Journal* (27/2/1914, 3).

171 *The Derry Journal* (21/10/1914, 3).

172 *The Derry Journal* (22/3/1915).

173 *The Derry Journal* (28/4/1915).
AOH (B.O.E.) Division 245, Glenties: ... A vote of condolence was also passed to Brothers James and Patrick Roarty over the death of their sister, Mrs. B. O'Keeney, Ardara.
T H A N K S: To the many kind friends who have sent messages of sympathy, as well as those who attended funeral of my dearly-beloved wife. I tender my sincerest thanks. 'We have loved her in life; let us not forget her in death.' O, Sacred Heart of Jesus, have mercy on her soul. B. O'Keeney. The Derry Journal (23/4/1915).

174 Tá cuntas ar an eagraíocht seo le fáil in Seosamh Ó Ceallaigh (eag.), *As Smaointe Tig Gníomh: Coláiste Uladh, an Ghaeilge agus 1916* (Coiste Cuimhneacháin Choláiste Uladh, 2017) 55–57. Féach, fosta, Liam McGinley, *Pádraic O'Beirn* (Glencolmcille Printing & Lulu, 2018) 138–44.

175 *The Derry Journal* (14/1/1916).

176 Tá cuntas ar an ócáid le fáil in '*Striking Tributes to Dr. Falvey,*' *The Derry Journal* (2/6/1916).

177 '*The Irish Homestead* and Public Boards,' *The Derry Journal* (18/12/1916).

178 *The Derry Journal* (14/1/1918).
179 *The Derry Journal* (1/6/1918).
180 *The Derry Journal* (16/12/1918).
181 *The Derry Journal* (8/1/1919).
182 *The Derry Journal* (31/1/1919).
183 *The Derry Journal* (12/11/1919).
184 *The Derry Journal* (20/2/1920).
185 *The Derry Journal* (30/4/1920).
186 *Partners: Brian O Cionaigh (sic!) and Philip O'Dwyer.*
187 *'Willie Riley Review,' The Donegal Democrat* (11/11 1921).
188 *Tús Maith (A Good Beginning). By Brian O Cianaigh. Dundealgan Press. 6d. This booklet, as we are told, is for school and home use, and contains the first six lessons of a complete course in simple Irish. There are also rhymes, etc. The booklet will be found useful by those beginning to learn the language. Irish Independent* (18/9/1922, 2).
189 *Derry People and Tirconaill News* (5/1/1929, 1). *Iona Hall Ardara: First Grand Production of* Under Three Flags *11 & 13 January, 1929: Grand Ball & Music by Sona Band and Orchestra. The Derry Journal* (5/1/1929).
190 *The Strabane Chronicle* (19/1/1929, 1).
191 Seo clann Shéamuis Mhic an Bhaird as Toraigh a bhí ina ndamhsóirí cáiliúla ar nós a n-athar Séamus.
192 *Derry People and Tirconaill News* (4/1/1930).
193 *Derry People and Tirconaill News* (22/2/1930, 1). *Cuntas eile: ARDARA NOTES: The Advertising Exhibition which opened at the Iona Hall on Monday is now in full swing, and may from every point of view be described as a most remarkable success. Visitors from near and far, attracted by the immense variety of the exhibits (and other attractions as well) continue to arrive by day and night in large and increasing numbers, and the town has assumed an air of gaiety and business activity. Special interest is centred at the moment in the dramatic production,* Come Back to Erin, *advertised for three nights only (namely, Feb.28th, March 1st and March 2nd). It is anticipated when the curtain falls on the last act action next Sunday night, the attendance for the week shall have constituted a record, of which any provincial town might be justly proud. Derry People and Tirconaill News* (28/2/1930).
194 *Derry People and Tirconaill News* (28/9/1929, 3).
195 *Derry People and Tirconaill News* (5/10/1929, 5).
196 *Derry People and Tirconaill News* (5/10/1929, 2).
197 *Derry People and Tirconaill News* (30/8/1930, 6).
198 Tá siad i gcló sa leabhar seo.

199 *Derry People and Tirconaill News* (15/3/1930, 9).

200 Féach, mar shampla, 7 Meitheamh, 5 Iúil, 2 Lúnasa.

201 *Derry People and Tirconaill News* (12/7/1930, 3).

202 *The Derry Journal* (17/11/1930).

203 *Derry People and Tirconaill News* (27/12/1930, 6).

204 *Derry People and Tirconaill News* (31/1/1931, 10). Bhí cuntas ar Louis ar an leathanach chéanna.

205 *Derry People and Tirconaill News* (7/3/1931, 9).

206 *Derry People and Tirconaill News* (20/6/1931, 6) *and, with correction* (27/6/1931, 10).

207 Tá an óráid i gcló sa leabhar Béarla.

208 *Derry People and Tirconaill News* (7/3/1931, 10).

209 *Derry People and Tirconaill News* (4/7/1931, 5).

210 *MRS. C. O'KEENEY, LOUGHROS POINT ARDARA: We regret to announce the death of Mrs. Catherine O'Keeney, Loughros Point, Ardara which took place on Saturday. Deceased, who was the mother of Brian O'Keeney (Irish teacher, author), had reached an advanced age, and the funeral at Ardara on Monday was one of the largest seen in this district for many years.*

Very Rev. Canon Byrne, P.P. (who officiated) delivered a beautiful panegyric in the course of which he outlined the saintly life and sterling qualities of the deceased. 'She was,' he said, 'a model of every form of Christian virtue, and the parish of Ardara was the poorer for the death of such a woman. She was a source of inspiration to all who knew her and the remarkable tribute of respect shown towards her today was not at all surprising. Her whole life was filled with good works and this thought together with that of her holy death cannot fail to comfort the members of her family in their present bereavement. May her soul rest in peace.' Derry People and Tirconaill News (21/11/1931, 5).

211 *Derry People and Tirconaill News* (28/11/1931, 4).

212 Tá an óráid i gcló sa leabhar Béarla.

213 *Derry People and Tirconaill News* (2/7/1932, 7). Bhain an dán seo duais ag Feis Thír Chonaill. Síleann an t-údar gur cheart do Ghaeil na hÉireann amhrán fíorGhaelach a bheith acu feasta (mar a deir an Béarla, *Rallying Song*) agus níl ceann ar bith againn chomh fóirsteanach fána choinne seo le fonn '*God Save Ireland.' The Strabane Chronicle* (27/8/1932, 8).

214 Niall Mac Giolla Bhríde, file cáiliúil as an Chraoslach.

215 *Derry People and Tirconaill News* (9/7/1932, 5).

216 *Irish Press* (24/8/1932, 6).

217 *Derry People and Tirconaill News* (21/1/1933, 11).

218 *Derry People and Tirconaill News* (11/2/1933, 1).

219 *The Derry Journal* (24/3/1933).

220 *Derry People and Tirconaill News* (25/3/1933, 1).

221 *The Derry Journal* (19/5/1933).

222 *Meeting of Loughros Point Cumann: There was a large meeting of Loughros Point ('Robert Emmett') Cumann, held on Sunday afternoon. The President (Brian O'Cianaigh) presided. Having first addressed the meeting in Irish, he said:* Tá an óráid i gcló sa leabhar Béarla. *Derry People and Tirconaill News* (10/6/1933, 9).

223 *The Derry Journal* (16/6/1933, 6)

224 *Derry People and Tirconaill News* (17/6/1933, 3).

225 *DONEGAL AUTHOR AS DRAMATIST*

BRIAN O'KEENEY'S PRIZE-WINNING DRAMA TO BE STAGED IN BELFAST

An interesting dramatic competition was opened in St. Mary's Hall. Belfast, last night under the auspices of Feis na Drámaidhacta Catoilige. There was a crowded audience which thoroughly enjoyed the production of the following Gaelic dramas which constituted the first round of the competition:

1 'Tá na Franncaigh ar Muir' from the pen of 'Cú Uladh,' staged by the pupils of St. Louis Convent, Kilkeel.

2 'Caitlin Ni Cluidhe,' by Pádraig Ó Conaire. (Pupils of St. Louis Convent, Kilkeel).

3 'Teachtaire Chríost go hÉireann,' by Rev. Father Gaffney, O.P. (pupils of St. Louis Convent, Middleton, Co. Antrim).

The final round of the competition will take place on Saturday next, March 3rd, at 7.30 p.m., when the following will be staged.

1 'Gríomhartha Lae san Ghaedhaltacht,' Brian O'Keeney ('Events of a day in the Gaeltacht'), Ardara, (produced by the 'Tír na nÓg' branch of the Gaelic League, Belfast).

2 'An Cleamhnas,' by Dr. Douglas Hyde (produced by 'Craobh Gaedheal Uladh')

3 'Buaidh an Ultaigh,' by Séamus Ó Néill (pupils of Ollsgoil na Rioghna).

It will be remembered that Mr. O'Keeney's drama won the Belfast Feis in 1933 and was hailed by competent Gaelic scholars as a 'masterpiece of dramatic art,' and hundreds of Donegal Gaels in Belfast and many other parts of Ulster will be present in St. Mary's Hall next Saturday evening to cheer the Tír na nÓg players and the popular Donegal author. It is significant to note that two of the dramas selected are in Donegal Irish. 'Cú Uladh,' one of the leading

Gaelic authors in Ireland, and President of the Gaelic League, is also a native of Donegal. The results of the competition are a-waiting, with more than ordinary interest. Irish News and Belfast Morning News (25/2/1935).

226 *The Derry Journal* (14/7/1933, 9).

227 *The Derry Journal* (12/8/1935, 6).

228 *ONE HUNDRED YEARS AGO: A GLIMPSE OF COUNTY DONEGAL IN PRE-FAMINE DAYS* ag Brian ar *The Derry Journal* (26/8/1935, 3). I gcló sa leabhar Béarla.
Prose and Poetry of a Bygone Age: Songs that Live Forever by Brian O'Cianaigh ar an *Derry People and Tirconaill News* (19/10/1935, 10). Tá an óráid i gcló sa leabhar Béarla.

229 *Derry People and Tirconaill News* (2/11/1935, 4).

230 *The Strabane Chronicle* (14/12/1935, 5).

231 *The Donegal Democrat* (29/2/1936, 7).

232 *Irish Press* (16/4/1936, 3).

233 Tá an óráid i gcló sa leabhar Béarla.

234 I gcló sa leabhar Béarla.

235 *Derry People and Tirconaill News* (5/12/1936, 3).

236 *The Derry Journal* (4/1/1937). Tá cuntas iomlán ar an ócáid ansin.

237 An tseachtain dheireanach de mhí Feabhra, 1937.

238 *Winner of first prize (All-Ireland) Oireachtas in Dublin, 1902 for best poem dealing with the battle of Benburb.*
(1) Winner of first prize (All-Ireland) for best essay on Cottage Industries (Oireachtas Dublin 1903)
(2) Winner of first prize (singing) for best rendering of Péarla and Bhrollaigh Bháin competition open to All-Ireland, Omeath Feis, 1904 (Cardinal Logue presiding).
(3) Winner of first prize (All-Ireland) for best short drama of Irish Life. Belfast Feis 1933.
(4) Winner of five first prizes at Feis Tirconaill since 1929. These include best poem to the air of 'The wearing of the Green,' best poem to the air of 'God save Ireland,' and the best poem on the beauties of Tirconaill (1937).

239 *Derry People and Tirconaill News* (10/7/1937, 3).

240 *Derry People and Donegal News* (2/4/1938, 4).

241 *The Derry Journal* (16/10/1937). *Negotiations are now in progress for the filming of Mr. Brian O'Cianaigh's well-known Anglo-Irish drama,* Under Three Flags *which has been produced on the stage with remarkable success in various centres in South-West Donegal*

during the past seven years. Derry People and Tirconaill News (16/10/1937, 1).

242 *Derry People and Tirconaill News* (23/10/1937, 1).

243 *Derry People and Tirconaill News* (30/10/1937, 5).

244 *The Derry Journal* (15/7/1938, 14).

245 *The Derry Journal* (5/10/1938).

246 *Derry People and Tirconaill News* (18/2/1939, 4).

247 *Mr. Brian O'Keeney O.G., Loughros Point ... has been a prizewinner in the Irish Literary section of the Feis for many years. Derry People and Tirconaill News* (6/7/1940, 3).

248 *Derry People and Tirconaill News* (20/3/1943, 6).

249 *Derry People and Tirconaill News* (20/3/1943, 2).

SCÉALTA BÉALOIDIS

Gadaí Dubh na Slóna agus Scéalta Eile

Cuireadh tús le sraith de scéalta béaloidis ar an *Derry People and Tirconaill News* ar an 30 Márta 1935 agus lean an tsraith ar aghaidh seachtain i ndiaidh seachtaine go dtí deireadh mhí Aibreáin 1937. Bhí aistriúchán leis na scéalta seo i gcónaí. Bhí an t-ábhar i gcló sa cholún *Easy Lessons in Irish with Condensed Grammar Notes,* colún teagaisc a bhí ag Brian Ó Cianaigh le fada roimhe sin ar an nuachtán. An t-am seo, áfach, ní ábhar teagaisc a bhí i gceist ná ní raibh aon nótaí gramadaí ag gabháil leis an cholún. Ar bhealach, áfach, d'fhéadfaí a mhaíomh ó tharla go raibh an chuid ba shaibhre de Ghaeilge na Gaeltachta sna scéalta go gcuideodh siad le barr feabhais agus slachta a chur ar Ghaeilge an lucht foghlama. Is scéalta iad seo a bhí ar eolas go forleathan i gceantar Bhriain agus é óg.

Gadaí Dubh na Slóna

Bhí Rí in Éirinn fada ó shin agus bhí dúil mhór aige i gcearrbhachas. Lá amháin tháinig seanchailleach go caisleán an Rí agus dúirt sí leis an doirseoir a d'fhoscail an doras gur mhaith léi an Rí a fheiceáil.

'Tá sé amuigh ag seilg inniu,' arsa an doirseoir.

'Tiocfaidh mé ar ais amárach,' ar sise.

'Cad é an gnoithe atá agat leis an Rí?' arsa an fear a raibh na cnaipí buí air.

'Tá sé faoi gheasa agam le bliain,' arsa an chailleach, 'agus caithfidh sé cluiche cártaí a imirt liom.'

Leis sin tháinig carráiste an Rí go dtí an geafta agus chonaic sé an tseanchailleach ina seasamh ag an doras. B'fhearr leis gan labhairt léi ach ní raibh teacht as aige.

'Cad é atá ag tabhairt trioblóide duit inniu?' arsa an Rí.

'Bliain agus an lá inniu,' arsa an chailleach, 'd'imir muid cluiche cártaí. Bhain mise an cluiche agus chuir mé de gheasa ort cluiche eile a imirt inniu. Tá na cártaí liom.'

D'aithin an Rí go han-mhaith go raibh dúil ag an chailleach dochar a dhéanamh dó ach bhí a cumhacht mhallaithe chomh mór sin is gurbh éigean dó tabhairt isteach. hImreadh an cluiche agus bhí an bhuaidh ag an chailleach.

'Tabhair do bhreithiúnas,' arsa an Rí.

'Tá triúr mac agat,' ar sise, 'agus caithfidh tú iad a chur go dtí an Domhan Thoir mar gheall ar an Ghearrán Óir a ghoid ó Rí na tíre sin.'

Nuair a chuala an Rí an breithiúnas míthrócaireach seo is beag nár thit sé i laige. Bhí aird mhór aige ar na trí prionsaí agus bhí a fhios aige an dainséar a bhí rompu.

'Nach dtig leat breithiúnas inteacht eile a thabhairt?' ar seisean leis an chailligh.

'Tá na focla ráite,' ar sise, 'agus ní thig iad a thabhairt ar ais.'

'Ag tórramh an diabhail go raibh tú,' arsa an Rí nuair a bhí an chailleach ag imeacht.

Ba bhrónach an scéal a bhí le hinsint ag an Rí an oíche sin nuair a bhí an bhanríon agus na trí prionsaí i gcuideachta a chéile. Bhí an t-iomlán acu ag gol go brónach ar feadh tamaill agus fá dheireadh labhair an prionsa ab óige mar a leanas: 'Rud nach bhfuil leigheas air, caithfear cur suas leis. Rachaimid i gceann siúil le misneach agus, más toil le Dia é, tiocfaimid abhaile slán.'

Cupla lá ina dhiaidh sin d'fhág na prionsaí slán ag an Rí agus an bhanríon agus chuir tús ar an turas go dtí an Domhan Thoir. Ní theachaigh siad i bhfad gur casadh fear orthu a raibh cosúlacht air go bhfaca sé laetha rua. Chuir sé ceist ar na prionsaí cá raibh siad ag gabháil agus d'inis siad an fhírinne dó.

'Tá garda saighdiúr thart fán Ghearrán Óir oíche agus lá,' arsa an fear, 'agus ní féidir é a ghoid. Ach ó tharla go gcaithfidh sibh a ghabháil ba mhaith liomsa a ghabháil libh. Tá an chuid is fearr de mo laetha thart agus, má tá an bás romhainn, chead againn é a roinnt go cothrom.'

'Táimid fíorbhuíoch duit,' arsa fear de na prionsaí. 'Cad é an t-ainm atá ort?'

'Tá aithne orm ar fud an domhain,' arsa an fear, 'mar Gadaí Dubh na Slóna.'

Shiúil siad leo i gcuideachta a chéile go dtáinig siad go dtí an fharraige. Chuaigh siad ar bord loinge agus fá dheireadh tháinig siad go dtí an tír ina raibh an Rí ar leis an Gearrán Óir.

'Is fada anois ó bhí mé sa tír seo,' arsa an Gadaí, 'ach tá a fhios agam nach bhfuil am ar bith le cailleadh againn. Caithfimid iarracht a dhéanamh an Gearrán Óir a ghoid anocht agus má sháraíonn orainn níl ag duine ar bith againn ach beatha amháin le cailleadh. Seo coill bheag ina dtig linn fanacht go dtí an meán oíche. Tá an Gearrán Óir cumhdaithe le cloigíní ón chluais go dtí an ruball agus siúd is go bhféadfadh na saighdiúirí a bheith ina gcodladh, musclóidh fuaim na gcloigín iad.'

'Bíodh sin mar atá sé,' arsa na prionsaí, 'tá an turas déanta againn agus caithfimid ár ndícheall a dhéanamh.'

Ag uair an mheán oíche tharraing siad ar an chaisleán go faichilleach ach, faraor, má bhí na saighdiúirí ina gcodladh, bhí an gearrán muscailte. Chroith sé é féin agus i mbomaite bhí an Gadaí Dubh agus na prionsaí i lámha na saighdiúr.

Maidin lá arna mhárach tugadh an ceathrar os comhair an Rí agus thug sé breithiúnas báis orthu. Dúirt sé leis na saighdiúirí an prionsa ba sine a cheangal de chrann, brosna a chur thart fána chosa agus ansin an brosna a chur le thinidh.

'Dóifear na prionsaí eile ina dhiaidh sin,' ar seisean, 'agus fágfaimid an Gadaí Dubh go dtí an duine deireanach.'

'A Rí uasail,' arsa an Gadaí, 'bhí mise níos comhgaraí don bhás seal blianta ó shin ná an prionsa atá ceangailte den chrann. Má bheir tú maithiúnas dó inseoidh mé an scéal duit.'

'Bíodh ina mhargadh,' arsa an Rí. 'Cuir chugainn an scéal.'

'A Rí uasail,' arsa an Gadaí Dubh, 'is iontach agus is ró-iontach an scéal atá le hinsint agam ach bheirim m'fhocal duit go bhfuil sé fíor. Uair amháin bhí mé ag siúl i dtír choimhthíoch agus nuair a tháinig an oíche orm ní raibh teach ar bith le feiceáil. Fá dheireadh tháinig mé fhad le coill agus chonaic mé tinidh faoi chrann mhór, ard. Tharraing mé ar an tinidh agus shuigh mé síos mar gheall ar mé féin a théamh. I gceann tamaill chuala mé gutha daonna agus d'aithin mé go raibh a n-aghaidh ar an tinidh. Bhí mé in mo dhreapaire chliste agus in am ghairid bhí mé in mo shuí ar ghéag den chrann, go díreach os cionn na tineadh. Leis sin, tháinig triúr de na cailleacha ba ghráice dá bhfaca mé riamh go dtí an tinidh, mála óir ag gach duine acu ar a droim. D'fhág siad síos na málaí comhgarach ag an tinidh agus shuigh gach duine acu ar a mála féin. Labhair bean amháin de na cailleacha leis an bheirt eile mar a leanas: 'Ar maidin amárach,' ar sise, 'caithfimid an t-ór seo a chur i bhfolach. Tá Gadaí Dubh na Slóna sa tír seo fá láthair agus caithfimid a bheith faichilleach.'

Níl ann ach go raibh na focla seo ráite nuair a d'amharc bean de na cailleacha in airde agus chonaic sí mé le solas na tineadh.

'Tá an Gadaí Dubh anseo,' ar sise.

D'éirigh an triúr ina seasamh. Thiontaigh bean acu í féin isteach ina fear mhór, láidir; rinne an dara bean tua di féin agus thiontaigh an tríú bean ina seabhac. Ba thrua mo chás, a Rí. Thoisigh an fear ag gearradh an chrainn leis an tua agus d'fhéach an seabhac na súile a phiocadh asam. Mhair an obair seo go bánú an lae agus fá dheireadh thoisigh an crann ag lúbadh. Dhéanfadh buille eile é a leagaint ach, ar an bhomaite sin, scairt an coileach agus thit an tua ó lámha an fhir. Ní raibh cumhacht acu fanacht níos faide agus d'imigh siad mar a bheadh séideán gaoithe ann. Sin deireadh mo scéil.'

'Is fíoriontach do scéal,' arsa an Rí. 'Bheirim pardún don phrionsa mar a gheall mé, ach caithfear na prionsaí eile agus tú féin a chur chun báis.'

Cheangail na saighdiúirí an dara prionsa den chrann agus ansin labhair an Gadaí Dubh arís.

'A Rí uasail,' ar seisean, 'an dtabharfaidh tú cead domh scéal eile a insint duit sula gcuirtear an prionsa seo chun báis?'

'Tá eagla orm go bhfuil an t-am suas,' arsa an Rí.

Bhí máthair an Rí láithreach san am seo agus d'iarr sí ar an Rí an scéal a éisteacht. Thug an Rí isteach agus d'inis an Gadaí Dubh an scéal a leanas.

'Tá mé fíorbhuíoch duit, a Rí, mar gheall ar cead a thabhairt domh an scéal seo a insint. Is cuma liom fá mo bheatha féin ach ba mhaith na prionsaí a shaoradh. Uair amháin, seal mór blianta ó shin, bhí mé ag siúl i dtír álainn nach bhfuil i bhfad ón áit ina bhfuil mé in mo sheasamh. Tháinig mé fhad le caisleán a bhí comhgarach don fharraige agus, de bhrí go raibh ocras orm, bhí dúil agam rud inteacht a ghoid mar gheall ar arán a cheannach. Chuaigh mé fhad le ceann de na fuinneogaí go faichilleach agus d'amharc mé isteach. Is é an chéad rud a chonaic mé bean an-dóighiúil ina suí i seomra mór, páiste ar a glúin agus í ag caoineadh. Rinne mé dearmad de mo bhuaireamh féin agus, mar bhí an doras foscailte, shiúil mé isteach.

'Cad é ábhar do chuid caointe?' arsa mise leis an mhnaoi.

'Banríon atá ionam,' ar sise, 'agus ar maidin inniu thug mé an páiste seo amach fá choinne aistir bhig. Agus tháinig an fathach ar leis an áit seo thart agus thug sé an péire againn anseo. Má thugaim iarracht imeacht cuirfidh sé chun báis mé.'

'Is trua do chás,' arsa mise. 'Cá bhfuil an fathach anois?' arsa mise.

'Amharc isteach ar an doras sin ar do chúl,' arsa an bhanríon.

'D'amharc mé isteach agus cinnte go leor bhí an fathach sínte ar urlár seomra an-mhór agus é ina chnap ina chodladh. Fuair mé bior iarainn agus choinnigh mé sa tinidh é go raibh sé dearg te. D'iarr mé ar an bhanrín an páiste a thabhairt léi agus a haghaidh a thabhairt ar an fharraige.

'Beidh mise 'do dhiaidh i mbomaite,' arsa mise.

'Fuair mé greim ar an bhior ansin agus chuaigh mé go ceann an fhathaigh. Ní raibh aige ach súil amháin agus bhí an tsúil sin i gclár a éadain. Sháith mé an bior dearg isteach sa tsúil agus thug mé áladh ar an doras. Fuair mé suas leis an bhanrín agus an páiste, ach bhí an fathach ar [mo] lorg agus é ag béicfigh mar a bheadh tarbh ann. Ar ndóiche, bhí sé dall ach bhí cumhacht mhallaithe inteacht á threorú. Is cosúil ina dhiaidh sin go raibh eagla air go gcaillfeadh sé sinn, agus tharraing sé amach fáinne draíochta agus chaith in airde sa spéir é. Bhí mise ag iompar an pháiste san am seo agus shonraigh mé gur thit an fáinne ar ladhair de chuid an pháiste. Theip sé orm an fáinne a bhogadh siúd is go dtearn mé mo dhícheall. Fá dheireadh, scairt an fathach go hard:

'Cá bhfuil tú anois?'

'Tá mé anseo,' arsa an fáinne.

'Thug an fathach áladh ar an áit a dtáinig guth an fháinne as agus shíl mé go raibh muid caillte. Ní raibh am ar bith le spáráil. Tharraing mé amach scian phóca agus ghearr mé an ladhair den pháiste. Bhí muid anois ag bruach na farraige agus chaith mé an ladhair ar a raibh an fáinne greamaithe amach san fharraige chomh fada is a bhí mé ábalta.

'Cá bhfuil tú anois?' arsa an fathach.

'Tá mé anseo,' arsa an fáinne.

'Tháinig an guth ó íochtar na farraige. Léim an fathach isteach san uisce, chuaigh sé as amharc go tobann agus báitheadh é.

'Agus anois, a Rí uasail, tá deireadh le mo scéal agus sin mar a shábháil mé an bhanríon óg agus an leanbh.'

Nuair a chríochnaigh an Gadaí an scéal shiúil máthair an Rí suas fhad leis agus d'amharc air go géar.

'An féidir,' ar sise, 'gur tusa an fear a shábháil mise agus an leanbh deich mbliana fichead ó shin?'

'Níl moill ort sin a fháil amach,' arsa an Gadaí. 'Más tusa an bhanríon a bhí i gcontúirt ar an ócáid sin, thig leat mé a cheistniú ina thaobh.'

'Níl agam le cur ort ach ceist amháin,' arsa máthair an Rí, 'agus beidh a fhios agam ansin an bhfuil do scéal fíor. Cad é a dúirt mé leat nuair a chonaic mé go raibh mé féin agus an leanbh sábháilte?'

'D'iarr tú orm an leanbh a iompar abhaile agus rinne mé sin. Thairg tú mé a choinneáil thart fán chaisleán ar feadh mo bheatha agus gan aon obair a bheith le déanamh agam. D'inis mé duit gurbh fhearr liom an bheatha a chleacht mé ó m'óige, agus ansin thug tú bia agus deoch domh agus i ndiaidh an oíche a chaitheamh in do chaisleán thug tú sparán óir domh agus thug mé m'aghaidh ar an domhan mhór, fhuar arís.'

'Tabhair domh do lámh,' arsa máthair an Rí. 'Tá an uile fhocal a deir tú fíor. Céad míle fáilte romhat féin agus na prionsaí seo.'

Thug sí a haghaidh ar an Rí ansin agus dúirt sí: 'Ba tusa an leanbh a bhí liom an lá sin. Sin mar a chaill tú an ladhair de do chois chlí.'

'Tá an t-am agam mo lánbhuíochas a thairgint duit,' arsa an Rí leis an Ghadaí. 'Is minic a chuala mé an scéal seo, ach is beag a shíl mé go gcasfaí orm go deo an fear cróga a shábháil mo mháthair agus mé féin. Ní fhéadaim a rá ach go bhfuil maithiúnas agat féin agus na prionsaí.'

Tugadh isteach sa chaisleán iad ansin agus d'ordaigh an Rí féasta seacht lá agus seacht n-oíche a chaitheamh ina n-onóir. Ag deireadh an ama sin thug sé an Gearrán Óir mar phronntanas do na prionsaí; thug sé mála óir don Ghadaí agus chuir sé a sheacht mbeannacht chuig Rí na hÉireann.

Ní féidir an lúcháir a bhí ar Rí agus Banríon na hÉireann a áireamh nuair a tháinig na prionsaí agus an Gadaí Dubh ar ais leis an Ghearrán Óir. Níor dhadaí an féasta a tionóladh sa Domhan Thoir le taobh an fhéasta a caitheadh in Éirinn. Cuireadh culaith sróil ar an Ghadaí agus tugadh an onóir chéanna dó a fuair na prionsaí iad féin. Lena chois sin dúirt an Rí leis fanacht sa chaisleán fhad is a bheadh sé beo.

'Dhéanfaidh mé sin,' arsa an Gadaí Dubh, 'ar choinníoll amháin.'

'Agus cad é do choinníoll?' arsa an Rí.

'Is dóigh liom,' arsa an Gadaí, 'go bhfuil mórán feirmeoirí ina gcónaí ar an dúiche seo.'

'Tá,' arsa an Rí. 'Thig leat céad teach a fheiceáil ó dhoras an chaisleáin.'

'Maith go leor,' arsa an Gadaí. 'Ní maith liom mo cheird a thabhairt suas ar fad. Ba mhaith liom rud inteacht a ghoid anois agus arís ó na feirmeoirí mura mbeadh ann ach cearc.'

'Ní thig liom tú a eitiú,' arsa an Rí le mothú gáire. 'Thig leis na searbhóntaí an chearc a chur ar ais lá arna mhárach.'

Bhí an Gadaí sásta agus d'fhan sé sa chaisleán go dtáinig an bás fána choinne.

NÓTA: *Derry People and Tirconaill News*, 30 March, 6, 13, 20, 27 April 1935. Foilsíodh leagan den scéal seo ar *An Claidheamh Soluis,* 1 August 1903, 1, 2, 3; 22 August 2, 3; 29 August 2; 12 September 3. Níorbh é sin críoch an scéil bhreá seo ach níor foilsíodh an chuid eile de ar *ACS*. Tá cuid den scéal seo ó *ACS* i gcló arís i gCorpas an RIA. Ní hionann amach is amach leagan *ACS* agus ceann an *Derry People*. Tá leagan *ACS* i gcló in Aguisín I anseo. Tá leagan eile den scéal i gcló in Mícheál Mac Giolla Easbuic (eag.), *Ón tSeanam Anall: Scéalta Mhicí Bháin Uí Bheirn* (Cló Iar-Chonnachta, 2008), 113–122.

Seán an Chóta Leathair

Bhí baintreach ina cónaí i gContae Dhún na nGall sa tseanam agus ní raibh aici ach mac amháin arbh ainm dó Seán. Ní raibh slí bheatha ar bith acu ach cá bith méid airgid a rinne an bhaintreach ag sníomh olla. Ní raibh aird ar bith ag Seán ar obair. Is annamh a d'éirigh sé go dtí an meán lae agus ón am sin go hoíche bhí sé sínte sa luaith. Mhair sé mar seo go dtí go raibh sé bliain agus fiche d'aois agus fá dheireadh dúirt a mháthair leis go mbrisfeadh sí a chnámha mura dtéadh sé i gceann oibre.

'Níl brosna ar bith agam le tinidh a dhéanamh,' ar sise, 'níl tuí ar bith ar an teach agus is gairid go dtitfidh sé.'

Leis sin, shiúil cailín óg as an chomharsanacht isteach.

'Tá mé ag iarraidh ar an chrionglach seo an luaith a fhágáil agus a ghabháil ag obair,' arsa an bhaintreach leis an chailín.

'Sin rud nach dtiocfadh leis a dhéanamh,' arsa an cailín. 'Níl láidreacht chait ann agus féadann tú a bheith ag dréim lena bhás lá ar bith.'

Chuir seo an oiread sin feirge ar Sheán gur léim sé ina sheasamh agus amach leis. Thoisigh sé á chroitheadh féin, an chéad uair ina shaol. Chroith sé an oiread luaithe de féin is a chumhdaigh acra talaimh roimhe, acra ina dhiaidh agus acra ar gach taobh de. Chuaigh sé ansin fhad le garraí a bhí leathmhíle ar shiúl agus chonaic sé stáca ocháin. Thug sé an uile phunann dá raibh sa stáca leis in ualach amháin. Ar a bhealach abhaile chonaic sé dréimire i ngarraí eile agus thug sé leis é faoina ascaill. Chuir sé an oiread sin tuí ar an teach is nach raibh sifín eile a dhíth air go ceann seacht mblian. I ndiaidh a dhinnéar a dhéanamh chuaigh sé go dtí an choill agus thug abhaile ualach de na crainn ba mhó a thiocfadh leis a fháil. Scoilt sé ina ngiotaí iad roimh luí na gréine agus ní raibh níos mó ábhar tineadh a dhíth ar an bhaintreach go ceann bliana.

Maidin lá arna mhárach dúirt Seán lena mháthair go raibh an t-am aige a ghabháil agus a fhortún a shaothrú.

'Ní thig leat an baile a fhágáil ins na seanéadaí sin,' arsa an bhaintreach. 'Thiocfadh liom culaith bháinín a fháil déanta fá do choinne,' ar sise, 'ach ní mhairfeadh sé lá amháin duit.'

'Faigh cóta leathair domh,' arsa Seán, 'agus ní iarrfaidh mé níos mó.'

Rinne an mháthair mar a hiarradh uirthi agus gléasadh Seán i gcóta leathair an oíche sin.

Lá arna mhárach ag éirí na gréine bhí Seán réidh leis an bhaile a fhágáil. Bhí toirtín gléasta ag a mháthair fána choinne agus d'fhiafraigh sí de cé acu ab fhearr leis an chuid ba mhó den toirtín agus a mallacht nó an chuid ba lú agus a beannacht.

'Is fearr liom an chuid is lú agus do bheannacht,' arsa Seán.

Bhí an mháthair sásta agus bhí sí ag doirteadh beannachtaí ina dhiaidh go dteachaigh sé as amharc.

Shiúil Seán leis go dtáinig sé fhad le ceárta. D'iarr sé ar an ghabha claíomh a dhéanamh dó a mhuirfeadh leathdhuisín leis an uile bhuille.

'Níl airgead ar bith agam,' arsa Seán, 'ach díolfaidh mé thú am inteacht eile.'

'Bhéarfaidh mé an claíomh duit mar phronntanas,' arsa an gabha.

'Go raibh maith agat,' arsa Seán. 'Nuair a tífeas tú mise arís beidh ainm Sheáin an Chóta Leathair thar an domhan agus ní dhéanfar dearmad ortsa.'

Ní theachaigh Seán i bhfad níos faide nó gur casadh fear air ar an bhealach mhór. Labhair an fear leis go macánta agus d'fhiafraigh de cá raibh sé ag gabháil.

'Tá mé ar lorg máistir,' arsa Seán.

'Agus tá mise ar lorg buachalla,' arsa an fear. 'Cad é an tuarastal atá a dhíth ort?'

'Fágfaidh mé sin agat féin,' arsa Seán. 'Beidh a fhios agat ag deireadh na bliana cad é an tuarastal is fiú mé.'

'Beidh iontas ort a chluinstin,' arsa an fear, 'gur Rí a bhí ionamsa siúd is go bhfuil mé ag caitheamh seanéadaí.'

'Is cuma liomsa,' arsa Seán, 'cad é an cineál éadaigh atá ort, agus más Rí atá ionat is dóiche go mbeidh tú 'do mháistir mhaith.'

'Ní bheidh obair ar bith agat le déanamh,' arsa an Rí, 'ach amháin aire a thabhairt do bha. Rachaimid abhaile anois agus thig leat a ghabháil i gceann oibre ar maidin amárach.'

Go moch lá arna mhárach cuireadh Seán amach leis na ba agus dúirt an Rí leis gan iad a ligint thar aon teorainn ar feadh an lae.

'Tá triúr fathach,' ar seisean, 'ina gcónaí i gcaisleán atá comhgarach ag an áit a mbeidh na ba ag ingilt agus is leo an talamh atá ar an taobh eile den teorainn. Ag luí na gréine,' arsa an Rí, 'cluinfidh tú fead ó gach duine de na fathaigh. Ar an bhomaite sin tiomáin na ba abhaile.'

Rinne Seán mar a hiarradh air agus nuair a bhí an ghrian ag gabháil síos chuala sé an chéad fhead. Níor chuala sé rud ar bith cosúil leis ina shaol. Tháinig dhá fhead eile ina dhiaidh sin. B'éigean do Sheán a mhéara a chur ina chluasa.

'Má fhanaim anseo ar feadh an tsamhraidh,' arsa Seán leis féin, 'cuirfidh mé deireadh leis an fheadalach.'

Nuair a chuaigh Seán amach leis na ba lá arna mhárach, d'amharc sé thar an sconsa agus chonaic sé go raibh féar breá ar ingilt na bhfathach. Rinne sé bearna in am ghairid agus thiomáin na ba isteach. 'Is mór an náire,' ar seisean leis féin, 'na ba a choinneáil i bpáirc lom agus féar mar seo ag gabháil amú.'

Fá thuairim an mheán lae d'amharc Seán in aice an chaisleáin agus chonaic sé fathach mór, gránna ag teannadh leis.

'Cé a thug cead duit,' arsa an fathach, 'na ba sin a chur isteach sa pháirc seo?'

'Má shíleann tú go bhfuil siad sa chasán,' arsa Seán, 'féach lena gcur amach.'

Chuir seo fearg ar an fhathach.

'Ní fiú domh,' arsa an fathach, 'mo lámha a shalú leat. Is mór liom de ghreim amháin thú; is beag liom de dhá ghreim thú, ach caithfidh mé deireadh a chur leat.'

'A bheathaigh ghránna,' arsa Seán, 'is í mo chomhairle dhuit a ghabháil abhaile má tá rud ar bith le déanamh agat.'

'Cad é an cineál báis is fearr leat?' arsa an fathach.

'Beidh faill agam m'intinn a dhéanamh suas nuair a bheas mé réidh leatsa,' arsa Seán. 'Ó tharla nach bhfuil claíomh ar bith leat, beidh cluiche coraíochta againn.'

Shíl an fathach go gcuirfeadh sé Seán faoi thalamh leis an chéad chasadh ach ba ghairid go bhfuair sé le fios go dtabharfadh Seán a sháith dó le déanamh. Mhair an choraíocht go dtí go dtearn siad bogán den chruán agus cruán den bhogán ach ní raibh an bhuaidh ag ceachtar acu. Fá dheireadh chuala Seán fead ó gach duine den dá fhathach a bhí sa chaisleán ach ní raibh fonn feadalaí ar an fhathach a raibh sé ag troid leis. Go dearfa, ní raibh sé ábalta fead a ligint. Bhí a fhios ag Seán go raibh an t-am ann leis na ba a thabhairt abhaile agus, leis sin, thug sé cor éifeachtach don fhathach agus chuir síos go dtína rúitíní é.

Le cor eile chuir sé go dtína ghlúine é agus chuir an tríú cor go dtína bhásta é.

'Stad, stad!' arsa an fathach, 'tá tú ró-chliste agam. Má ligeann tú domh a ghabháil abhaile bhéarfaidh mé each dubh duit a chuideos leat an domhan a shiúl gan dainséar.'

'Nuair a d'iarr mé ort a ghabháil abhaile,' arsa Seán, 'ní rachfá, ach tá tú mall anois. Gheobhaidh mé an t-each dubh lá inteacht eile. Tá obair an lae seo ar bhealach a bheith thart.'

Fuair Seán an claíomh a bhí ina luí ar an talamh agus leis an chéad bhuille sciob sé an ceann den fhathach. Chuir sé air a chóta ansin agus thiomáin na ba abhaile. Cheisnigh an Rí é fá mar a chaith sé an lá ach dúirt Seán go raibh sé tuirseach agus go dtabharfadh sé tuilleadh tuairisce dó ar maidin.

Nuair a d'éirigh Seán ar maidin chuir an Rí ceist air an raibh a fhios aige cad é an fáth nár lig fear amháin de na fathaigh aon fhead an oíche roimhe sin.

'Ní raibh sé ábalta,' arsa Seán.

'Cad chuige sin?' arsa an Rí.

'Bhí sé ag troid liomsa,' arsa Seán, 'agus chuir mé deireadh lena chuid feadalaí.'

'Más mar sin atá an scéal,' arsa an Rí, 'is fearr duit fanacht sa bhaile inniu. Muirfidh an bheirt eile thú.'

'Ní bheidh a shaothar orthu,' arsa Seán. 'Ní bhainfidh mise leo má choinníonn siad ar shiúl uaim, ach má bhíonn troid a dhíth orthu, gheobhaidh siad a sáith de.'

Thug Seán na ba leis agus thiomáin isteach iad i bpáirc na bhfathach. Tamall beag ina dhiaidh sin chonaic sé fathach ag teannadh leis. Bhí an fathach dhá uair chomh mór leis an fhathach a mharbh sé an lá roimhe sin.

'An tusa an fear a mharbh mo dheartháir?' arsa an fathach.

'Is mé,' arsa Seán, 'agus éireoidh an rud céanna duitse mura dté tú abhaile go socair.'

Leis sin, chuir an fathach mionna as a chuir crith ar na cnoic. Bhí claíomh mór, fada leis agus thóg sé in airde sa spéir é mar gheall ar Seán a mharbhadh le buille amháin. Nuair a chonaic Seán an buille ag titim léim sé i leataobh agus chuaigh barr an chlaímh síos ins an talamh. Sula raibh faill ag an fhathach an claíomh a tharraingt ar ais, ghearr Seán an lámh dheas de. D'fhéach an fathach greim a fháil ar Sheán lena láimh chlí ach ar an bhomaite sin thit sé agus sula raibh faill aige éirí sciob Seán an ceann de.

Nuair a bhí an ghrian ag gabháil faoi chuala Seán fead ón fhathach a bhí beo agus thiomáin sé na ba abhaile. Bhí an Rí ag fanacht leis agus chuir sé ceist ar Sheán cén fáth nár chuala sé ach fead amháin ag luí na gréine.

'Nach leor sin?' arsa Seán. 'Mura bhfuil seachrán ormsa,' ar seisean, 'ní chluinfidh tú fead ar bith san oíche amárach.'

Chuaigh Seán a luí ach bhí sé ag brionglóidigh ar na fathaigh ar feadh na hoíche. Nuair a d'éirigh sé ar maidin lá arna mhárach thug sé na ba leis mar ba ghnách agus chuir isteach in ingilt na bhfathach iad. In am ghairid tháinig an fathach ba mhó den iomlán chun troda leis.

'Mharbh tú mo dhá dheartháir,' arsa an fathach, 'ach cuirfidh mise deireadh leat.'

'Is orthu féin a bhí an locht,' arsa Seán. 'D'iarr mé orthu a ghabháil abhaile ach níor ghlac siad mo chomhairle.'

'Cé a thug seilbh duit ar an pháirc seo?' arsa an fathach.

'Beidh seilbh iomlán agam,' arsa Seán, 'nuair a bheas mé réidh leatsa.'

D'fhéach an fathach greim a fháil ar Sheán mar gheall ar é a mharbhadh ach bheadh sé chomh maith aige iarracht a thabhairt greim a fháil ar ghiorria. Bhí Seán ag damhsa thart fá dtaobh de go dtí go raibh an fathach sáraithe aige. Thit sé sa deireadh agus sciob Seán an ceann de. Thiomáin sé na ba abhaile ag luí na gréine agus níor chuala an Rí fead ar bith an oíche sin, ach shonraigh sé go raibh Seán an-tuirseach agus nach raibh ann ach go raibh sé ábalta siúl.

Lá arna mhárach cheistnigh an Rí Seán i dtaobh na bhfathach.

'Níor chuala mé fead ar bith aréir,' arsa an Rí.

'Tá an fheadalach thart,' arsa Seán. 'Mharbh mé na trí fathaigh.'

'Cad é mar atá dúil agat an lá seo a chur isteach?' arsa an Rí.

''Fhad is a bheas na ba ag ithe,' arsa Seán, 'tá dúil agam cuairt a thabhairt ar an chaisleán ina raibh na fathaigh. Tá each dubh ansin agus is dóigh liom go bhfuil sé ina cheann mhaith.'

'Níl each ar bith sa domhan atá inchurtha leis,' arsa an Rí, 'ach má théann tú ar a lorg ní thiocfaidh tú ar ais go deo.'

'Má tá sin mar sin,' arsa Seán, 'beidh mé tamall maith ar shiúl.'

I ndiaidh na ba a chur i bpáirc na bhfathach thug Seán a aghaidh ar an chaisleán. D'aithin sé go raibh contúirt inteacht roimhe ar siocair an rud a dúirt an Rí. Ar an ábhar sin shiúil sé go faichilleach. Bhí crainn ag fás thart fán chaisleán agus sheas Seán, a chlaíomh ina láimh aige, ar scáth na gcrann. Bhí doras an chaisleáin foscailte agus bhí tormán iargúlta ag gabháil chun tosaigh taobh istigh. Fá dheireadh chonaic sé seanchailleach ag teacht amach agus ar siocair an droch-chuma a bhí uirthi, is beag nár thit Seán i laige. Bhí adharc ag fás as barr a cinn. Bhí an adharc deich dtroigh ar fad. Bhí fiacla aici a bhí dhá throigh déag ar fad agus ingne ar a cuid méar a bhí níos faide ná fiacla. Chonaic sí Seán ina sheasamh faoi chrann agus tháinig sí comhgarach.

'An tusa an diabhal saolta a mharbh mo chuid páistí?' ar sise.

'Ba bhreá, mór na páistí iad,' arsa Seán. 'An bhfuil troid ar bith a dhíth ortsa?' ar seisean.

'Tá d'am thuas,' arsa an chailleach ag tabhairt áladh ar Sheán mar gheall ar é a strócadh ina ghiotaí.

Bhí na crainn an-ramhar agus comhgarach ag a chéile agus d'aithin Seán nach dtiocfadh leis an chailligh greim a fháil air, go mbeadh sí ina dhiaidh go Lá an Luain. Thoisigh an ruaig i measc na gcrann, Seán ag gáirí agus ag magadh ar an chailligh agus ise ag gabháil ar mire ag an uile thiontó. Mhair siad mar seo go dtí go raibh leath an lae caite. Fán am seo bhí an chailleach as anál ar fad agus d'aithin Seán go mbeadh an bhuaidh leis ag an deireadh. Chuir sé a chúl le crann agus sheas ansin go dtí go dtáinig an chailleach comhgarach. Chrom sí a ceann agus thug iarracht Seán a pholladh leis an adharc. Thug sé céim i leataobh agus chuaigh an adharc dhá throigh isteach sa chrann. Bhí an chailleach chomh sáraithe sin nach raibh sí ábalta an adharc a tharraingt ar ais. Leis sin, thug Seán buille den chlaíomh di i gcúl an mhuinéil agus ba é sin deireadh na caillí.

'Ag tórramh an diabhail go raibh tú,' arsa Seán nuair a chonaic sé marbh í ag bun an chrainn. Chuaigh Seán isteach sa chaisleán agus thoisigh ag siúl ó sheomra go seomra. I ngach ceann acu bhí mála óir.

'Is liomsa an caisleán anois,' ar seisean leis féin, 'agus nuair a thiocfas deireadh na bliana thig liom an t-ór a thabhairt abhaile liom agus beidh mé ábalta an gabha a dhíol ar son an chlaímh.'

Fuair Seán buinse mór eochrach agus chuir sé an glas ar gach doras dá raibh sa chaisleán. Bhí sé ar tí na ba a thabhairt abhaile nuair a smaoinigh sé ar an each dhubh. Chuaigh sé fhad leis na stáblaí ach ní raibh each ar bith ansin. Bhí páirc ghlas in aice leis na stáblaí agus shiúil Seán isteach sa pháirc. Chuala sé monamar srutháin agus dúirt sé leis féin go dtiocfadh leis deoch uisce a fháil agus is cinnte go raibh sin a dhíth air. Ní raibh soitheach ar bith leis ach ina dhiaidh sin d'éirigh leis a sháith den uisce a ól agus é ina luí ar a bhéal faoi. Nuair a d'éirigh sé ina sheasamh bhí an t-each dubh ag a thaobh.

'A bheathaigh bhoicht,' arsa Seán, 'níl do leithéid eile ar dhroim an domhain. Is fearr liom thú ná an méid óir atá sa chaisleán agus beidh mise 'mo mháistir mhaith agat.'

Ansin chumail sé ceann an ghearráin agus dúirt: 'Is trua nach dtig leat labhairt liom.'

'Thig liom labhairt leat,' arsa an t-each, 'agus beidh iontas ort a chluinstin gur mac Rí mise. Chuir na fathaigh a mharbh tusa sa chruth seo mé, agus caithfidh mé fanacht mar seo go dtí go mbuailfear trí bhuille orm den tslat draíochta a rinne each díom.'

'Cá bhfuil an tslat anois?' arsa Seán.

'Sa tseomra is mó sa chaisleán tá an tslat crochta ar an bhalla.'

'Maith go leor,' arsa Seán, 'is gairid go mbeidh tú 'do phrionsa arís.'

Sheas an t-each ar bhruach an tsrutháin agus in oiread bomaití tháinig Seán ar ais leis an tslat draíochta. Bhuail sé trí bhuille ar an each agus, leis sin, bhí prionsa óg, dóighiúil ina sheasamh lena thaobh. Thug an prionsa póg do leiceann Sheáin agus ansin d'inis dó gurbh é a athair an Rí a raibh Seán ar aimsir aige. Bhí lúcháir mhór ar Sheán nuair a chuala sé gur shábháil sé mac a mháistir.

'Tá an t-am agamsa na ba a thabhairt abhaile,' arsa Seán. 'Is dóigh liom go bhfuil deifir abhaile ortsa fosta.'

'Tá, go dearfa,' arsa an prionsa. 'Tá sé trí bliana ó cuireadh faoi dhraíocht mé agus síleann m'athair go bhfuil mé marbh.'

'Síleann sé go bhfuil mise marbh mar an gcéanna,' arsa Seán. 'Dúirt sé liom dá dtéinn ar lorg an ghearráin nach dtiocfainn ar ais choíche. Beidh iontas air an péire againn a fheiceáil.'

Tháinig an prionsa agus Seán abhaile leis na ba. Nuair a chonaic an Rí a mhac a shíl sé a bhí marbh, thit sé i laige. Ba ghairid go dtáinig sé chuige féin agus d'ordaigh sé féasta seacht lá a chaitheamh sa chaisleán.

'An bhfuil daoine muinteartha ar bith agat?' arsa an Rí le Seán, 'ar mhaith leat cuireadh a thabhairt dóibh chun an fhéasta?'

'Tá,' arsa Seán, 'mo sheanmháthair. Is dóigh liom go bhfuil sí beo ar bhrachán ó d'fhág mise an baile.'

'Thig léi slán a fhágáil ag an bhrachán ó seo amach,' arsa an Rí. 'An bhfuil duine ar bith eile ar mhaith leat cuireadh a thabhairt dó?'

'Tá,' arsa Seán, 'an gabha a rinne an claíomh fá mo choinne.'

Cuireadh carráiste fá choinne na beirte agus bhí siad ag an fhéasta lá arna mhárach. Bhí an gabha tugtha don ól agus ní raibh sé leathuair sa chaisleán go dtí go raibh sé ar meisce. Mhair sé mar seo ar feadh na seacht lá ach níor dhúirt aon duine drochfhocal leis.

Nuair a bhí an féasta thart chuir Seán ceist ar an Rí i dtaobh chaisleán na bhfathach.

'Má bhí seilbh agatsa air in am ar bith,' ar seisean, 'ní bheidh dadaí agamsa le déanamh leis.'

'Ní raibh aon seilbh agam ar an chaisleán sin agus níl mé ag dréim le seilbh air anois. Throid tusa na fathaigh agus is leat iomlán a gcuid saibhris. Ba mhaith liom tú a bheith mar chomharsa agam ar siocair go mbeidh do chuidiú úsáideach dá dtigeadh trioblóid ar bith in mo bhealach.'

'Tá mé buíoch duit,' arsa Seán, 'agus ó tharla go bhfuil tú sásta, rachaidh mé féin agus mo mháthair a chónaí sa chaisleán.'

Shásaigh seo an Rí go mór ach, ina dhiaidh sin, chonacthas do Sheán go raibh rud inteacht ag tabhairt trioblóide dó.

'Is minic a bhí dúil agam,' arsa Seán, 'a fhiafraí duit cé acu a bhí níon ar bith agat riamh agus, má tá, cá bhfuil sí?'

'Is maith liom,' arsa an Rí, 'gur chuir tú an cheist sin orm. Tá níon amháin agam ach tá sí ó bhaile le dhá bhliain. Lá amháin bhí sí thíos fán tráigh agus tháinig ollphéist amach as an fharraige agus hobair go gcuirfeadh sí deireadh léi. Go dearfa, ach ab é go raibh baicle de mo chuid saighdiúr ar bhruach na farraige san am ní bhainfeadh mo níon an baile amach. Am ar bith ina dhiaidh sin nuair a rachadh an cailín ar amharc na farraige, thiocfadh an phéist amach agus bhéarfadh iarracht í a shlogadh. Fá dheireadh, b'éigean domh an cailín a chur go tír choimhthíoch agus tá sí ansin go fóill.'

'Má ghlacann tú mo chomhairle,' arsa Seán, 'cuirfidh tú scéala chuig do níon a theacht abhaile.'

'Chuirfeadh sin lúcháir ar mo chroí,' arsa an Rí, 'ach ab é go bhfuil eagla orm roimh an phéist.'

'An bhfacthas an phéist ó d'imigh do níon?' arsa Seán.

'Uair amháin,' arsa an Rí. 'San earrach a chuaigh thart bhí beirt de mo chuid fear ag treabhadh sa pháirc atá in aice leis an fharraige. Ní raibh siad i bhfad i gceann oibre nuair a chonaic siad an phéist ag teacht amach as an fharraige. Rith na fir an méid a bhí siad ábalta. Thug an phéist áladh ar an dá ghearrán a bhí sa tseisreach agus i ndiaidh an bheirt a shlogadh, chuaigh isteach san fharraige arís. Ní fhacthas ó shin í.'

'Tabhair seanghearrán domhsa amárach,' arsa Seán, 'agus rachaidh mé i gceann oibre sa pháirc chéanna.'

'Ní bheifeá ach ag cur do lámh in do bhás féin,' arsa an Rí. 'Níl do chlaíomh fada go leor. Dá dtigtheá fá fhad claímh don phéist ní shábhóladh m'arm ar fad thú.'

'Ar chuala tú riamh,' arsa Seán, 'go bhfuil 'claíomh solais' i gcaisleán na bhfathach agus nach bhfuil a leithéid le fáil ar dhroim an domhain?'

'Chuala mé in m'óige,' arsa an Rí, 'go raibh claíomh iontach ag na fathaigh ach ní raibh a fhios agam go raibh sé sa chaisleán go fóill.'

'Tá, maise,' arsa Seán, 'agus tífidh tú é anocht nuair a thiocfas mise abhaile leis na ba.'

'Fan ort,' arsa an Rí, 'má tá dúil agat a ghabháil chun troda leis an phéist amárach, cuirfidh mé buachaill eile leis na ba.'

'Maith go leor,' arsa Seán. 'Ag bánú an lae amárach beidh mise ag cois na farraige agus tífidh tú cad é a éireos don ollphéist.'

Maidin lá arna mhárach d'éirigh Seán ag breacadh an lae. D'ith sé bricfeasta maith agus ansin chuaigh sé fhad leis an stábla mar gheall ar diallait a chur ar an tseanghearrán bhán a gheall an Rí dó. Nuair a d'fhoscail sé an doras chonaic sé an gabha ina luí ar dhornán féir sa choirnéal.

'An féidir,' arsa Seán, 'nach dteachaigh tú abhaile nuair a bhí an féasta thart?'

'Tá mé anseo go fóill,' arsa an gabha. 'Níl dúil agam aon deor a ól ón lá seo amach.'

'Is iontach liom,' arsa Seán, 'má tá aon deor fágtha agus an méid a d'ól tú ó tháinig tú anseo.'

'Cá bhfuil tú ag gabháil leis an ghearrán?' arsa an gabha.

'Tá obair mhór lae romham,' arsa Seán. 'Tá agam le péist farraige a throid agus cluinim go bhfuil sí chomh mór le seacht gcruach mónadh. Má chuireann sí chun báis mé, abair le mo mháthair gur léise caisleán na bhfathach agus an méid atá ann.'

'Rachaidh mise leat,' arsa an gabha.

'Amaidí,' arsa Seán. 'Tá tú leath ar meisce agus ní bheifeá ach sa chasán agam.'

Thug Seán a aghaidh ar an pháirc a bhí in aice leis an fharraige.

'Cá bhfuair tú an claíomh sin?' arsa guth ar a chúl. Ba é an gabha a labhair. Bhí an seanchlaíomh a rinne sé fá choinne Sheáin ina láimh aige.

'Nár dhúirt mé leat fanacht ag an chaisleán?' arsa Seán.

'Bhí dúil agam sin a dhéanamh,' arsa an gabha, 'ach nuair a d'imigh tusa leis an ghearrán fuair mé an claíomh sa stábla agus lean mé thú.'

'Bheadh sé chomh maith agat maide pota a thabhairt leat,' arsa Seán. 'Tá an 'claíomh solais' cúig throigh déag ar fad agus féadann sé a bheith gairid go leor.'

Níl ann ach go raibh na focla seo ráite ag Seán nuair a chuala siad béic iargúlta. Bhí an phéist ag teacht amach as an fharraige.

'Bain chugat go tapaidh,' arsa Seán leis an ghabha, 'agus téigh i bhfolach in áit inteacht.'

'Ná bac liomsa,' arsa an gabha. 'Nach bhfeiceann tú nach bhfuil sí ró-achmair ina cuid siúil?'

'Beidh sí ró-achmair agatsa,' arsa Seán.

Bhí an phéist ag teacht isteach sa pháirc fán am seo agus d'aithin Seán gurbh é an rud ab fhearr a dhéanamh í a choinneáil ag reathaigh thart fán pháirc go tráthnóna nó go dtí go mbeadh sí sáraithe. Bheadh sé amaideach a ghabháil i gceann troda léi amach díreach. Bhí Seán níos gaiste ná aon ghiorria dár tógadh riamh ar Chnoc na Binne Báine ach ní raibh an phéist chomh gasta le seanbhó. Thoisigh an rása thart fán chuibhreann, Seán fá thuairim céad slat i dtoiseach. Bhí seacht n-acra agus fiche sa pháirc. Nuair a bhí siad ag gabháil thart an tríú huair chonaic an phéist an gabha faoi thom agus shlog sí siar é gan fiacal a leagaint air. Ina dhiaidh sin bhí sí ag éirí níos fadálaí an uile thiontó agus d'aithin Seán go raibh sí á cloí. Thoisigh sé ag caitheamh cloch uirthi mar gheall ar í a choinneáil ag reathaigh agus ag an mheán lae ní raibh sí ag gabháil mórán níos gaiste ná seilide.

D'aithin Seán sa deireadh nach raibh contúirt ar bith a theacht comhgarach don phéist. Bhí géibheann air an 'claíomh solais' a chur in úsáid. Bhí a fhios aige go raibh teangaidh na péiste dainséarach agus go dtiocfadh léi í a shíneadh amach fiche troigh agus í ina luí ar an talamh. Tháinig sé chun tosaigh, an claíomh ina láimh aige, agus d'fhan go foighdeach go dtí gur chuir an phéist amach a teangaidh. D'éirigh le Seán an teangaidh a ghearradh ina dhá leith. 'Coinneoidh tú do theangaidh agat féin ó seo amach,' ar seisean. D'aithin sé fán am seo nach raibh dadaí le himeacht ar an 'chlaíomh solais' agus ghlac sé misneach úr. Thit an phéist, sáraithe amach, agus chuaigh Seán a mharcaíocht ar a dhroim. Thoisigh buillí an chlaímh ag titim ar a ceann agus in oiread leathuaire bhí sí chomh marbh le scadán.

'Chaith an beathach gránna seo na céadtaí bliain san fharraige,' arsa Seán leis féin, 'agus ní chuirfeadh sé iontas orm dá mbeadh lán seacht mála de sheoda luachmhara ina corp.' D'fhoscail sé taobh na péiste leis an chlaíomh ach ba é an chéad 'seod' a chonaic sé: an gabha ina shuí go sócúlach agus é ag gabháil 'Éamann an Chnoic.'

'An bhfuil a fhios agat cá bhfuil tú?' arsa Seán.

'Níl a fhios,' arsa an gabha, 'agus is cuma liom. Níl a dhíth orm ach lasán.'

'Tar amach,' arsa Seán, 'agus chead againn réiteach a dhéanamh le a ghabháil abhaile. Tá obair an lae seo thart.'

'Tá am fada idir deochannaí,' arsa an gabha ag teacht amach ar thaobh na péiste.

'B'fhéidir gurb agat atá an chiall is fearr,' arsa Seán, 'ach ba cheart duit gan níos mó a ól.'

'Ní dhéanfaidh gloine nó beirt eile dochar d'fhear ar bith nuair atá sé leath ar meisce,' arsa an gabha. 'Cá bhfuil an gearrán bán?' ar seisean le Seán.

'Bhí níos mó céille ag an ghearrán ná agatsa,' arsa Seán. 'D'imigh sé ar cosa in airde nuair a chonaic sé an phéist ag teacht.'

'Sin an rud a níos díobháil ólacháin,' arsa an gabha. 'Dá mbeadh braon ólta aige sheasfadh sé a thalamh.'

D'amharc Seán in aice an chaisleáin agus chonaic sé carráiste ag teacht. I mbomite eile bhí an Rí ina sheasamh ag a thaobh.

'Tabhair domh do lámh,' arsa an Rí le Seán. 'Thóg tú lód de mo chroí. Bhí mé ag amharc ar an troid ó thús go deireadh agus d'aithin mé ar an dóigh a dteachaigh tú i gceann oibre go mbeadh an bhuaidh leat.'

Shiúil an Rí agus Seán leo go dtáinig siad fhad leis an chaisleán. Chuir an bhanríon slabhradh óir ar mhuineál Sheáin agus chuir an prionsa a shábháil sé fáinne ar a mhéar.

'Tá pronntanas agamsa le tabhairt duit fosta,' arsa an Rí, 'ach ní tháinig an t-am go fóill.'

Thug Seán buíochas don Rí agus ansin d'fhiafraigh sé de an raibh obair ar bith eile le déanamh.

'Tá,' arsa an Rí, 'ba mhaith liom mo níon a bheith sa bhaile agam.'

'Cá bhfuil sí?' arsa Seán.

'In Albain,' arsa an Rí. 'Tá sí faoi chúram Rí na tíre sin agus tá eagla mhór orm gur thit sé i ngrá léi agus nach bhfuil dúil aige scarúint léi. Chuirfinn an prionsa fána coinne ar maidin amárach ach ab é go bhfuil eagla orm go gcuirfí chun báis é.'

'Más mar sin atá an scéal,' arsa Seán, 'tá mise sásta a ghabháil leis. Tá mé [i ndiaidh] na fathaigh agus an tseanchailleach [a mharbhadh].'

'Agus an phéist,' arsa an Rí.

'Go díreach,' arsa Seán.

Nuair a d'inis an Rí don bhanríon go raibh Seán sásta a ghabháil go hAlbain leis an phrionsa, bhí lúcháir an domhain uirthi. 'Ní thiocfadh linn an prionsa a ligint ar shiúl leis féin,' ar sise, 'ach faoi chúram Sheáin ní bheidh aon ábhar imní orainn.'

'Sin mo bharúil féin,' arsa an Rí.

Maidin lá arna mhárach chuir an prionsa agus Seán tús ar an turas go hAlbain. Ní raibh aon chlaíomh le Seán ach mar sin féin ní raibh a dhath d'eagla air. Bhí an prionsa imníoch ar siocair go raibh a fhios aige go gcuirfeadh Seán deireadh le duine ar bith a bhéarfadh iarracht an cailín a choinneáil uathu, bíodh sé ina Rí nó ina bhacach, ach go raibh dainséar go dtitfeadh an péire isteach i lámha na saighdiúr.

Nuair a tháinig siad go caisleán an Rí, bhuail Seán ag an doras. D'fhoscail doirseoir é agus d'fhiafraigh cad é a bhí a dhíth orthu.

'Tá gnoithe againn leis an Rí,' arsa Seán, 'agus má tá sé sa bhaile, abair leis a theacht chun tosaigh.'

'Bíodh sé sa bhaile nó i gcéin,' arsa an doirseoir, 'ní fheicfidh tusa é.'

Chuir sé a lámh leis an doras mar a bheadh sé ar tí é a bhualadh amach ina n-éadan ach fuair Seán greim scornaí air, tharraing amach é agus ansin chaith thar sconsa é a bhí deich dtroigh ar airde. Chonaic saighdiúir ó fhuinneoig an rud a rinne Seán agus tháinig sé chun tosaigh, claíomh ina láimh. Chuaigh Seán ina araicis agus nuair a thóg an saighdiúir an claíomh in airde thug Seán léim mar a dhéanfadh cat, fuair greim ar an láimh a raibh an claíomh inti agus lena láimh eile fuair seilbh ar an chlaíomh. Ansin shín sé an claíomh chuig an phrionsa, fuair greim ar an tsaighdiúir agus chaith trasna sconsa é san áit chéanna ar chaith sé an doirseoir trasna.

'Coinneoidh sé cuideachta leis an fhear eile,' ar seisean leis an phrionsa.

Bhí doras an chaisleáin foscailte agus shiúil Seán isteach, an prionsa ina dhiaidh. Casadh cailín orthu sa halla agus d'fhiafraigh Seán di cá raibh níon Rí na hÉireann.

'Tá sí sa tseomra is airde sa chaisleán,' arsa an cailín, 'agus tá glas ar an doras.'

'Cá bhfuil an Rí é féin?' arsa Seán.

'Tá sé sa pharlús,' arsa an cailín, 'ach níl cead ag an doirseoir duine ar bith a ligint isteach.'

'Níl a chead a dhíth orainne,' arsa Seán.

Chuaigh sé ansin go doras an pharlúis, chuir a ghualainn leis agus chuir leath bealaigh trasna an tseomra é. Bhí an Rí ina shuí i gcathaoir shócúlach agus léim sé ina shuí go feargach. Bhí feadóg ar an tábla agus thug sé iarracht í a shéideadh ach sciob Seán an fheadóg uaidh. Tharraing sé anuas na cuirtíní síoda a bhí ar an fhuinneoig agus leo seo cheangail sé lámha agus cosa an Rí agus d'fhág sínte ar an urlár é.

'Fan thusa anseo,' ar seisean leis an phrionsa, 'agus coinnigh Rí na hAlbana san áit a bhfuil sé go dtige mise ar ais. Má bheir sé iarracht scairt a ligint, tabhair buille den chlaíomh dó i mbun na cluaise.'

I mbomaite eile bhí Seán ar ais, greim láimhe aige ar níon Rí na hÉireann. Phóg sí a deartháir go gráúil agus d'fhág siad an caisleán fá dheifir.

'Níl am ar bith againn le cailleadh,' arsa Seán agus iad ag teannadh leis an chladach. 'Beidh an t-arm ar ár lorg in am ghairid.'

B'fhíor dó. Ní raibh ann ach go raibh siad ar bord loinge go bhfaca siad na saighdiúirí ag teacht. Chroch siad suas na seoltaí móra bocóideacha comhfhada comhdhíreacha go barra na gcrann nach bhfágfadh téad tíre gan tarraingt ná maide rámha gan róbhriseadh, ag treabhadh na farraige folcanta falcanta, míolta móra ag déanamh ceoil sí agus seirbhíse dóibh, ag cur gaineamh mín in íochtar, gaineamh garbh in uachtar, gur shroich siad cuan agus caladh in Éirinn.

Nuair a chonaic Rí agus banríon na hÉireann go dtáinig Seán agus an prionsa agus an cailín óg abhaile slán, ba mhór a gcuid lúcháire. Pósadh Seán agus níon an Rí seachtain ina dhiaidh sin agus bhí na céadtaí daoine ag an bhainis. Chuaigh Seán agus a bhean chéile a chónaí i gcaisleán na bhfathach agus rinneadh ardmhaor den ghabha.

Agus is é sin deireadh scéil 'Sheáin an Chóta leathair.'

NÓTA

1 *Derry People and Tirconaill News*, 4, 11, 18, 25 May, 1, 8, 15, 22, 29 June, 6, 13, 20 July 1935. Tá leagan den scéal seo i gcló ar *ACS*: 25 Iúil, 1, 8, 15, 22 Lúnasa 1903. Tá an scéal le fáil i gcolún a bhfuil OIDEACHAS mar theideal air.

Craiceann na Bó

Bhí beirt deartháir ina gcónaí sa tsean-am fá mhíle nó mar sin de bhaile Dhún na nGall, agus má thig linn an seanscéal a chreidbheáil bhí fear acu bocht agus an fear eile saibhir. Bhí seacht mba ag an fhear shaibhir ach ní raibh ag an fhear bhocht ach seanbhó amháin a chonaic laetha níos fearr. Ní raibh aonach ar bith dá raibh cuntas air riamh i bhFéilire Uí Mhóra nach raibh sí aige ach ní thiocfadh leis an fhear bhocht luach a dhinnéara a fháil uirthi. Lá amháin thit sí isteach i ndíogaidh agus bomaite ina dhiaidh sin bhí bó amháin níos lú ar thalamh na hÉireann. Ar ndóiche bhí an fear bocht buartha ina diaidh, nó, mar a dúirt sé féin, 'Is fearr cineál ar bith bó ná a bheith folamh.'

D'éirigh sé go moch maidin lá arna mhárach, fuair scian agus d'fheann sé an bhó. Thug sé an craiceann abhaile agus nuair a bhí sé tirim dúirt sé lena mhnaoi go raibh dúil aige a ghabháil go Doire agus é a dhíol.

'Ní bhfaighidh tú oiread air is a dhíolfas do bhealach,' ar sise.

'Ná bac leis,' arsa an fear bocht. 'Má tá airgead ar bith agat, tabhair domh é.'

'Níl airgead ar bith agam,' arsa an bhean, 'ach trí phíosa leathchoróin. Beidh sin beag go leor le bia a cheannach.'

'Nuair a thiocfas mise abhaile,' arsa an fear, 'ní bheidh ganntanas bídh ort go ceann tamaill. Tabhair domh an t-airgead agus beidh mé ag imeacht.'

Thug an bhean bhocht an t-airgead dó agus thug sé a aghaidh ar Dhoire. Ag titim na hoíche d'fhág sé Srath an Urláir ina dhiaidh agus shuigh sé go maidin faoi chrann mhór a bhí ag fás san áit a bhfuil Teach na Contae fá láthair. Bhí solas breá gealaí ann agus chuir sé trí pholl i gcraiceann na bó agus chuir píosa leathchoróin go faichilleach i ngach ceann acu. Bhí sé ina shuí leis an fhuiseoig agus gan mhoill i ndiaidh an mheán lae bhí sé i nDoire. Sheas sé i lár na sráide, an craiceann i láimh amháin agus bata sa láimh eile, agus é ag scairtigh amach: 'An craiceann draíochtach, an craiceann draíochtach.' Ba ghairid go raibh mórán mór daoine cruinnithe. Thoisigh sé ag bualadh an chraicinn leis an bhata. Thoisigh na leathchoróineacha ag titim. Bhí Sasanach láithreach agus chuir sé ceist ar an fhear cad é an luach a bhí sé a iarraidh ar an chraiceann.

'Ní maith liom é a dhíol ar chor ar bith de bhrí go dtig liom leathchoróin a chnagadh as le gach buille,' arsa an fear.

'Bhéarfaidh mise mála óir duit air,' arsa an Sasanach.

'Bíodh ina mhargadh,' arsa an fear ó Dhún na nGall.

Cheannaigh an fear bocht (fear saibhir a bhí ann anois) seanghearrán ó fhear a casadh air i nDoire agus chuir sé an t-ór ar dhroim an ghearráin agus tháinig abhaile. Nuair a chonaic a bhean é ag teacht, ar ndóiche bhí iontas uirthi.

'Tím,' ar sise, 'go bhfuair tú luach maith ar an chraiceann ach nach mó a bheadh bó a dhíth orainn ná gearrán?'

'Tá sin fíor,' arsa an fear, 'ach thig linn bó a cheannach amárach ag aonach Dhún na nGall.'

Thug sé dornán féir don ghearrán agus ansin d'fhág sé an mála óir síos ag cois na tineadh. Nuair a chonaic an bhean bhocht go raibh an mála lán de ghiníocha is beag nár thit sí i laige.

'A Chonaill, a stór,' ar sise, 'cad é an t-ádh a tháinig ort ó d'fhág tú an baile?' (Bhí Conall mar ainm ar an fhear bhocht).

'Thug tú an méid airgid a bhí agat domh nuair a bhí mé ag imeacht,' ar seisean, 'agus thig liom do dhíol go maith inniu. Líon d'aprún anois agus cuirfidh mé an sreangán ar bhéal an mhála arís.'

Rinne an bhean mar a hiarradh uirthi agus chuir Conall an mála i gcórtha a bhí lán go minic de mhin choirce. Lá arna mhárach chuaigh an péire chun aonaigh agus cheannaigh siad ceithre ba bainne.

Nuair a chuala Muiris (an deartháir saibhir) go raibh neart airgid ag Conall, bhí éad dáiríre air. Chuir sé a bhean go teach Chonaill mar gheall ar go bhfaigheadh sí amach cá has a dtáinig an t-ór. D'inis Conall di go bhfuair sé luach na mbó a cheannaigh sé agus a sheacht n-oiread lena chois ar chraiceann na bó a fuair bás.

'Inseoidh mé sin do Mhuiris,' ar sise. D'inis, agus i ndiaidh comhrá fada rinne siad réiteach an bhó ba sine a bhí acu a mharbhadh agus an craiceann a dhíol i nDoire.

'Beidh oiread airgid againn le Conall nuair a thiocfas mise abhaile,' arsa Muiris.

'Beidh, ar ndóiche,' arsa an bhean.

Cupla lá ina dhiaidh sin bhí fear i nDoire ag siúl ó theach go teach ag iarraidh craiceann bó a dhíol. Fá dheireadh casadh fear air a bhí ag ceannach craicne agus chuir sé ceist ar Mhuiris (nó ba é Muiris an díoltóir) cad é an luach a bhí sé a iarraidh.

'Luach ceithre bhó agus a sheacht n-oiread eile,' arsa Muiris.

'An dtig leat réasún ar bith a thabhairt [cén] fáth go bhfuil tú amuigh?' arsa an fear.

'Níl mé ag iarraidh ach an luach a fuair mo dheartháir ar chraiceann nach raibh chomh maith,' arsa Muiris.

'Arbh é do dheartháir a dhíol an craiceann le Sasanach ar an bhaile seo fá thuairim seachtain ó shin?' arsa an fear.

'Is dóigh liom gurbh é,' arsa Muiris.

'Ar chuala tú gur thit píosa leathchoróin as an chraiceann an uile uair a bhuail sé é le bata?'

'Níor chuala,' arsa Muiris.

'Níl tú chomh cliste le do dheartháir,' arsa an fear. 'Nuair a d'imigh do dheartháir leis an airgead chaith an Sasanach agus fear eile leath lae ag bualadh an chraicinn ach sin a raibh ar a shon acu.'

'Tím,' arsa Muiris. 'Rinne mo dheartháir amadán díom ach beidh mé inchurtha leis go fóill. Cá mhéad is fiú an craiceann?'

'Trí scillinge,' arsa an fear.

'Is leat é,' arsa Muiris. 'Tabhair domh an t-airgead.'

Nuair a tháinig an deartháir saibhir abhaile i ndiaidh an craiceann a dhíol ar luach bheag dúirt sé lena mhnaoi go raibh dúil aige Conall a mharbhadh.

'Ní bheadh sin ceart,' arsa an bhean. 'Ní thearn sé dochar ar bith ort.'

'Rinne sé amadán díom,' arsa Muiris. 'Ach ab é a chuid agallaí ní bheinnse i nDoire ag iarraidh luach feirm talaimh ar chraiceann seanbhó. Shíl daoine go raibh mé as mo mheabhair.'

'Shíl, ar ndóiche,' arsa an bhean, 'ach caithfidh tú tabhairt isteach nár iarr Conall ort a ghabháil go Doire. Nuair a chuaigh seisean go Doire tá a fhios ag an tsaol nach raibh dadaí le díol aige ach craiceann bó a bhí chomh sean leis an cheo agus go dtáinig sé abhaile ina fhear shaibhir. Bhí tusa chomh santach sin gur chuir tú mise le tuairisc a chur cad é mar a fuair sé an saibhreas agus tá mé cinnte gur inis sé an fhírinne.'

'Ach níor inis sé iomlán na fírinne,' arsa Muiris. 'Dá n-insíodh sé duit gur chuir sé píosaí leathchoróin sa chraiceann agus go raibh sé ag cnagadh ceann acu amach le gach buille go dtí go dtug fear saibhir mála óir dó, ní rachainnse go Doire ar chor ar bith. Sin an fáth go bhfuil dúil agam é a mharbhadh.'

'Cad chuige nár imir tusa an cleas céanna?' arsa an bhean.

'Is maith domh féin nár imir,' arsa Muiris. 'An chéad fhear a imreos an cleas sin i nDoire beidh rópa fána mhuineál in am ghairid.'

'Féadann sin a bheith fíor,' arsa an bhean.

Maidin lá arna mhárach chuaigh Muiris go teach Chonaill agus a sháith feirge air.

'Cá bhfuil Conall?' ar seisean nuair a chonaic sé a bhean ag an doras.

'Beidh sé sa bhaile gan mhoill,' arsa an bhean.

'Cad é an fáth nár inis sé an fhírinne fán dóigh a bhfuair sé an saibhreas?' arsa Muiris.

'Níl a fhiachadh air a ghnoithe a insint duitse ná do dhuine ar bith eile,' arsa bean Chonaill. 'Is iomaí lá a chaith muid i mboichtineacht agus ní thearn muid casaoid ar bith leatsa. Coinnigh do bhean sa bhaile feasta más rud é nach bhfuil tú sásta leis an tuairisc a fuair sí. Coimheád do ghnoithe féin agus ní bhainfidh Conall leat.'

Shiúil Conall isteach ar an bhomaite sin agus chuir sé ceist cad é a bhí contráilte.

'Tá a fhios agat go maith cad é atá contráilte,' arsa Muiris. Thug sé áladh ar Chonall agus thoisigh an bheirt ag coraíocht. Thit siad ar chleith fuirste a bhí i gcoirnéal na cisteanaí agus chaill Conall ceann dena shúile. Sula raibh faill ag Muiris éirí thug bean Chonaill buille den mhaide bhriste dó agus d'fhág cnap ar a cheann chomh mór le fód móna.

'Ní bheidh deifir ar ais ort,' ar sise.

Tháinig an deartháir saibhir abhaile ach ní raibh mórán suaimhnis intinne aige. Bhí a fhios aige go maith gur thuill sé an méid trioblóide a fuair sé agus is trom an lód intinn mhíshuaimhneach. Bhí trioblóid i dteach Chonaill mar an gcéanna de bhrí go raibh an duine bocht ar leathshúil. Ach ní raibh sé gan dóchas. Chuala sé ina óige go raibh lios fá thuairim míle ar shiúl agus gur leigheasadh mórán daoine sa lios seo a raibh amharc na súl caillte acu.

'Rachaidh mé fhad leis an lios anocht,' ar seisean lena mhnaoi, 'agus b'fhéidir go dtabharfadh Dia ar ais amharc na súl.'

'Beidh mise sásta leis an réiteach sin,' arsa a bhean. 'Dhéanfaidh mé toirtín aráin duit agus coinneoidh sin an t-ocras uait go dtige tú abhaile.'

Ag uair an mheán oíche chuaigh Conall fhad leis an doras agus chonaic sé go raibh an ghealach ag soilsiú.

'Seo an t-am ceart le a ghabháil chuig an lios,' ar seisean lena mhnaoi.

'Mo bheannacht leat,' ar sise, 'go dtige tú ar ais.'

Tamall gairid ina dhiaidh sin tháinig Conall fhad leis an lios. Ag ligint osna trom as shuigh sé síos ar charraig. Bomaite beag ina dhiaidh sin tháinig caitín beag chuige agus d'fhiafraigh sí cad é a bhí contráilte leis. D'inis sé don chat cad é mar a tharla.

'Marbhfáisc air,' arsa an cat, 'nach aige a bhí an droch-chroí! Ach, ná bac leis,' ar sise, 'cuirfimid múineadh air. Beidh mise ar ais i gceann leathuaire agus rachaidh tusa agus mise go dtí an tobar íocshláinte atá sa ghleann sin thall agus beidh do dhá shúil chomh maith is a bhí siad riamh.'

Choinnigh an cat a gealltanas. D'iarr sí ar Chonall a shúile a ní in uisce an tobair agus i mbomaite bhí sé leigheasta.

'Tar abhaile liom anois,' arsa an cat, 'go bhfeice tú na cait eile atá ina gcónaí sa ghleann seo. Tá siad amuigh ag seilg anois ach beidh siad ar ais gan mhoill. D'fhág siad mise i mbun an tí ach dá mbeadh a fhios acu go dtug mé amharc na súl ar ais duitse, chuirfeadh siad deireadh liom.

Caithfidh tusa a ghabháil i bhfolach san áit a n-abróidh mise leat agus, ar a bhfaca tú riamh, ná déan aon tormán.'

'Glacfaidh mé do chomhairle,' arsa Conall.

Nuair a tháinig na cait abhaile is é an chéad rud a d'fhiafraigh siad: 'An bhfuil duine ar bith sa teach?'

'Níl duine ar bith anseo ach mé féin,' arsa an cat beag.

Thoisigh siad ag caint eatarthu féin agus bhí Conall ina sheasamh ar chúl an dorais ag éisteacht leis an uile fhocal a dúirt siad.

'Cluinim,' arsa ceann de na cait, 'go bhfuil fear saibhir i mBaile Átha Cliath agus go bhfuil mac aige atá an-tinn. Thairg sé cúig mhíle punta do dhuine ar bith a leigheasfadh é.'

'Dá mbeadh a fhios aige,' arsa cat eile, 'go leigheasfadh lán spanóige den uisce atá sa tobar íocshláinte é, ba ghairid go gcuirfeadh sé fána choinne.'

Tamall ina dhiaidh sin thit siad ina gcodladh agus ansin dúirt an cat beag le Conall go dtiocfadh leis a ghabháil abhaile.

'Ba mhaith liom sin a dhéanamh,' arsa Conall, 'ar siocair go mbeidh mo bhean ag dréim liom. Ach caithfidh mé buíochas a thabhairt duitse ó mo chroí ar son do chuid cineáltais.'

'Ná habair é,' arsa an cat beag. 'Tá croí maith agat agus sin an fáth ar chuidigh mé leat. Má thigeann trioblóid ar bith in do bhealach in am ar bith eile, tar go dtí an lios agus beidh lúcháir orm tú a fheiceáil.'

Tháinig Conall abhaile le croí éadrom agus bhí lúcháir an domhain ar a mhnaoi nuair a chuala sí uaidh go raibh amharc na súl chomh maith aige is a bhí riamh.

'Caithfimid an Paidrín Páirteach a rá,' ar sise, 'mar gheall ar buíochas a thabhairt do Dhia ar son an méid a rinne Sé dúinn.'

'Níor chuala tú deireadh an scéil go fóill,' arsa Conall. 'Chaith mé tamall den oíche i dteach na gcat sa cheann íochtarach den ghleann agus fhad is a bhí mé ansin fuair mé le fios go leigheasfadh an t-uisce atá sa tobar draíochta an uile aicíd ar an domhan. Tá dúil agam braon den uisce a fháil amárach.'

Gan mhoill i ndiaidh éirí na gréine chuaigh Conall fhad leis an tobar agus fuair lán crúiscín den uisce agus thug abhaile é. Bhí bean tinn sa chomharsanacht agus bhí an uile chomhartha báis uirthi. Leigheas lán spanóige den uisce í i mbomaite. Spréigh an scéal ar fud na contae go dtiocfadh le Conall aicíd ar bith a leigheas. In am ghairid bhí daoine ag teacht ionsair ina gcéadtaí. Chuaigh an t-iomlán abhaile leigheasta. Na daoine nach raibh airgead acu thug siad bearach nó caora nó b'fhéidir muc do Chonall agus i gceann bliana nó mar sin bhí níos mó stoic aige ná aon tiarna talaimh in Éirinn.

Lá amháin tháinig fear coimhthíoch go dtí an ceantar i gcóiste ghalánta. Ba é Muiris an chéad fhear a casadh air.

'An tusa an fear,' ar seisean, 'a dteachaigh a chliú fhad le Baile Átha Cliath mar gheall ar an méid daoine a leigheas sé?'

'Ní mé,' arsa Muiris, 'ach tím mórán daoine ag teacht go teach mo dhearthár an uile lá.'

'Sin an fear atá mise a chuartú,' arsa an fear uasal. 'Níl agam ach mac amháin agus tá sé tinn le fada. Tá cúig mhíle punta agam in mo phóca agus má thig le do dheartháir mo mhac a dhéanamh slán arís, is leis an t-airgead.'

D'aithin Muiris go han-mhaith go mbeadh na cúig mhíle punta i bpóca Chonaill in am ghairid agus chuir seo leath ar mire é. D'fhéach sé ar an uile dhóigh fios a fháil ar an rún a rinne ainm Chonaill cliúúil ar fud na tíre. Dhiúltaigh a bhean a ghabháil ar ais go teach Chonaill agus d'fhág sin Muiris ar bheagán suaimhnis intinne. Bhí fear sa chomharsanacht a bhí go han-mhór le Conall agus bhí a fhios ag Muiris seo go maith. Thairg sé cúig phunta don fhear dá n-éiríodh leis an tuairisc a fháil. D'fhéach an fear bocht na cúig phunta a shaothrú agus thug sé cuairt ar theach Chonaill an oíche sin. D'inis Conall an fhírinne dó ó thús go deireadh.

'Tá mé in m'fhear shaibhir anois,' ar seisean, 'agus is cuma liom cé a chluinfeas mo rún.'

Nuair a chuala Muiris scéal an fhir rinne sé suas a intinn i mbomaite. Bhain sé ceann de na súile as féin an oíche sin agus chuaigh sé fhad leis an lios. Ba ghairid gur casadh an caitín air agus d'fhiafraigh sí cad é a bhí contráilte leis. Thóg sé cloch agus d'fhéach sé í a mharbhadh.

'Ná bac leis,' arsa an cat, 'cuirfidh mise múineadh ort.'

I mbomaite bhí sí as amharc ach ba ghairid go dtáinig sí agus na cait eile léi. Thug siad áladh ar Mhuiris agus stróc siad an craiceann de. Bhí a éadan agus a lámha cumhdaithe le fuil agus nuair a d'fhág na cait é bhí lúcháir air teacht abhaile. Bhí drochdhóigh ar fad air. Shíl a bhean go raibh contúirt bháis air agus ní thabharfadh sí suaimhneas ar bith dó go dtéadh sé léi go teach Chonaill. Fá dheireadh thug sé isteach. Chuir Conall agus a bhean fáilte roimh an phéire agus ba ghairid go bhfuair Conall braon d'uisce an tobair íocshláinte agus bhí Muiris leigheasta le caochadh súile. Leis sin, chuaigh Muiris ar a ghlúine agus d'iarr pardún ar Chonall.

'Dhíol mé go cruaidh ar son mo chuid gníomhartha,' ar seisean.

'Dhéanfaimid dearmad ar an méid atá thart,' arsa Conall agus rinne an bheirt croitheadh lámh.

Nuair a bhí Muiris agus a bhean ag imeacht thug Conall lán canna d'ór dóibh agus ina dhiaidh sin bhí siad go hanmhór lena chéile go dtí go dtáinig an bás fána gcoinne.

Nóta

1 *Derry People and Tirconaill News*, 27 July, 3, 10, 17, 24, 31 August 1935.

Conall na Méanfach

Bhí Rí in Éirinn ins an tsean-am agus ní raibh aige ach mac amháin. D'fhás an mac suas go dtí go raibh sé bliain agus fiche d'aois. Bhí an duine bocht aimhleasta agus siúd is go raibh siamsa go leor aige sa bhaile rinne sé suas a intinn go rachadh sé ag iarraidh a fhortúin. D'fhág sé an baile maidin amháin ag éirí na gréine agus shiúil sé leis gan a fhios aige cá raibh sé ag gabháil go dtí go dtáinig sé fhad le coill uaigneach. Chonaic sé teach beag in imeall na coilleadh agus bhuail sé ag an doras. D'fhoscail bean an doras agus d'iarr air a theacht isteach.

'Níl a dhíth orm,' ar seisean, 'ach foscadh an tí go maidin. Ba chuma liom codladh sa choill ach ab é go bhfuil eagla orm roimh bheathaigh allta.'

'Níl iontas ar bith ansin,' arsa an bhean. 'Is iomaí fear breá a cailleadh sa choill seo agus bhí an t-ádh ort nuair a tháinig tú fhad leis an bhothán seo.'

'Tá neart bídh agam sa mhála,' arsa mac an Rí.

Ba ghairid ina dhiaidh seo go dtáinig fear eile isteach agus é ar lorg lóistín.

'Féadann tú fanacht ag cois na tineadh,' arsa an bhean, 'ach níl leabaidh ar bith agam fá do choinne.'

'Níl leabaidh ar bith a dhíth orm,' arsa an fear.

'Gheall an bhean seo leabaidh domhsa i gcomhair na hoíche,' arsa mac Rí Éireann, 'agus má tá tú 'd'fhear níos fearr ná mise, bíodh an leabaidh agat.'

Leis sin, thoisigh an bheirt ag coraíocht. Mhair siad mar seo ar feadh leathuaire agus fán am seo ní raibh greim ná giota foireann tí sa teach nach raibh briste acu. D'fhéach an bhean bhocht réiteach a dhéanamh eatarthu ach ní raibh faill acu éisteacht léi. Fá dheireadh nuair a bhí an péire sáraithe amach shuigh siad síos ar an urlár. Bhí siad i mbarr anála.

'Díolfaidh mise ar son an damáiste,' arsa mac Rí Éireann.

'Caithfidh tú a chruthú go bhfuil tú 'd'fhear níos fearr ná mise sula ndíola tú leithphingin,' arsa an fear a tháinig isteach go deireanach.

Chonacthas do bhean an tí go raibh siad ag magadh uirthi agus tháinig fearg dáiríre uirthi. Fuair sí greim ar an mhaide bhriste agus dúirt: 'Go haitheann (= ifreann) leis an phéire agaibh má shíleann sibh nach bhfuil dadaí agamsa le déanamh ach ag amharc oraibh ag troid. Díolaigí ar son an méid a bhris sibh, sin nó beidh faire dhúbailte anseo go maidin.'

Thug siad iarracht éirí ón urlár ach chuir buille den mhaide bhriste gach duine acu ar shlait a dhroma. D'aithin siad go raibh lámh an uachtair ag an mhnaoi agus dhíol siad an méid a d'iarr sí.

'Tá mo chead agaibh anois,' ar sise, 'troid libh go maidin ó tharla nach bhfuil rud ar bith eile le briseadh ach bhur gcnámha féin.'

'Ní bheidh níos mó troda againn,' arsa mac an Rí, 'go dtí go mbeidh a fhios agam ainm an fhir a bhfuil mé ag troid leis.'

'Níl moill ar bith an tuairisc sin a fháil,' arsa an fear. 'Is mise Conall na Méanfach.'

'Ní thearn tú mórán méanfaí ó tháinig tú anseo,' arsa mac an Rí.

'Ní thug tú faill domh,' arsa Conall. 'Is tú an fear is cliste a casadh orm riamh.'

'Go raibh maith agat,' arsa mac an Rí. 'Cuirfimid stad leis an troid agus imreoimid cluiche cártaí.'

D'imir, agus bhain Conall an cluiche.

'Cuir do gheasa anois,' arsa mac an Rí.

Is é an freagar a thug Conall dó: 'An chéad bhuille gan chosaint as Éirinn amach.'

'Maith go leor,' arsa mac an Rí.

Ag éirí na gréine d'fhág an péire teach na mná. Thug Conall a aghaidh ar an ghréin agus thug mac an Rí a chúl léi, is é sin le rá, chuaigh fear acu soir agus an fear eile siar. Ní raibh a fhios ag ceachtar acu go raibh cailín óg, dóighiúil sa teach a d'fhág siad, ach bhí. Bhí sí sa tseomra in aice na cisteanaí ina raibh an troid agus fhad is a bhí sí ag amharc fríd pholl na heochrach thit sí i ngrá le mac an Rí. Rinne sí suas a hintinn é a leanúint agus nuair a bhí mac an Rí míle nó mar sin ón teach, rug sí suas leis. Bhí iontas air nuair a chonaic sé í agus d'fhiosraigh sé di cá raibh sí ag gabháil.

'Tá mé ag gabháil leatsa,' ar sise, 'agus an áit a gcaillfear thusa, caillfear mise in éineacht leat.'

'A bhean gan chéill,' ar seisean, 'níl teach ná áras agamsa fá do choinne.'

'Is cuma liom,' ar sise, 'níl a dhíth orm ach a bheith in do chuideachta.'

'C'ainm atá ort?' arsa mac an Rí.

'Féadann tú Deirdre a thabhairt orm,' ar sise.

Thóg mac an Rí ar a ghualainn í agus shiúil leis go tapaidh. In am ghairid casadh Fionn Mac Cumhaill orthu agus leathscór de na Fianna ag siúl ina dhiaidh. Bhí aithne ag mac an Rí ar Fhionn agus d'fhiafraigh sé de c'áit a raibh a thriall.

'Táimid ag gabháil go dtí an Domhan Thoir,' arsa Fionn, 'le briseadh a throid le Rí na tíre sin agus leathscór dá chuid laochraí.'

'Ní mhairfidh an briseadh i bhfad,' arsa mac an Rí.

'Féadann sin a bheith fíor,' arsa Fionn, 'ach ina dhiaidh sin ba mhaith liom tusa a bheith linn.'

'Rachaidh mise leat go cinnte,' arsa mac an Rí, 'má ligeann Deirdre domh an aistear a dhéanamh.'

'Ligfidh mé dó a ghabháil leat,' arsa Deirdre, 'má gheallann tú gan é a thabhairt as Éirinn amach.'

'Tá an áit ina bhfuil muid ag gabháil i bhfad ó Éirinn,' arsa Fionn Mac Cumhaill.

'Más mar sin atá an scéal,' arsa Deirdre, 'ní thig liom cead a thabhairt dó.'

Chaoch mac an Rí ar Fhionn agus dúirt: 'Fágfaimid an scéal mar sin go maidin.'

'Bíodh ina mhargadh,' arsa Fionn Mac Cumhaill.

Tharla sé go raibh áras mór, folamh sa chomharsanacht agus chaith siad an oíche sin san áras. Thoisigh Deirdre ag cíoradh a cinn agus bhí a fhios ag mac an Rí nach dtiocfadh léi achainí ar bith a eitiú fhad is a bheadh sí i gceann na hoibre seo. D'iarr sé uirthi cead a thabhairt dó a ghabháil le Fionn go dtí an Domhan Thoir agus b'éigean di tabhairt isteach. Thug sí grá a croí do mhac an Rí agus ba doiligh léi scarúint leis. Bhí a fhios aici go raibh an 'chéad bhuille gan chosaint' ag Conall dá gcasfaí mac an Rí air 'as Éirinn amach.' Ar an ábhar sin bhí eagla uirthi nach bhfeicfeadh sí mac an Rí go deo arís. Rinne sí réiteach le Fionn dá gcaillfí mac an Rí go gcuirfeadh sé suas bratacha dubha ar theacht abhaile dó agus, dá maireadh sé, go gcuirfeadh sé suas seoltaí bána.

D'fhág siad slán ag Deirdre agus ansin thug siad a n-aghaidh ar an chuan, an áit a raibh long ag fanacht leo. Nuair a tháinig siad go dtí an Domhan Thoir bhí tinneas cinn ar fhear de na Fianna agus d'fhiafraigh Fionn de mhac an Rí an nglacfadh sé a áit.

'Is é sin mian mo chroí,' arsa mac an Rí. 'Thug Deirdre claíomh domh nuair a bhí mé ag fágáil slán aici agus ní baol domh fhad is atá an claíomh in mo láimh.'

'Maith go leor,' arsa Fionn. 'Is tusa an fear a bhuailfeas an cuaille comhraic.'

Shiúil mac an Rí chun tosaigh agus bhuail sé an cuaille comhraic leis an chlaíomh. Chroith an talamh seacht míle ar gach taobh. Tháinig teachtaire an Rí agus chuir ceist air cad é a bhí a dhíth air.

'Teach fá choinne mo mháistir agus a chuid fear go maidin,' arsa mac an Rí.

'Níl teach ar bith le fáil agaibh ach teach na n-amhas.'

Chuaigh mac an Rí fhad leis an teach agus d'amharc isteach. Chuntas sé amhas agus fiche.

'Tá sé chomh maith agam iad a mharbhadh ar an bhomaite,' ar seisean le Fionn.

'Tá mé den bharúil,' arsa Fionn, 'go mbeidh an tasc sin trom go leor ag an iomlán againn.'

'Beidh mé níos fearr liom féin,' arsa mac an Rí.

'Cad chuige sin?' arsa Fionn. 'Ní maith liom tú a chailleadh.'

'Tá,' arsa mac an Rí, 'nuair a bheas mise ag gabháil fríothu, b'fhéidir go mbuailfinn i ngan fhios domh féin fear dár gcuid féin.'

'Tá an ceart agat,' arsa Fionn.

Chuaigh mac an Rí isteach agus thoisigh an t-ármhach. Bhí seanbhean i gContae Chiarraí a raibh éisteacht an-ghéar aici agus chuala sí béicfeach na n-amhas fhad is a bhí mac an Rí ag baint na gcinn díobh. Chuaigh sé fríothu mar a rachadh seabhac fríd scaifte éanlaithe. Nuair a bhí an duine deireanach acu marbh chaith sé amach ar chúldoras iad. Leis sin, shiúil Fionn agus na Fianna isteach agus rinne siad croitheadh lámh leis go croíúil.

'Beidh foscadh againn go maidin,' arsa mac an Rí.

'Dá mbeadh tinidh againn anois,' arsa Fionn, 'b'fhéidir go n-éireodh linn beagán bídh a fháil.'

'Ní bheimid i bhfad gan tinidh,' arsa mac an Rí. Chuaigh sé fhad le teach an Rí agus tháinig ar ais i mbomaite le neart ábhar tineadh. D'iarr sé ar na Fianna an tinidh a dheargadh agus go rachadh seisean ar lorg bídh agus dí i gcomhair na hoíche.

'Níor casadh comrádaí orm i rith mo shaoil atá inchurtha leat,' arsa Fionn.

'Ní thearn mé mórán go fóill,' arsa mac an Rí, 'ach tá obair mhór lae romhainn amárach. Sin an fáth a mbeidh suipéar maith a dhíth orainn.'

Chuaigh sé go teach an Rí athuair agus d'inis don doirseoir cad é a bhí a dhíth air.

'Tá neart bídh sa tsoiléar,' arsa an doirseoir.

Fuair mac an Rí bairille agus líon sé é den bhia is fearr agus thug fhad le Fionn agus na Fianna é.

'Ní bheidh ganntanas bídh orainn go dtí go mbeidh an troid thart,' arsa Fionn.

'Níl fonn troda ar bith ar an Rí,' arsa fear de na Fianna.

'Cé a d'inis sin duit?' arsa Fionn.

'Teachtaire de chuid an Rí,' arsa an fear.

'Creidim an scéal,' arsa mac an Rí. 'D'iarr sé ormsa gan bia ná deoch a spáráil agus tá mé ag gabháil ar ais anois fá choinne bairille beorach.'

'Tá sin iontach,' arsa Fionn Mac Cumhaill.

Maidin lá arna mhárach chuir Rí an Domhain Thoir teachtaire chuig Fionn. 'Ba mhaith leis an Rí,' arsa an teachtaire, 'dá dtigtheá féin agus do chuid fear fhad leis an chaisleán.'

'Abair leis go bhfuil lúcháir orainn a leithéid de chuireadh a fháil,' arsa Fionn.

Tamall beag ina dhiaidh sin tháinig siad i láthair an Rí.

'A Fhinn Mhic Cumhaill,' ar seisean, 'níl aon dúil agam a ghabháil i gceann troda leat féin agus do chuid fear. Chuir mé fiche fear fá thuairim seachtain ó shin leis na hamhais a mharbhadh agus níor tháinig fear amháin acu ar ais beo. Chuir tusa fear amháin le iad a throid agus chuir sé deireadh leo i gcúig bhomaite. Má tá aon rud a dhíth ort ar son do chuid trioblóide, abair an focal.'

'Ba mhaith liom,' arsa Fionn, 'Smólach an Chinn Óir a fháil.'

'Féadann tú an Smólach a thabhairt leat,' arsa an Rí, 'agus mo bheannacht ina cuideachta.'

D'fhág siad slán ag an Rí agus thug siad a n-aghaidh ar an chuan an áit a raibh an long a bhí le iad a thabhairt abhaile go hÉirinn feistithe. Chonaic siad bád ag teacht isteach.

'Níl sa bhád ach fear amháin,' arsa Fionn, 'agus b'fhéidir go bhfuil sé ag dréim a bheith linn go hÉirinn.'

Ar an bhomaite sin d'aithin mac an Rí gurbh é Conall a bhí sa bhád.

'A Fhinn Mhic Cumhaill,' ar seisean, 'tá mé caillte. Seo mo namhaid agus tá 'an chéad bhuille aige gan chosaint.' Tabhair mo chorp abhaile chuig Deirdre. Beidh a fhios aici cad é is fearr a dhéanamh.'

Leis sin tháinig Conall i dtír agus shiúil sé suas fhad leis an áit a raibh mac an Rí ina sheasamh. Bhuail sé buille trom air i gclár an éadain agus thit mac an Rí marbh ag cosa Fhinn Mhic Cumhaill. Bhí na Fianna ag brath deireadh a chur le Conall ach dúirt Fionn leo gan baint leis.

'Bainfidh mise sásamh as ar thalamh na hÉireann,' ar seisean.

Chuaigh Conall isteach sa bhád arís agus ba ghairid go raibh sé as amharc. Cuireadh corp mhac an Rí i gcónair agus cuireadh é ar bhord na loinge. Thóg siad na seoltaí agus thug siad a n-aghaidh ar thír na hÉireann.

Bhí Deirdre ag fanacht lá ar lá ar son theacht abhaile na loinge. Maidin amháin chonaic sí an long ag teannadh leis an talamh agus na seoltaí bána in airde. Chuir seo lúcháir an domhain uirthi agus bhí an oiread sin deifre uirthi mac an Rí a fheiceáil gur shiúil sí go dtína com san fharraige in araicis na loinge. Nuair a chonaic sí an chónair bhris an gol uirthi.

'A Fhinn Mhic Cumhaill,' ar sise, 'níor shíl mé go ndéanfá bréag liom. Gheall tú na bratacha dubha a chur suas dá mbeadh mac an Rí marbh.'

'Bhí eagla orm,' arsa Fionn, 'go gcuirfeá ceo draíochta orainn dá bhfeictheá na bratacha dubha.'

'Is cinnte go gcuirfinn,' arsa Deirdre. 'Is maith go dtug tú an corp abhaile. Tabhair domhsa an long anois agus rachaidh mé chun farraige arís.'

Sheol Deirdre léi go dtáinig sí fhad le hoileán sa Domhan Thoir. Ba le beirt deartháir an t-oileán agus nuair a shroich sí an cuan chuir siad fáilte roimpi. D'fhiafraigh siad fáth a turais agus d'inis sí dóibh gur marbhadh a fear agus go dtug sí an corp léi sa chónair.

'Chuala mé,' ar sise, 'go bhfuil uisce íocshláinte ar an oileán seo a dhéanfadh duine marbh beo.'

'Chuala tú an fhírinne,' arsa fear de na deartháireacha. Chuaigh sé isteach sa chaisleán agus tháinig ar ais i mbomaite le buidéal den uisce. Chuir sé braon ar cheann mhac an Rí agus d'éirigh sé ina sheasamh i mbláth beatha agus sláinte. Phóg Deirdre é go cineálta agus ansin chuaigh an t-iomlán acu isteach sa chaisleán, an áit a raibh neart bídh agus dí ag fanacht leo.

Nuair a bhí an dinnéar thart dúirt an deartháir is sine le mac an Rí: 'Tá mé cinnte gur gaiscíoch éifeachtach atá ionat agus tá do chuidiú a dhíth orainne go cruaidh. Gach oíche i ndiaidh luí na gréine tigeann dream mallaithe go dtí an oileán seo a throid linn agus, gí go n-éiríonn linn iad a mharbhadh roimh an lá, ní duine inteacht beo arís iad agus tigeann siad ar ais san oíche.'

'Ní thig liomsa níos lú a dhéanamh ná mo chuidiú a thabhairt daoibh anocht,' arsa mac an Rí.

'Beidh mise ansin fosta,' arsa Deirdre.

Ag titim na hoíche tháinig an dream i dtír agus thoisigh an troid. Chuaigh mac an Rí fríothu mar a dhéanfadh séideán gaoithe agus in am ghairid bhí an duine deireanach acu sínte ar mháigh an áir. Thug na deartháireacha buíochas do mhac an Rí agus dúirt siad go raibh an t-am acu pilleadh ar an chaisleán.

'Ní bheadh sin ceart,' arsa Deirdre. 'Is fearr dúinn fanacht anseo go bhfeicimid cad é mar a thugtar na daoine seo chun beatha arís.'

'Sin mo chomhairlese fosta,' arsa mac an Rí.

Thaitin an réiteach seo leis na deartháireacha go hanmhaith. Oíche réabghealaí a bhí ann agus thoisigh na fir ag caint eatarthu féin ach bhí Deirdre ag amharc in aice na farraige. Ba ghairid go bhfaca sí cailleach ag teacht amach as an fharraige. Bhí pota crochta fána muineál agus cleite ina láimh aici a bhí deich dtroigh ar fad.

'Cé hí féin?' arsa mac an Rí le Deirdre.

'Sin cailleach an chleite phoitín,' ar sise. 'Tá uisce na híocshláinte léi sa phota agus má thigeann sí fhad leis na daoine atá marbh ar an léana, dhéanfaidh sí beo arís iad. Níl bomaite le cailleadh.'

Rug mac an Rí ar a chlaíomh agus d'ionsaigh sé an chailleach. Sula raibh faill aige buille a bhualadh rinne sí cat di féin agus thug sí a sháith dó le déanamh. Fá dheireadh chuir sé an claíomh fríd a brollach agus thit sí marbh. Bhí aghaidh agus lámha mhac an Rí cumhdaithe le fuil ach thom Deirdre an cleite sa phota agus leigheas sé é i mbomaite.

'Tá bhur gcuid trioblóide thart anois,' ar sise leis na deartháireacha.

'Má tá,' ar siadsan, 'féadann muid a bheith buíoch duitse agus do d'fhear chróga. Má fhanann sibh againn bhéarfaimid leath an oileáin daoibh saor go deo.'

'Táimid buíoch daoibh,' arsa Deirdre, 'ach caithfimid pilleadh go hÉirinn.'

Chaoin na deartháireacha mar a dhéanfadh páistí nuair a d'fhág mac an Rí agus Deirdre slán acu lá arna mhárach.

Gí nach raibh Fionn agus na Fianna ag dréim go bhfeicfeadh siad mac an Rí go deo arís, bhí siad ag fanacht lá ar lá le Deirdre a fheiceáil ar thalamh na hÉireann. Ní féidir an lúcháir a bhí orthu a áireamh nuair a tháinig an péire abhaile slán. Tionóladh féasta a mhair seacht lá agus seacht n-oíche i gCaisleán Fhinn i nDún na nGall. Tá lorg an chaisleáin le feiceáil go fóill in aice leis na Cealla Beaga.

An lá deireanach den fhéasta tháinig fear ar dhroim capaill fhad leis an gheafta. Chuir fear de na Fianna ceist air cad é a bhí a dhíth air agus d'fhreagair an marcach: 'Má tá do mháistir sa bhaile abair leis go dtáinig mise le troid a chur air.'

Chuala Deirdre na focla seo agus chuaigh sí isteach sa tseomra ina raibh Fionn agus mac an Rí ag imirt cluiche cártaí. D'inis sí an scéal mar a chuala sí é agus thug Fionn áladh ar a chlaíomh.

'Fan bomaite,' arsa Deirdre. 'Má tá Conall na Méanfaí beo, is é atá ag an gheafta.'

'Má tá sin mar sin,' arsa mac an Rí, 'beidh focal agamsa leis.'

Rug sé ar a chlaíomh agus d'ionsaigh sé an marcach. Bhí Fionn ar tí cuidiú le mac an Rí ach dúirt Deirdre leis moill a dhéanamh ar feadh bomaite. Leis sin, thit ceann Chonaill chun talaimh agus bhí an bhuaidh ag mac an Rí.

Cupla lá ina dhiaidh seo dúirt mac an Rí le Fionn go raibh dúil ag Deirdre agus é féin cuairt a thabhairt ar a athair.

'Ba mhaith liomsa Rí na hÉireann a fheiceáil fosta,' arsa Fionn.

'Níor mhaith linne a ghabháil gan tú,' arsa mac an Rí.

Bhí lúcháir as miosúr ar Rí na hÉireann a mhac a fheiceáil arís. Shíl sé go raibh sé marbh. Níor lú ná sin an fháilte a chuir sé roimh Dheirdre agus Fionn. D'ordaigh sé féasta a thionóladh ach caithfimid slán a fhágáil anois ag mac an Rí, Deirdre agus Fionn Mac Cumhaill.

NÓTA: *Derry People and Tirconaill News*, 7, 14, 21, 28 September, 5, 12 October 1935.

Fionn Mac Cumhaill agus Seachtar de Laochraí na bhFiann

Lá dá raibh Fionn Mac Cumhaill ag triall i gCúige Uladh tháinig sé fhad le caisleán a bhí suite ag bun sléibhe. Bhí seanchailleach ina cónaí sa chaisleán agus chuir sí ceist ar Fhionn ar mhaith leis cluiche cártaí a imirt.

'Ní raibh mé riamh nach n-imreoinn,' arsa Fionn.

In am ghairid bhain an chailleach an cluiche.

'Cuir do gheasa,' arsa Fionn, 'ó tharla go bhfuil an bhuaidh agat.'

'Cuirim de gheasa ort,' arsa an chailleach, 'go rachaidh tú go dtí an Domhan Thoir agus go dtabharfaidh tú abhaile chuig Rí na hÉireann an páiste a ghoid fathach uaidh trí bliana agus an oíche anocht.'

'Is trom do gheasa,' arsa Fionn, 'ach níl neart air anois. Ní thig leat diúltú cluiche eile a imirt anois.'

'Níl mé ag diúltú,' arsa an chailleach.

Thoisigh an cluiche ach bhí an bhuaidh ag Fionn an t-am seo.

'Cuir do gheasa,' arsa an chailleach.

'Cuirim de gheasa ort,' arsa Fionn, 'go mbeidh tú 'do shuí ar an tsimléar láir den chaisleán seo go dtige mise ar ais ón Domhan Thoir. Beidh punann coirce ar an tsimléar ar thaobh do láimhe deise agus tobán uisce ar an tsimléar ar thaobh do láimhe clí. Ní bhfaighidh tú bia ná deoch ar feadh an ama sin ach an méid a cheapfas tú in do bhéal ón phunann agus ón tobar nuair a bheas an ghaoth ag séideadh.'

Leis sin tógadh an chailleach in airde go dtí an simléar agus b'éigean do Fhionn tús a chur ar a thuras fhada. Shiúil sé leis go dtáinig sé fhad le carraig ar thaobh an bhealaigh mhóir. Shuigh sé síos le scríste a dhéanamh agus leis an osna a lig sé scoilt an charraig ina dhá leith faoi. Bomaite ina dhiaidh sin chonaic sé seachtar fear ag teannadh leis. Bhí fear beag, bídeach fá thuairim dhá throigh ar airde ag siúl ina ndiaidh. Labhair Fionn leis na fir go carthanach agus chuir ceist orthu c'áit a raibh a dtriall.

'Táimid ar lorg máistir,' arsa fear acu.

'Is maith mar a tharla,' arsa Fionn. 'Tá cuidiú a dhíth ormsa. C'ainm atá ort?' arsa Fionn leis an fhear a labhair ar dtús.

'Eolaí Mac Eolaí,' arsa an fear.

'Cad é a thig leatsa a dhéanamh?' arsa Fionn.

'Tá eolas agam ar gach ball ar an domhan,' arsa an laoch.

'Is maith agus is rómhaith thú,' arsa Fionn. 'Beidh tusa liom. C'ainm atá ortsa?' ar seisean leis an dara fear.

'Fios Mac Fios,' arsa an fear.

'Cad é a thig leatsa a dhéanamh?' arsa Fionn.

'Thig liom a insint duit cad é atá ag gabháil chun tosaigh in áit ar bith ar an domhan,' arsa Fios Mac Fios.

'Is maith agus is rómhaith thú,' arsa Fionn. 'Beidh tusa liom. C'ainm atá ortsa?' ar seisean leis an tríú fear.

'Neart Mac Neart.'

'Cad é a thig leatsa a dhéanamh?' arsa Fionn.

'Is mise an fear is láidre ar éadan na cruinne,' arsa an laoch.

'Is maith agus is rómhaith thú,' arsa Fionn. 'Beidh tusa liom.'

Cheistnigh Fionn an ceathrú fear agus d'fhreagair sé: 'Is mise Slis Mac Slis.'

'Cad é a thig leatsa a dhéanamh?' arsa Fionn.

'Tabhair domh giota adhmaid, beag nó mór, agus dhéanfaidh mé long de.'

'Is maith agus is rómhaith thú,' arsa Fionn. 'Beidh tusa liom.'

'Is mise Fead Mac Fead,' arsa an cúigiú fear.

'Cad é a thig leatsa a dhéanamh?' arsa Fionn.

'Dhéanfaidh fead uaimse na mílte de na Fianna a chruinniú i mbomaite,' ar seisean.

'Is maith agus is rómhaith thú,' arsa Fionn. 'Beidh tusa liom.'

Thug an seisiú fear a ainm mar Dreapaire Mac an Dreapaire. Dúirt sé go dtiocfadh leis dreapaireacht a dhéanamh ar shnáithe síoda.

'Beidh tusa liom,' arsa Fionn.

'C'ainm atá ortsa?' arsa Fionn leis an seachtú fear.

'Gadaí Mac an Ghadaí,' ar seisean.

'Ní bheidh baint ar bith agam leatsa,' arsa Fionn.

'An áit a mbeidh na fir seo, beidh mise,' arsa an gadaí.

'Má tá sin mar sin,' arsa Fionn, 'beidh tú linn. Ach, ní iarrfaidh mé ort aon rud a dhéanamh.'

'C'ainm atá ortsa?' arsa Fionn leis an fhear bheag.

'Níl ainm ar bith orm,' arsa an fear beag.

'Bhéarfaidh mise Ceasán ort,' arsa Fionn. 'Thig leat a theacht linn.'

'Anois, a chairde,' arsa Fionn, 'tá turas fada romhainn. Caithfimid a ghabháil go dtí an Domhan Thoir. Trí bliana ó shin rugadh mac óg i gcaisleán Rí na hÉireann agus deirtear go dtáinig fathach agus gur ghoid sé an páiste. Cá bhfuil an fathach anois?'

'Tá sé sa Domhan Thoir,' arsa Fios Mac Fios.

'An bhfuil an páiste beo?' arsa Fionn.

'Tá,' arsa an laoch.

'Maith go leor,' arsa Fionn, 'chead againn a ghabháil ar aghaidh. Inis domh, a Eolaí Mac Eolaí, an bhfuil caisleán Rí na hÉireann ar an bhealach?'

'Tá,' arsa Eolaí Mac Eolaí. 'Rachaidh mise i dtoiseach.'

Shiúil siad leo idir oíche agus lá go dtáinig siad fhad leis an chaisleán. Cuireadh fáilte fhlaithiúil rompu agus dúirt an Rí le Fionn nach dtiocfadh leis a theacht in am ní b'fhearr.

'Rugadh níon óg anseo ar maidin inniu,' ar seisean, 'agus deir an seandall atá in mo chuid seirbhíse go ngoidfear an páiste seo fosta.'

'Ní gan troid a mbeidh cuimhne air,' arsa Fionn. 'Tá mise agus mo chuid fear ag fanacht anseo go maidin agus féadann tú cúram an chaisleáin a fhágáil orainn.'

'Tógann sin lód de mo chroí,' arsa an Rí.

'Bheinn buíoch duit, a Rí,' arsa Fionn, 'dá n-inseofá domh cad é mar a goideadh an páiste eile.'

'Is brónach an scéal é,' arsa an Rí, 'ach is furast é a insint. Rugadh an leanbh ar an mheán lae agus bhí mórán d'uaisle na tíre cruinnithe sa chaisleán an oíche sin agus féasta mór ar bun. Ag uair an mheán oíche thoisigh thart fán chaisleán an ceol ba truacánta a chuala cluas riamh. In am ghairid thit sinn uilig inár gcodladh. Mhair an codladh draíochta seo go maidin agus ní fhacthas an leanbh ón bhomaite sin go dtí anois.'

'Beidh lúcháir ort a chluinstin,' arsa Fionn, 'go bhfuil an leanbh beo slán agus go bhfuil sinne ar ár mbealach go dtí an Domhan Thoir lena thabhairt abhaile.'

Ní féidir an lúcháir a chuir na focla seo ar an Rí a insint. 'Chuir tú misneach úr ionam,' ar seisean le Fionn.

Bhí siad ag ithe agus ag ól go subhach go dtáinig an t-am le réiteach a dhéanamh i gcomhair na hoíche. D'ordaigh Fionn go gcuirfí an naíonán i gcliabhán sa tseomra ba mhó sa chaisleán. Rinneadh seo go tapaidh agus shuigh Fionn agus a chuid fear thart fán chliabhán.

Ag uair an mheán oíche thoisigh an ceol truacánta amuigh agus in am ghairid bhí gach duine dá raibh sa chaisleán i dtromchodladh taobh amuigh de Fhionn agus laochraí na bhFiann.

'An bhfuil an fathach comhgarach anocht?' arsa Fionn le Fios Mac Fios.

'Tá sé ar mhullach an chaisleáin anois,' arsa an laoch.

Leis sin chuir an fathach a lámh dheas anuas an simléar. Bhí an lámh chomh ramhar le corp fir agus sular shroich sí an cliabhán fuair Neart Mac Neart greim uirthi. D'fhéach an fathach an lámh a tharraingt ar ais ach níor bhaol go ligfeadh Neart Mac Neart amach a ghreim. Fá dheireadh tháinig an sciathán leis amach ón ghualainn agus thit sé ar gcúl sa cheann eile den tseomra. Sula raibh faill aige éirí chuir an fathach anuas a lámh chlí agus sciob an leanbh ar shiúl. Lean Fionn agus a chuid fear an fathach ach chuaigh sé as amharc i mbomaite, agus nuair a mhuscail an Rí ar maidin ní raibh dadaí le feiceáil sa tseomra ach sciathán an fhathaigh.

D'inis Fios Mac Fios do Fhionn go raibh an fathach ar a bhealach go dtí an fharraige mar gheall ar a ghabháil ar bord loinge.

'Coinneoimid ar a lorg,' arsa Fionn.

Ag bánú an lae bhí siad ar amharc na farraige agus chonaic siad seoltaí na loinge.

'Ní theachaigh sé chun farraige go fóill,' arsa Fios Mac Fios.

'Cad chuige sin?' arsa Fionn.

'Tá díobháil na láimhe ag tabhairt trioblóide dó,' arsa an laoch, 'agus tá scaifte fear ag caitheamh uisce ar a ghualainn.'

'Cá has a dtáinig na fir?' arsa Fionn.

'Daoine as an Domhan Thoir a chuir an fathach faoi dhraíocht. Thug sé céad go leith acu leis ins an loing.'

'Má tá sin mar sin,' arsa Fionn, 'bheadh sé amaideach againn iad a ionsaí.'

'Ná déan dearmad,' arsa Fead Mac Fead, 'go bhfuil mise anseo.'

Leis sin, lig sé fead agus i mbomaite bhí míle de na Fianna lena dtaobh.

'Ní bheidh eagla orainn a ghabháil chun tosaigh anois,' arsa Fionn agus in am ghairid bhí siad comhgarach ag an chladach. Chonaic an fathach iad ag teacht agus shiúil sé go dtína bhásta san fharraige agus chuaigh ar bhord na loinge. Thug na fir a bhí leis an fhathach iarracht an rud céanna a dhéanamh ach báitheadh an duine deireanach acu sula dtáinig siad fhad leis an loing.

'Níl gnoithe linne,' arsa fear de na Fianna a tháinig nuair a chualathas an fead agus d'imigh siad mar a tháinig siad.

Bhí long an fhathaigh faoi sheol i mbomaite agus dúirt Fionn le Fios Mac Fios: 'An féidir linn fáil suas leis?'

'Ní féidir,' arsa an laoch, 'ach ó tharla go gcaithfimid a ghabháil go dtí an Domhan Thoir i gcás ar bith, is fearr dúinn gan am ar bith a chailleadh.'

Rinne Slis Mac Slis long de ghiota adhmaid a fuair sé ar an tráigh agus chuaigh siad ar bord.

'An bhfuil muid uilig anseo?' arsa Fionn.

'Níl,' arsa Fios Mac Fios. 'Tá Ceasán neamhláithreach.'

'Cá bhfuil sé?' arsa Fionn.

'Chuaigh sé ar lorg bídh agus dí,' arsa an laoch. 'Seo é ag teacht.'

D'amharc Fionn ar an chladach agus chonaic sé Ceasán ina shuí ar bhairille.

'Caithfidh mise a ghabháil i dtír agus an bairille a chur ar bhord na loinge,' arsa Neart Mac Neart.

Gan mhoill ina dhiaidh seo thóg siad na seoltaí agus thug Fionn buíochas do Cheasán ar son a chuid oibre. 'Ach ab é thú,' ar seisean, 'dhéanfaí dearmad ar an bhia.'

Is fada an turas ó Éirinn go dtí an Domhan Thoir ach chríochnaigh Fionn agus a chuid fear é chomh gasta is ab fhéidir leo.

'An bhfuil i bhfad againn le a ghabháil anois?' arsa Eolaí Mac Eolaí. 'Rachaidh mise ar dtús,' ar seisean.

Nuair a bhí siad ag ceann an turais, labhair Eolaí Mac Eolaí le Fionn mar a leanas: 'Níl gnoithe dúinn siúl níos faide. An bhfeiceann tú an snáithe seo atá ag crochadh ón spéir?'

'Tím,' arsa Fionn.

'Tá caisleán an fhathaigh trí mhíle ón bhall seo.'

'In airde san aer?' arsa Fionn.

'Sea,' arsa an laoch. 'Tá an caisleán dofheicseanach ón talamh agus níl dóigh ar bith le fáil fhad leis ach dreapaireacht a dhéanamh ar an snáithe seo.'

'An bhfuil comhairle ar bith agatsa le tabhairt?' arsa Fionn le Fios Mac Fios.

'Tá,' arsa an laoch. 'Thig le Dreapaire Mac an Dreapaire a ghabháil in airde ar an snáithe agus nuair a thiocfas sé ar ais beidh a fhios againn cad é is fearr a dhéanamh.'

'Maith go leor,' arsa Fionn.

Chuaigh an Dreapaire suas an snáithe mar a rachadh fuiseog in airde sa spéir. Tháinig sé ar ais in am ghairid agus thug cuntas ar an méid a chonaic sé.

'Tá doras an chaisleáin druidte,' ar seisean, 'agus ní féidir é a fhoscailt ach ón taobh istigh. Tá poll ar íochtar an dorais ach níl sé mór go leor le go dtiocfadh liom a ghabháil isteach. Tá an fathach ina luí ar a dhroim ar an urlár agus bean mhór ag tabhairt aire dó. Tá gasúr beag fá thuairim trí bliana ag bogadh cliabháin agus tá naíonán sa chliabhán.'

'Sin dhá pháiste Rí na hÉireann,' arsa Fios Mac Fios.

'An féidir na páistí a ghoid?' arsa Fionn.

'Níl ach fear amháin ar éadan na cruinne a bheadh ábalta na páistí a ghoid fhad is atá an fathach sa bhaile,' arsa Fios.

'Agus cé hé an fear sin?' arsa Fionn.

'Gadaí Mac an Ghadaí,' arsa an laoch.

'Nach bhfuil an Gadaí anseo?' arsa Fionn.

'Má tá,' arsa an Gadaí, 'dúirt tú liom nach n-iarrfá orm aon rud a dhéanamh.'

'Tá mé i dtrioblóid,' arsa Fionn. 'Ní thig liom pilleadh go hÉirinn gan na páistí. Déan dearmad de na focla a dúirt mé agus tabhair domh do chuidiú.'

'Tá mé sásta,' arsa an Gadaí, 'ach cuir i gcás go dtiocfadh liom a ghabháil suas ar dhroim an Dreapaire, níorbh fhéidir liom fáil isteach sa chaisleán fhad is atá an doras druidte.'

'Fanaigí oraibh,' arsa Ceasán, 'ba mhaith liomsa mo lámh a chur leis an obair seo.'

'An síleann tú,' arsa Fionn, 'go dtiocfadh leat a ghabháil isteach ar an pholl atá sa doras?'

'Rachainn isteach fríd pholl na heochrach,' arsa Ceasán, 'ach b'fhéidir nach mbeadh an Dreapaire ábalta mé a thabhairt leis.'

'Cuirfidh mé in mo phóca thú,' arsa an Dreapaire.

'Maith go leor,' arsa Ceasán. 'Fosclóidh mise an doras is cuma cé a dhruidfeas é.'

Chuaigh an Dreapaire suas ar an snáithe síoda agus bhí an Gadaí agus Ceasán leis ar a dhroim.

'Inis domh,' arsa Fionn le Fios Mac Fios, 'cad é mar atá siad ag gabháil ar aghaidh.'

'Tá siad ag doras an chaisleáin anois,' arsa Fios Mac Fios. 'Tá an fathach ina chodladh. Tá an bhean ag cur síos tineadh. Tá a cúl leis an chliabhán. Tá Ceasán ag gabháil isteach ar an pholl atá sa doras. Tá sé ag foscailt an dorais anois ón taobh istigh. D'éirigh leis. Siúd isteach an Gadaí. Tá an dá pháiste leis. Tá sé ag gabháil ar dhroim an Dreapaire, na páistí faoi ascaill amháin agus Ceasán faoin ascaill eile. Tá siad ar a mbealach go dtí an talamh.'

Nuair a chuala Fionn an nuaíocht mhaith chaith sé a hata in airde sa spéir. Lig sé scread áthais as a cluineadh in

Éirinn. I mbomaite eile bhí an Dreapaire, an Gadaí, Ceasán agus páistí an Rí lena thaobh.

Phóg Fionn na páistí go cineálta agus ansin labhair sé le Fios Mac Fios mar a leanas: 'An bhfuil an chuid is measa dár gcuid buartha thart?' ar seisean.

'Is fada uainn,' arsa an laoch. 'Is gairid go mbeidh an fathach ar ár lorg.'

Thug siad a n-aghaidh ar an fharraige agus in am ghairid bhí siad ar bhord na loinge.

'Ní bhfaighidh an fathach suas linn anois,' arsa Fionn.

'Ní fada uainn é,' arsa Fios Mac Fios.

D'amharc Fionn thart agus chonaic sé an fathach ag teannadh leis an loing. Bhí sé ag siúl san fharraige, a cheann fá thuairim sé troithe os cionn an uisce. Bhí Eolaí Mac Eolaí ag stiúrú na loinge agus dúirt sé le Fionn nach dtiocfadh leis a ghabháil níos gaiste.

'Cad é do chomhairle?' arsa Fionn le Fios Mac Fios.

'Gheobhaidh an fathach suas linn,' arsa an laoch, 'ach tá fear anseo a bheas inchurtha leis.'

B'fhíor dó. Tháinig an fathach chun tosaigh agus d'fhéach a theacht ar bhord na loinge. Shín sé a cheann amach uaidh ach bhí Neart Mac Neart ag fanacht leis. Thug sé buille dó i gclár an éadain agus thit sé ar gcúl san fharraige agus níor éirigh ó shin.

'An bhfuil sé marbh?' arsa Fionn.

'Chomh marbh le scadán,' arsa Fios Mac Fios. 'Scoilt an buille a chloigeann ina dhá chuid.'

'Ó tharla go bhfuil an bhuaidh linn,' arsa Fionn, 'tá an t-am agam buíochas a thabhairt daoibh go léir. Ním sin amach ó mo chroí.'

Sheol siad leo go dtáinig siad go talamh na hÉireann. 'Rachaimid go caisleán an Rí ar dtús,' arsa Fionn.

Thaitin an réiteach seo leis na laochraí ar siocair go raibh siad tuirseach, agus nuair a tháinig siad ar amharc an chaisleáin bhí lúcháir an domhain orthu. Chonaic an Rí iad ag teacht agus tháinig sé ina n-araicis.

'A Rí uasail,' arsa Fionn, 'seo chugat an dá pháiste a goideadh uait.'

Ní raibh aon scéalaí riamh in Éirinn a dtiocfadh leis an lúcháir a bhí ar an Rí a chur i bhfocla. Níor lú ná sin an lúcháir a bhí ar an bhanríon. Cuireadh féasta ar bun agus mhair an féasta lá agus bliain. Ag deireadh an ama sin dúirt Fionn leis an Rí go raibh an t-am acu slán a fhágáil aige.

'Is trua liom scarúint leat féin agus na fir chróga seo,' arsa an Rí. 'Beidh an caisleán seo ina áit chónaithe agaibh am ar bith a mbeidh sibh ag teacht an bealach seo.'

'Rachaimid anois go dtí an áit ar casadh orm sibh ar dtús,' arsa Fionn leis na Fianna.

'Táimid sásta,' arsa na laochraí.

Shiúil siad leo go dtáinig siad fhad leis an áit ar cuireadh Fionn faoi gheasa. Chonaic an tseanchailleach iad ag teacht agus thit sí marbh. Thiontaigh Fionn thart mar gheall ar labhairt leis na Fianna ach ní raibh aon duine acu le feiceáil. Bhí sé leis féin arís agus bhí na laochraí imithe go brách. Bhí a gcuid oibre déanta.

NÓTA: *Derry People and Tirconaill News*, 19, 26 October, 2, 9, 16 November 1935. The following story is written exactly as taken down from the oral narration of one of Donegal's best storytellers, now deceased. This story was regarded by old-time storytellers as the finest in Irish folklore. Tá leagan den scéal i gcló in Mícheál Mac Giolla Easbuic (eag.), *Ón tSeanam Anall: Scéalta Mhicí Bháin Uí Bheirn* (CIC, 2008) 38–45 agus tá leagan ó Ard an Rátha i mBailiúchán na Scol, Iml. 1040: 255–266.

Athair agus a Chuid Níonach

Bhí feirmeoir ina chónaí in Inis Eoghain mórán blianta ó shin agus fuair a bhean bás. Bhí triúr níonach aige arbh ainm dóibh: Róise, Síle agus Máire. Fán am a thoisíos an scéal bhí na níonacha inphósta agus bhí Éamann (an t-athair) fonnmhar iad a fheiceáil pósta. Oíche amháin nuair a bhí siad ina suí thart fán tinidh dúirt Róise, an níon ba sine, lena hathair go raibh cleamhnas déanta idir í féin agus feirmeoir sa chomharsanacht. D'inis sí ainm an fheirmeora d'Éamann agus bhí sé sásta i gceart. 'Níl fear níos fearr sa pharóiste,' ar seisean, 'agus tá feirm bhreá talaimh aige lena chois sin.'

Rinneadh réiteach i gcomhair na bainise agus pósadh Róise cupla lá ina dhiaidh sin. Oíche na bainise thug Éamann fá dear go raibh siopadóir ag caitheamh mórán den am ag comhrá le Síle, an dara níon, agus rinne sé suas a intinn go raibh siad ag caint ar níos mó ná an aimsir. Ní raibh sé i bhfad ar seachrán. Lá arna mhárach d'fhág Róise slán acu agus chuaigh abhaile lena fear. Thug Éamann dhá bhó di mar spré.

An Domhnach ina dhiaidh sin tháinig an siopadóir go teach Éamainn. D'aithin Éamann go maith go raibh rud inteacht san aer.

'Más rud é nach bhfuil dadaí agat in m'éadan,' arsa an siopadóir, 'ba mhaith liom do níon a phósadh.'

'Níl aon rud agam in d'éadan,' arsa Éamann. 'Tá aithne agam ort ó bhí tú 'do pháiste agus má tá tú féin agus Síle sásta, ní sheasfaidh mise in bhur gcasán.'

Bhí neart airgid ag an tsiopadóir agus thug sé cuireadh chun bainise do gach duine dá raibh aithne aige air. Ní raibh mangaire, gréasaí, tincéir ná táilliúir ins na trí pharóiste ba chomhgaraí nach dtug cuireadh dóibh féin agus, roimh luí na gréine, bhí teach agus scioból Éamainn lán go dtí na doirse.

'Má thigeann níos mó,' arsa Éamann, 'caithfidh mé iad a chur san úllghort.'

'Ná bac leo,' arsa an siopadóir. 'D'ordaigh mé oiread bídh is dí is a dhéanfadh cúis d'arm na Sasana.'

Bhí siad ag ithe agus ag ól, ag damhsa agus ag gabháil cheoil go bánú an lae. Iad siúd a bhí ábalta siúl san am sin, chuaigh siad abhaile, ach ní bhfuair Éamann réitithe leis an iomlán acu go deireadh na seachtaine. D'ith siad cearca agus lachain, caoirigh agus gabhair agus muc a bhí dhá chéad ar meáchan.

Ní bréag a rá go raibh lúcháir ar Éamann nuair a chonaic sé an péire deireanach ag imeacht ar thrucail asail.

Nuair a chuaigh Éamann agus Máire ar a nglúine an oíche sin leis an Phaidrín Pháirteach a rá, bhí uaigneas orthu. Bhí Róise agus Síle imithe agus ní raibh duine ar bith lena gcuid áiteach a ghlacadh.

'Thig linn paidir a rá ar a son,' arsa Éamann, 'agus iad a fhágáil i gcúram Dé.'

Chuaigh bliain nó beirt thart ar an nós seo ach bhí eagla ar Éamann go bpósfadh Máire agus go bhfágfaí leis féin é. Thug sé fá dear go raibh táilliúir sa chomharsanacht a bhí go han-mhór le Máire, ach níor chuir seo imní ar bith air de bhrí go raibh an táilliúir ina bhuachaill mhúinte, mhacánta. Bhí a fhios aige ina dhiaidh sin nach raibh saibhreas ar bith á dhéanamh ar tháilliúireacht i ndúiche chúlriascach agus go raibh an táilliúir gan teach gan talamh.

Maidin amháin nuair a d'éirigh Éamann óna leabaidh ní raibh Máire le fáil. Chuaigh sé fhad le teach comharsan ag iarraidh tuairisce.

'Níl do níon caillte,' arsa an comharsa, 'ach tá sí pósta ar an táilliúir fán am seo.'

'Toil Dé go raibh déanta,' arsa Éamann. 'Sin mar a pósadh mé féin.'

Tháinig an lánúin óg go teach Éamainn an tráthnóna sin agus chuir sé fáilte rompu.

'Bhí eagla orm,' arsa Máire, 'go mbeadh fearg ort ach iarraim do phardún.'

'Níl fearg ar bith orm,' arsa Éamann. 'Tá mise ag éirí sean,' ar seisean, 'agus is leatsa agus d'fhear an teach agus an talamh seo ón lá seo amach. Tá an teach mór go leor ag an iomlán againn.'

'Bhí dúil againn an teach beag ag an chroisbhealach a ghlacadh,' arsa an táilliúir, 'ach fágfaidh mise an réiteach ag Máire.'

'Tá an réiteach déanta,' arsa Éamann. 'Cuideoidh Dia linn.'

Bhí lúcháir ar Mháire nuair a chuala sí nach mbeadh aici leis an bhaile a fhágáil agus gí nach raibh mórán airgid acu bhí gach duine den triúr chomh sásta leis an duine eile. Is iomaí uair a dúirt Éamann: 'Fhad is atá grásta Dé againn is cuma fá rud ar bith eile.'

Mhair an scéal mar seo ar feadh cupla bliain agus lá amháin dúirt Éamann le Máire go raibh dúil aige cuairt a thabhairt ar an dá níon eile.

'Níl sé ceart agam,' ar seisean, 'iomlán mo chuid ama a chaitheamh anseo ó tharla nach bhfuil mé ag saothrú airgid ar bith.'

'Ná smaoinigh air sin,' arsa an táilliúir. 'Bheadh uaigneas ar Mháire agus mé féin gan tú agus tá ár ndóchas i nDia.'

'Tá mé buíoch duit,' arsa Éamann. 'Bhí tú mar mhac agam ón lá a tháinig tú go dtí an teach seo agus ní bheidh tú níos measa lena linn. Tá an croí agat san áit cheart. Tá m'intinn déanta suas agam ina dhiaidh sin cuairt a thabhairt ar mo dhá níon eile mar gheall ar fios a fháil an bhfuil fáilte ar bith acu romham.'

'Ní dhéanfaidh sin dochar ar bith,' arsa Máire, 'ach tar ar ais gan mhoill.'

Maidin lá arna mhárach bhuail Éamann isteach i dteach Róise. Chonaic sé i mbomaite gur fuar an fháilte a bhí roimhe. Ní raibh faill ag Róise labhairt leis agus níor thairg sí oiread is cupa tae dó.

'Beidh níos mó fáilte romham nuair a thiocfas mé ar ais,' arsa Éamann. 'Fágaim slán agat.'

Thug Éamann an dara ruaig go teach Shíle agus ba ghairid go bhfuair sé le fios nach raibh mórán fáilte roimhe.

'Is fada ó bhí mé anseo anois,' ar seisean.

'Sin mar is fearr é,' arsa Síle. 'Thug tú an teach agus an talamh do Mháire agus tá sé beag go leor aici tú a chothú.'

'Ach ab é Máire, bheadh drochdhóigh orm anois,' arsa Éamann. 'B'fhéidir go mbeadh sí chomh saibhir leatsa lá inteacht. Fágaim slán agat.'

Nuair a tháinig Éamann abhaile shuigh sé go tostach ag cois na tineadh. D'inis sé do Mháire nach raibh fáilte ar bith ag an dá níon eile fána choinne.

'Ba cheart dóibh náire a bheith orthu,' arsa Máire. 'Is maith go dtig leat a bheith beo gan iad,' ar sise. 'Is fíor nach bhfuil muid saibhir ach ní fheicfidh Dia ar an anás sinn. Tá Sé chomh láidir is a bhí Sé riamh agus tá máthair mhaith Aige. Bíodh braon tae agat agus coinnigh suas do chroí.'

'Sin comhairle mhaith,' arsa an táilliúir. 'Fhad is atá an tsláinte ag Máire agus agamsa ní bheidh anás ar bith ortsa.'

'Go raibh beannacht Dé ar an phéire agaibh,' arsa Éamann.

Bhí Éamann ar an bhaile mhór cupla lá ina dhiaidh sin agus cheannaigh sé páipéar nuaíochta. Nuair a bhí siad ina suí thart fán tinidh an oíche sin thoisigh Máire ag léamh an pháipéir. 'Tím,' ar sise, 'go bhfuil imirce shaor ag toiseacht ón tír seo go Meiriceá.'

'Sin nuaíocht mhaith,' arsa Éamann.

'An síleann tú sin?' arsa an táilliúir.

'Sílim,' arsa Éamann. 'Bhí mé ag brionglóidigh aréir go raibh saibhreas ag fanacht liom sa tír sin agus le cuidiú Dé beidh mé ar an chéad long a fhágfas Doire.'

'Nach fearr domhsa a ghabháil?' arsa an táilliúir. 'Tá mé níos óige ná thusa agus níl mórán le déanamh ar tháilliúireacht fá láthair.'

'Má bhíonn mo dhóigh féin agamsa,' arsa Máire, 'ní rachaidh ceachtar agaibh.'

'Is dóigh liom,' arsa Éamann, 'nach mbeimid ábalta an cheist a shocrú anocht. Beidh tuilleadh agam le rá amárach.'

'Go gcuire Dia ar ár leas sinn,' arsa an táilliúir.

Rinne an táilliúir agus a bhean a ndícheall Éamann a choinneáil sa bhaile ach ní raibh gar ann. Bhí long na himirce i ndán dó agus thug sé a aghaidh ar an Oileán Úr. Nuair a shroich sé Nua-Eabhrac bhí drochnuaíocht ag fanacht leis. Bhí pláigh ar siúl sa chathair agus na daoine ag fáil bháis ina gcéadtaí. Thairg lucht stiúrtha na cathrach dhá phunta sa lá do dhuine ar bith a chuideodh na coirp a chur i gcónair. Fuair siad cead mar an gcéanna an méid airgid agus éadaí a gheobhadh siad i dteach ar bith ina mbeadh corp a choinneáil. Ní raibh eagla ar bith ar Éamann roimh an phláigh agus thoisigh sé i gceann na hoibre seo dáiríre. Fuair sé mórán mór airgid i gcuid de na tithe agus idir seo agus a pháighe (dhá phunta déag sa tseachtain), bhí sé ina fhear shaibhir nuair a bhí an phláigh thart. Fuair sé leathdhuisín de bhocsaí móra agus líon sé iad leis na héadaí agus bróga ab fhearr. Chuir sé an t-ór i mbocsa eile agus tháinig ar ais go hÉirinn. Nuair a bhí sé fá thuairim leathmhíle ón bhaile chuir sé air an tseanchulaith a chaith sé an lá a d'imigh sé agus thug sé an chéad ruaig go teach

Róise. Rinne sé réiteach na bocsaí a chur go teach an táilliúra an lá ina dhiaidh sin.

[*Píosa ar iarraidh.*]

[Ó tharla go raibh an chuma ar Éamann nár éirigh go maith leis thall i Meiriceá, a chruthú sin go raibh sé gléasta i gcifleogaí, níor chuir Róise fáilte ar bith roimhe. A athrach ar fad.]

Thug Éamann an dara cuairt ar theach Shíle.

'Is maith a rinne tú an baile a bhaint amach,' arsa Síle. 'Ó tharla go bhfuil na seanéadaí céanna ort a chaith tú sular imigh tú ní dóigh liom gur éirigh leat go rómhaith san Oileán Úr.'

'Ná déan breithiúnas ar an leabhar de réir an chumhdaigh,' arsa Éamann.

'Caint amaideach,' arsa Síle. 'Tá súil agam go mbeidh fáilte ag Máire agus an táilliúir romhat.'

'Tá mé cinnte go mbeidh,' arsa Éamann. 'Ní ag amharc ar mo chuid seanéadaigh a bheas siad murar athraigh siad go mór.'

'Bheadh beagán airgid a dhíth orthu,' arsa Síle.

'Is dóigh liom go mbeadh,' arsa Éamann. 'An gcuirfeadh sé iontas ort a chluinstin go dtig liomsa cuidiú beag a thabhairt dóibh?' ar seisean.

'Chuirfeadh, go dearfa,' arsa Síle.

'Maith go leor,' arsa Éamann. 'Beannacht leat.'

Ag luí na gréine tháinig Éamann go teach an táilliúra, a sheanbhaile féin. Bhí lúcháir mhór ar Mháire agus an táilliúir é a fheiceáil sa bhaile slán. Ní raibh acu de mhaoin an tsaoil seo ach scilling amháin.

'Téigh fhad leis an tsiopa,' arsa Máire lena fear, 'agus ceannaigh builín aráin agus cupla ubh.'

'Rachaidh mise leis,' arsa Éamann.

Nuair a bhí an péire ar an bhealach go dtí an siopa chuir Éamann a lámh ina phóca agus shín sé nóta chúig phunta chuig an táilliúir.

'Ceannaigh cá bith atá a dhíth ort,' ar seisean, 'agus gheobhaimid braon biotáilte fosta a bheas abhaile linn. Beidh am pléisiúrtha againn go dtí an meán oíche.'

'Tá seo barraíocht ar fad,' arsa an táilliúir.

'Ná habair é,' arsa Éamann.

Cheannaigh siad luach punta d'earraí lón tí, buidéal biotáilte, tobac agus snaoisín, agus tháinig abhaile. Nuair a chonaic Máire an méid a bhí leo bhí iontas agus lúcháir uirthi. Shín an táilliúir ceithre phunta chuici agus is beag nár thit sí i laige. Ní fhaca sí an oiread sin airgid ón lá a pósadh í.

'Sin pronntanas ó d'athair,' arsa an táilliúir.

'Beannacht Dé agus Mhuire air,' arsa Máire.

'Fan ort,' arsa Éamann leis an táilliúir. 'Is leatsa an briseadh sin. Cuir in do phóca é. Seo pronntanas Mháire.'

Leis sin, shín sé fiche punta ionsar Mháire.

'Níl anseo ach tús,' ar seisean. 'Bain an corca as an bhuidéal sin agus beidh deoch againn.'

D'ól siad sláinte a chéile go lúcháireach agus in am ghairid bhí béile maith réidh ag Máire. Ní raibh níos mó áthais i dteach ar bith in Éirinn.

Nuair a bhí an béile thart shuigh Éamann agus an táilliúir ag cois na tineadh le toit a chaitheamh. Shiúil Máire isteach sa tseomra a bhí in aice na cisteanaí agus tháinig ar ais i mbomaite, páiste sé mhí ar a gualainn.

'Cé seo?' arsa Éamann.

'Seo Éamann Óg,' arsa Máire.

Shín Éamann Óg a lámh bheag chuig a athair mór.

'Shíl mé,' arsa Éamann, 'nárbh fhéidir an lúcháir a bhí orainn a mhéadú ach buaileann seo amach deireadh.'

Nuair a chuala na comharsanaigh go dtáinig Éamann abhaile tháinig siad le fáilte a chur roimhe. Bhí siad ag ithe agus ag ól go dtí go raibh sé anonn go maith san oíche.

'Tá an t-am againn an Paidrín Páirteach a rá,' arsa Éamann nuair a chuaigh na comharsanaigh abhaile.

'Tá sin ceart,' arsa an táilliúir. 'Nuair a bheas an Paidrín thart,' ar seisean, 'caithfidh mise péire brístí a chríochnú do mhac Phaidí Mhóir.'

'Rachaidh mac Phaidí Mhóir gan bhrístí amárach,' arsa Éamann. 'Tá do scríste a dhíth ort agus nuair a thiocfas na bocsaí anseo ar maidin bhéarfaidh mise péire brístí do mhac Phaidí mar phronntanas.'

'An bhfuil bocsaí leat?' arsa Máire.

'Ní choinneoidh an chisteanach an t-iomlán acu,' arsa Éamann.

'Glóir don Rí,' arsa Máire.

'Áiméan,' arsa an táilliúir.

Maidin lá arna mhárach tháinig na bocsaí. Bhí ainm Mháire scríofa ar cheann amháin acu. D'fhoscail sí féin é agus ní fhaca sí le linn a saoil radharc ar bith le cur i gcomórtas leis. Ní cheannódh céad punta na gúnaí síoda a bhí sa bhocsa. B'fhiú an oiread sin eile na hataí agus bróga ban a bhí ann. Tháinig mac Phaidí isteach nuair a bhí Éamann agus an táilliúir ag foscailt bocsa eile. Thug Éamann culaith éadaigh dó a bheadh maith go leor ag prionsa.

'Gheobhaidh tú na brístí atá mise a dhéanamh ag deireadh na seachtaine,' arsa an táilliúir.

'Beidh siad in am go leor,' arsa an buachaill. Thug sé buíochas d'Éamann agus tháinig abhaile go lúcháireach. Ach, le scéal fada a dhéanamh gairid, nuair a bhí na bocsaí uilig foscailte thiocfadh le hÉamann culaith úr agus péire bróg a thabhairt do leath a raibh de dhaoine sa pharóiste.

Maidin Dé Domhnaigh ina dhiaidh sin chuaigh Éamann, an táilliúir agus Máire chun aifrínn. Níl ann ach gur aithin na comharsanaigh iad, bhí siad cóirithe chomh maith sin. Ní raibh bean ná cailín sa phobal nár sheas mar gheall ar an ghúna síoda a bhí ar Mháire a fheiceáil. Agus is cinnte nach raibh beirt fhear ar bith eile sa pharóiste a bhí gléasta chomh maith le hÉamann agus an táilliúir an lá sin. Tharla go raibh Róise agus Síle agus a gcuid fear ag an Aifreann an lá céanna agus tháinig siad chun cainte le hÉamann. Labhair sé leo go carthanach ach bhí a intinn déanta suas aige gan mórán tuairisce a thabhairt dóibh.

'Tá lúcháir orm,' arsa an feirmeoir (fear Róise), 'gur éirigh leat go maith i Meiriceá.'

'Níl mé ag déanamh casaoide ar bith,' arsa Éamann.

'Tar abhaile linne,' arsa an siopadóir, 'agus caith an tráthnóna againn. 'Dhéanfaidh Síle dinnéar maith fánár gcoinne.'

'Is dóigh liom,' arsa Éamann, 'go dtáinig athrú mór ar Shíle le cupla lá. Thug mé cuairt uirthi an lá a tháinig mé abhaile agus níor thairg sí oiread is cupa tae domh.'

'An bhfuil sin fíor, a Shíle?' arsa an siopadóir.

'Tá,' arsa Síle. 'Bhí mé gnoitheach san am.'

'Seo an Domhnach,' arsa Éamann, 'agus níl dúil agam a bheith ag trácht ar rudaí den chineál sin. Tá réiteach déanta agam i gcomhair dinnéara agus tá mé ag gabháil a thabhairt cuireadh don tsagart paróiste cuairt a thabhairt orainn. Ní bheidh ganntanas ar bith bídh ná dí agus beidh fáilte roimh gach duine agaibh má tá dúil agaibh ann.'

D'imigh Róise agus Síle agus a gcuid fear abhaile agus chuaigh Éamann, an táilliúir agus Máire go teach an tsagairt. Bhí lúcháir ar an tsagart iad a fheiceáil.

'Tím,' arsa Éamann, 'go bhfuil tú ag gabháil ar aghaidh go maith leis an teach pobail úr ó chuaigh mé go Meiriceá.'

'Táimid ag déanamh ár ndíchill,' arsa an sagart, 'ach tá airgead gann.'

'Thug tú do bheannacht domh an lá a d'imigh mé,' arsa Éamann, 'agus chuir Dia ádh mór orm. D'fhág muid beirt bhan sa bhaile mar gheall ar dinnéar maith a dhéanamh réidh agus ba mhaith linn do chuideachta fá thuairim an trí a chlog. Cuir m'ainm síos ar son céad punta agus beidh an t-airgead abhaile leat.'

'Go dtuga Dia a luach duit,' arsa an sagart. 'Beidh mé ansin ag a trí a chlog agus tá mé an-bhuíoch duit.'

'Slán leat, a Athair,' arsa Éamann.

'Go dté sibh slán,' arsa an sagart.

Bhí an dinnéar réidh ag an trí a chlog agus tháinig an sagart paróiste mar a gheall sé. D'inis Éamann dó fán phláigh i Nua-Eabhrac agus an dóigh ar éirigh sé saibhir.

'I gcuid de na tithe,' ar seisean, 'fuair mé níos mó ná céad punta agus bhí cead agam an t-airgead a choinneáil.'

'Nach raibh eagla ort,' arsa an sagart, 'a ghabháil isteach ins na tithe agus fios agat gur leis an phláigh a fuair muintir an tí bás?'

'Ní raibh aon eagla orm,' arsa Éamann. 'Thairg mé mé féin do Dhia an uile mhaidin agus chuir mé mo dhóchas Ann ar feadh an lae. Bhí mé ag saothrú mórán airgid agus níor chuir mé aird ar bith ar an aicíd. Ach go dearfa bhí lúcháir orm nuair a bhí cúrsa na haicíde thart agus nuair a mhothaigh mé mé féin ar mo bhealach ar ais go hÉirinn.'

'Tá mé cinnte go raibh,' arsa an sagart.

Nuair a bhí an dinnéar thart shuigh siad ag cois na tineadh. Ba é an Domhnach roimh an Nollaig é agus bhí an aimsir fuar. Tháinig marcach go dtí an doras agus chuaigh an táilliúir chun cainte leis. Cé a bhí ann ach an siopadóir. Cuireadh fáilte chineálta roimhe agus shuigh sé síos ag taobh an tsagairt.

'Cad chuige nach dtáinig Síle?' arsa Éamann.

'Tá tinneas cinn uirthi ó tháinig sí abhaile ón Aifreann,' arsa an siopadóir.

'Tá braon sa bhuidéal seo,' arsa Éamann, 'a leigheasfadh tinneas cinn in am ghairid. An dtig leat gloine de a ól?'

'Thig liom go dearfa,' arsa an siopadóir. Nuair a rug sé ar an ghloine ina láimh thóg sé in airde é.

'Seo do shláinte, a Athair,' ar seisean leis an tsagart, 'agus tá súil agam go rachaidh cúis na measarthachta chun tosaigh go bríomhar ar fud na paróiste seo.'

'Má fhaigheann tú cupla ceann eile acu sin,' arsa an sagart, 'ní bheidh cúis na measarthachta ag tabhairt mórán trioblóide duit.'

'Is maith liom dearmad a dhéanamh ar bhuaireamh an tsaoil corruair,' arsa an siopadóir. 'Tá an Nollaig comhgarach,' ar seisean, 'agus ní Nollaig ar bith Nollaig gan braon de dhrúcht an tsléibhe.'

'Ní as an Teagasc Chríostaí a fuair tú an chaint sin,' arsa an sagart.

'Tá tú ceart ansin,' arsa an siopadóir, 'ach braon níos fearr níor bhlais mé riamh. '

'Go ndéana sé maith duit,' arsa Éamann.

Leis an fhírinne a dhéanamh bhí croí maith ag an tsiopadóir. Bhí náire air smaoineamh nach dtug sé tarrtháil ar bith don táilliúir agus Máire fhad is a bhí Éamann i Meiriceá. B'fhéidir gurbh é an imní a bhí air ina thaobh seo a thug air níos mó a ól ar an ócáid seo ná a bhí maith aige. Bíodh sin mar atá sé b'éigean d'Éamann agus an táilliúir é féin agus an gearrán a thabhairt abhaile ag am codlata. Chuaigh an sagart abhaile ag titim na hoíche agus ní thearn Éamann dearmad céad punta a chur ina láimh nuair a bhí sé ag fágáil an tí.

Nuair a d'éirigh an siopadóir maidin lá arna mhárach thoisigh Síle, a bhean, á cheistniú fán dóigh ar chaith sé oíche Dhomhnaigh.

'An raibh an sagart paróiste ansin?' ar sise.

'Bhí,' arsa a fear, 'agus is breá an sagart é.'

'Is dóigh liom,' arsa Síle, 'nach raibh sé sásta tú a fheiceáil ar meisce.'

'Chuaigh an sagart abhaile ag titim na hoíche,' ar seisean, 'agus ní raibh muid ach ag toiseacht an t-am sin. Bheirim isteach go raibh braon maith ólta agam nuair a tháinig mé abhaile.'

'Níor tháinig tú abhaile,' arsa Síle. 'Tugadh abhaile ar thrucail thú.'

'Tá sin níos fearr ná gan a theacht abhaile ar chor ar bith,' arsa an siopadóir.

'B'fhéidir,' arsa Síle, 'go mbeadh faill agat, anois féin, a insint domh an dtáinig athrú ar bith ar theach m'athara ó tháinig sé as Meiriceá.'

'Tháinig,' ar seisean. 'Tá ceann de na seomraí lán d'éadaí agus bróga.'

'Go moltar an Rí,' ar sise, 'an féidir go bhfuil tú ag insint na fírinne?'

'Is féidir go dearfa,' arsa an siopadóir.

'Ní fiú mórán na héadaí,' arsa Síle, 'mura bhfuil airgead leis. Ní thig leo na héadaí a ithe.'

'Tá mé fíorchinnte,' arsa an siopadóir, 'go bhfuil na mílte punta ag d'athair ar an bhomaite. Thug sé céad punta don tsagart le haghaidh an tí úir pobail.'

'Tá mé buartha anois nár thairg mé cupa tae dó an lá a tháinig sé abhaile,' arsa Síle.

'Tá tú mall,' arsa a fear. 'Shíl tú nach raibh pingin rua aige nuair a chonaic tú na seanéadaí air.'

'Shíl, ar ndóiche,' arsa Síle.

'Bhéarfaidh mé comhairle do leasa duit,' arsa an siopadóir. 'Téigh fhad le d'athair agus iarr a phardún. Abair leis go bhfuil náire ort é a chastáil ort agus b'fhéidir go dtabharfadh sé maithiúnas duit.'

'Má thigeann tusa liom,' ar sise, 'dhéanfaidh mé sin.'

Chuaigh laetha saoire na Nollag thart go suaimhneach ach níor tháinig Róise ná Síle go teach Éamainn. Bhí imní orthu agus éad ina cuideachta. Bhí aonach ar an bhaile ba chomhgaraí an chéad lá den Bhliain Úr agus chuala siad gur cheannaigh Éamann an dá bhó ab fhearr ar an aonach.

Tamall gearr ina dhiaidh seo tháinig bacach go teach Éamainn lá amháin agus é ag cruinniú buidéal.

'Tháinig tú go dtí an teach ceart,' arsa Éamann. 'Tá lán mála de bhuidéil folmha anseo agus airdigh leat iad.'

'Cé acu is fearr leat dornán cnaipí a fháil nó ar mhaith leat cupla ró de bhioráin?' arsa an bacach. 'Tá sé beag go leor agam rud inteacht a thabhairt ar son na mbuidéal.'

'Níl rud ar bit a dhíth orm,' arsa Éamann. 'Tá lúcháir orm a bheith réitithe leo. Ar chuala tú nuaíocht ar bith ar do shiúl?' ar seisean leis an bhacach.

'Chuala mé scéal a chuir iontas orm,' arsa an bacach. 'Tá an caisleán seo thall agus an méid talaimh atá i bhfostó leis le díol ag deireadh na míosa. Tá an fear ar leis é ag gabháil a chónaí i mBaile Átha Cliath.'

'An féidir sin?' arsa Éamann. 'Sin an fheirm is fearr sa chontae.'

'Níl feirm níos fearr ó seo go Béal Feirste,' arsa an bacach.

'Cad é an méid is fiú an áit?' arsa Éamann.

'Bheadh an talamh saor ar chúig chéad déag punta agus tá a fhios agat féin gur fiú cúig chéad punta an caisleán,' arsa an bacach.'

'Sin mórán airgid,' arsa Éamann.

'Táimid ag caint anois ar luach na háite,' arsa an bacach, 'ach níl fear ar bith sa taobh seo den chontae a bheadh ábalta an oiread sin airgid a dhíol.'

'Is deacair sin a insint,' arsa Éamann, 'ach beidh a fhios againn an scéal go hiomlán roimh an Fhéile Bhríde.'

Tháinig an lá a raibh an caisleán le díol. D'éirigh Éamann go luath ar maidin agus dúirt sé leis an táilliúir a theacht leis ionsar an díol phoiblí. Bhí lúcháir ar an táilliúir sin a dhéanamh ach ní raibh a fhios aige cad é a bhí in intinn Éamainn.

'Cuirfidh sé isteach tamall den lá,' arsa Máire nuair a bhí an péire ag fágáil an tí.

Tháinig an díoltóir poiblí ag an mheán lae agus bhí lúcháir air nuair a chonaic sé go raibh cruinniú mór daoine láithreach. Sheas sé ar bhocsa agus rinne óráid ag moladh na háite a bhí sé ag gabháil a dhíol.

'Ní gach lá,' ar seisean, 'a bhfuil tithe mar seo á ndíol sa chontae seo agus má fhaighim luach measartha tá cead agam an margadh a chríochnú inniu. Cé a bhéarfas an chéad tairiscint domh?'

Bhí fear mór, ard ina sheasamh comhgarach ag an bhocsa agus dúirt sé: 'Bhéarfaidh mise míle punta duit ar an áit.'

'Sin tús i gcás ar bith,' arsa an díoltóir poiblí. 'Níor thóg míle punta an caisleán,' ar seisean, 'gan trácht ar an talamh. Tá mé ag fanacht ar thairiscint níos fearr.'

Níor labhair duine ar bith ar feadh cupla bomaite agus fá dheireadh dúirt Éamann: 'Bhéarfaidh mise aon chéad déag punta duit.'

Bhí aithne ag an díoltóir ar Éamann agus bhí a fhios aige go maith nach dtiocfadh leis poll muinchille veiste a cheannach an lá a d'fhág sé an baile le a ghabháil go Meiriceá.

'Tar isteach sa chaisleán bomaite,' ar seisean le hÉamann. 'Beidh mé ar ais i mbomaite,' a dúirt sé leis na daoine a bhí cruinnithe. Nuair a chuaigh siad isteach sa chaisleán labhair an díoltóir le hÉamann go híseal.

'Tá a fhios agam,' ar seisean, 'gur fear ionraice atá ionat agus ba mhaith liom a chluinstin sula dté mé níos faide chun tosaigh an féidir go bhfuil tú ábalta aon chéad déag punta a dhíol ar son na háite seo?'

'Níl mé ag iarraidh ort m'fhocal a ghlacadh,' arsa Éamann. Leis sin tharraing sé amach leabhar bainc agus shín chuig an díoltóir phoiblí é.

'Ní ghlacfainn mionna aon fhir dá bhfuil anseo inniu go bhfuil tú chomh saibhir is atá tú,' arsa an díoltóir nuair a d'fhoscail sé an leabhar.

'Gread leat,' arsa Éamann, 'agus má cheannaímse an áit cuirfidh mé síos an t-airgead i ndíolaíocht amháin.'

'Tá aon chéad déag tairgthe domh,' arsa an díoltóir poiblí nuair a chuaigh sé suas ar an bhocsa arís.

'Dhá chéad déag,' arsa an fear mór a thug an chéad tairiscint.

'Dhá chéad déag go leith,' arsa Éamann. Níor labhair an fear mór ní ba mhó agus, fá dheireadh, dúirt an díoltóir poiblí: 'Is leat an caisleán, a Éamainn, agus an méid talaimh atá i bhfostó leis. Cuirfidh mé síos d'ainm agus tá súil agam gur fada a bheas do réim sa chaisleán seo.'

'Go raibh maith agat,' arsa Éamann, 'ach ó tharla go bhfuil mise ag éirí sean ba mhaith liom ainm an fhir seo a chur síos ar son na háite.'

Bhí a lámh aige ar ghualainn an táilliúra fhad is a bhí sé ag caint agus thuig an díoltóir poiblí cad é mar a bhí. Is beag nár thit an táilliúir bocht i laige. Ní raibh a fhios aige cé acu a bhí sé ina sheasamh ar a cheann nó ar a chuid cos. Díoladh an t-airgead ina chnap amháin agus tháinig Éamann agus an táilliúir abhaile leis an nuaíocht a insint do Mháire.

'Coinnigh suas do chroí, a Mháire,' arsa Éamann nuair a tháinig sé isteach ar an doras. 'Is gairid go mbeidh tú 'do chónaí sa chaisleán.'

'Chuala mé,' arsa Máire, 'go bhfuil an fear ar leis an caisleán ag gabháil a chónaí i mBaile Átha Cliath.'

'Tá an fear ar leis an caisleán anseo,' arsa Éamann. 'Féadann tú comhghairdeachas a dhéanamh leis.'

'An ag déanamh grinn atá an péire agaibh?' arsa Máire.

'Beidh iontas ort a chluinstin,' arsa an táilliúir, 'gur cheannaigh d'athair an caisleán inniu, agus gur chuir sé síos m'ainmse ar son na háite. Ní féidir linn buíochas a thabhairt dó mar ba chóir dúinn ach guím go dtabharfaidh Dia saol agus sláinte dó agus glóir na bhflaitheas nuair a fhágfas sé an saol seo.'

'A athair dhílis,' arsa Máire, 'inis domh cad é an dóigh a dtig liom mo chuid buíochais a thaispeáint ar son do chuid cineáltais.'

'Tuilleann do chroí maith a sheacht n-oiread,' arsa Éamann. 'Chuir Dia comrádaí maith chugat agus ní thearn mé dearmad ar an dóigh ar chaith sibh bhur scilling dheireanach le bia a cheannach fá mo choinne an lá a tháinig mé abhaile as Meiriceá gí gur shíl sibh de réir mo chuma nach raibh pingin rua agam. Faigh an buidéal, a Mháire, go n-ólaimid do shláinte.'

Shuigh Éamann agus an táilliúir ag cois na tineadh agus rinne Máire dhá ghloine scoiltín fána gcoinne. Ansin chuaigh sí isteach sa tseomra ina raibh an páiste ina chodladh. Ba é an chéad rud a rinne sí í féin a chaitheamh ar a glúine le buíochas a thabhairt do Dhia. Shonraigh sí go raibh Éamann Óg muscailte agus thóg sí ar a gualainn é.

'Rugadh bocht thú,' ar sise leis an pháiste, 'ach níl tú bocht inniu.'

Nuair a chuala Róise agus Síle gur cheannaigh Éamann an caisleán bhí siad ar an daoraí. Leis an fhírinne a insint ar an tsiopadóir ní raibh éad ar bith ina chroí agus dúirt sé le Síle go raibh dúil aige a ghabháil go teach Éamainn agus comhghairdeachas a dhéanamh leo.

'Ar mhaith leat a theacht abhaile am eile ar thrucail?' arsa Síle.

'Tá a fhios agat nach bhfuil mé ag ól aon rud níos láidre ná uisce ón Nollaig,' arsa a fear.

'Agus tá a fhios agam mar an gcéanna,' arsa Síle, 'go gcuireann braon biotáilte biseach mór ar an uisce.'

'Dhéanfaidh mé margadh leat,' arsa an siopadóir. 'Gheall tú a theacht liom le d'athair a fheiceáil agus anois an t-am.'

'Tá tú ceart,' arsa Síle. 'Rachaidh mé leat.'

Bhí lúcháir ar na comharsanaigh a chluinstin gur cheannaigh Éamann an caisleán de bhrí go raibh meas mór ag an iomlán acu air. Nuair a bhí siad cruinnithe an oíche sin tháinig an siopadóir agus a bhean go teach Éamainn mar a bhí leagtha amach acu. Chuir Éamann fáilte rompu agus d'iarr orthu dearmad a dhéanamh ar an am a bhí thart.

Bhí siad ag gabháil cheoil agus ag rince go dtí go raibh sé anonn go maith san oíche. Díoladh an méid foireann tí a bhí sa chaisleán gan mhoill ina dhiaidh sin agus ba é Éamann an ceannaitheoir.

Sula dtáinig an chuach bhí Éamann, an táilliúir agus Máire ina gcónaí sa chaisleán. Thug an táilliúir suas gnoithe na táilliúireachta agus thiontaigh sé amach ina fheirmeoir chliste. Cuireadh stoc mór ar an talamh agus cuireadh cuid mhaith de faoi churaíocht. Níor ligeadh d'Éamann obair ar bith a dhéanamh ach ba é a phléisiúr a bheith ag tabhairt aire do na huain óga agus na gamhna. In am ghairid bhí Éamann Óg ábalta a ghabháil amach ar fud na bpáirceann lena athair mhór agus sin mar a chaith siad mórán den am.

Bíonn deireadh le gach scéal agus táimid ag deireadh an scéil seo anois. Bhí aois mhór ag Éamann sula bhfuair sé bás agus d'fhág sé iomlán a chuid saibhris ag an táilliúir agus a bhean, taobh amuigh de chúig chéad punta a chuir sé sa bhanc in ainm Éamainn Óig.

NÓTA

1 *Derry People and Tirconaill News*, 23, 30 November, 7, 14, 21, 28 December 1935; 4, 11, 18, 25 January, 1 February 1936. Tá leagan eile den scéal seo faoin teideal 'An Old Donegal Story' chomh maith le haistriúchán i gcló ar an *Derry People and Tirconaill News* ar 26/1/1935, 8, 2/2/1935, 7, 9/2/1935, 8, 16/2/1935, 8, 23/2/1935, 8. Tá leagan gearr eile den scéal seo i gcló in *ACS* 29 Lúnasa, 5, 12, 19, 26 Meán Fómhair, 1903. Tá sé i gcló in Aguisín II.

Cathal Amaideach

Bhí baintreach ina cónaí fada ó shin comhgarach do bhaile Dhún na nGall. Bhí mac amháin aici agus thug na comharsanaigh Cathal Amaideach air de bhrí nach raibh mórán céille aige riamh. Ní thiocfadh leis rud ar bith a dhéanamh go ceart agus is iomaí greadadh a thug a mháthair dó. Dá gcuirfeadh sí go dtí an portach é fá choinne cliabh mónadh, thiocfadh sé abhaile le fód nó beirt faoina ascaill agus an cliabh ar a dhroim ar a bhéal faoi. Lá amháin d'iarr sí air a ghabháil go dtí an siopa agus builín aráin a cheannach.

'Seo dhuit trí pingne,' ar sise. 'Tabhair an t-airgead don tsiopadóir agus bhéarfaidh sé an t-arán duit.'

Nuair a tháinig Cathal fhad leis an tsiopa sheas sé tamall gan focal ar bith a labhairt. Tháinig cailín beag isteach agus cheannaigh sí dhá bhuilín aráin. Thug Cathal na pingneacha don tsiopadóir gan mhoill ina dhiaidh sin agus fuair sé builín mar a d'iarr a mháthair air. Nuair a thiontaigh fear an tsiopa thart thóg Cathal trí bhuilín eile agus thug a aghaidh ar an bhaile. Bhí a mháthair ag fanacht leis agus nuair a chonaic sí ag teacht é leis na ceithre bhuilín d'aithin sí go raibh rud inteacht contráilte.

'Cé a d'iarr ort an méid sin aráin a cheannach?' ar sise.

'Ná bac liomsa,' arsa Cathal. 'Nuair a bhí mé sa tsiopa tháinig cailín beag isteach agus fuair sí dhá bhuilín gan airgead ar bith, agus rinne mise suas m'intinn go raibh sé beag go leor agam ceithre cinn a fháil ar thrí scillinge.'

'Cé a d'inis duit go raibh trí scillinge leat?' arsa a mháthair.

'Ní amadán ar bith mise,' arsa Cathal. 'Bhí píosa airgid ar an drisiúr inné agus dúirt tú liom gur scilling a bhí ann. Bhí na rudaí a bhí liom inniu i bhfad níos mó.'

'Níl gar a bheith ag caint,' arsa an mháthair. 'Tá mo chroí briste agat.'

Tamall ina dhiaidh seo chuaigh an mháthair go dtí an baile mór agus cheannaigh sí ceathrú laofheola. Thug sí abhaile í agus d'inis do Chathal go mbeadh giota den laofheoil agus clogad cáil acu an uile lá go ceann seachtaine. Bhí Cathal sásta leis an réiteach seo.

Tharla go raibh páiste sa chomharsanacht a bhí go dona leis an triuch agus chuaigh máthair Chathail le tuairisc a fháil i dtaobh an pháiste. Nuair a bhí sí imithe fuair Cathal scian agus ghearr sé an laofheoil ina giotaí beaga, bídeacha. Chuir sé na giotaí i mbascóid, chuaigh isteach i ngarraí an cháil agus chuir giota den laofheoil ar mhullach gach cinn de na clogadaí. Nuair a tháinig an mháthair abhaile ní raibh aon mhadadh sa chomharsanacht nach raibh cruinnithe sa gharraí, Cathal ina measc ag iarraidh iad a choinneáil ó throid. Nuair a chuala a mháthair fán dóigh ar chaith Cathal an t-am fhad is a bhí sí ar shiúl, lean sí é le súiste agus ach ab é gur léim sé isteach i bpoll uisce is dóiche go gcuirfeadh sí deireadh lena chuid gníomhartha.

'Beidh agat le a theacht abhaile am inteacht,' ar sise, 'agus creid mise, beidh spuaiceacha go leor ort nuair a bheas mise réidh leat.'

'Lig domh a ghabháil abhaile,' arsa Cathal, 'agus ní chuirfidh mé cos i ngarraí an cháil go brách arís.'

Deirtear go ndearcann duine simplí níos géire ar mhórán rudaí ná mar a níos daoine a bhfuil níos mó céille acu. Ba é sin do Chathal. Lá amháin tháinig beirt fhear go teach na baintrí agus dúirt siad go raibh siad ag cruinniú airgid fá choinne balla a chur thart fán reilig. Bhí an bhaintreach ar tí síntiús beag a thabhairt do na bailitheoirí ach dúirt Cathal léi gan pingin amháin a thabhairt dóibh.

'Tá tú ag tabhairt droch-chomhairle do do mháthair,' arsa duine de na fir.

'Nílim,' arsa Cathal.

'An síleann tú,' arsa a mháthair, 'nach mbeadh sé ceart balla a chur ar an reilig?'

'Níl gnoithe ar bith leis,' arsa Cathal.

'Cad chuige sin?' arsa an mháthair.

'Nach bhfuil a fhios agat,' arsa Cathal, 'nach bhfuil baol ar bith go dtiocfaidh na daoine atá istigh amach, agus níl duine ar bith amuigh a bhfuil dúil aige a ghabháil isteach.'

'Tá tú ceart uair amháin in do shaol,' arsa an mháthair agus chuir sí an t-airgead ar ais ina póca.

Oíche amháin ag am codlata tháinig dhá ghasúr ón chomharsanacht go teach na baintrí. Bhí a gcuid pócaí lán d'úllaí.

'Cá bhfuair sibh na húllaí breátha sin?' arsa an bhaintreach.

'In úllghort Shéamais Uí Chasaide,' arsa fear acu.

'Má fhaightear sin amach, muirfear sibh,' arsa an bhaintreach.

'Níl a fhios ag duine ar bith é ach thú féin agus Cathal,' arsa na buachaillí. Thug siad leathdhuisín do Chathal agus chuir seo lúcháir mhór air. Nuair a chuaigh sé a luí an oíche sin rinne sé suas a intinn go dtabharfadh sé cuairt ar an úllghort. D'éirigh sé ag bánú an lae agus thug leis rópa cnáibe agus tua agus ba ghairid go raibh sé san úllghort. Bhain sé duisín nó mar sin d'úllaí móra de na crainn agus d'fhéach iad a cheangal leis an rópa ach sháraigh sé air. Ansin smaoinigh sé ar an tua. Ghearr sé na trí crainn úllaí ba mhó san úllghort, cheangail leis an rópa iad agus tháinig abhaile. Nuair a d'éirigh a mháthair chonaic sí Cathal ina shuí ag cois na tineadh, lámh amháin leagtha ar a ghoile agus an lámh eile ag coinneáil suas a chinn.

'Cad é atá ort?' ar sise.

'Na húllaí, na húllaí,' arsa Cathal. 'Is dóigh liom,' ar seisean, 'go raibh siad beo nuair a d'ith mé iad agus níl siad marbh go fóill. Má fhaighim bás anois, cé a íosfas an chuid eile acu?'

Shíl a mháthair gurbh iad na húllaí a d'ith Cathal an oíche roimhe sin a rinne tinn é ach bhí tuilleadh tuairisce i ndán di. Chuala sí guth fir amuigh agus nuair a chuaigh sí fhad leis an doras chonaic sí na crainn úllaí ina luí ar an tsráid agus iad ceangailte le rópa. Bhí Séamas Ó Casaide ina sheasamh ag amharc orthu. Is beag nach raibh seachrán intinne air.

'Cá bhfuil an diabhal saolta,' ar seisean, 'a chreach m'úllghort agus a ghearr na crainn?'

'An féidir,' arsa an bhaintreach, 'go dteachaigh Cathal amach ar maidin inniu nuair a bhí mé 'mo chodladh?'

'Féidir?' arsa Séamas. 'Nach bhfaca mé é ag teacht trasna na páirce leis an lód ar a dhroim. Dá mbeadh ciall aige mar dhuine eile ní fhágfainn cnámh slán ina chorp.'

'Is cuma fá sin,' arsa an bhaintreach, 'díolfaidh mise luach na gcrann.'

'Thig linn an cás a shocrú ar dhóigh eile,' arsa Séamas. 'Tá mise ag gabháil a thógáil scioból úr agus má bheir tú cead domh an gaineamh atá in uachtar na páirce seo a thabhairt liom, cuirfidh sin deireadh leis an scéal.'

'Ná spáráil an gaineamh,' arsa an bhaintreach.

Bhí Séamas sásta.

Lá amháin chuaigh máthair Chathail go dtí an baile mór agus d'fhág sí cúram an tí air go dtigeadh sí ar ais. Bhí cearc ghoir sa scioból agus í ina suí ar dhuisín uibheach. Bhí doras an sciobóil foscailte agus chuaigh an chearc amach ar fud na bpáirceann. D'inis duine inteacht do Chathal go dtiocfadh le duine greim a fháil ar éan fiáin dá gcuirfeá gráinnín beag salainn ar a ruball agus shíl an duine bocht go mbeadh sé ábalta greim a fháil ar an chirc ar an nós seo agus í a chur ar ais ar na huibheacha. Thug sé fá thuairim cloch salainn leis i gcanna agus amach leis ar lorg na circe. Lean sé í suas agus síos go dtí go raibh sé [rite as anáil]. Bhí an chearc míle ó bhaile nuair a bhí an salann uilig scabtha agus b'éigean do Chathal a theacht abhaile gan í. Ní dóiche go dtáinig an chearc ar ais ón lá sin go dtí an lá inniu.

Chuaigh Cathal isteach sa scioból agus dhearc sé ar na huibheacha. Chuala sé a mháthair a rá go rachadh siad amú dá bhfaigheadh siad faill fuaradh. Chuir sé sa channa iad agus ansin d'fhág sé iad ag cois na tineadh. Bhí uisce te sa chiteal agus dhoirt sé an t-uisce anuas ar na huibheacha.

'Beidh lúcháir ar mo mháthair,' ar seisean leis féin, 'nuair a chluinfeas sí gur choinnigh mé na huibheacha te.' Tamall ina dhiaidh sin bhí eagla air go raibh an t-uisce ag éirí fuar agus smaoinigh sé ar chleas úr. Chuir sé na huibheacha i bpota agus chroch sé an pota ar an tinidh. Nuair a thoisigh an t-uisce ag goil thoisigh Cathal ag gáirí. Mhair an scéal mar seo go dtáinig a mháthair abhaile.

'Rinne mé dearmad a insint duit,' ar sise, 'súil a choinneáil ar an chirc ghoir. An bhfuil sí ina suí ar na huibheacha ó d'imigh mé?'

'Níl,' arsa Cathal. 'Lean mise í go mullach an chnoic agus ach ab é gur rith an salann amach, gheobhainn greim uirthi.'

'Cad é fá na huibheacha?' arsa an mháthair. 'Cuirfidh mé geall go bhfuil siad chomh fuar le clocha sneachta.'

'Níl a shaothar orthu,' arsa Cathal, ag tógáil an chláir den phota. 'Cuir do lámh sa phota anois,' ar seisean, 'agus beidh a fhios agat an bhfuil siad fuar.'

Níor chuir an mháthair a lámh sa phota ach thug sí áladh ar an mhaide bhriste. Bhain Cathal an doras amach agus cuireann sin deireadh leis an scéal.

Nóta

1 *Derry People and Tirconaill News*, 8, 15, 22 February 1936.

Séamas agus an Bhean a d'Fhuadaigh na Siógaí

Bhí buachaill i dTír Eoghain sa tsean-am agus bhí sé tugtha go mór do shiúl san oíche. Ba chuma leis cé acu a bhí an oíche dorcha nó geal agus is minic nach dtáinig sé abhaile go bánú an lae. Ba ghnách leis amhráin a ghabháil mar gheall ar cuideachta a choinneáil leis féin nuair a bheadh sé amuigh go mall. Nuair a chluinfí ceol ar bith amuigh i lár na hoíche déarfadh gach duine: 'Sin Séamas Bán ag teacht abhaile ó dhamhsa inteacht.'

Lean sé den obair seo go dtí go raibh sé corradh le fiche bliain d'aois. Oíche amháin ag an mheán oíche bhí sé ag teacht abhaile mar ba ghnách leis agus chonaic sé an slua sí ag teannadh leis. Bhí siad ag teacht ó Chúige Laighean i ndiaidh níon an Rí a fhuadach. Siúd is nach raibh eagla ar bith ar Shéamas rompu chuaigh sé i bhfolach ar chúl crainn nuair a tháinig siad comhgarach. Bhí lóchrann le gach duine acu agus bhí siad ag iompar cónair. Labhair duine acu go hard agus dúirt leis an chuid eile: 'Caithfimid an chónair a fhágáil anseo go ceann tamaill. Tím siógaí Dhún na nGall sa pháirc sin thall agus tháinig siad le troid a chur orainn. Chead againn iad a ruaigeadh amach as an chontae seo. Is linne Tír Eoghain agus deirtear gur teann madadh ar a theallach féin.'

Leis sin, d'imigh siad i measc na bpáirceann agus fágadh an chónair ar an bhóithrín cupla slat ón áit a raibh Séamas ina sheasamh ar chúl an chrainn. 'Tífidh mé anois le solas na gealaí cé atá sa chónair,' arsa Séamas leis féin.

Shonraigh sé go raibh an chónair gan chlár agus chuir seo iontas air. Chrom sé síos le hamharc ar an chorp, mar a shíl sé, ach chonaic sé aghaidh mná óige, álainne gan aon chosúlacht báis uirthi.

'Chuir siad faoi gheasa í,' ar seisean leis féin, 'agus sin an fáth a bhfuil sí ina codladh.'

Bhí croí maith ag Séamas agus ba bhocht leis í a fhágáil i lámha na sióg. Bhí aithne aige ar fhear sa chomharsanacht a raibh gearrán aige agus rith sé go dtína theach. Bhí an fear ina luí ach nuair a bhuail Séamas ar an doras tharraing sé air a chuid éadaigh go tapaigh.

'Cad é atá contráilte?' ar seisean, 'nó cad é an fáth ar mhuscail tú mé?'

'Bhí mé ar mo bhealach abhaile,' arsa Séamas, 'nuair a casadh an slua sí orm agus iad ag iompar cónair. Tá an chónair anois ar an bhóithrín comhgarach don droichead cham agus cailín óg, dóighiúil ina codladh inti.'

'Agus cá bhfuil an slua sí?' arsa fear an tí.

'Tá siad ag troid le siógaí Dhún na nGall agus nuair a bheas an troid thart tá súil agam go mbeidh an cailín slán, folláin faoi chúram mo mháthara,' arsa Séamas.

'Beidh mo chuidiúsa a dhíth ort,' arsa an fear. 'Bhéarfaimid an gearrán linn.'

'Go raibh míle maith agat,' arsa Séamas. 'Is dóigh liom gur níon Rí atá inti agus díolfar go maith thú ar son do chuid trioblóide.'

Nuair a thug siad an cailín abhaile go teach Shéamais d'inis sé dá mháthair cad é mar a tharla. Cuireadh a luí í agus d'fhan an mháthair ag taobh na leapa go maidin.

'Caithfimid aire mhaith a thabhairt di,' ar sise, 'agus nuair a mhusclós sí inseoidh sí dúinn cé hí féin agus cad é an dóigh ar thit sí isteach i lámha na sióg.'

'Ní dhéanfadh siad í a fhuadach,' arsa Séamas, 'ach ab é gur níon Rí atá inti.'

'Tá tú ceart,' arsa máthair Shéamais. 'Ní fhaca mé le linn mo shaoil aon chailín a bhí leath chomh dóighiúil is atá sí.'

Mhair an scéal mar seo go dtí lár an tsamhraidh.

'Tá sí tamall fada ina codladh,' arsa Séamas lena mháthair. 'Rachaidh mé síos anocht ionsar an bhóithrín an áit ar fhág muid an chónair agus b'fhéidir go gcluinfinn na siógaí ag caint eatarthu féin.'

'Tá fearg orthu leat,' arsa an mháthair, 'agus caithfidh tú a bheith faichilleach.'

'Níl aon eagla orm rompu,' arsa Séamas. 'Rachaidh mé faoin droichead agus má bhíonn siad amuigh anocht is dóiche go mbeidh siad ag caint fán chailín.'

Ag uair an mheán oíche bhí Séamas ina sheasamh faoin droichead. Go díreach mar a shíl sé chruinnigh na siógaí ar an droichead agus thoisigh siad ag caint.

'Táimid comhgarach ag an áit anois,' arsa ceann acu, 'inar fhág muid níon Rí Laighean ina codladh sa chónair.'

'Tá sí ina codladh ó shin,' arsa duine eile acu.

'Tá sin fíor,' arsa sióg eile, 'ach dá mbeadh ciall ag an amadán bhocht a thug leis í an biorán suain atá ina folt a bhaint as, is gairid go mbeadh sí muscailte.'

Chuala Séamas an uile fhocal dár dhúirt siad agus d'fhan sé faoin droichead go bánú an lae. D'imigh na siógaí agus tháinig Séamas abhaile go lúcháireach. D'inis sé don mháthair an uile fhocal a chuala sé.

'Is gairid go mbeidh a fhios againn,' arsa a mháthair, 'an raibh siad ag insint na fírinne.'

Thóg Séamas ceann an chailín in airde agus cinnte go leor fuair a mháthair an biorán suain. Tharraing sí amach é agus ar an bhomaite sin mhuscail an cailín.

'Níl a fhios agam,' ar sise, 'cé sibh féin ach tá a fhios agam gur shábháil sibh mé ó na siógaí.'

'Tá do scéal fíor,' arsa Séamas. 'Is tusa níon Rí Laighean agus nuair a bheas tú rud beag níos láidre bhéarfaidh mé abhaile thú go caisleán d'athara.'

Nuair a chuala níon an Rí na focla seo ba mhór a lúcháir. Thug sí buíochas do Shéamas agus a mháthair arís agus arís.

'Ba mhaith liom,' ar sise, 'fanacht anseo go ceann míosa eile agus ansin rachaimid go Cúige Laighean mar gheall ar féasta a chaitheamh i gcaisleán m'athara.'

Ag deireadh na míosa dúirt níon an Rí go raibh an t-am aici cuairt a thabhairt ar a hathair agus a máthair.

'Tá lúcháir orm a bheith ag gabháil abhaile,' ar sise, 'ach is trua liom scarúint le do mháthair.'

'Beidh mo mháthair buartha 'do dhiaidh,' arsa Séamas, 'agus is cinnte go mbeidh sí uaigneach lena chois sin. Tá a fhios aici nach bhfeiceann sí thú go deo arís.'

'Ní mar sin atá an scéal,' arsa níon an Rí. 'Ní thig liom ar an bhomaite a insint duit cad é atá in m'intinn ach beidh tuilleadh agam le hinsint duit nuair a tífeas mé m'athair.'

Thug seo misneach mór do Shéamas siúd is gur beag a shíl sé go raibh níon an Rí i ngrá leis ach thug a mháthair fá dear ar feadh na míosa gur thaitin sé léi a bheith i gcuideachta Shéamais agus go mbíodh uaigneas uirthi lá ar bith a mbeadh sé ó bhaile. I gcás Shéamais é féin thug sé suas cuartaíocht na hoíche ón am a mhuscail níon an Rí ón tromchodladh a dhorchaigh a beatha ar feadh leathbhliana. Bhí a fhios ag Séamas go raibh dúil mhór aici a bheith ina chuideachta. Is iomaí uair a chaith an péire ag cruinniú sabharcán agus ag amharc ar na bric ag snámh ins an tsruthán a bhí in aice leis an teach. Shonraigh sé mar an gcéanna nach raibh fonn uirthi labhairt leis na buachaillí sa chomharsanacht, ach ina dhiaidh sin is uilig níor shíl sé riamh go dtiocfadh le grá ar bith a bheith eatarthu ar siocair a chuid ísleachta féin. Bhí sé ró-umhal le smaoineamh nach bhfuil ach coiscéim idir an Rí agus an bacach agus go rachaidh siad chun na huaighe mar an ionann.

Tháinig an lá nuair ab éigean don phéire acu slán a fhágáil ag Contae Thír Eoghain agus aghaidh a thabhairt ar Chúige Laighean. Bhí an scarúint idir máthair Shéamais agus níon an Rí croíréabach.

'Tiocfaidh tusa ar ais, a Shéamais,' arsa a mháthair, 'nuair a tífeas tú níon an Rí slán sa bhaile ach ní fheicfidh mé an spéirbhean uasal seo go deo arís.'

'Ná bí ag caoineadh anois, a mháthair,' arsa níon an Rí. 'Sin an chéad uair a thug mé máthair ort ach tá súil agam nach é an t-am deireanach é.'

Thuig máthair Shéamais ar an bhomaite cad é a bhí in intinn níon an Rí agus phóg sí í go dúthrachtach. Bhí Séamas rud beag faiteach ach chuaigh míniú na bhfocal a dúirt an cailín go dtína chroí. Ag an bhomaite chéanna smaoinigh sé ar chomh hamaideach is a bhí sé.

'Nuair a tífeas an Rí a níon slán sa bhaile,' ar seisean leis féin, 'cuirfidh sé deireadh leis an charthanas atá idir an cailín agus mé féin agus ansin beidh mé níos measa ná a bhí mé riamh. Bíodh sin mar atá, beidh mé ábalta a rá ar feadh mo shaoil gur ghráigh níon Rí mé.'

Ní bréag a rá go raibh lúcháir mhór ar fud Chúige Laighean nuair a chuaigh an scéala thart go dtáinig níon an Rí abhaile slán. Is iomaí seanbhean a dúirt ag cois na tineadh: 'Má thug na sióg aí ar shiúl í, níor chuir siad chun báis í agus tiocfaidh sí abhaile lá inteacht.'

D'inis níon an Rí dona hathair agus a máthair gurbh é Séamas a shábháil í agus ar an ábhar sin bhí oiread fáilte roimhe is dá mbeadh sé ar dhuine den mhuirín. Bhí féasta sa chaisleán a mhair seacht lá agus seacht n-oíche. Ag deireadh an ama sin dúirt Séamas leis an Rí go mbeadh a mháthair uaigneach gan é agus go raibh an t-am aige pilleadh ar an bhaile.

'Ní dóigh liom,' arsa an Rí, 'go bhfuil dúil ag mo níon scarúint leat. Níl mac ar bith agamsa,' ar seisean, 'agus an fear a phósfas mo níon, beidh sé ina Rí ar Chúige Laighean nuair a bheas mo lásа thart.'

'Níl sé fóirsteanach ag duine chomh híseal liomsa níon Rí a phósadh,' arsa Séamas.

'Ní shíleann mo níon sin,' arsa an Rí. 'Shábháil tusa í ón bhás agus dúirt sí liom nach bpósfadh sí duine ar bith eile go deo. Cuirfidh mé cóiste fá choinne do mháthara agus beidh sí anseo fá choinne na bainise.'

Tamall ina dhiaidh sin pósadh Séamas agus níon an Rí. Tionóladh féasta eile agus ní fhacthas a leithéid i gCúige Laighean ón lá sin go dtí an lá inniu. Rinneadh ardmhaor den fhear a chuidigh le Séamas níon an Rí a thabhairt as lámha na sióg agus nuair a fuair an seanRí bás ba é Séamas an Rí ar Chúige Laighean ar feadh mórán blianta.

NÓTA

1 *Derry People and Tirconaill News*, 29 February 7, 14, 21 March 1936. Tá leagan gearr Béarla den scéal seo i gcló in *Pull Up a Chair*, 113–4.

Dreoilín Rí na nÉan

Ins na laetha fadó chruinnigh éanlaith an aeir lá amháin mar gheall ar rí a thógáil a bheadh os a gcionn. Ghlac an t-iolar an chathaoir agus thug óráid uaidh.

'Tá a fhios agaibh uilig,' ar seisean, 'gur mise Rí na nÉan. Tá eagla ar gach éan sa tír romham agus tá sin mar is cóir.'

'Druid suas,' arsa seanphréachán a bhí ina shuí ar ghéag crainn. 'Níl ionat ach scriosadóir,' ar seisean, 'agus ach ab é go bhfuil drochshlaghdán orm phiocfainn na súile as do cheann.'

Thoisigh na héanacha eile ag gáirí agus chuir seo fearg ar an iolar.

'Ná cuir aird ar an amadán dubh sin,' ar seisean. 'Is maith leis a bheith ag éisteacht leis féin ag caint.'

'Fan ort,' arsa an fhuiseog. 'An bhfuil aon fáth le gur chóir dúinn tusa a thógáil mar Rí?'

'An í sin an fhuiseog atá ag caint?' arsa an t-iolar.

'Is mé,' arsa an fhuiseog.

'Ba mhaith liom a rá,' arsa an t-iolar, 'nach bhfuil éan ar bith láithreach a bhfuil níos mó measa agam uirthi ná an fhuiseog. Musclann a cuid ceoil mé go moch ar maidin agus éirím in am mhaith le a ghabháil ar lorg bídh.'

'In am mhaith le cearca a ghoid,' arsa an préachán.

'Coinnigh go socair,' arsa an t-iolar. 'Má abrann tú focal eile cuirfidh mé an seabhac ar do lorg.'

'Is cuma liom sifín cocháin fán phéire agaibh,' arsa an préachán. 'Fhad is atá vóta agamsa ní bheidh ceachtar agaibh ina Rí.'

'Níl ach amaidí dúinn a bheith ag caitheamh an lae anseo ó tharla nach bhfuil muid ag déanamh obair ar bith,' arsa an spideog.

'Dhéanfaidh mise réiteach a shásós an t-iomlán agaibh,' arsa an t-iolar. 'An t-éan is airde a rachas ins an spéir, bíodh an t-éan sin ina Rí.'

Taobh amuigh den phréachán shásaigh seo na héanacha eile go léir agus thoisigh siad ag eitilt.

'An bhfuil tusa ag gabháil suas?' arsa an t-iolar leis an phréachán.

'B'fhearr liom an bás ná do chuideachtasa,' arsa an préachán.

'Dá mbeinnse 'mo phréachán,' arsa an t-iolar, 'bháithfinn mé féin.'

'Ba mhór an trua an t-uisce a shalú le do chorpán,' arsa an préachán.

'Suas linn,' arsa an t-iolar, agus ba ghairid go raibh siad as amharc.

Fhad is a bhí an t-iolar ag scansáil leis an phréachán shocraigh an dreoilín í féin ar a dhroim. Ní raibh a fhios ag an iolar go raibh sí ansin ar chor ar bith. Nuair a bhí na héanacha eile uilig sáraithe bhí an t-iolar níos airde suas ná aon cheann acu. Ansin scairt sé amach: 'Is mise Rí na nÉan.'

'Fan ort,' arsa an dreoilín. 'Tá mise níos airde ná thusa agus ar an ábhar sin is mise Rá na nÉan.'

Bhí an t-iolar ró-sháraithe le a ghabháil suas níos faide agus bhí an bhuaidh ag an dreoilín.

NÓTA

1 *Derry People and Tirconaill News*, 28 March, 1936.

Diarmaid agus na Siógaí

Deirtear go raibh siógaí fairsing in Éirinn ins na laetha fadó agus sin an fáth a bhfuil an oiread sin de sheanscéaltaí againn a bhaineas leo. Bhí cuid acu maith ach bhí cuid eile acu a chaith a gcuid ama ag imirt cleasanna ar dhaoine nár thaitin leo. Baineann an scéal a leanas le ceann de na siógaí maithe.

I gcaorán uaigneach i gceartlár Dhún na nGall bhí fear arbh ainm dó Diarmaid an Chnoic ina chónaí seal mór blianta ó shin. Thóg sé teach beag sa chaorán agus ní raibh teach ar bith eile fá chúig mhíle den áit. Chaith sé gach lá ar a leabaidh agus bhíodh sé ina shuí ag déanamh poitín san oíche. Is annamh a bhíodh sé leis féin aon oíche sa tseachtain. Daoine a raibh aird acu ar bhraon de Dhainí an tSléibhe thigeadh siad chuige ag titim na hoíche leis an eorna i málaí ar a ndroim agus choinneodh siad leis an ól go bánú an lae.

Bhí dhá oíche sa bhliain ar ghnách le Diarmaid a bheith leis féin. Ba iad seo Oíche Shamhna agus Oíche Bhealtaine. Bhí réasún leis seo. Ar an dá oíche seo bhíodh na siógaí ar a gcois agus is iomaí duine a dúirt gur ghnách leo mórán ama a chaitheamh thart fá bhothán Dhiarmada.

Tháinig Oíche Bhealtaine thart agus bhí Diarmaid leis féin. D'ól sé cupla gloine poitín agus ansin shuigh sé ag cois na tineadh lena phíopa a chaitheamh. Ag uair an mheán oíche tháinig sióg isteach agus shuigh ar stól a bhí comhgarach don tinidh.

'Ba mhaith liom ceist a chur ort,' arsa Diarmaid, 'cé acu a tháinig tú le cleas a imirt orm nó le cuidiú liom?'

'Ní imríonn an dream ar díobh mise cleasanna ar bith,' arsa an tsióg. 'Ach b'fhéidir,' ar seisean, 'nach bhfuil aon dóigh arbh fhéidir liomsa cuidiú leat.'

'Ní mar sin atá an scéal,' arsa Diarmaid. 'Níl mé ach ag cur mo chuid ama amú anseo.'

'Shíl mise,' arsa an tsióg, 'go raibh tú ag déanamh neart airgid.'

'Níl mé,' arsa Diarmaid. 'Na daoine a leanas den ól, bíonn siad gan airgead. Sin na daoine a thigeas anseo san oíche agus tá mise ag éirí tuirseach díobh. Cuidigh liom airgead a dhéanamh ar dhóigh inteacht eile agus cuideoidh mise leatsa má thig liom é.'

Bhí an tsióg tostach ar feadh tamaill agus ansin labhair sé mar a leanas: 'Tá luibh ag fás ar chúl an tí seo agus is fiú mórán óir é. Tá fear saibhir i gCúige Chonnacht a bhfuil níon an-dóighiúil aige. Chaill an cailín amharc na súl dhá bhliain ó shin agus gheobhaidh fear ar bith a leigheasfas í mála óir. Tar amach liomsa anois agus tífidh tú an luibh a bhfuil mé ag caint air.'

'Fan bomaite,' arsa Diarmaid, 'go bhfaighe mé fód leathdhóite. Tá eagla orm go bhfuil an oíche dorcha.'

'Ná bac leis,' arsa an tsióg, 'tá lóchrann agamsa a bhéarfas solas dúinn.'

Lean Diarmaid an tsióg agus fuair sé an tuairisc a bhí a dhíth air. Rinne sé suas a intinn aghaidh a thabhairt ar Chonnachta lá arna mhárach.

'Bhéarfaidh mé comhairle amháin duit,' arsa an tsióg. 'Ná caith oíche ar bith in aon teach ina mbeidh cailín óg agus í ag caitheamh fáinní cluas.'

'Glacfaidh mé do chomhairle,' arsa Diarmaid, 'agus tá an t-am agam anois mo mhíle buíochas a thabhairt duit.'

'Agus tá an t-am agamsa a bheith ag imeacht,' arsa an tsióg. 'Seo feadóg,' ar seisean, 'agus má bhíonn tú i dtrioblóid ar bith séid í agus tiocfaidh mise chugat.'

'Maith go leor,' arsa Diarmaid.

Ag bánú an lae lá arna mhárach d'fhág Diarmaid an baile agus thoisigh ar an aistear fhada go Connachta. Ní thearn sé aon réiteach le duine ar bith i dtaobh an tí a choimheád go dtigeadh sé ar ais.

'Beidh mé 'm'fhear shaibhir,' a dúirt sé leis féin, 'agus ní dóiche go gcaithfidh mé aon oíche eile sa chaorán.'

Thug sé lón bídh leis mar gheall ar nach mbeadh sé riachtanach air scairtint ag aon teach ar feadh an lae. Nuair a tháinig an meán lae shuigh sé in aice le sruthán le greim bídh a ithe agus scríste a dhéanamh. Nuair a chuir sé a lámh ina phóca lena phíopa a fháil smaoinigh sé go dtearn sé dearmad an luibh a thabhairt leis agus bhí drochdhóigh air ar fad. Mhothaigh sé an fheadóg ina phóca agus thug seo misneach úr dó. Shéid sé an fheadóg agus i mbomaite bhí an tsióg lena thaobh.

'Rinne mé dearmad,' arsa Diarmaid, 'an luibh a thabhairt liom nuair a bhí mé ag fágáil an bhaile ar maidin agus deirtear go mbeidh drochádh ar dhuine ar bith a thiontaíos ar ais.'

'Tá an luibh chéanna ag fás ar bhruach an tsrutháin seo,' arsa an tsióg.

'Tá sin ádhúil,' arsa Diarmaid. 'Ach ab é go dtáinig tú chugam bheadh agam le pilleadh ar an bhaile.'

Fuair an tsióg an luibh agus thug do Dhiarmaid é.

'Ná déan dearmad,' ar seisean, 'ar an chomhairle a thug mé duit.'

'Ní baol domh,' arsa Diarmaid, 'agus anois fágfaidh mé slán agat.'

'An bhfuil tú ag imeacht?' arsa an tsióg.

'Tá,' arsa Diarmaid, 'tá aistear fada romham.'

'Tá eagla orm,' arsa an tsióg, 'go bhfuil tú ag déanamh dearmaid eile.'

'Níl mé,' arsa Diarmaid. 'Tá an luibh in mo phóca.'

'Cá bhfuil an fheadóg?' arsa an tsióg.

'Tá sí caillte agam,' arsa Diarmaid.

'Níl,' arsa an tsióg. 'Tá an fheadóg agus do phíopa ar an bhruach san áit a raibh tú 'do shuí.'

'Tá tú ceart,' arsa Diarmaid.

'Tabhair aire mhaith don fheadóg.'

Shiúil Diarmaid leis, a aghaidh ar Chúige Chonnacht, go dtí go raibh solas an lae ag claonadh. Chonaic sé solas ag bun cnoic agus dúirt sé leis féin go raibh teach san áit a raibh an solas. B'fhíor dó. Teach beag, bídeach a bhí ann agus, mar bhí an doras foscailte, shiúil sé isteach. Bhí bean ina suí ag cois na tineadh agus í ag cíoradh a cinn.

'An dtig liom foscadh an tí seo a bheith agam go maidin?' arsa Diarmaid.

'Thig leat agus fáilte,' arsa an bhean.

'An bhfuil duine ar bith sa teach ach thú féin?'

'Mé féin agus mo níon,' arsa an bhean. 'Beidh sí anseo i mbomaite. Chaill sí fáinne a bhí ar a méar agus thug sí lóchrann léi agus chuaigh amach á chuartú.'

'Más mar sin atá an scéal,' arsa Diarmaid, 'rachaidh mise ar lorg tí eile.'

Leis sin tháinig an níon isteach agus dúirt lena máthair gur sháraigh sé uirthi an fáinne a fháil.

Bhí a intinn déanta suas ag Diarmaid gan an oíche a chaitheamh sa teach. Dúirt sé leis féin gur dóiche, ó tharla go raibh an cailín ag caitheamh fáinne ar a méar, go mbeadh sí ag caitheamh fáinní cluas fosta.

'Suigh síos,' arsa an cailín, 'má tá dúil agat an oíche a chaitheamh sa teach seo.'

'Is fada go meán oíche,' arsa Diarmaid, 'agus tá solas breá gealaí ann.'

'Bíodh do dhóigh féin agat,' arsa an cailín, 'ach ba mhaith liom a insint duit go bhfuil an teach is comhgaraí ceithre mhíle ar shiúl.'

Fhad is a bhí an cailín ag caint bhí Diarmaid ag amharc uirthi go géar. Bhí sí an-dóighiúil agus ba deacair le Diarmaid an cuireadh a eitiú. Bhí a folt órga ag croitheadh go trom thart fána cluasa. Ar an ábhar sin ní raibh a fhios aige cé acu a bhí sí ag caitheamh fáinní cluas nó nach raibh. Bhí an chomhairle a thug an tsióg dó ag cur mórán imní air agus ní raibh a fhios aige cad é ab fhearr dó a dhéanamh. Fá dheireadh d'inis an cailín dó go raibh scriosadóirí ins na coillte agus má bhí airgead ar bith leis go mbeadh sé dainséarach aige a bheith amuigh go mall san oíche. Ní raibh airgead ar bith ag Diarmaid arbh fhiú labhairt air ach smaoinigh sé ar an luibh a bhí aige ina phóca agus an fheadóg a thug an tsióg dó.

'Má chaillim iad seo,' ar seisean leis féin, 'tá mé caillte go deo.'

Shocraigh sé ar fanacht go maidin.

'Suigh anseo ag cois na tineadh,' arsa an cailín. 'Coinneoidh mo mháthair comhrá leat fhad is a bheas mise ag déanamh réidh do shuipéar.'

'Níl ocras ar bith orm,' arsa Diarmaid. 'Tá neart aráin agam in mo mhála agus níl a dhíth orm ach braon beag bainne.'

'Beidh an t-arán a dhíth ort amárach,' arsa an tseanbhean, 'agus bhéarfaidh mo níon an tráth bídh is fearr duit a fuair tú ón lá a rugadh thú.'

Ní raibh Diarmaid sásta ina intinn go raibh an bhean a bhí sa choirnéal ina máthair ag an chailín. Ní fhaca sé riamh aon phéire a bhí chomh neamhchosúil lena chéile. Choinnigh sé a intinn aige féin ach choinnigh sé a shúil ar gach duine acu. Bhí tábla i lár na cisteanaí agus thoisigh an cailín á líonadh suas le bia den uile chineál. Fá dheireadh bhí oiread bídh ar an tábla is a d'íosfadh fiche fear.

'Tá do shuipéar réidh anois,' arsa an cailín.

'Inis domh,' arsa Diarmaid, 'cad é an fáth ar chuir tú an carnán bídh seo ar an tábla. Má tá sibh ag dréim le cuideachta, ní maith liomsa a bheith sa chasán.'

'Sin gnás an tí,' arsa an cailín. 'Níl muid ag dréim le cuideachta ar bith.'

Shuigh Diarmaid ag an tábla ach d'aithin sé go maith nach raibh an cailín ag insint na fírinne. Shuigh an cailín ag an tinidh agus thoisigh an tseanbhean ag cíoradh a cinn. Chuir sí na cuacha órga i leataobh lena láimh agus chonaic Diarmaid go raibh an cailín ag caitheamh fáinní cluas den ór ba ghile.

'Tá mé i dtrioblóid dáiríre anois,' arsa Diarmaid leis féin. 'Tá siad ag dréim abhaile leis na scriosadóirí agus sin an fáth ar hiarradh ormsa fanacht.'

D'éirigh sé ón tábla, thóg aibhleog as an tinidh agus las a phíopa.

'Is cosúil nach bhfuil aird agat ar an bhia,' arsa an tseanbhean.

'Sin an chéad tráth de bhia ghoidte a bhlais mé riamh,' arsa Diarmaid.

Las an cailín suas mar a bheadh rós ann ach tháinig fearg ar an tseanbhean.

'Sin an doras a dtáinig tú isteach air,' ar sise, 'agus bain chugat anois sula dtige na fir anseo.'

'Ní fhágfaidh mé an teach seo,' arsa Diarmaid, 'go dtí go bhfaighe mé le fios cé hí an cailín seo agus cad é atá á coinneáil anseo.'

Níor luaithe a bhí na focla seo ráite ag Diarmaid ná gur chuala siad caint daoine taobh amuigh den teach.

'Coinneoidh tú do bhéal druidte anois,' arsa an tseanbhean le Diarmaid.

'Ná bí róchinnte de sin,' arsa Diarmaid. 'Níl eagla ar bith orm romhat féin ná na scriosadóirí.'

Leis sin, tháinig seisear fear isteach agus ní raibh deachuma ar aon duine acu.

'Cá has a dtáinig an fear seo?' arsa duine acu leis an tseanbhean.

'Níl a fhios agam,' ar sise, 'ach is fear gan mhúineadh é agus ach ab é go dtáinig sibh isteach in am tá mé cinnte go gcuirfeadh sé deireadh liom.'

'An bhfuil airgead ar bith agat?' arsa fear de na scriosadóirí le Diarmaid.

'Má tá,' arsa Diarmaid, 'is liom féin é.'

'Faigh rópa,' arsa an scriosadóir leis an chúigear eile, 'agus ceangail lámha agus cosa an fhir seo.'

Shéid Diarmaid an fheadóg agus, leis sin, tháinig an tsióg agus scór eile ina chuideachta isteach sa teach. Bhí dosán fraoich le gach duine acu agus bhí an fraoch le thinidh. Scanraigh seo na scriosadóirí agus rith siad isteach i gcoirnéal. Shonraigh Diarmaid go raibh an cailín óg ag caoineadh agus dúirt sé léi gan eagla a bheith uirthi.

'Sábháil mise fosta,' arsa an tseanbhean.

'Sin rud nach dtig leis a dhéanamh,' arsa an tsióg a raibh aithne ag Diarmaid air. 'Seo an oíche dheireanach de do shaol,' arsa an tsióg.

Bhí fear de na scriosadóirí níos dána ná an chuid eile agus d'fhéach sé an lasóg a sciobadh ó dhuine de na siógaí. Bhí an tsióg ró-achmair aige agus chuir sé brístí an scriosadóra le thinidh. Thoisigh an scriosadóir ag béicfigh. Chaith sióg eile braon uisce air agus chuir an tinidh as.

'Cuirfidh sin múineadh ort,' arsa an tsióg.

'Cad é atá dúil agaibh a dhéanamh linn?' arsa fear de na scriosadóirí leis an tsióg a bhí mar cheannfort ar an chuid eile.

'Beidh a fhios agat sin i mbomaite,' arsa an tsióg. 'Inis domh ar dtús cé hí an cailín seo agus cá has a dtáinig sí.'

'Níon fir uasail i gConnachta,' arsa an scriosadóir.

'Sin bréag,' arsa an tsióg. 'Níon Rí Theamhra an cailín seo agus rinne sibh í a fhuadach mí ó shin. An dtig leat sin a shéanadh?'

'Ní thig liom,' arsa an scriosadóir, 'ach má bheir tú cead dúinn an áit seo a fhágáil ní dhéanfaimid aon rud go deo a mbeadh náire orainn as.'

'Beidh faill an cheist sin a shocrú amárach,' arsa an tsióg. 'Rachaidh an cailín abhaile chuig a hathair i gcuideachta an fhir a bhí sibh ag gabháil a cheangal le rópa, agus má bheir aon duine agaibh iarracht an teach seo a fhágáil go dtige sinne ar ais san oíche amárach, dóifear sibh chomh tapaidh is a dhóifeadh tinidh sifín cocháin. I dtaobh na seanmhná,' arsa an tsióg, 'gheobhaidh sí bás roimh éirí na gréine.'

Thoisigh an tseanbhean ag béicfigh agus tháinig critheagla ar na scriosadóirí. Dúirt níon an Rí nach n-iarrfadh sí ar Dhiarmaid fanacht go maidin ach ab é go raibh a fhios aici go n-inseodh an tseanbhean do na scriosadóirí dá ndéanadh sí a athrú de réiteach. 'Chuirfeadh siad chun báis mé,' ar sise.

'Creidim do scéal,' arsa an tsióg.

'Tabhair cead domhsa imeacht liom i measc na gcnoc,' arsa an tseanbhean, 'agus bhéarfaidh mé mála óir daoibh.'

'Ní fhágfaidh tú an coirnéal sin go brách,' arsa an tsióg, agus nuair a chuala an tseanbhean na focla seo thit sí marbh.

D'fhág Diarmaid agus na siógaí an teach agus thug siad an cailín leo.

'Ach ab é an fheadóg,' arsa Diarmaid, 'chuirfeadh siad deireadh [liom.' Chuir Diarmaid ceist ar an tsióg a bhí ina chara aige sular fhág sé an baile. 'Chuir tú comhairle orm a ghabháil go Connachta ach cad é mar gheall uirthi féin?'][2]

'Caithfidh tú í a thabhairt leat go Connachta,' arsa an tsióg. 'Ní féidir níon an fhir uasail i gConnachta a leigheas gan an luibh atá agat in do phóca. Tá Rí Theamhra i gConnachta fá láthair ar lorg a níona agus casfar ort é ansin. Tabhair aire mhaith don fheadóg de bhrí go mbeidh tú i dtólamh i gcontúirt. Caithfidh sinne thú a fhágáil anois.'

D'fhág na siógaí slán ag Diarmaid agus níon an Rí agus ba ghairid go raibh siad as amharc.

'Má shíleann tú,' arsa Diarmaid leis an chailín, 'go dtig leat an baile a bhaint amach gan mise, níl gnoithe duit a theacht liom go Connachta.'

'Nár dhúirt an tsióg leat,' arsa níon an Rí, 'go raibh m'athair i gConnachta fá láthair agus cad é an fáth a scarfainn leat?'

'Hobair domh dearmad a dhéanamh de sin,' arsa Diarmaid. 'Tá sé chomh maith againn a ghabháil ar aghaidh.'

Shiúil siad leo ar feadh an lae agus ag titim na hoíche tháinig siad fhad le teach iascaire. Tháinig Diarmaid chun tosaigh go cúramach agus d'amharc isteach ar an fhuinneoig. Bhí fear ina shuí ag cois na tineadh agus cuma air go raibh sé míshuaimhneach ina intinn. D'aithin Diarmaid go maith nach fear tíre a bhí ann agus dúirt sé sin leis an chailín.

'Fan,' ar sise, 'go bhfeice mise é.'

Chuaigh sí fhad leis an fhuinneoig agus tháinig ar ais i mbomaite.

'Is é m'athair dílis,' ar sise, 'atá ina shuí ag an tinidh.'

'Fan anseo, 'arsa Diarmaid, 'faoi scáth na gcrann, agus labharfaidh mise le d'athair.'

Chuaigh sé isteach sa teach agus dúirt sé leis an Rí: 'Más tusa Rí Theamhra is dóigh liom go bhfuil tú ar lorg do níona.'

'Tá,' arsa an Rí, 'agus má tá tuairisc ar bith agat le tabhairt domh beidh mé buíoch duit.'

'Is é an tuairisc atá agam le tabhairt duit,' arsa Diarmaid, 'go bhfuil do níon anseo.'

Leis sin, shiúil an cailín isteach agus i mbomaite bhí a ceann leagtha ar ghualainn a hathara.

'Cá raibh tú, a níon mo chroí?' arsa an Rí.

'Beidh faill agam [sin a insint duit nuair] a bhéarfas tú buíochas don fhear a shábháil mé.'

'Mo bheannachtsa agus beannacht Teamhra go raibh ort,' arsa an Rí le Diarmaid.

'A athair,' arsa an cailín, 'cén fáth a bhfuil tú ag fanacht in áit mar seo?'

'Seo teach iascaire,' arsa an Rí, 'agus d'iarr sé orm fanacht go maidin. Thig linn fanacht go bánú an lae. Beidh fear an tí anseo i mbomaite. Beidh iasc úr againn fá choinne an tsuipéara agus rachaidh an t-am thart go tapaidh.'

D'fhan siad i dteach an iascaire go dtí go raibh grian na maidine le feiceáil sa spéir.

'Is fada an aistear ó seo go Teamhair,' arsa an Rí, 'ach nach cuma fhad is a thig liom mo níon a thabhairt abhaile chuig a máthair. An dtiocfaidh tusa linn?' ar seisean le Diarmaid.

'Ní féidir liom sin a dhéanamh fá láthair,' arsa Diarmaid. 'Fiche míle ón áit seo tá cailín óg atá i gcontúirt bháis. Tá súil agam a bheith ábalta a beatha a shábháil.[3] Dúirt an uile dhochtúir a chonaic í le bliain nach féidir í a leigheas ach níor dhúirt mise sin go fóill. Má éiríonn liom leanfaidh mé thú féin agus do níon álainn go Teamhair.'

'Beidh fáilte fhlaithiúil romhat,' arsa an Rí, 'agus tionólfar féasta in d'onóir.'

'A Rí uasail,' arsa Diarmaid, 'níl mise ag dréim le féasta ná onóir de bhrí nach dtearn mé aon rud ar fiú labhairt air. Is é an rud is mian liom onóir a thabhairt duit féin agus an bhanríon ins an ríocht a bhfuil tú os a cionn.'

'Ní bheidh moill an cheist a shocrú nuair a thiocfas tú go Teamhair,' arsa an Rí.

Nuair a bhí Diarmaid ag fágáil slán acu thug níon an Rí dlaoi dá cuid gruaige dó. Thaitin seo go mór leis agus thug sé buíochas lánchroíoch di.

'Beidh tú in mo chuimhne i dtólamh,' ar sise.

'Is fearr sin ná ór ná airgead,' arsa Diarmaid.

'Is fearr,' arsa an Rí. 'Beidh sé deacair againn ár mbealach a dhéanamh amach.'

'Is maith liom gur thrácht tú air sin,' arsa Diarmaid. 'B'fhéidir go dtiocfadh liom cuidiú beag a thabhairt daoibh.'

Leis sin, shéid sé an fheadóg agus i mbomaite bhí an tsióg lena thaobh. Nuair a chonaic níon an Rí an tsióg dúirt sí lena hathair gur chuidigh sé le Diarmaid í a shábháil ó na scriosadoirí agus thug an Rí buíochas don tsióg.

'Is é an fáth gur shéid mé an fheadóg,' arsa Diarmaid, 'le go n-inseofá don Rí cad é an bealach is giorra ón áit seo go Teamhair.'

'Rinne tú an rud a bhí ceart,' arsa an tsióg. 'Tá an aistear fada agus contúirteach.'

Chuir an tsióg a lámh faoina chóta agus tharraing amach giota éadaigh a bhí déanta mar éadach cláir. Spréigh sé an t-éadach ar an talamh ag cosa an Rí. D'iarr sé ar an Rí agus a níon seasamh ar an éadach agus dúirt go mbeadh siad i dTeamhair i mbomaite. Ansin d'fhág an tsióg slán ag Diarmaid agus ag cur a choise ar an éadach chuaigh an triúr as amharc le caochadh súile.

'Nach trua,' arsa Diarmaid leis féin, 'nár iarr mé ar an tsióg mé a thabhairt fhad leis an teach ina bhfuil an cailín tinn sular imigh sé go Teamhair.'

Shiúil sé leis go tapaidh agus ag luí na gréine bhí an aistear críochnaithe aige. D'inis sé don fhear uasal go dtiocfadh leis a níon a leigheas in am ghairid. Bhí dochtúir ag freastal ar an chailín agus dhiúltaigh sé Diarmaid a ligint isteach sa tseomra.

'Cuirfidh sé an cailín chun báis,' arsa an dochtúir le hathair an chailín.

Chreid an fear an dochtúir agus dúirt sé leis na searbhóntaí Diarmaid a chur isteach i seomra dhorcha go dtí go mbeadh faill aige breithiúnas a thabhairt air.

'Ar mhaith leat féin tamall a chaitheamh sa tseomra dhorcha?' arsa Diarmaid. Chuir seo fearg ar an fhear uasal agus thug sé ordú an ceann a bhaint de Dhiarmaid. Shéid Diarmaid an fheadóg agus bhí dhá chéad de na siógaí ag a thaobh i mbomaite. Thiomáin siad fear an tí, an dochtúir agus na searbhóntaí isteach sa tseomra dhorcha agus choinnigh ansin iad go dtí go dteachaigh Diarmaid ionsar an tseomra ina raibh an cailín ina luí. D'iarr sé uirthi an luibh bheag a ithe agus rinne sí sin. I gcúig bhomaite bhí sí chomh maith is a bhí sí riamh. Tháinig máthair an chailín isteach sa tseomra agus nuair a chonaic sí go raibh a níon leigheasta ba mhór a lúcháir. D'iarr Diarmaid ar an chailín í féin a ghléas ins na héadaí ab fhearr a bhí aici agus a ghabháil chuig a hathair. 'Is dóigh liom,' ar seisean, 'go bhfuil sé fada go leor sa tseomra dhorcha.'

Tugadh cead do na daoine a bhí sa tseomra é a fhágáil agus bhí lúcháir mhór ar an fhear uasal a níon a fheiceáil ag siúl lena máthair. Nuair a chonaic an dochtúir an cailín dhearbh sé gurbh é féin a leigheas í. Bhuail duine de na siógaí é le slait agus thit sé ar an talamh ina fhear thinn.

'Leigheas thú féin anois,' arsa Diarmaid, 'agus creidfimid thú.'

'Lig domh éirí,' arsa an dochtúir, 'agus rachaidh mé abhaile.'

Rinneadh sin agus ba ghairid gur fhág an dochtúir slán acu.

'Tá náire orm,' arsa an fear uasal, 'nár chreid mé focal an fhir seo.'

'Déan dearmad ar an méid atá thart,' arsa Diarmaid. 'Is maith liom go bhfuil do níon slán.'

'Caithfidh tú fanacht againn,' arsa an fear, 'agus má tá mo níon sásta dhéanfaidh mé cleamhnas idir an péire agaibh.'

'Tá sé riachtanach agam a ghabháil go Teamhair ar dtús,' arsa Diarmaid. 'Beidh an Rí agus a níon ag dréim liom.'

'Caithfidh sibh féin an cás sin a shocrú,' arsa fear de na sióga í, 'de bhrí nach dtig linne fanacht níos faide.'

Chuaigh siad as amharc chomh tapaidh is a tháinig siad.

D'fhan Diarmaid i dteach an fhir uasail ar feadh seachtaine agus chaith an cailín óg mórán ama ina chuideachta. Bhí Diarmaid i ngrá léi agus ach ab é gur casadh níon an Rí air bhéarfadh sé isteach í a phósadh. Ní raibh a fhios aige cad é ab fhearr a dhéanamh.

'Rachaidh mé go Teamhair,' ar seisean leis féin, 'agus dhéanfaidh mé suas m'intinn ansin.'

Nuair a chuala an cailín go raibh dúil ag Diarmaid scarúint léi thoisigh sí ag caoineadh. Chuir seo imní air ach ghlac sé trua di. Sular fhág sé slán aici thug sé gealltanas pósta di.

'Tá dúil agam dearmad a dhéanamh ar níon an Rí,' ar seisean, 'agus tá buaireamh orm go bhfaca mé riamh í.'

'Glac mo chomhairle,' arsa an cailín, 'agus fan anseo. Beidh tú i dtrioblóid má théann tú go Teamhair.'

'Ná bíodh eagla ar bith ort,' arsa Diarmaid. 'Tiocfaidh mise ar ais i gceann cupla lá agus rachaimid ar aghaidh leis an phósadh.'

Shéid Diarmaid an fheadóg agus tháinig an tsióg chuige.

'Ba mhaith liom a ghabháil go Teamhair,' arsa Diarmaid.

'Bíodh do dhóigh féin agat,' arsa an tsióg, 'ach ní rachaidh mise leat.'

'Cad é atá contráilte?' arsa Diarmaid.

'Pósadh níon an Rí inné ar phrionsa ó Shasain agus tá fearg ar an Rí nuair nach dteachaigh tú chuige níos luaithe. Is fearr duit coinneáil as a bhealach,' arsa an tsióg.

'Más mar sin atá an scéal,' arsa Diarmaid, 'ní fheicfidh mé níon an Rí go deo. Gheall mé an cailín a leigheas mé a phósadh.'

'Tá ciall leis sin,' arsa an tsióg. 'Níl cailín níos fearr ar thalamh na hÉireann.'

Fhad is a bhí siad ag caint tháinig an fear uasal agus a níon chun tosaigh.

'Chuala mé,' arsa athair an chailín, 'go raibh dúil agat a ghabháil go Teamhair.'

'Tháinig athrú intinne orm,' arsa Diarmaid. 'Thug mé grá mo chroí do do níon agus gealltanas pósta agus ní bhrisfidh mé m'fhocal. Níl a dhíth orm anois ach cead a fháil uait féin agus ó do mhnaoi.'

'Beidh ár gcead agus ár mbeannacht agat,' arsa an fear uasal. 'Tá mála óir agam fá do choinne mar an gcéanna agus thig leat do rogha rud a dhéanamh leis.'

'Is fearr bean mhaith,' arsa Diarmaid, 'ná ór ná airgead. Agus anois,' arsa Diarmaid, 'ba mhaith liom a insint duit gur sióg an fear beag seo atá ag mo thaobh. Ach ab é a chuidiú, ní bheinn ábalta do níon a leigheas.'

Thug an fear uasal agus a níon buíochas don tsióg. Thug siad cuireadh chun na bainise dó fosta agus gheall sé go rachadh sé láithreach. Tionóladh an bhainis lá arna mhárach agus mura bhfuair Diarmaid agus a bhean chéile bás dhá chéad bliain ó shin ó sheanaois, bain an chluas chlí den scéalaí.

NÓTAÍ

1 *Derry People and Tirconaill News*, 4, 11, 18, 25 April, 2, 9, 16, 23 May 1936.

2 Tá praiseach déanta de chúpla líne anseo ag na clódóirí.

3 Cúpla líne anseo nach ndéanann ciall.

Na Deartháireacha agus an Stocaire

Bhí baintreach ann fada ó shin a raibh dhá mhac aici. Bhí an péire cosúil lena chéile ach bhí an fear ba sine níos intleachtaí ná an fear eile. Bhí fear sa chomharsanacht a raibh níon inphósta aige. Bhí an fear seo ina stocaire; ní raibh aird aige ar aon rud ach ag cruinniú saibhris. Ba mhaith leis a níon a fheiceáil pósta ach bhí a intinn déanta suas aige pingin mhaith airgid a fháil ón fhear a phósfadh í. Fá dheireadh fuair sé le fios go raibh dhá mhac na baintrí i ngrá leis an chailín. Chuir seo imní air ach choinnigh sé a intinn aige féin. Thug sé fá dear go dtigeadh an deartháir ba sine fhad leis an teach gach oíche gan mhoill i ndiaidh luí na gréine agus gur fhan sé ar feadh uaire nó mar sin. Tamall ina dhiaidh sin thigeadh an deartháir ab óige agus ní minic a chuaigh sé abhaile go meán oíche.

Mhair an scéal mar seo ar feadh bliana nó mar sin. Oíche amháin tharla sé go dtáinig an dá dheartháir ag amharc ar an chailín fá thuairim an ama chéanna. Chuir an cailín fáilte rompu ach chonacthas dóibh nach raibh a hathair rócharthanach.

'Bhí dúil agamsa,' arsa an deartháir ba sine i ndiaidh tamaill, 'do níon a phósadh dá mbeifeá thusa agus ise sásta.'

'Bhí dúil agamsa an rud céanna a dhéanamh,' arsa an deartháir ab óige.

'Ní fhéadaim a rá,' arsa fear an tí, 'nach dtig le mo níon an péire agaibh a phósadh, ach thig liomsa an cás a shocrú i bhfocal amháin. Chead agaibh araon a theacht anseo bliain ón oíche anocht agus an fear is mó a mbeidh airgead leis beidh sé ina chliamhain agamsa.'

Tháinig na deartháireacha abhaile i gcuideachta a chéile. Chuir an bhaintreach ceist orthu cad é mar a chaith siad an oíche. D'inis Dónall, an mac ba sine, di cad é mar a tharla ach níor labhair Seán, an mac ab óige, focal ar bith.

'An bhfuil dúil agaibh,' arsa an bhaintreach, 'a ghabháil amach ar fud an domhain le airgead a shaothrú mar gheall ar níon an stocaire a phósadh?'

'Níl aon dúil againn rud ar bith den chineál sin a dhéanamh,' arsa Dónall, 'ach iarraim ortsa, a mháthair, an cás a fhágáil in mo lámhasa. Níl locht ar bith le fáil ar an chailín agus thug Seán gealltanas pósta di. Ní ligfidh a hathair di Seán a phósadh ar siocair nach bhfuil airgead ar bith aige ach, ina dhiaidh sin, ní bheadh sé ceart aige a fhocal a bhriseadh. Lig mise orm go raibh mé féin i ngrá léi ach bhí sé i bhfad ó mo chroí. Dhéanfaidh Seán anois an rud a iarrfas mise air agus má éiríonn leis cleamhnas a dhéanamh le cailín chomh breá sin, beidh sé ádhúil. Thug mé comhairle do Sheán fostó a dhéanamh le feirmeoir inteacht go ceann bliana agus tá sé sásta. Fanóidh mise sa bhaile go dtige sé ar ais agus beidh mo chuidiú úsáideach aige.'

'Tá cloigeann fada ort, a Dhónaill,' arsa an bhaintreach.

Ar maidin lá arna mhárach d'éirigh Seán go moch agus d'imigh leis ar lorg máistir. Bhí sé cúig mhíle ó bhaile ag an mheán lae agus bhuail sé isteach i dteach feirmeora agus d'iarr sé deoch uisce. Chuir fear an tí ceist air cá raibh a thriall agus d'inis Seán dó gur mhaith leis fostó a dhéanamh le feirmeoir go ceann bliana.

'Is maith mar a tharla,' arsa an feirmeoir, 'de bhrí go bhfuil mise ar lorg buachalla.'

'Maith go leor,' arsa Seán, 'tá mise sásta margadh a dhéanamh leat.'

In am ghairid bhí an margadh críochnaithe.

'An bhfuil ocras ort?' arsa an feirmeoir.

'Tá,' arsa Seán, 'ach tá oiread bídh in mo mhála is a dhéanfas cúis domh go dtí an oíche.'

Nuair a bhí Seán réidh ag ithe dúirt an feirmeoir go rachadh siad amach leis na ba agus nach mbeadh siad ar ais go titim na hoíche.

'Bíodh do dhóigh féin agat,' arsa Seán. 'Ní bheidh ocras ar bith ormsa fhad is atá arán ar bith fágtha sa mhála a thug mé liom nuair a bhí mé ag fágáil an bhaile.'

Thug gach duine acu spád leis agus thoisigh siad ag cóiriú na gclaíoch a bhí thart ar ingilt an fheirmeora. D'oibir siad leo go dteachaigh an ghrian as amharc agus ansin tháinig siad abhaile. Cheisnigh an feirmeoir bean an tí fán tsuipéar.

'Tá an suipéar réidh,' ar sise.

Bhí tábla i gcoirnéal na cisteanaí ar a raibh pláta lán de bhrachán lom. Bhí trí ghogán ina raibh bláthach ar an tábla fosta. Shuigh an feirmeoir, a bhean agus Seán síos agus thoisigh siad ag ithe. Ní raibh ann ach go raibh tús déanta acu nuair a labhair an feirmeoir mar a leanas: 'Tá mé féin agus mo mhuirín sásta; tóg thart an bia.'

Leis sin d'éirigh bean an tí agus thóg sí an pláta ar a raibh an brachán agus chuir isteach i gcórtha é. Ba é sin an deireadh a bhí leis an tsuipéar. Dúirt sí le Seán go raibh a leabaidh réidh sa tseomra a bhí in aice na cisteanaí agus go raibh an t-am aige a ghabháil a luí.

Chuaigh Seán isteach sa tseomra ach bhí iontas air nach dteachaigh an feirmeoir a luí san am chéanna. Ba ghairid gur chuala sé an feirmeoir agus a bhean ag caint thart fán tinidh agus choinnigh sé a chluas le poll na heochrach.

'Is dóigh liom,' arsa an fear, 'go bhfuil an brachán fuar anois.'

'Tá sé ceart go leor go fóill,' arsa an bhean. 'Téigh thusa ionsar do shuipéar fhad leat.'

'Tá mo sháith tuairisce agam anois,' arsa Seán leis féin agus, siúd is go raibh ocras air, chodail sé go maidin.

Ag bánú an lae bhí an feirmeoir ina shuí agus mhuscail sé Seán. Rinne bean an tí bricfeasta réidh agus shuigh an triúr síos mar a rinne siad an oíche roimhe sin. I mbomaite nó mar sin dúirt an feirmeoir: 'Tá mé féin agus mo mhuirín sásta; tóg thart an bia.'

Nuair a d'éirigh Seán ón tábla bhí ocras dáiríre air.

'Ní dhéanfaidh seo cúis ar chor ar bith,' arsa an feirmeoir. 'Ba cheart dúinn a bheith i gceann oibre uair ó shin,' ar seisean.

'Rachaidh tú i gceann oibre leat féin inniu,' arsa Seán. 'Caithfidh mise a ghabháil abhaile fá choinne mo chuid éadaigh oibre.'

'Ní raibh sin sa mhargadh a rinne muid,' arsa an feirmeoir. 'Ní bhfaighidh tú páighe ar bith ar son an lae seo má théann tú abhaile.'

'Ná bac leis an pháighe,' arsa Seán. 'Ní raibh sé sa mhargadh ach oiread go rachadh fear amach ag obair agus é ina throscadh. Fágfaimid an scéal mar seo go dtige mise ar ais.'

Tháinig Seán abhaile go hardtráthnóna agus d'inis do Dhónall cad é mar a tharla ó d'fhág sé an baile.

'Glacfaidh mise d'áit amárach,' arsa Dónall. 'Thig leatsa fanacht sa bhaile go dtige mise ar ais. Inseoidh mé don fheirmeoir go bhfuil tú tinn.'

'Sin réiteach maith,' arsa Seán, 'ach ní bheidh tú in innimh oibriú gan bhia.'

'Fág sin agamsa,' arsa Dónall.

Maidin lá arna mhárach tháinig Dónall go teach an fheirmeora.

'Tá mo dheartháir tinn,' ar seisean, 'agus tá dúil agamsa a áit a ghlacadh go ceann seachtaine.'

'Cad é a tháinig air?' arsa an feirmeoir.

'Tá mé den bharúil,' arsa Dónall, 'gur ith sé barraíocht bídh ach níor dhúirt sé sin.'

'Tím,' arsa an feirmeoir. 'An bhfuil tú réidh le a ghabháil i gceann oibre?'

'Níl,' arsa Dónall. 'Caithfidh mé mo dhinnéar a fháil ar dtús.'

'B'fhéidir,' arsa an feirmeoir, 'go bhfuil tú ceart. Is dóigh liom go bhfuil an dinnéar ar bhealach a bheith réidh.'

Shiúil siad isteach sa chisteanach agus bhí an dinnéar ar an tábla. Shuigh siad síos i gcuideachta bhean an tí agus in oiread bomaití dúirt an feirmeoir: 'Tá mé féin is mo mhuirín sásta, tóg thart an bia.'

'Is mise an seirbhíseach anseo,' arsa Dónall, 'agus ní ligfidh mé don mhnaoi seo mo chuid oibre a dhéanamh.'

Leis sin thóg sé an uile ghreim bídh a bhí ar an tábla agus shiúil sé amach ar an doras.

'Cá bhfuil tú ag gabháil?' arsa an feirmeoir.

'Sin mo ghnoithe féin,' arsa Dónall. 'Dúirt tú go raibh tú féin agus do bhean sásta agus creidimse do scéal. Níl mise ach ag toisiú ach nuair a bheas mé réidh tiocfaidh mé ar ais leis an éadach cláir.'

Shuigh Dónall ar an chlaí a bhí os coinne an dorais agus d'ith sé tráth maith. Ní raibh mórán bídh fágtha nuair a tháinig sé ar ais chun na cisteanaí.

'Tá mé réidh fá choinne oibre anois,' ar seisean leis an fheirmeoir. D'aithin sé go maith go raibh an feirmeoir ina throscadh agus go raibh náire air tabhairt isteach.

'Téigh thusa fhad leis an phortach,' arsa an feirmeoir, 'agus tug abhaile cliabh mónadh.'

'Níl a fhios agamsa cá bhfuil an portach,' arsa Dónall. 'Caithfidh tusa a theacht liom.'

'Thig leat siúl suas an bealach mór,' arsa an feirmeoir, 'agus leanfaidh mise thú.'

Bhí a fhios ag Dónall nach raibh a dhíth ar an fheirmeoir ach leithscéal fanacht sa bhaile go bhfaigheadh sé beagán bídh.

'Ní thig liom a ghabháil gan tú,' arsa Dónall. 'Bhí mé ag brionglóidigh aréir gur fhág mé leat féin thú agus gur stróc madadh crosta na héadaí de do dhroim. Ní thig liom tú a ligint amach as m'amharc go dtige mo dhearthháir ar ais.'

'Bhí do dhearthháir ina fhear uasal ach tá tusa in d'amadán,' arsa an feirmeoir.

Chonaic an feirmeoir go raibh Dónall róchliste aige agus ní raibh dadaí le déanamh aige ach a ghabháil leis chun an phortaigh. D'oibir siad i gcuideachta a chéile go dtí go raibh an [oíche ann] agus bhí an suipéar ar an tábla. Bhí dhá ubh os coinne an fheirmeora agus ubh amháin os coinne Dhónaill. Shuigh Dónall síos san áit ar ghnách le fear an tí suí agus d'ith sé an dá ubh.

Bhí an feirmeoir cloíte leis an ocras agus d'aithin sé go maith nach raibh gar an bia a thógáil de bhrí go mbeadh a sháith ag Dónall i gcás ar bith. Ón bhomaite sin go dtí deireadh na seachtaine fuair Dónall neart bídh.

'An bhfuil dúil agat a ghabháil abhaile?' arsa an feirmeoir ar maidin Dé Sathairn.

'Tá mé sásta fanacht seachtain eile,' arsa Dónall.

'Níl mise sásta tú a choinneáil níos faide,' arsa an feirmeoir. 'Tá do dhearthháir ina bhuachaill mhacánta agus má thigeann sé ar ais coinneoidh mé é go deireadh na bliana.'

'Más mar sin atá an scéal,' arsa Dónall, 'rachaidh mise abhaile inniu agus beidh mo dhearthháir anseo maidin Dé Luain. Tá rud amháin ba mhaith liom a insint duit agus ba chóir duit é a choinneáil i gcuimhne. Má thógann do bhean an bia ón tábla fhad is atá mo dhearthháir ag ithe beidh ordú aige a theacht abhaile agus tiocfaidh mise ina áit.'

Nuair a tháinig Dónall abhaile d'inis sé do Sheán an méid a tharla.

'Chuir tú múineadh air,' arsa Seán.

'Féadann tú a bheith cinnte go dtearn,' arsa Dónall. 'Beidh tú ábalta do thuarastal a shaothrú gan níos mó trioblóide.'

'Agus nuair a bheas an t-am thuas,' arsa Seán, 'is dóiche nach mbeidh go leor airgid agam leis an stocaire a shásamh.'

'Fág sin agamsa,' arsa Dónall. 'Bhí mise inchurtha leis an fheirmeoir agus beidh mé inchurtha leis an stocaire.'

Le scéal fada a dhéanamh gairid chaith Seán bliain ag an fheirmeoir agus tháinig abhaile lena thuarastal.

'Cad é mar a chuir tú isteach an t-am?' arsa Dónall.

'Go han-mhaith,' arsa Seán. 'Fuair mé neart bídh agus ní raibh an obair róchruaidh.'

'An bhfuil dúil agat go fóill níon an stocaire a phósadh?' arsa Dónall.

'Tá,' arsa Seán. 'Thig liom deich bpunta a dhíol síos.'

'Níl sin riachtanach,' arsa Dónall. 'Cuirfidh mise an méid a shílim ceart isteach i sparán agus thig leat é a fhágáil ar an tábla. Beidh mise leat agus féadann tú an chuid eile a fhágáil agamsa.'

'Maith go leor,' arsa Seán.

Cupla oíche ina dhiaidh sin tháinig Dónall agus Seán go teach an stocaire. Ní raibh duine ar bith sa teach ach amháin an níon agus chuir sí fáilte chroíúil rompu.

'An bhfuil d'athair ó bhaile?' arsa Dónall.

'Níl,' arsa an cailín, 'beidh sé anseo ar an bhomaite.'

'Sin mar is fearr é,' arsa Dónall. 'Ba mhaith liom cleamhnas a dhéanamh idir thú féin agus mo dheartháir.'

Leis sin shiúil an stocaire isteach ar an doras.

'Tá lúcháir orm an péire agaibh a fheiceáil,' ar seisean.

'Go raibh maith agat,' arsa na deartháireacha.

'Cuir do chuid airgid ar an tábla,' arsa Dónall le Seán. Chuir Seán an sparán ar an tábla.

'Cuntas airgead Sheáin ar dtús,' arsa Dónall leis an stocaire, 'agus ansin cuirfidh mise síos mo chuid féin.'

Thóg an stocaire an sparán ina láimh.

'Tá sé trom go leor,' ar seisean le Seán, 'agus más rud é nach bhfuil ann ach ór rinne tú cúis mhaith.'

D'fhoscail sé an sparán agus dhoirt an t-airgead amach ar an tábla. Ní raibh dadaí sa sparán ach ocht bpingin déag in airgead rua. Tháinig taom feirge ar an stocaire.

'An ag iarraidh amadán a dhéanamh díom atá tú?' ar seisean le Seán. Ní raibh a fhios ag Seán go dtí an bomaite sin cad é an méid airgid a chuir Dónall sa sparán.

'Fan ort,' arsa Dónall leis an stocaire. 'Thig liomsa an cás a shocrú. Níor chuir mise mo chuid airgid síos go fóill.'

Leis sin chuir sé a lámh ina phóca agus d'fhág dhá phingin ar an tábla.

'An cluiche cártaí atá a dhíth oraibh?' arsa an stocaire.

'Ní hea,' arsa Dónall. 'Gheall tú do níon a thabhairt do cá bith duine againn is mó a mbeadh airgead aige i gceann bliana. Tá an bhuaidh le Seán agus is leis do níon. Is tú féin a rinne an réiteach. Má théann tú chun dlí nó fiú do níon féin nach mbeidh in d'éadan.'

'Beidh go cinnte,' arsa an cailín. 'Dlí ann nó as,' ar sise, 'ní phósfaidh mé fear go deo ach Seán.'

'Tá mé buailte agus scriosta,' arsa an stocaire.

'Tá an chuid is fearr den mhargadh agat,' arsa Dónall, 'dá mbeadh ciall agat amharc ar an cheist mar is cóir. Níl mac ar bith agat leis an talamh seo a oibriú agus tá an fheirm ag gabháil amú. Beidh Seán mar mhac agat agus ba chóir duit buíochas a thabhairt do Dhia in ionad a bheith ag cur in aghaidh A thola. Is í do níon atá a dhíth ar Sheán agus ní hé do chuid airgid.'

'Tá an méid a deir tú fíor,' arsa an stocaire. 'Chead ag an phéire réiteach a dhéanamh i gcomhair na bainise agus díolfaidh mise an costas.'

'Tabhair domh do lámh,' arsa Dónall. 'Tá bród orm asat.'

'Tá bród orm féin,' arsa an stocaire, 'mac mar Sheán a bheith agam ó seo amach.'

Pósadh an lánúin cupla lá ina dhiaidh sin agus cuireann sin deireadh leis an scéal.

NÓTA

1 *Derry People and Tirconaill News,* 30 May, 6, 13, 20, 27 June 1936.

An Bhean Déirce agus an Meisceoir

Oíche amháin ins an tsean-am tháinig bean déirce go teach feirmeora i bparóiste na nGleanntach. Bhí fear an tí, a bhean agus seachtar páistí i ndiaidh an Paidrín Páirteach a chríochnú agus bhí siad ina suí thart fán tinidh.

'Tá sé náireach,' ar sise, 'scairtint ag teach ar bith chomh mall seo san oíche ach níl dlí ar an riachtanas.'

'Tá sin fíor,' arsa fear an tí, 'agus tá mé cinnte nach gan réasún inteacht atá tú ar do chois ar uair an mheán oíche.'

'Tá tú ceart,' arsa an bhean déirce. 'Má fhaighim foscadh an tí seo go maidin geallaim duit go dtitfidh beannacht Dé ort féin agus ar do chúram.'

'Tá sé comhgarach ag fiche bliain ó tógadh an bothán seo agus níor tiontaíodh aon duine bocht ón doras ó shin,' arsa an feirmeoir.

'Go dtuga Dia a luach duit,' arsa an bhean déirce. 'Is trua liom,' ar sise, 'nach dtig le cuid de do chomharsanaigh an scéal céanna a insint. Tháinig mise fhad le teach sa chomharsanacht seo ag titim na hoíche agus leis an fhírinne a insint bhí fáilte ag bean an tí romham. Nuair a bhí muid ag déanamh réidh le a ghabháil a luí tháinig fear an tí isteach. Bhí sé ar meisce agus d'iarr sé orm an teach a fhágáil agus gan a theacht ar ais ní ba mhó. Thoisigh an bhean ag caoineadh ach níor chuir seo bac ar bith air. Chuir mé mo mhála ar mo dhroim agus tháinig mé anseo.'

'Cuireann an scéal sin iontas orm,' arsa an feirmeoir. 'Beidh drochdheireadh leis.'

'Beidh,' arsa an bhean déirce, 'ach caithfimid an bhean a shábháil.'

'An síleann tú go bhfuil sí i gcontúirt?'

'Tá mé cinnte de,' arsa an bhean. 'Tá sé as a mheabhair anois agus níl bomaite le cailleadh. Tá tusa 'd'fhear láidir agus ní bheidh moill ort an bhuaidh a fháil air. Cuir ort do hata agus rachaidh mise leat.'

'Nach fearr duitse fanacht anseo?' arsa an feirmeoir.

'Ní fearr,' arsa an bhean déirce. 'Sábháil thusa an bhean agus bhéarfaidh mise iarracht anam an fhir a shábháil.'

'Beidh lóchrann a dhíth orainn,' arsa an feirmeoir. 'Tá an oíche dorcha.'

'Ná bac leis an lóchrann,' arsa an bhean. 'Tiocfaidh solas ó neamh chugainn.'

Shiúil siad amach ar an bhealach mhór an áit a raibh gasúr beag ag fanacht leo, lóchrann ina láimh. Shiúil an gasúr rompu.

'Ní fhaca mé an gasúr sin riamh roimhe,' arsa an feirmeoir.

'Chonaic tú é go cinnte,' arsa an bhean déirce, 'ach rinne tú dearmad de. Sin mac an fhir atá ar meisce, an gasúr a fuair bás cúig bliana ó shin.'

'Moladh do Dhia,' arsa an feirmeoir.

Nuair a tháinig siad fhad leis an teach ina raibh an meisceoir ina chónaí chuaigh an buachaill beag agus an lóchrann as amharc. Bhí doras an tí foscailte agus shiúil an feirmeoir agus an bhean déirce isteach. Chonaic siad an fear a bhí ar meisce ina luí i gcoirnéal den chisteanach. Bhí a bhean ina suí ar stól lena thaobh agus í ag caoineadh go brónach.

'Cad é atá contráilte?' arsa an feirmeoir.

'Thit sé de chathaoir,' arsa an bhean, 'agus bhuail sé a cheann in éadan an bhalla. Tá eagla orm go bhfuil sé marbh.'

D'amharc an feirmeoir ar an fhear a bhí ina luí. 'Níl sé marbh go fóill,' ar seisean, 'ach tá mé den bharúil go bhfuil an chuid is fearr dá chuid laetha thart. Is dóiche go bhfuil a chloigeann scoilte ach mar sin féin tiocfaidh sé chuige féin sula bhfaighidh sé bás.'

'Arbh fhéidir linn é a thógáil ón urlár?' arsa an bhean.

'Bheadh sé dainséarach é a chorrú go fóill,' arsa an feirmeoir. 'Is cosúil gur ól sé an mhórchuid poitín.'

'Bhí sé ar meisce nuair a tháinig sé abhaile,' arsa an bhean, 'agus d'ól sé leathphionta as buidéal ó shin.'

'Níl sé iontach gur thit sé,' arsa an feirmeoir. 'Cá bhfuil an bhean déirce?' ar seisean.

'Níl a fhios agam,' arsa an bhean. 'Ní fhaca mé í ag imeacht.'

'Ní dóigh liom gur duine saolta atá inti,' arsa an feirmeoir. 'Dá mbeadh sí anseo anois le cuideachta a choinneáil leatsa rachainnse fá choinne sagairt.'

'Abróimid cúig dheichniúr den Phaidrín,' arsa an bhean. 'Cuideoidh Dia linn,' ar sise.

Sula raibh an Paidrín críochnaithe shiúil an bhean déirce agus sagart isteach ar an doras.

'Tá mo chuid oibre déanta anois,' arsa an bhean déirce. Shiúil sí amach agus ní fhaca aon duine sa pharóiste í ón lá sin go dtí an lá inniu.

D'inis an sagart don fheirmeoir go raibh sé i dteach fá thuairim míle ar shiúl an áit a raibh bean ag fágáil an tí gur casadh an bhean déirce air. 'Dúirt sí liom a theacht anseo,' arsa an sagart, 'agus tá lúcháir orm go dtáinig mé.' Leis sin d'fhoscail an fear a bhí ina luí ar an urlár a shúile. 'Glóir do Dhia,' ar seisean, 'tím sagart.'

Uair ina dhiaidh sin bhí a shíocháin déanta aige leis an Dia a chruthaigh é agus ag éirí na gréine bhí sé ar shlua na marbh.

'Beidh cuimhne agam ar an oíche seo go deo,' arsa an sagart nuair a bhí sé ag imeacht.

NÓTA

1 *Derry People and Tirconaill News*, 4, 11 July 1936.

GLEANN DOMHAIN

Fá thuairim trí mhíle ó bhaile Ard an Rátha tá baile talaimh ar a dtugtar Gleann Domhain. Fuair an áit an t-ainm seo ar siocair go bhfuil gleann domhain in aice leis agus gleann beag níos deise níl le fáil i gContae Dhún na nGall. Deir na seandaoine gur fhan na siógaí seal mór blianta san áit seo i ndiaidh a ndíbeartha ó áiteacha eile i nDún na nGall agus Tír Eoghain. Rachadh cuid de na seandaoine a fhad agus a rá go bhfuil siógaí le feiceáil sa ghleann chéanna go dtí an lá inniu, go háirithe ag am na Samhna agus ag bánú an lae an chéad lá de mhí na Bealtaine. Tá sruthán uisce ag reathaigh ar fud an ghleanna agus is é seo an teorainn idir Gleann Domhain agus Carraig an tSléibhe. Tá carraigeacha móra ar gach taobh agus uaimh ansiúd agus anseo atá mór go leor le gearrán a cheangal iontu.

Fá thuairim céad go leith bliain ó shin bhí fear ina chónaí i gCarraig an tSléibhe arbh ainm dó Séamas Ó Maoilchiaráin. Lá amháin tháinig sé fhad leis an ghleann ar lorg caorach a bhí caillte aige. Ba leis an talamh ar thaobh amháin den ghleann. Shonraigh sé gur hitheadh an féar a bhí idir na carraigeacha isteach go dtí an talamh siúd is nach raibh lorg coise aon chineál beathaigh le feiceáil. 'Seo obair na sióg,' ar seisean leis féin, 'cá bith atá siad a dhéanamh leis an fhéar.'

Tháinig sé abhaile leis an chaora agus d'inis dona bhean an méid a chonaic sé. 'Tá dúil agam,' ar seisean, 'a ghabháil go dtí an gleann anocht go bhfeice mé cad é atá ag teacht ar an fhéar.'

'B'fhearr liom an féar a chailleadh ná titim amach leis na siógaí,' arsa an bhean.

'Ní bheidh mé róchruaidh orthu,' arsa Séamas, 'má chruthaíonn siad go bhfuil an féar a dhíth orthu.'

Oíche réabghealaí a bhí ann agus ar an mheán oíche bhí Séamas ina shuí ar thomóg luachra sa ghleann ag dréim na siógaí a fheiceáil. Chuala sé fá dheireadh fuaim mar a bheadh ba ag ithe féir thart fá dtaobh de ach ní fhaca sé dadaí. Ní raibh a fhios aige cad é ab fhearr dó a dhéanamh. Chuaigh sé fhad leis an aill ab airde sa ghleann. Bhí uaimh ag bun na haille agus nuair a d'amharc sé isteach chonaic sé solas ag an cheann ab fhaide uaidh. Tháinig sé chun tosaigh go faichilleach agus seo an rud a chonaic sé: bean bheag ag sníomh ar thuirne óir agus fiche páiste ag imirt ar an urlár.

'Nach mall atá tú ag obair?' arsa Séamas.

'Níl tú féin 'do chodladh,' arsa an bhean sí.

'Níl,' arsa Séamas. 'Ní thig liom codladh go dtí go bhfaighe mé le fios cé ar leis na ba atá ag ithe mo chuid féir.'

Ar an bhomaite sin tháinig fear beag a raibh bearád dearg air isteach.

'Is linne na ba,' ar seisean le Séamas, 'ach ní fhaca tusa iad de bhrí go bhfuil siad ar dhath an fhéir.'

'Nach bhfuil a fhios agat,' arsa Séamas, 'go bhfuil do chuid ba ag ithe mo chuid féirse an uile oíche agus nach bhfuil tú ag díol cíosa ná *tax*aí?'

'Tá sin fíor ar dhóigh ach níl ar dhóigh eile,' arsa an fear beag. 'Siúil amach,' ar seisean le Séamas, 'agus tífidh tú go bhfuil mé féin agus mo mhuirín ag díol ar son an fhéir.'

Tháinig siad amach as an uaimh agus ansin dúirt an fear beag sí: 'An bhfeiceann tú aon rud ar bharr na haille?'

Bhí solas breá gealaí ann agus chonaic Séamas bearach dá chuid féin ar imeall na haille.

'Tím an bearach is fearr in mo sheilbh ach ní thig liom í a shábháil anois. Titfidh sí anuas go cinnte agus brisfear a cnámha.'

'Ní baol di titim,' arsa an tsióg. 'An bhfeiceann tú go bhfuil gasúr beag ina sheasamh ag a ceann?'

'Tím go cinnte,' arsa Séamas.

'Maith go leor,' arsa an fear sí. 'Sin gasúr beag de mo chuidse agus dhéanfaidh sé an bearach a thiomáint ar gcúl go dtí an talamh cothrom. Tá sé ag tabhairt aire do do chuid eallaigh le dhá bhliain agus ach ab é sin chaillfí mórán acu.'

'Cad é mar a thig liom buíochas a thabhairt duit?' arsa Séamas.

'Níl gnoithe duit buíochas ar bith a thabhairt domh,' arsa an tsióg. 'Níl a dhíth orm ach cead a fháil uait mo chuid ba a chothú leis an fhéar atá ag fás idir na carraigeacha seo. Ní bheadh na páistí beo gan braon beag bainne.'

'Tá mo chead agat,' arsa Séamas, 'na ba a chothú oíche agus lá ar an uile throigh de thalamh ó seo go Cuiscreachán.'

'Ní itheann siad mórán féir,' arsa an tsióg. 'Ar mhaith leat iad a fheiceáil?' ar seisean.

'Ba mhaith liom,' arsa Séamas.

'Tá an ghealach faoi néal anois,' arsa an fear beag, 'ach thig leat iad a fheiceáil le solas an lóchrainn seo.'

Shiúil siad go bruach an tsrutháin an áit a raibh na ba beaga ag ól.

'Níl agam ach triúr anois,' arsa an tsióg. 'Ba ghnách liom ceithre cinn a choinneáil ach dhíol mé ceann acu le bean sí i gCor an Easa.'

D'amharc Séamas ar na ba. Ní raibh aon cheann acu níos mó ná coinín agus bhí dath an fhéir orthu.

'Rathúnas orthu,' arsa Séamas. 'Ní fhaca mé le linn mo shaoil beathaigh bheaga níos deise. Inis domh,' ar seisean leis an tsióg, 'cad é an fáth nach n-itheann siad an féar ar an taobh eile den ghleann?'

'Tá réasún leis sin,' arsa an tsióg. 'Rinne muintir Ghleann Domhain sconsa ar a dtaobh féin den ghleann agus níl coimheád ar bith a dhíth ar a gcuid ba. Ní fhágann sin leithscéal agamsa ná ag mo chlann na ba a chur ar a gcuid ingilte.'

'Tá mé den bharúil,' arsa Séamas, 'nach bhfuil iomlán na sióg chomh hionraice leatsa.'

'Féadann sin a bheith fíor,' arsa an tsióg.

'Caithfidh mé buíochas a thabhairt do bhean an tí agus an buachaill beag atá ag tabhairt aire do mo chuid bearach sula dté mé abhaile,' arsa Séamas.

Chuaigh siad isteach san uaimh arís agus shuigh Séamas ar stacán giúise a bhí i lár an urláir.

'Tá mórán páistí agat,' ar seisean leis an mháthair.

'Níl againn ach fiche cloigeann anois,' arsa an bhean. 'Bhí beirt agus fiche againn anuraidh ach fuair an bheirt ab óige den mhuirín bás an geimhreadh seo a chuaigh thart leis an bhruitíneach. Tá luibh ag fás ins an ghleann seo a leigheasfadh an aicíd sin i mbomaite ach bhí sneachta ar an talamh agus ní raibh an luibh le fáil.'

'Tá páiste agamsa,' arsa Séamas, 'atá ina luí leis an aicíd chéanna san am atá i láthair.'

'Má tá sin mar sin,' arsa an bhean, 'beidh an leigheas abhaile leat.'

'Beidh lúcháir orm an leigheas a fháil,' arsa Séamas, 'ach caithfidh mé cineáltas inteacht a thaispeáint duit féin agus iomlán na muiríne seo.'

'Tá do chuid cineáltais le feiceáil anseo cheana féin,' arsa an bhean. 'Amharc cad é atá na páistí a dhéanamh.'

D'amharc Séamas thart. Bhí gach duine de na páistí ag ól bainne as méaracán. Ní raibh an duine ab airde acu níos mó ná troigh ar airde agus bhí mórán acu i bhfad níos lú.

'Tím,' arsa Séamas, 'nach bhfuil siad deacair a shásamh.'

'Níl fán am seo den bhliain,' arsa an bhean, 'ach bíonn bia gann ins an gheimhreadh.'

'Bíonn neart min choirce agamsa ar feadh an gheimhridh,' arsa Séamas, 'agus má tá sé fóirsteanach agaibh, ná spáráil é.'

'Go raibh maith agat,' arsa an bhean, 'ach b'fhearr linn an coirce a fháil de bhrí go dtig linn min a dhéanamh de ar ár ndóigh féin.'

'Maith go leor,' arsa Séamas. 'Gheobhaidh sibh mála coirce roimh Oíche Shamhna. Sin an tuarastal atá mé ag gabháil a thabhairt don ghasúr a shábháil an bearach.'

'Ní bheidh gnoithe againn leis an oiread sin coirce,' arsa an bhean. 'Is dóiche go mbeimid ag imeacht as an áit seo ag tús na Bealtaine.'

'Ba mhór an trua sibh imeacht choíche,' arsa Séamas. 'Ní iarrfainn comharsanaigh níos fearr.'

'Nuair a thiocfas an scairt,' arsa an bhean, 'ní bheidh sé inár gcumhacht fanacht níos faide. Tiocfaidh sióga eile go dtí an gleann seo ach beidh siad dofheicseanach ag daoine saolta. Tiocfaidh do lása fosta. Beidh an taobh seo agus dhá cheann an ghleanna i seilbh na mBreisleán agus an taobh eile i seilbh Chlann tSuibhne. Beidh an loch seo thoir ag coinneáil solais le muintir Ard an Rátha agus beidh dearmad déanta ortsa agus ormsa.'

'Tigeann deireadh le gach ní ar an tsaol seo,' arsa Séamas. 'Tá an t-am agam a ghabháil abhaile.'

'Ná himigh gan an luibh,' arsa an bhean. 'Cuideoidh m'fhear leat é a phiocadh.'

Bhí an lá ag glanadh nuair a tháinig Séamas agus an fear beag amach as an uaimh. Phioc siad an luibh agus thug Séamas a aghaidh ar an bhaile. Thug sé an leigheas do mhórán daoine sa chomharsanacht agus sin an fáth nach bhfuair aon pháiste bás le bruitíneacht i gCarraig an tSléibhe ná i nGleann Domhain ón lá sin go dtí an lá inniu. Tháinig tarngaireacht na mná sí isteach fíor agus sin deireadh an scéil.

NÓTA

1 *Derry People and Tirconaill News*, 18, 25 July, 1 August 1936.

An Táilliúir agus a Mhac

Ins na laetha fadó bhí táilliúir ina chónaí i ngleanntán uaigneach fá thuairim dhá mhíle ó Leitir Ceanainn. Fán am a thoisíos ár scéal bhí mac amháin aige a bhí fiche bliain d'aois. D'fhéach sé a cheird féin a fhoghlaim dó ach bhí a intinn déanta suas ag an mhac gan a bheith ina tháilliúir go deo.

Lá amháin dúirt an mac lena athair go raibh dúil aige a ghabháil go Contae Ard Mhacha ar lorg oibre.

'Tá sin greannmhar,' arsa an t-athair. 'Ní thearn tú obair lae ó rugadh thú agus tá eagla orm go mbeidh tú mar sin.'

'Ní raibh obair ar bith le déanamh anseo ach táilliúireacht agus níl sin fóirsteanach agamsa.'

'Bíodh do dhóigh féin agat, a Éamainn,' arsa an t-athair. 'Mura bhfuil ciall go leor agat le aire a thabhairt duit féin ó seo amach, rinne tú drochúsáid de do chuid ama.'

'Ná bíodh eagla ar bith ort, a athair,' arsa Éamann. 'Tiocfaidh mé ar ais lá inteacht le molltraí saibhris agus gheobhaidh tú scríste in do sheanlaetha.'

'Ba mhaith liom go dtiocfadh do scéal isteach fíor,' arsa an t-athair, 'ach ní chuirfidh caint den chineál seo cnaipí ar phéire úr brístí.'

Lá arna mhárach, i ndiaidh beannacht a athara a fháil, thug Éamann a aghaidh ar Chontae Ard Mhacha. Chaith sé cupla lá ar lorg oibre ach sin a raibh aige ar a shon. Fá dheireadh tháinig sé fhad le tobar a bhí faoi charraig agus d'ól sé deoch uisce. Bhí tom sceiche in aice leis an tobar agus chonaic sé fear beag ina sheasamh faoin tom. Labhair an fear beag leis go carthanach agus chuir ceist air cad é an fáth ar fhág sé Dún na nGall.

'Tháinig mé anseo ar lorg oibre,' arsa Éamann, 'agus más sióg mhaith thusa ba mhaith liom do chuidiú a fháil.'

'Ní thig liom mórán a dhéanamh ar do shon,' arsa an tsióg, 'ach thig liom comhairle do leasa a thabhairt duit.'

'Sin a bhfuil mé a iarraidh,' arsa Éamann.

'Maith go leor,' arsa an fear beag sí. 'An bhfeiceann tú an caisleán atá ar bharr an chnoic sin thall?' ar seisean.

'Tím go cinnte,' arsa Éamann.

'Tá fathach ina chónaí ansin,' arsa an tsióg, 'agus tá an caisleán lán den troscán is luachmhaire ar an domhan.'

'Cad é an mhaith a dhéanfas sin domhsa?' arsa Éamann.

'Más rud é nach bhfuil dúil agat saibhreas a chruinniú,' arsa an tsióg, 'cad chuige a dtáinig tú anseo?'

'Mura bhfuil dóigh ar bith le saibhreas a fháil,' arsa Éamann, 'ach ag goid troscán tí, tá eagla orm go bhfaighidh mé bás 'm'fhear bhocht.'

'Ná bí in d'amadán,' arsa an tsióg. 'Níl aon rud sa chaisleán nár ghoid an fathach ó Ríte na hÉireann agus níl dochar duitse do chuid den chreach a fháil.'

'Cuireann sin athrú ar an scéal,' arsa Éamann. 'Cad é an t-am is fearr domh tús a chur ar an obair?'

'Anocht,' arsa an tsióg. 'Rachaimid fhad leis an chaisleán ag titim na hoíche.'

Gan mhoill i ndiaidh luí na gréine tháinig Éamann agus an tsióg fhad leis an chaisleán.

'Cad é do chomhairle anois?' arsa Éamann.

'Tá mé ag gabháil a thabhairt clóca duit,' arsa an tsióg, 'agus creid mise go mbeidh sé a dhíth ort. Coinnigh seo i gcuimhne: fhad is a bheas an clóca ort beidh tú dofheicseanach ach, sin is uilig, caithfidh tú a bheith faichilleach. Ná tabhair iarracht aon rud a thabhairt leat nach mbeidh tú ábalta a iompar.'

'Sin comhairle mhaith,' arsa Éamann. 'An mbeidh tusa liom?'

'Ní bheidh,' arsa an tsióg. 'Tá dúil agam fanacht anseo faoi scáth na gcrann agus má thig mí-ádh ar bith ort dhéanfaidh mé mo dhícheall tú a shábháil.'

Chuir Éamann air an clóca agus i mbomaite bhí sé sa chaisleán. Shiúil sé leis ó sheomra go seomra ach ní fhaca sé duine ar bith. Fá dheireadh tháinig sé fhad le cisteanach an-mhór agus chonaic sé an fathach ina shuí ag cois na tineadh. Sheas Éamann ar chúl an dorais. Tháinig cat mór, dubh thart agus ghreamaigh a chuid crúb ann. Bhí lúcháir air an chisteanach a fhágáil ach lean an cat é go dtí an chuid íochtarach den halla. Shíl an fathach gur ar lorg luchóige a bhí an cat agus níor chorraigh sé.

'Cuirfidh an cat seo deireadh liom,' arsa Éamann leis féin. Bhí solas an lae ag claonadh agus ba deacair an cat a fheiceáil.

'Coinnigh suas do mhisneach,' arsa guth lena thaobh.

Ba é an tsióg a labhair. 'Seo tua,' ar seisean, 'agus nuair a gheobhas mise greim rubaill ar an chat, buail thusa buille sa chloigeann air.'

Leis sin thug an cat áladh eile ar Éamann ach bhí greim ag an tsióg ar a ruball. Bhuail Éamann sa cheann é agus thit sé marbh.

'Níl ach cat amháin sa chaisleán,' arsa an tsióg, 'agus féadann tú a ghabháil ar ais go dtí an chisteanach.'

Rinne Éamann mar a hiarradh air agus sheas sé ar chúl an dorais. Bhí an fathach ina shuí ag an tábla san am seo agus bean mhór ag freastal air.

'Cá bhfuil an t-éadach draíochta?' arsa an fathach. Chuaigh an bhean fhad le bocsa sa choirnéal, an áit a raibh an t-éadach, agus chuir ar an tábla é. Shíl Éamann nach raibh ann ach éadach cláir coitianta ach ba ghairid go bhfuair sé le fios nach mar sin a bhí an scéal.

'Bia agus deoch,' arsa an fathach. I mbomaite bhí an t-éadach cumhdaithe leis an uile chineál bídh agus dí. Thoisigh an péire ag ithe. D'ith siad agus d'ith siad go dtí gur shíl Éamann go bpléascfadh siad.

'Go leor,' arsa an fathach fá dheireadh.

D'amharc Éamann ar an éadach. Ní raibh bia ná deoch le feiceáil. Chuir an bhean an t-éadach sa bhocsa athuair agus ansin shuigh sí ag an tinidh. Thit an fathach ina chodladh ar an bhomaite chéanna.

Ní raibh solas ar bith sa chaisleán ach amháin solas na tineadh agus ar an ábhar sin ní raibh moill ar bith ar Éamann an t-éadach cláir a ghoid agus a chúl a thabhairt ar an chaisleán. Bhí an oíche dorcha ach tháinig an tsióg chuige le lóchrann agus shiúil siad i gcuideachta a chéile go dtáinig siad go dtí an áit ar casadh ar a chéile iad ar dtús.

'Rinne tú do chuid oibre go maith,' arsa an tsióg.

'Ní raibh moill orm,' arsa Éamann, 'ach chaillfí mé ach ab é an clóca.'

'Níor shábháil an clóca thú ón chat,' arsa an tsióg.

'Tá tú ceart,' arsa Éamann.

'Cad é atá dúil agat a dhéanamh anois?' arsa an tsióg.

'Dhéanfaidh mé rud ar bith a iarrfas tusa orm,' arsa Éamann. 'Ní thig liom níos lú a dhéanamh ná do chomhairle a ghlacadh.'

'Maith go leor,' arsa an tsióg. 'Is fiú na mílte punta an t-éadach cláir ach caithfidh tú aire mhaith a thabhairt dó. Is fearr duit pilleadh abhaile chuig d'athair. Is fada an aistear ó seo go Dún na nGall agus beidh ort lóistín a fháil gach oíche go dtí go sroiche tú do theach féin. Ná taispeáin an t-éadach do dhuine ar bith ar an bhealach ar eagla go ngoidfí uait é. Má thigeann mí-ádh ort, tar ar ais go dtí an áit a bhfuil tú 'do sheasamh anois agus bhéarfaidh mise comhairle do leasa dhuit. Codail anseo go bánú an lae agus ansin tabhair d'aghaidh ar Dhún na nGall.'

Rinne Éamann mar a hiarradh air agus ag éirí na gréine bhí sé ar a bhealach chun an bhaile. Scairt sé ag teach ansiúd is anseo ar feadh an lae agus fuair sé an méid bídh agus dí a bhí a dhíth air. Bhí eagla air úsáid a dhéanamh den éadach cláir ar siocair an chomhairle a thug an tsióg dó. Nuair a bhí an oíche ag titim tháinig sé fhad le teach mór a bhí suite in imeall coilleadh. Ba le fear saibhir an teach agus hinseadh d'Éamann go raibh fáilte roimhe fanacht go maidin.

'Is trua liom,' arsa fear an tí, 'go bhfuil an suipéar thart. Chuaigh mo bhean amach a chuartaíocht agus tá na searbhóntaí ina gcodladh.'

'Ná bac leis,' arsa Éamann. 'Beidh suipéar maith ar an tábla i mbomaite.' Tharraing sé amach an t-éadach cláir agus spréigh ar an tábla é.

'Suigh thusa ag ceann an tábla,' ar seisean le fear an tí, 'agus suífidh mise anseo.'

Rinne an fear mar a hiarradh air agus ansin dúirt Éamann: 'Bia agus deoch.'

Níor luaithe a bhí na focla ráite aige ná bhí an t-éadach cumhdaithe leis an uile chineál bídh agus dí.

D'ith siad agus d'ól siad go raibh siad sásta.

'Go leor,' arsa Éamann fá dheireadh agus d'imigh na neathannaí maithe as amharc.

'Bhéarfaidh mé míle punta dhuit ar an éadach cláir,' arsa an fear saibhir.

'Ní dhíolfainn é ar ór ná airgead,' arsa Éamann.

Gan mhoill ina dhiaidh sin tháinig bean an tí abhaile. Chóirigh sí leabaidh mhaith d'Éamann agus chodail sé go suaimhneach go maidin.

I lár na hoíche tháinig fear an tí go dtí an seomra ina raibh Éamann ina chodladh. Bhí an t-éadach cláir ar chathaoir ag taobh na leapa. Thug sé leis é go socair agus d'fhág éadach cláir eile a bhí cosúil leis ina áit.

Nuair a d'éirigh Éamann ar maidin bhí a bhricfeasta ar an tábla. 'Cad chuige nár fhan tú go mbeadh an bricfeasta againn ón éadach draíochta?' arsa Éamann.

'Thug tú suipéar maith domhsa aréir,' arsa fear an tí, 'agus tá sé beag go leor againne costas an bhricfeasta a bheith orainn.'

Nuair a bhí an béile thart d'fhág Éamann slán acu agus thug aghaidh ar an bhaile. 'Bhí mé 'mo bhuachaill bhocht an lá a d'fhág mé teach m'athara,' ar seisean leis féin, 'ach tá mé 'm'fhear shaibhir anois agus beidh fhad is a bheas an t-éadach cláir seo in mo sheilbh.' Is beag a shíl sé nárbh fhiú dhá phingin an t-éadach a bhí faoina ascaill aige. Ansin smaoinigh sé ar an chomhairle a thug an tsióg dó agus rinne sé suas a intinn gan an t-éadach a thaispeáint do dhuine ar bith eile go sroichfeadh sé an baile.

Tráthnóna Dé Sathairn tháinig sé ar amharc an tí inar rugadh é agus chuir seo lúcháir ar a chroí. Chonaic a athair ag teacht é agus tháinig sé giota den bhealach ina araicis.

'Nár dhúirt mé leat an lá a d'fhág mé an baile,' arsa Éamann, 'go dtiocfainn ar ais in m'fhear shaibhir?'

'Dúirt tú sin go cinnte,' arsa an t-athair, 'agus tá súil agam go dtáinig do scéal isteach fíor.'

'Beidh a fhios agat an t-iomlán anocht,' arsa Éamann. 'Bhéarfaimid cuireadh do na comharsanaigh uilig agus nuair a bheas siad cruinnithe cuirfidh mise iontas orthu.'

'Caithfidh tú bia a cheannach fána gcoinne,' arsa an t-athair, 'má bheir tú cuireadh dóibh.'

'Tá bia agus deoch anseo ar son na mílte,' arsa Éamann ag tógáil an t-éadach cláir ina láimh.

'Is maith do scéal má tá sé fíor,' arsa athair Éamainn.

Gan mhoill i ndiaidh thitim na hoíche chruinnigh na comharsanaigh isteach. Chuir Éamann fáilte rompu agus d'inis dóibh gur éirigh leis go maith i gContae Ard Mhacha. Ansin chuir sé tábla i lár an urláir. 'Féadann sibh suí thart fán tábla anois,' ar seisean. Spréigh sé an t-éadach cláir agus dúirt: 'Bia agus deoch.'

Níor tháinig bia ná deoch.

'Bia agus deoch,' ar seisean arís. Ní raibh gar ann.

'Tá rud inteacht contráilte,' arsa Éamann sa deireadh.

'D'fhéach duine inteacht amadán a dhéanamh díot,' arsa an táilliúir.

'Beidh mé inchurtha leis go fóill,' arsa Éamann.

'Ná bac leis,' arsa an t-athair. 'Seo nóta punta a cheannós neart tae agus siúcra agus an méid aráin atá a dhíth orainn.'

'Ní thig linn níos fearr a dhéanamh fá láthair,' arsa Éamann. 'Gheobhaidh mise an méid lón tí atá riachtanach agus ag éirí na gréine beidh mé ar mo bhealach go hArd Mhacha arís.'

D'imigh leis go dtí an siopa ba chomhgaraí agus fhad is a bhí sé imithe dúirt an táilliúir leis na comharsanaigh go raibh eagla air go raibh seachrán intinne ag teacht ar a mhac. 'Níor thug sé aon rud abhaile leis,' ar seisean, 'ach an seanéadach cláir sin agus ní fiú trí leithphingne é.'

'Cuirfidh mé geall,' arsa fear a bhí ina shuí ag ceann an tábla, 'gur casadh na siógaí air agus go dtug siad an t-éadach dó mar gheall ar cleas a imirt air.'

'Tá mise den bharúil chéanna,' arsa comharsa eile.

'Bíodh sin mar is mian leis,' arsa an táilliúir, 'ní chuirfidh mise bac air imeacht athuair. Tá mé cinnte go bhfuil saibhreas i ndán dó agus go n-éireoidh leis go fóill.'

Tháinig Éamann ar ais leis an lón tí agus in am ghairid bhí suipéar maith ar an tábla. Bhí siad ag ithe, ag ól agus ag gabháil cheoil go meán oíche, ach thug siad fá dear nach raibh fonn ar bith grinn ar Éamann. Nuair a chuaigh na comharsanaigh abhaile chuaigh sé a luí go tostach.

Ag breacadh an lae ar maidin lá arna mhárach d'éirigh an táilliúir mar gheall ar tinidh a dhéanamh agus bricfeasta a ghléas fá choinne Éamainn. Gan mhoill ina dhiaidh sin d'éirigh Éamann agus nuair a d'amharc a athair air d'aithin sé nach raibh sé róshásta ina intinn.

'Ar chodail tú néal ar bith?' arsa an táilliúir.

'Féadaim a rá nár chodail,' arsa Éamann. 'Níl suaimhneas ar bith i ndán domh go bhfaighe mé le fios cad é atá contráilte leis an éadach cláir. Cupla lá ó shin thairg fear saibhir míle punta domh air agus anois ní fiú dadaí é.'

'Sin scéal iontach,' arsa an táilliúir. 'Má tá dúil agat imeacht arís ith bricfeasta maith agus ní bheidh ocras ort go dtí go mbeidh sé anonn go maith sa lá.'

Nuair a bhí an bricfeasta thart chuir Éamann tús ar a aistear. Thug sé a aghaidh ar Ard Mhacha mar a rinne sé cheana agus ba bheag an scríste a fuair sé go dtáinig sé fhad leis an áit ar casadh an tsióg air ar dtús. Shuigh sé faoin tom sceiche agus thit ina chodladh. Nuair a mhuscail sé bhí an tsióg ina sheasamh lena thaobh.

'Tá mé buartha,' arsa Éamann, 'go raibh agam le a theacht ar ais agus is brónach an scéal atá agam le hinsint.'

'Cad é atá contráilte?' arsa an tsióg.

'Tá an uile rud contráilte,' arsa Éamann. 'Thug mé an t-éadach cláir abhaile agus tá sé chomh neamhúsáideach le seanphéire stocaí.'

'Cuirfidh mé geall,' arsa an tsióg, 'nár ghlac tú an chomhairle a thug mise dhuit. Ar thaispeáin tú an t-éadach do dhuine ar bith ar do bhealach?'

'Faraor,' arsa Éamann, 'rinne mé dearmad ócáid amháin. Chaith mé oíche i dteach inar chónaigh fear saibhir agus bhí suipéar againn ón éadach cláir. D'fhág mé an t-éadach ar chathaoir ag taobh na leapa inar chodail mé agus thug mé liom é ar maidin. Is dóigh liom gur chaill sé an draíocht de bhrí nach dtigeann bia ná deoch air anois is cuma cad é na focla a deirtear.'

'Cá bhfuil an t-éadach a bhí abhaile leat?' arsa an tsióg.

'Seo é,' arsa Éamann, á tharraingt amach as a phóca.

'Bhí an fear saibhir róchliste agat,' arsa an tsióg. 'D'fhág sé an tseanbhratóg sin in do sheomra nuair a bhí tú 'do chodladh agus choinnigh sé an t-éadach draíochta.'

'Ag tórramh an diabhail go raibh sé,' arsa Éamann. 'Chreach sé mé ar son mo chuid cineáltais.'

'Níor thuill tú rud ar bith eile,' arsa an tsióg. 'Dúirt mé leat a bheith faichilleach.'

'Tá sin fíor,' arsa Éamann. 'Tá náire orm a aidmheáil go raibh mé chomh neamartach is a bhí mé.'

'Ná bac leis,' arsa an tsióg. 'Is fearr é ná drochphósadh,' ar seisean. 'Cuirfidh tú níos mó suime sa chéad chomhairle eile a gheobhas tú. Cad é atá dúil agat a dhéanamh anois?' ar seisean le hÉamann.

'Rud ar bith a inseos tusa domh,' arsa Éamann.

'Téigh fhad leis an chaisleán,' arsa an tsióg. 'Coinnigh do shúile foscailte agus tífidh tú mórán neathannaí a chuirfeas iontas ort. Bí cinnte gan amharc 'do dhiaidh nuair a bheas tú ag teacht ar ais an bealach seo.'

'Maith go leor,' arsa Éamann.

In am ghairid bhí Éamann istigh sa chaisleán. Sheas sé ar chúl doras na cisteanaí agus i mbomaite shiúil an fathach isteach agus shín sé é féin ar an urlár. Bhí an bhean mhór a chonaic Éamann ar an chéad chuairt a thug sé ar an chaisleán ina suí ag an tinidh.

'Faigh an casúr draíochta,' arsa an fathach léi, 'agus déan an méid óir is a cheannós bológ fá choinne mo dhinnéara.'

D'fhoscail an bhean bocsa agus tharraing amach casúr beag agus cloch a bhí fá thuairim cúig phunta ar meáchan. Bhuail sí an chloch leis an chasúr agus thiontaigh an chloch isteach ina ór.

Chuir an bhean mhór an casúr ar ais ins an bhocsa. Ansin thug sí an t-ór léi ina haprún agus chuaigh amach ar fud na comharsanachta le bológ a cheannach. Thit an fathach ina chodladh ar an bhomaite chéanna. D'fhoscail Éamann an bocsa agus chuir sé an casúr faoina ascaill. Nuair a bhí sé ag teacht amach ar an doras d'amharc sé ina dhiaidh agus d'fhoscail an fathach a shúile. Siúd is nach bhfaca sé Éamann chonaic sé an casúr agus lig sé béic as féin a cluineadh sa Domhan Thoir. Rith Éamann síos an cabhsa agus rith an fathach ina dhiaidh. Fá dheireadh chuaigh Éamann ar fhoscadh crainn agus ní fhaca an fathach é ní ba mhó.

Tháinig an tsióg le tarrtháil a thabhairt ar Éamann agus thug leis é go dtí an tom sceiche.

'Cad chuige nár ghlac tú an chomhairle a thug mé dhuit?' ar seisean. 'Cad chuige ar amharc tú 'do dhiaidh?'

'Cad é an dóigh a dtiocfadh liom amharc 'mo dhiaidh nuair a bhí an fathach ar mo shála?' arsa Éamann.

'D'amharc tú 'do dhiaidh nuair a bhí tú ag teacht amach ar dhoras na cisteanaí,' arsa an tsióg.

'Rinne go cinnte,' arsa Éamann.

'Cad é a fuair tú sa chaisleán?' arsa an tsióg.

'Casúr a thiontós carraig isteach ina ór,' arsa Éamann.

'Téigh abhaile anois,' arsa an tsióg, 'agus ná déan amadán díot féin mar a rinne tú ar an aistear dheireanach. Ná lig d'aon duine an casúr a fheiceáil go raibh tú sa bhaile i dteach d'athara. Ná caith aon oíche i dteach ar bith ar an bhealach. Déan scríste agus codladh faoi scáth na gcrann agus ná déan carantas ar bith leis na daoine a chastar ort.'

'Maith go leor,' arsa Éamann. 'Cad é an dóigh a dtig liom buíochas a thabhairt duit ar son do chuid cineáltais?'

'Déan ór den charraig seo ar a bhfuil muid inár suí,' arsa an tsióg. Bhuail Éamann an charraig leis an chasúr agus rinne ór di.

'Bain chugat anois,' arsa an tsióg, 'agus coinnigh cuimhne ar an méid a dúirt mé.'

I ndiaidh slán a fhágáil ag an tsióg thug Éamann a aghaidh ar an bhaile. Shiúil sé go tapaidh agus ag deireadh an lae bhí sé tuirseach agus shuigh sé faoi chrann. 'D'fhanfainn anseo go maidin,' ar seisean leis féin, 'ach ab é go bhfuil ocras orm.' Leis sin chonaic sé cailín óg ina suí ar charraig giota beag ón áit a raibh sé ag déanamh a scríste. Is cosúil go bhfaca an cailín Éamann ag amharc uirthi agus labhair sí leis go carthanach. Cailín an-dóighiúil a bhí inti agus chonacthas d'Éamann go mba cheart dó fios a fháil cé hí féin. I mbomaite eile bhí sé lena taobh agus labhair mar a leanas: 'Tá mise in m'fhear shaibhir agus tá mé ar lorg mná. Má gheallann tusa mé a phósadh ní rachaidh mé níos faide.'

'A dhuine bhoicht,' ar sise, 'an bhfuil a fhios agat cé leis a bhfuil tú ag caint? Is níon fir uasail mise agus cad é an dóigh a mbeadh a fhios agam nach bhfuil tusa 'do bhacach? Caithfidh tú a chruthú domh go bhfuil tú saibhir sula dté tú níos faide le do chuid suirí.'

'Thig liom sin a dhéanamh i mbomaite,' arsa Éamann. Bhain sé an casúr as a phóca agus bhuail an charraig ar a raibh an cailín ina suí. Thiontaigh an charraig ina ór.

'Cad é do bharúil anois?' arsa Éamann.

'Barúil mhaith,' arsa an cailín. 'Tabhair domh an casúr agus bhéarfaidh mé grá mo chroí duit.'

'Grá ann nó as,' arsa Éamann, 'ní thig liom scarúint leis an chasúr.'

'Cá bhfuil do thriall?' arsa an cailín.

'Tá mé ar mo bhealach go Dún na nGall,' arsa Éamann. 'Má thig tusa liom beidh fáilte romhat. Tógfaidh mé caisleán fá do choinne agus bhéarfaidh mé gealltanas pósta dhuit.'

'Tar fhad leis an áras ina bhfuil mise 'mo chónaí,' arsa an cailín, 'agus má bheir m'athair cead domh rachaidh mé leat. Tá an oíche ag teannadh linn agus ní thig leat a ghabháil níos faide go maidin.'

'Níl dúil agam a ghabháil níos faide,' arsa Éamann, 'ach mar sin féin ní thig liom oíche a chaitheamh i dteach ar bith go raibh mé sa bhaile. Tím go bhfuil teach ag bun an chabhsa seo agus má fhaighim bia ann tiocfaidh mé ar ais go dtí an áit seo agus caithfidh mé an oíche faoin chrann sin ar bhruach an tsrutháin.'

'Tá sé iontach,' arsa an cailín, 'go bhfuil sé riachtanach ag fear a dtig leis ór a dhéanamh as carraigeacha codladh faoi scáth crainn.'

'Níl sé níos iontaí ná cailín deas a fheiceáil ag tairgint grá a croí ar chasúr,' arsa Éamann.

'Mo bheannacht leat,' arsa an cailín agus i mbomaite chuaigh sí as amharc i measc na gcrann.

Chuaigh Éamann fhad leis an teach ba chomhgaraí agus tugadh a sháith bídh dó. Tháinig sé ar ais agus chodail sé go sámh faoin chrann. Chuir sé an casúr go cúramach faoina veist agus rinne suas a intinn a bheith ar an bhealach abhaile ag bánú an lae.

Ar uair an mheán oíche tháinig an cailín ar ais agus chonaic sí Éamann ina chodladh ag taobh an tsrutháin. Bhí sé ag brionglóidigh agus gan a fhios aige cad é a bhí sé a dhéanamh tharraing sé an casúr as faoina veist agus d'fhág lena thaobh é. I mbomaite eile bhí sé i dtromchodladh agus ba ghairid go raibh an cailín ar an bhealach go háras a hathara agus an casúr ina seilbh.

Mhuscail Éamann bocht ag breacadh lae ach faraor ní raibh an casúr le fáil. Ní raibh a fhios aige cad é ab fhearr dó a dhéanamh agus chaoin sé go dúthrachtach. 'Ní thig liom a ghabháil abhaile le lámha folmha,' ar seisean leis féin, 'agus ní dóiche go gcuideoidh an tsióg liom níos mó.'

Fá dheireadh rinne sé suas a intinn cuairt eile a thabhairt ar an tsióg. Shiúil sé leis gan bia ná deoch agus bhí sé ar amharc chaisleán an fhathaigh roimh luí na gréine. Casadh an tsióg air agus d'iarr sé a phardún.

'Níor ghlac mé do chomhairle go hiomlán,' arsa Éamann, 'siúd is gur chodail mé faoi chrann.'

'Níor iarr mé ort titim i ngrá le cailín,' arsa an tsióg.

'Tá sin fíor,' arsa Éamann. 'Is orm féin atá an locht.'

'Sea, ar ndóiche,' arsa an tsióg.

'Tabhair comhairle amháin eile domh,' arsa Éamann, 'agus sin a n-iarrfaidh mé go deo.'

'Bíodh ina mhargadh,' arsa an tsióg. 'Cuir ort an clóca arís agus téigh fhad le caisleán an fhathaigh. Coinnigh do shúile foscailte agus tiocfaidh tú ar ais in d'fhear shaibhir.'

Chuir Éamann air an clóca draíochta agus thug an tríú cuairt ar chaisleán an fhathaigh. Nuair a chuaigh sé isteach bhí an fathach agus an bhean mhór ag díospóireacht. Bhí an fathach ag caint go feargach.

'Is dóigh liom,' ar seisean, 'gur duine inteacht atá muintearach agatsa a thug leis an t-éadach cláir agus an casúr.'

'Níl daoine muintearacha ar bith agamsa,' arsa an bhean. 'Nár dhúirt tú liom go bhfaca tú an casúr ag gabháil amach ar an doras agus gan duine ar bith á iompar?'

'Is ortsa atá an locht,' arsa an fathach. Bhí bata ag an fhathach ina láimh agus d'fhág sé ar an tábla é. 'Anois,' ar seisean leis an bhata, 'déan do chuid oibre.' Thoisigh an bata ag bualadh na mná go trom agus bhí trua ag Éamann di. Fá dheireadh dúirt an fathach: 'Sin go leor,' agus tháinig an bata ar ais go dtí an tábla.

Bhí Éamann ina sheasamh ar chúl an dorais ar feadh an ama seo agus dúirt sé leis féin go mbeadh an bata an-úsáideach dá dtigeadh leis é a fháil. Gan mhoill ina dhiaidh sin thit an fathach ina chodladh, agus nuair a bhí cúl na mná tiontaithe ar Éamann, sciob sé an bata agus tháinig go dtí an áit a raibh an tsióg ag fanacht leis.

'Fuair tú an rud a bhí a dhíth ort,' arsa an tsióg. 'Coinnigh ort an clóca agus má níonn tú úsáid mhaith den bhata beidh an t-éadach cláir agus an casúr abhaile leat.'

Thug Éamann buíochas don tsióg agus ag titim na hoíche bhí sé i dteach an fhir uasail a ghoid an t-éadach cláir uaidh. Bhí mórán uaisle cruinnithe agus bhain Éamann de an clóca. Dúirt sé leis an bhata: 'Déan do chuid oibre.' Thoisigh an bata ag bualadh an fhir. Ba ghairid go raibh lúcháir air an t-éadach a thabhairt d'Éamann. Tháinig cailín óg amach as seomra agus shín sí an casúr draíochta dó.

'B'éigean domh an casúr a ghoid uait,' ar sise, 'ar eagla go muirfeadh m'athair mé. Tá mé sásta anois a ghabháil abhaile leat go Dún na nGall.'

'Bíodh ina mhargadh,' arsa Éamann.

Tháinig siad abhaile go teach an táilliúra agus pósadh iad. Thóg siad caisleán mór agus bhí siad beo go sona ar feadh mórán blianta.

NÓTA

1 *Derry People and Tirconaill News*, 8, 15, 22, 29 August 1936, 5, 12, 19, 26 September 1936.

Tomás agus an tSióg

Oíche amháin sa tsean-am bhí fear arbh ainm dó Tomás Ó Dochartaigh ag teacht abhaile go mall san oíche. Bhí an ghealach ag soilsiú agus ní raibh eagla ar bith air riamh roimh thaibhsí. Is iomaí uair a dúirt a bhean leis gur cheart dó a theacht abhaile níos luaithe ach fuair sí an freagar céanna i gcónaí óna fear: 'Ní fhaca mé taibhse le linn mo shaoil agus níl eagla ar bith orm rompu.'

Nuair a bhí Tomás fá thuairim leath bealaigh sa bhaile tháinig néal ar an ghealaigh agus tháinig dorchadas ar éadan na tíre.

'Tá seo iontach ar fad,' arsa Tomás leis féin. Bhí eolas maith aige ar an bhealach agus shiúil sé go tapaidh. Fá dheireadh chonaic sé solas ar an bhóthar agus thug seo misneach dó. 'Tá duine inteacht eile amuigh go mall,' ar seisean leis féin. Tháinig sé go dtí an áit a raibh an solas. Lóchrann a bhí ann agus fear beag, féasógach á iompar.

'Más duine saolta atá ionat,' arsa Tomás, 'ba cheart duit a theacht liom giota den bhealach.'

'Tá dúil agam sin a dhéanamh,' arsa an fear beag. 'Tá bean sa chomharsanacht agat atá ina luí tinn,' ar seisean.

'Tá sin fíor,' arsa Tomás, 'ach chuala mé go raibh sí ag bisiú.'

'Níl sí ag bisiú,' arsa an fear beag. 'Tháinig dorchadas na hoíche seo mar chomhartha chuig a bunadh. Má tá sé i ndán di bás a fháil anocht cluinfidh tú caoineadh na mná sí nuair a bheas muid comhgarach ag an teach. Beidh sí marbh, sin nó i bhfad níos fearr roimh éirí na gréine.'

D'aithin Tomás ar sheanchas an fhir bhig gur sióg a bhí ann ach níor chuir sin imní ar bith air. Shiúil siad míle nó mar sin gan focal a labhairt. Fá dheireadh sheas an fear beag ar an bhóthar agus chuir an lóchrann ar mhullach a chinn. Ar an bhomaite sin thoisigh an ceol ba truacánta dár chuala Tomás riamh. 'Tá an bhean sí anseo go cinnte,' arsa Tomás.

'Tá,' arsa an fear beag. 'Sin teach na mná atá tinn ins na toim os ár gcoinne.'

'Is iomaí míle a shiúil mé,' arsa Tomás, 'ach níor chuala mé riamh go dtí an bomaite seo caoineadh na mná sí.'

'Creidim sin,' arsa an fear beag.

Mhair an caoineadh go dtí go dtáinig an ghealach amach as na néaltaí. Bhí an dorchadas imithe agus ba mar sin don fhear bheag i gcaochadh súile. Níor lig Tomás don fhéar fás faoina chosa go dtáinig sé abhaile. 'Tabhair domh deoch uisce,' ar seisean nuair a shuigh sé ag an tinidh. Thug a bhean an t-uisce dó agus d'aithin sí go bhfuair sé scanradh.

'Tá eagla orm,' ar sise, 'go raibh na taibhsí amuigh anocht.'

'Tá na sióga amuigh i gcás ar bith,' arsa Tomás. 'Chuala mé caoineadh na mná sí.'

'Chreidfinn sin,' arsa an bhean. 'Ghlac Máire Mhór drochthaom ag an deich a chlog. Níor chualathas an bhean sí sa chomharsanacht seo ó fuair a hathair bás. Ba chóir dúinn a ghabháil ag amharc uirthi agus má tá sí marbh thig linn paidir a rá ar son a hanama.'

'Tá mé sásta,' arsa Tomás, 'ach níl dúil agam a bheith amuigh i ndiaidh na hoíche liom féin ó seo amach.'

'Sin mar is fearr é,' arsa bean Thomáis.

Cupla bomaite ina dhiaidh sin bhí an péire ag doras an tí ina raibh an bhean tinn ina luí.

'Tar isteach,' arsa an fear a d'fhoscail an doras. 'Tá Máire marbh,' ar seisean, 'agus tá an t-am againn an Paidrín Páirteach a rá.'

NÓTA

1 *Derry People and Tirconaill News*, 24 October 1936.

Proinsias Mac Suibhne agus an Púca

Ní chluintear ach an fíorbheagán i dtaobh an Phúca le seal maith blianta ach deir na seandaoine go raibh a leithéid ann fá thuairim céad bliain ó shin.

Bhí fear arbh ainm dó Proinsias Mac Suibhne ina chónaí fada ó shin i bparóiste na nGleanntach. Bhí sé tugtha do chearrbhachas agus is minic a tháinig sé abhaile idir an meán oíche agus an lá. Ba chuma leis an oíche geal nó dorcha agus ní raibh eagla ar bith air roimh thaibhsí. Oíche amháin bhí sé ag teacht abhaile ó bhaile Dhún na nGall agus d'aithin sé ar na réaltaí go raibh bánú an lae ag teannadh leis. Nuair a bhí sé ag gabháil trasna ar dhroichead a bhí míle nó níos mó ó áit ar bith chónaithe tháinig seanghearrán bán roimhe ar an bhóthar.

'Nach mall atá tú ar do chois?' arsa an gearrán.

'Tá mé chomh luath leat féin,' arsa Proinsias. 'Más tú an Púca ní bheidh baint ar bith agam leat, ach más gearrán macánta, dóighiúil atá ionat ba mhaith liom a ghabháil ar do dhroim ar feadh míle nó beirt.'

'Ó tharla go bhfuil muid ag gabháil an bealach céanna,' arsa an gearrán, 'tá sé chomh maith agat a bheith ag marcaíocht ná ag siúl.'

Chuaigh Proinsias ar dhroim an ghearráin agus thug an gearrán a aghaidh ar na cnoic.

'Cá bhfuil an diabhal ag gabháil leat?' arsa Proinsias. 'Cé a d'inis duit go raibh mo chónaí i lár na sléibhte?'

'Caithfidh tú an oíche seo ins na sléibhte,' arsa an gearrán.

Bhí siad ag gabháil chomh gasta sin is go raibh eagla ar Phroinsias léimint anuas. Mhair siad mar seo go dtí gur scairt an coileach agus ansin chaith an gearrán an marcach chun talaimh. Nuair a d'éirigh Proinsias bhí an gearrán ina eala agus bhí ag snámh ar loch a bhí in aice leo.

'Sin an chéad Phúca a casadh orm riamh,' arsa Proinsias leis féin, 'agus tá súil agam gurb é an ceann deireanach é.'

Bhí Proinsias fá dhá mhíle den bhaile nuair a casadh an Púca air ach anois bhí sé dhá mhíle dhéag eile níos faide ó bhaile. Thug sé a chúl leis an ghréin a bhí ag éirí agus chuir tús ar an aistear fhada a bhí roimhe. Ní bréag a rá go raibh sé tuirseach nuair a tháinig sé abhaile an tráthnóna sin ach chuir an Púca deireadh leis an chearrbhachas.

NÓTA

1 *Derry People and Tirconaill News*, 28 November 1936.

An Rí agus a Chuid Mac

Bhí Rí in Éirinn fada ó shin agus bhí triúr mac aige, Brian, Diarmaid agus Art. Lá amháin dúirt sé leo: 'Tá tusa, a Bhriain, sé bliana agus fiche, tá Diarmaid ceithre bliana agus fiche agus tá Art bliain agus fiche inniu. Níor chaith aon duine agaibh oíche ó bhaile ó rugadh sibh ach tá mé ag gabháil a thabhairt cead daoibh anois turas a dhéanamh ar fud na hÉireann. Caithfimid an Nollaig i gcuideachta a chéile agus cuirfidh sibh tús ar an turas an lá ina dhiaidh sin. Beidh mé ag dréim libh ar ais bliain ó inniu. Tá mo chead ag gach duine agaibh pósadh agus bean a thabhairt abhaile leis. Tá mise ag éirí sean,' ar seisean, 'agus tá dúil agam an choróin a chur ar an phrionsa a phósfas an cailín is dóighiúla. An bhfuil sibh uilig sásta leis an réiteach sin?'

'Táimid sásta agus buíoch,' arsa na prionsaí.

Chaith siad Nollaig phléisiúrtha agus ar maidin lá arna mhárach thug an Rí a bheannacht dóibh agus d'iarr orthu tús a chur ar an tasc a bhí leagtha amach aige. Chaoin Art, an mac ab óige, go brónach nuair a bhí sé ag fágáil slán ag a athair ach níor shil Brian ná Diarmaid aon deor. Bhí an bhanríon tinn an mhaidin sin agus chuaigh na prionsaí go dtí an seomra ina raibh sí ina luí agus phóg í sular fhág siad. Cupla bomaite ina dhiaidh sin bhí siad as amharc an chaisleáin. Ag luí na gréine bhí siad fiche míle ó bhaile.

Shuigh siad síos faoi chrann a bhí ag fás ar bhruach srutháin agus d'ith cuid den arán a bhí leo ó bhaile. Nuair a bhí an béile thart tháinig spideog anuas ón chrann agus thoisigh ag piocadh na ngrabhróg (*cromógaí* sa bhuntéacs) a bhí ar an talamh.

'A éinín bhig, bhoicht,' arsa Art, 'tá tusa cosúil linn féin. Níl aon fhoscadh os do chionn ach an spéir ghorm.'

'Ní mar sin atá an scéal,' arsa an spideog. 'Tá caisleán ar chúl an ardáin seo ar thaobh na láimhe deise agus beidh fáilte romhaibh an oíche a chaitheamh ann. Gheobhaidh sibh an seomra is fearr sa teach agus má fhágann sibh an fhuinneog foscailte caithfidh mise an oíche in bhur gcuideachta.'

Thug na prionsaí buíochas don spideog agus ba ghairid go raibh siad ag doras an chaisleáin. Ba é fear an tí é féin a d'fhoscail an doras agus dúirt sé: 'Tá fáilte romhaibh an oíche a chaitheamh sa chaisleán seo ach ba mhaith liom fios a fháil cé sibh féin nó ar shiúil sibh i bhfad?'

'Is sinne triúr mac Rí na hÉireann,' arsa Brian.

'Má tá sin mar sin,' arsa an fear uasal (nó fear uasal a bhí ann), 'tá fáilte agus fiche romhaibh. Taraigí isteach,' ar seisean, 'agus suígí ag cois na tineadh. Beidh sneachta trom againn roimh an mheán oíche.'

'Go raibh míle buíochas agat,' arsa Brian, 'agus go raibh beannacht Dé ort féin agus ar do chúram.'

'Tá lúcháir orm,' arsa an fear uasal, 'go mbeidh mé ábalta a rá amárach gur chaith trí phrionsa óga oíche san áras seo.' Ansin scairt sé ar sheirbhíseach agus dúirt: 'Abair le mo bhean agus mo chuid iníonach gur mhaith liom iad a theacht anseo i mbomaite. Is mór an onóir dóibh triúr mac Rí na hÉireann a chastáil orthu. Beidh féasta againn anocht a mbeidh cuimhne air ar feadh blianta.'

Gan mhoill ina dhiaidh sin tháinig bean an fhir uasail agus a triúr iníonacha láithreach. Ní raibh ar thalamh na hÉireann trí chailín a bhí leath chomh dóighiúil leo agus ní thiocfadh leis an tsúil is géire aon difear a dhéanamh eatarthu.

Fhad is a bhí an féasta ag gabháil ar aghaidh b'fhurast a fheiceáil go raibh carthanas dáiríre ag éirí idir na prionsaí agus níonacha an fhir uasail. Bhí sé anonn go maith san oíche sular smaoinigh aon duine dá raibh sa chaisleán go raibh an t-am ann a ghabháil a luí. Fá dheireadh dúirt fear an tí go raibh scríste a dhíth ar na prionsaí agus, mar a dúirt an spideog, tugadh 'an seomra ab fhearr sa chaisleán' dóibh. D'fhoscail Art an fhuinneog agus tháinig an spideog isteach.

'Tá an sneachta ag titim go trom,' ar sise, 'agus is maith liom foscadh a fháil go maidin.'

'Tá lúcháir orainn a bheith in do chuideachta,' arsa na prionsaí. Ansin d'inis siad don spideog an réiteach a rinne an Rí sular fhág siad an baile.

'Ní fhéadaim a rá libh,' arsa an spideog, 'ach go bhfuil na trí cailíní is áille in Éirinn sa chaisleán seo. Chaith sibh tamall den oíche seo ina gcuideachta. Tá scéal agamsa le hinsint a chuirfeas iontas oraibh. Bhí deirfiúr agaibh nach bhfaca aon duine agaibh riamh. Síleann bhur n-athair agus bhur máthair go bhfuair sí bás an lá a rugadh í ach ní mar sin atá an scéal. Goideadh í agus fágadh páiste marbh ina háit.'

'An bhfuil sí beo go fóill?' arsa na prionsaí.

'Tá,' arsa an spideog. 'Beidh sí ocht mbliana déag amárach.'

'Arbh fhéidir linn í a fháil?' arsa na prionsaí.

'Ní gan trioblóid,' arsa an spideog. 'Níor chuala sibh iomlán an scéil go fóill. Rugadh mac óg sa chaisleán seo an oíche ar rugadh bhur ndeirfiúr agus d'éirigh leisean ar an dóigh chéanna. Síleann muintir an tí seo go bhfuair an páiste bás ina naíonán ach, dálta bhur ndeirfiúir, tá sé beo agus faoi dhraíocht.'

'Is iontach do scéal,' arsa na prionsaí. 'An gcuideoidh tú linn eisean a fháil fosta?'

'Cuideoidh,' arsa an spideog. 'Rinne mé dearmad a insint daoibh,' ar sise, 'gur Nuala an t-ainm a bhí ar bhur ndeirfiúr. Inseoidh mé daoibh ar maidin cad é atá le déanamh agaibh, ach tá codladh a dhíth oraibh anois.'

Luigh na prionsaí síos, gach duine acu ina leabaidh féin, agus in am ghairid thit Brian agus Diarmaid ina gcodladh. Níorbh é sin d'Art. Thoisigh sé ag smaoineamh ar laetha a óige agus fá dheireadh bhí sé ag caint os ard agus gan a fhios aige air. 'Mo Nuala bhocht,' a deireadh sé. 'Bhí mise níos óige ná Brian ná Diarmaid agus ar an ábhar sin bheinn níos minice i gcuideachta Nuala dá bhfágfaí agam í. Dhéanfainn coróin fána coinne, an uile lá, de na blátha ba deise. Ach, faraor, ní fhaca mé mo Nuala bhocht riamh.' Leis sin thoisigh sé ag caoineadh agus bhí trua ag an spideog dó. Tháinig sí agus luigh ar a bhrollach agus dúirt: 'Ná bí ag caoineadh, a Airt. Tá Nuala níos comhgaraí ná a shíleas tú agus tífidh tú gan mhoill í. Codail go sámh go maidin agus inseoidh mé scéal rúin duit.'

Ag bánú an lae mhuscail Art agus bhí lúcháir air nuair a chonaic sé go raibh an spideog go fóill sa tseomra. Chuir sé air a chuid éadaigh go tapaidh mar bhí deifir air scéal rúin na spideoige a chluinstin.

'Tá a fhios agam,' arsa an spideog, 'go raibh tú ag brionglóidigh fá Nuala agus caithfidh mé anois mo gheall a choinneáil. Is mise Nuala,' ar sise, 'ach caithfidh mé fanacht sa chruth seo go dtí go bhfaighidh tú féin agus do dhá dheartháir eile an páiste a rugadh sa chaisleán seo an oíche a rugadh mise. Tá sé anois ocht mbliana déag d'aois ach tá sé faoi dhraíocht agus i gcruth éin fosta. Tá aistear fada romhainn sula raibh muid ag an áras ina bhfuil sé faoi ghlas agus eochair agus caithfimid tús a chur ar an aistear sin inniu. Ná hinis do Bhrian nó Diarmaid an méid a chuala tú. Muscail anois iad agus inis dóibh go gcaithfidh siad imeacht ón chaisleán seo ag an mheán lae.'

Mhuscail Art a dhá dheartháir agus d'inis dóibh a bheith réidh leis an chaisleán a fhágáil ar uair an mheán lae.

'Ní bheidh muintir an tí seo sásta sinn a ligint ar shiúl chomh luath sin,' arsa Brian.

'Is cuma,' arsa Art, 'caithfear comhairle na spideoige a iompar amach.'

Bhí an bricfeasta réidh nuair a tháinig siad anuas na staighrí agus shuigh an fear uasal, a bhean agus na trí níonacha ag an tábla amháin. 'Tá súil agam,' arsa fear an tí, 'go gcaithfidh sibh mí nó beirt sa chaisleán seo.'

'Faraor,' arsa an prionsa ba sine, 'ní thig linn fanacht ach cupla uair eile.'

'An féidir go bhfuil sibh ag gabháil abhaile chomh tobann sin?' arsa an fear uasal.

'Níl muid ag gabháil abhaile go dtí an lá roimh an Nollaig seo chugainn,' arsa Brian.

'Cuirfidh sé iontas ort a chluinstin go bhfuil muid ag gabháil ar lorg do mhic,' arsa Art.

'Ní raibh agam riamh ach mac amháin agus fuair sé bás ina naíonán.'

'Tá do mhac beo,' arsa Art. 'Goideadh an páiste agus fágadh páiste marbh ina áit.'

Nuair a chuala muintir an chaisleáin na focla seo chaoin gach duine acu go brónach.

'Ní cúis bhróin é seo,' arsa na prionsaí. 'Nuair a thiocfas sinne ar ais, beidh do mhac linn.'

'Tá mé féin agus mo mhuirín sárbhuíoch daoibh,' arsa an fear uasal. 'Iarr orm anois aon ní atá in mo chumhacht a thabhairt daoibh agus gheobhaidh sibh é.'

'Níl aon ní ar an domhan seo ab fhearr linn,' arsa Brian, 'ná cleamhnas idir sinn féin agus do chuid níonach.'

'Agus níl aon ní ar an domhan is mó a bhéarfadh pléisiúr domhsa agus mo bhean ná an cleamhnas céanna,' arsa an fear uasal.

'Go raibh maith agat,' arsa na prionsaí, 'ach caithfimid do mhac a fháil ar dtús.'

D'fhág na prionsaí an caisleán agus in am ghairid casadh an spideog orthu.

'Ní bheimid ag deireadh an aistir,' ar sise, 'go dtí an oíche amárach.'

'Is cuma linn,' arsa Art, 'nuair atá tusa linn.'

'Tím,' arsa an spideog, 'nach bhfuil claíomh ag duine ar bith agaibh.'

'Níl,' arsa Brian. 'Ní raibh a fhios againn go mbeadh troid ar bith le déanamh againn.'

'Tá dhá bhriseadh le troid agaibh,' arsa an spideog. 'Ar maidin amárach sroichfimid teach ar bhruach locha. Tá fathach ina chónaí in uaimh atá idir an teach agus an loch. Tá trí chlaíomh aige agus caithfidh sibh iad a fháil sula dtéimid níos faide ar aghaidh. Níl ach súil amháin ag an fhathach agus muirfidh buille sa tsúil sin é i mbomaite.'

Shiúil siad leo gan bhia ná scríste go dtí gur éirigh an ghrian an mhaidin ina dhiaidh sin. Nuair a tháinig siad go teach an fhathaigh chonaic siad an fathach ag folcadh sa loch.

'Anois an t-am,' arsa an spideog, 'deireadh a chur leis.'

Chuaigh siad go bruach an locha agus nuair a tháinig an fathach comhgarach acu scaoil gach duine acu cloch. Bhuail ceann de na clocha an fathach sa tsúil agus thit sé marbh. Chuaigh siad isteach sa teach agus fuair na claímheacha. Bhí neart bídh sa teach agus d'ith na prionsaí agus an spideog béile maith.

Shiúil siad leo arís agus ag titim na hoíche tháinig siad fhad le caisleán in imeall coilleadh. Tháinig triúr fear, gach duine seacht dtroigh ar airde, agus chuir troid orthu. Tharraing na prionsaí na claímheacha agus thoisigh an briseadh. Bhí bata iarainn ag gach duine de na fir agus i gceann uaire ní raibh buaidh ag aon taobh. Fá dheireadh thoisigh an spideog ag tógáil dusta an bhealaigh mhóir lena cuid eiteog agus á chaitheamh isteach i súile na bhfear go dtí go raibh siad dall. I mbomaite eile sciob na prionsaí na cinn díobh.

Chuaigh siad isteach sa chaisleán ansin agus d'iarr an spideog orthu leac a bhí san urlár a thógáil. Bhí eochair faoin leic.

'Anois,' arsa an spideog, 'caithfimid an doras seo ar thaobh na láimhe deise a fhoscailt.'

D'fhoscail Brian an doras agus shiúil siad isteach. Ní raibh aon rud sa tseomra ach tábla ar a raibh éan deas ina sheasamh.

'Sin slat draíochta faoin tábla,' arsa an spideog le Brian. 'Tóg í agus leag í ar cheann an éin.'

Rinne Brian mar a hiarradh air agus thiontaigh an t-éan isteach ina fhear chomh breá is a chonaic na prionsaí riamh.

'Tabhair domhsa an tslat anois,' arsa Art. Thug Brian an tslat dó agus leag sé í ar cheann na spideoige. Thiontaigh an spideog isteach ina cailín óg, dhóighiúil. Phóg Art í go cineálta.

'Mo Nuala, mo Nuala,' ar seisean. Bhí iontas an domhain ar Bhrian agus Diarmaid.

'Seo bhur ndeirfiúr,' arsa Art.

Phóg siad í mar a rinne Art agus ansin dúirt Nuala leis an fhear óg: 'An tusa Éamann, mac Ridire na Mumhan?'

'Is mé,' arsa an fear óg.

'Maith go leor,' arsa Nuala. 'Caithfimid uilig an oíche seo i gcuideachta d'athara agus do mháthara agus do thriúr deirfiúrach. Tá cóiste draíochta sa chaisleán seo a bhéarfas abhaile sinn in uair ach fanóimid le solas lae.'

Go luath lá arna mhárach tháinig na prionsaí, Nuala agus Éamann, go teach an Ridire. Bhí fáilte mhór roimh na prionsaí agus chuir an fear uasal ceist orthu an raibh siad sásta lena dturas.

'Táimid sásta go mór,' arsa Brian. 'Amharc bomaite ar an fhear óg seo agus ansin inseoidh mé duit cé hé féin.'

Bhí bean an Ridire agus na níonacha láithreach agus bhí gach súil leagtha ar Éamann. Fá dheireadh ghlaoigh bean an Ridire os ard: 'Mo leanbh bán,' agus chaith sí a cuid lámh thart fá mhuineál Éamainn. Rinne an t-athair agus na cailíní mar an gcéanna agus ní féidir an lúcháir a bhí orthu a áireamh.

'Anois,' arsa an Ridire, 'ó tharla nach dtig liom mo bhuíochas a chur i bhfocla, inis dúinn cé hí an cailín álainn seo atá in bhur gcuideachta.'

'Níon Rí na hÉireann,' arsa Brian.

'Bhur ndeirfiúr?' arsa an Ridire.

'Go díreach,' arsa na prionsaí. 'Goideadh í mar a goideadh Éamann ach tá a gcuid draíochta thart.'

Rinne an Ridire, a bhean agus na níonacha dearmad ar Éamann ar feadh bomaite agus phóg siad Nuala go carthanach. D'ordaigh an Ridire féasta seacht seachtainí a chur ar bun agus ba iad sin na seacht seachtainí ba phléisiúrtha dár caitheadh riamh in Éirinn.

Bhí an t-earrach ann nuair a bhí an féasta thart agus lá amháin chuir na prionsaí ceist ar an Ridire an raibh sé sásta cead a thabhairt do na cailíní iad a phósadh.

'Tá mo chead agus mo bheannacht acu,' arsa an Ridire. 'D'inis tú domh,' ar seisean le Brian, 'gur mian leis an Rí gach duine agaibh bean a bheith chun an bhaile leis.'

'Tá sin ceart,' arsa na prionsaí.

Fhad is a bhí siad ag caint tháinig Éamann agus Nuala go dtí an áit a raibh siad ina seasamh. Ba é Art a labhair ar dtús.

'An bhfuil tusa sásta, a Nuala,' ar seisean, 'cead a thabhairt dúinn pósadh?'

'Tá,' arsa Nuala, 'má phósann sibh níonacha an fhir uasail seo. Sin mian mo chroí.'

'Tá mé buíoch duit,' arsa an Ridire. 'Iarr orm anois aon rud a thig liom a thabhairt duit agus gheobhaidh tú é.'

'Maith go leor,' arsa Nuala. 'Tabhair domh do mhac. Ní phósfaidh mé go deo ach é.'

Chuir seo lúcháir mhór ar na prionsaí agus dúirt an Ridire: 'Aontaím, a Nuala.'

'Go raibh maith agat, a athair,' arsa Éamann.

'Míle buíochas,' arsa Nuala.

Sula raibh an samhradh thart pósadh na prionsaí agus níonacha an Ridire agus níl gnoithe a rá gur pósadh Éamann agus Nuala an lá céanna. Mhair an féasta a cuireadh ar bun lá na bainise go dtí go raibh an Nollaig comhgarach.

Ní féidir an lúcháir a bhí ar an Rí agus an Bhanríon a insint nuair a tháinig na prionsaí agus a gcuid ban, agus Éamann agus Nuala abhaile ag troscadh na Nollag. Choinnigh an Rí cuimhne ar a ghealltanas ach sháraigh sé air aon difear a dhéanamh idir mná na bprionsaí. Chuir sé Brian os cionn Chúige Laighean, Diarmaid os cionn Chúige Chonnacht, agus Art os cionn Chúige Uladh. D'fhág Ridire na Mumhan iomlán dá raibh ina sheilbh ag Éamann agus Nuala.

NÓTA

1 *Derry People and Tirconaill News*, 5, 12, 19, 26 December 1936, 2 January 1937.

An tÉan agus an Crann Cuilinn

Geimhreadh fuar, fliuch a bhí ann ins na laetha fadó. Bhí mórán d'éanacha beaga, fiáine na tíre ag fáil bháis agus lá amháin tháinig siad i gceann a chéile i gContae na Mí.

'Ní bheimid ábalta an geimhreadh seo a chur isteach in Éirinn,' arsa ceann de na héanacha. 'Beidh an talamh cumhdaithe le sneachta amárach agus beimid gan bhia.'

'Is fearr dúinn,' arsa éan eile, 'an tír seo a fhágáil go dtí go mbeidh an geimhreadh thart. Thig linn a ghabháil go tír inteacht ina mbíonn sé ina shamhradh i gcónaí.'

Leis sin d'éirigh siad in airde sa spéir agus d'fhág slán ag Éirinn. Ach bhí éan beag amháin ina measc nach raibh ábalta eiteal agus b'éigean dó fanacht sa bhaile.

'Níl samhradh ar bith i ndán domhsa,' ar seisean leis féin, 'go mí na Bealtaine agus ní dóiche go mbeidh mé beo ansin.'

Ar ndóiche, bhí an t-éinín bocht uaigneach nuair a d'imigh a chuid comrádaithe. Ní raibh a fhios aige cad é ab fhearr a dhéanamh. Tháinig sé fhad le teach feirmeora agus d'fhan sé tamall ar ghéag crainn a bhí os coinne an dorais. Chonaic níon an fheirmeora é fá dheireadh agus bhí trua aici dó. Scab sí grabhróga faoin chrann agus bhí tráth maith ag an éan. Bhí dúil aige an oíche a chaitheamh sa chrann ach chonaic sé cat mór, dubh ag amharc suas air agus chonacthas dó go mbeadh sé críonna an oíche a chaitheamh i gcoill a bhí comhgarach.

Bhí an oíche ag titim nuair a tháinig sé fhad leis an choill. Chonaic sé crann fuinseoige agus d'iarr sé ar an chrann foscadh a thabhairt dó go maidin.

'Imigh leat,' arsa an crann fuinseoige, 'ní bheidh mé gaibhte leat. Gheobhaidh tú foscadh in áit inteacht eile.'

'Ná bac leis,' arsa an t-éinín. 'Ní bheidh tú chomh bródúil nuair a bheas an geimhreadh thart.'

Ansin chuaigh sé fhad le crann mór darach agus dúirt: 'A chrainn uasail darach, an dtabharfaidh tú áit bheag domh i measc do chuid duilliúir leis an oíche seo a chaitheamh? Is gairid go mbeidh sneachta ag titim agus is fada an t-am go maidin.'

'Imigh leat,' arsa an crann darach. 'Tá mo sháith agamsa le déanamh aire a thabhairt domh féin. Téigh isteach i bpoll sa chlaí sin thall go raibh an doineann thart.'

'Nuair a bheas an doineann seo thart,' arsa an t-éinín, 'ní bheidh tusa chomh bródúil is atá tú anois.'

D'imigh an t-éinín beag, bocht leis arís ar fud na coilleadh.

'Cad é is fearr domh a dhéanamh ar chor ar bith?' ar seisean leis féin. 'Is trua nach bhfuair mé bás ins an tsamhradh.'

Is cosúil gur chuala crann cuilinn an rud a dúirt an t-éinín agus go raibh trua aige dó.

'Cad é atá ag cur imní ort?' arsa an crann cuilinn.

'Inseoidh mé sin duit,' arsa an t-éinín. 'Dhiúltaigh na crainn mhóra foscadh a thabhairt domh i gcomhair na hoíche agus tá eagla orm go gcuirfidh an geimhreadh deireadh liom.'

'Ná bíodh aon eagla ort,' arsa an crann cuilinn.

'Ní bheinn anseo anois,' arsa an t-éan, 'ach ab é go bhfuil sciathán de mo chuid briste agus ní raibh mé ábalta a ghabháil thar sáile le mo chuid comrádaithe.'

'Níl gnoithe duit fanacht níos faide amuigh san fhuacht,' arsa an crann cuilinn. 'Déan thú féin sa bhaile i measc mo chuid duilliúir. Cruinnigh beagán olla agus déan nead duit féin. Coinneoidh mo chuid duilleog an sioc agus an sneachta ar shiúl uait.'

'An gcoinneoidh tú mé ar feadh an gheimhridh?' arsa an t-éan.

'Ar feadh do shaoil,' arsa an crann cuilinn, 'má tá dúil agat fanacht. 'Thig leat na caora atá ag fás ar mo ghéaga a ithe agus ní fhéadann tú eagla a bheith ort roimh fhuacht ná ocras.'

'Go raibh maith agat,' arsa an t-éinín. 'Níl eagla ar bith orm roimh an gheimhreadh anois.'

Rinne an t-éan nead mar a hiarradh air agus bhí sé chomh compordach is dá mbeadh an nead déanta i scioból.

'Ní bhfaighidh cat ná madadh fhad liom anseo,' ar seisean leis féin, agus bhí sin fíor.

Oíche amháin gan mhoill ina dhiaidh sin tháinig stoirm iargúlta isteach ón fharraige. Lúb sé na crainn mhóra síos go talamh beagnach, agus nuair a tháinig an mhaidin ní raibh duilleog amháin fágtha ar aon cheann acu. Shonraigh an crann cuilinn nár chaill sé duilleog ar feadh na hoíche.

Ansin labhair an crann cuilinn leis an éan agus dúirt: 'Is ádhúil an rud é go dtáinig tú chugam ag iarraidh foscaidh. Níl duilleog amháin fágtha ar na crainn mhóra ach tá mo chótasa chomh deas is a bhí riamh.'

'Beidh tú mar sin go deo,' arsa an t-éinín. 'Bhí croí maith agat agus sin an fáth a bhfuil do dhuilliúr slán.'

'Inis domh,' arsa an crann darach leis an chrann cuilinn, 'cad é an dóigh ar shábháil tú thú féin ó dhoineann na hoíche aréir? Chaill mise na duilleogaí a bhí ag déanamh cóta geimhridh fá mo choinne agus tá drochdhóigh orm. Tá mo ghéaga lom agus tá mé bearaiste leis an fhuacht.'

'Is é do dhroch-chroí is ciontaí leis sin,' arsa an crann cuilinn. 'Tháinig éinín beag, bocht chugat an lá fá dheireadh agus d'iarr foscadh ort i gcomhair na hoíche. Dúirt tú leis a bheith ag imeacht ar siocair go raibh go leor le déanamh agat aire a thabhairt duit féin. Is olc an aicíd an bród agus is minic a thigeann deireadh tobann leis.'

'Ní chreidim do scéal,' arsa an crann darach. 'Féach an crann giúise. Níl seisean ag tabhairt aire d'éinín ar bith agus níor baineadh lena chuid duilliúir.'

'Fan ort,' arsa an crann cuilinn, 'go gcluine tú iomlán an scéil. Bhí comhrá fada agamsa leis an chrann giúise inné agus dúirt sé liom go raibh sé buartha nach dtáinig an t-éinín chuige nuair a bhí sé ar lorg foscaidh. An té a bhfuil croí fial aige gheibheann sé díolaíocht ar son na nithe a bhí dúil aige a dhéanamh chomh maith leis na nithe a d'iompair sé amach. Caithfidh tusa agus an crann fuinseoige cur suas le bhur gcuid trioblóide anois. Caillfidh sibh bhur nduilliúr an uile gheimhreadh ach beidh an crann giúise agus mé féin glas go deo agus beidh cuideachta na n-éan againn nuair a bheas tusa agus an crann fuinseoige ag fáil bháis le huaigneas.'

NÓTA

1 *Derry People and Tirconaill News*, 9, 16, 23 January 1937.

Cailleach an Ardáin Ghlais

Sula dtáinig Naomh Pádraig go hÉirinn bhí Rí i gCúige Laighean a raibh níon an-dóighiúil aige. Lá amháin nuair a bhí sí ag cruinniú sabharcán tháinig seanchailleach fhad léi agus dúirt: 'Tá níon agam sa bhaile atá ar aon aois leatsa agus caithfidh tusa cuidiú liom cleamhnas a dhéanamh di a bheas taitneamhach agamsa.'

'Níl baint ar bith agamsa le do ghnoithese,' arsa níon an rí. 'Níl aithne ar bith agam ar do níon agus chomh beag aithne agam ort féin.'

'Beidh na seacht n-aithne agat orm sula bhfágfaidh tú an gleann seo,' arsa an chailleach. Leis sin chonaic siad cailín ag teannadh leo. Bhí sí beagnach chomh sean i gcuma leis an chailligh í féin agus bhí aghaidh uirthi chomh gránna le peacadh marfa.

'Seo mo níon,' arsa an chailleach. 'Bhí sí ina cailín álainn nuair a bhí sí fiche bliain d'aois ach lá amháin chuir sí fearg ormsa agus chuir mé deireadh lena cuid áilleachta le buille den tslaitín seo atá in mo láimh. Éireoidh an rud céanna duitse má dhiúltaíonn tú an rud atá mise ag iarraidh ort a dhéanamh.'

Ar chluinstin na bhfocla seo di tháinig eagla mhór ar níon an Rí. Is dóiche go dtitfeadh sí i laige ach ab é go bhfaca sí a deartháir (an mac ba sine ag an Rí) ag teannadh léi.

'Cé hiad na mná seo?' arsa an prionsa.

'Is mise Cailleach an Ardáin Ghlais agus is í seo mo níon,' arsa an tseanbhean. 'Tá mé ag iarraidh ar do dheirfiúr cuidiú liom fear a fháil fá choinne an chailín seo.'

'Níl fear ar an domhan a dhéanfadh cleamhnas den chineál sin,' arsa an prionsa.

'Ná bí róchinnte de sin,' arsa an chailleach. 'Tá aithne agamsa ar fhear,' ar sise, 'agus beidh lúcháir air í a phósadh roimh luí na gréine.'

'Má tá,' arsa an prionsa, 'is fearr duit a ghabháil ar a lorg.'

'Níl gnoithe leis sin,' arsa an chailleach. 'Is tusa an fear atá in m'intinn.'

Chuir seo fearg ar an phrionsa agus dúirt sé: 'Bain chugat go tapaidh agus ná feicim go deo arís thú. Tá duisín saighdiúr ar an taobh eile den sconsa sin agus má scairtim orthu is gairid go mbeidh tú féin agus do níon sa loch udaí thall.'

Leis sin bhuail an chailleach níon an Rí sa ghualainn leis an tslaitín draíochta agus i gcaochadh súile bhí sí níos gráice ná níon na caillí. Ní raibh a fhios ag níon an Rí go dtáinig athrú ar a cuma ach ar siocair an rud a dúirt an chailleach tháinig crith trom uirthi.

'A dheirfiúr mo chroí,' arsa an prionsa, 'is é an mí-ádh a thug anseo thú inniu. Cad é an dóigh a dtig liom tú a thabhairt abhaile chuig d'athair agus do mháthair?'

'Dhéanfaidh mise álainn arís í,' arsa an chailleach, 'má phósann tú mo níon.'

Ansin bhuail an chailleach a níon féin leis an tslait agus rinne cailín dóighiúil di arís.

'An bpósfaidh tú anois í?' ar sise leis an phrionsa.

'Ní phósfaidh mé anois ná go brách í,' arsa an prionsa, 'agus níl dúil agam codladh dhá oíche sa leabaidh amháin go dtí go ndíbrítear thusa agus gach duine de do chineál ó éadan na tíre seo.'

Scairt sé ar na saighdiúirí agus d'imigh an chailleach agus a níon chomh tapaidh le séideán gaoithe.

Ba le croí brónach a thug mac an Rí a dheirfiúr abhaile. Chonaic an Rí ag teacht iad agus tháinig sé giota ina n-araicis. 'An í seo Cailleach an Ardáin Ghlais atá leat?' ar seisean leis an phrionsa.

'Faraor, a athair, ní hí,' arsa an prionsa. 'Seo do níon féin ach caithfidh mé a insint duit gurb í an chailleach a chuir sa chrot sin í.'

'Mo leanbh, mo níon,' arsa an Rí. 'Ba bhrónach an lá é a chuaigh tú amach le sabharcáin a chruinniú. Ach ná bac leis. Tiontóidh an t-arm amach amárach agus bhéarfaidh siad an chailleach ghránna go dtí an caisleán seo. Dóifear í mar fhód mónadh ach bhéarfaidh mé uirthi ar dtús áilleacht mo níona a thabhairt ar ais.'

'An dtabharfaidh tú cead domhsa a ghabháil leis an arm?' arsa mac an Rí.

'Cinnte,' arsa an Rí. 'Ní rachaidh siad ar lorg na caillí gan tú. Ach ná déan dearmad go gcaithfear í a thabhairt anseo beo. Ní bhfaighidh mé suaimhneas intinne go deo go dtuga mé breithiúnas báis uirthi.'

'Dhéanfar sin uilig,' arsa an prionsa.

'Tá súil agam go n-éireoidh leat,' arsa an Rí, 'ach caithfidh tú a bheith cúramach. Tá mé beagnach cinnte go rachaidh sí as amharc in uaimh inteacht faoin talamh nuair a gheobhaidh sí le fios go bhfuil an t-arm ar a lorg. Déan fáinne thart fán áit a bhfaca tú í agus ná lig di imeacht.'

'Sin an dóigh is fearr,' arsa an prionsa. 'Tá cú agam a rachas isteach san uile uaimh agus ní baol go dtiocfaimid abhaile gan í. Tabhair aire mhaith, a athair, do mo dheirfiúr dhílis go dtige mise ar ais.'

Maidin lá arna mhárach gléasadh dhá mhíle de na saighdiúirí ab fhearr a bhí ag an Rí agus chuir siad tús ar an aistear, an prionsa ag a gceann. Shílfeadh duine go raibh a fhios ag an chú cad é a bhí riachtanach. Chuaigh sé isteach san uile uaimh a casadh orthu agus is rómhinic a tháinig sé amach cumhdaithe le clábar. Thug obair an mhadaidh uchtach úr don phrionsa agus na saighdiúirí agus d'aithin siad go mbeadh an chailleach ina príosúnach in am ghairid.

Mhair an cuartú ar feadh seachtaine ach ní raibh an chailleach ná a níon le feiceáil. Ag éirí na gréine maidin amháin chuaigh an prionsa, an cú leis, fhad le gleann beag ina bhfaca sé giorria cupla lá roimhe sin. Bhí sé imníoch ar siocair nach raibh tuairisc ar bith aige le cur chuig an Rí agus ba é sin an fáth a dteachaigh sé leis féin. Chuaigh an cú isteach in uaimh agus tháinig amach go tapaidh, giota éadaigh leis ina bhéal.

'An áit ina bhfuil éadaí féadann daoine a bheith,' arsa an prionsa leis féin. Shéid sé adharc agus in am ghairid tháinig baicle saighdiúr chuige. 'Tá Cailleach an Ardáin Ghlais anseo,' arsa an prionsa, 'ach ní thiocfaidh sí amach i dtobainneacht.'

'Thig linn an talamh a thochailt ar an dá thaobh,' arsa fear de na saighdiúirí.

Leis sin, tháinig an chailleach amach as an uaimh. Thug cupla saighdiúir léim cun tosaigh le greim a fháil uirthi ach d'iarr an prionsa orthu seasamh ar gcúl go ceann bomaite.

'Cad é atá a dhíth oraibh?' arsa an chailleach.

'Tusa agus do níon agus an slaitín draíochta,' arsa an prionsa.

'Má éiríonn leat,' arsa an chailleach, 'beidh lúcháir ort fáil réite linn.'

'Gheobhaimid réite libh gan mórán trioblóide,' arsa an prionsa. 'An bhfuil sibh ag teacht linn go socair nó an mbeidh sé riachtanach againn brosnach a chruinniú agus sibh a dhódh anseo?'

'Tug do dheirfiúr anseo,' arsa an chailleach, 'agus dhéanfaidh mise chomh dóighiúil í is a bhí riamh.'

Ar an bhomaite sin thug an cú léim ar aghaidh agus sular mhothaigh an chailleach é sciob sé an slaitín draíochta as a láimh.

'Tá mo chumhacht imithe anois,' arsa an chailleach. 'Fhad is a bhí an slaitín agam in mo sheilbh ní raibh binn agam ort féin ná d'arm.'

Bheir beirt de na saighdiúirí ar an chailleach agus cheistnigh an prionsa í fána níon.

'Níl sí i bhfad uainn,' arsa an chailleach.

'Ní fhágfaimid an gleann seo gan í,' arsa an prionsa.

'Tá mise anseo,' arsa níon na caillí ag teacht amach as an uaimh. Chuir a cuid áilleachta iontas ar an phrionsa agus rinne sé suas a intinn a iarraidh ar an Rí gan í a chur chun báis. Bhí sí go díreach chomh hálainn lena dheirfiúr féin sular buaileadh í leis an tslaitín draíochta.

'Cuirfidh mé ceist amháin ort,' arsa an prionsa, 'sula dtéimid chun tosaigh. An í seo do mháthair?' ar seisean.

'Ní hí,' arsa an cailín álainn.

'Ní chuireann an freagar sin iontas orm,' arsa an prionsa. Thug sé ordú do na saighdiúirí aghaidh a thabhairt ar an bhaile agus an chailleach a thabhairt leo. 'Siúlfaidh an cailín seo le mo thaobh féin,' ar seisean.

Nuair a tháinig an prionsa agus na saighdiúirí fhad leis an chaisleán d'ordaigh an Rí go gcuirfí an chailleach agus a níon i seomra dhorcha go maidin. 'Bhéarfaidh mé breithiúnas orthu,' ar seisean, 'ag éirí na gréine.'

'Cá bhfuil mo dheirfiúr?' arsa an prionsa leis an Rí.

'Tá sí ina seomra féin ó d'imigh tú ar lorg na caillí,' arsa an Rí. 'Níl sí ag ithe ná ag ól,' ar seisean, 'ach is fearr dúinn a ghabháil chun cainte léi.'

'An bhfuil tú tinn, a Úna?' arsa an prionsa nuair a chuaigh sé isteach sa tseomra. Níor labhair an cailín. Ansin bhuail an prionsa sa ghualainn í leis an tslaitín draíochta agus le caochadh súile bhí sí chomh dóighiúil, álainn is a bhí sí riamh. Tháinig athrú iontach uirthi i mbomaite agus phóg sí an prionsa agus a hathair.

'Beidh lúcháir ort a chluinstin,' arsa an Rí, 'gur éirigh le do dheartháir agus an t-arm greim a fháil ar an chailligh agus a níon agus go bhfuil siad le cur chun báis amárach.'

'B'fhéidir, a athair,' arsa an cailín, 'nach bhfuil a fhios agat go bhfuil níon na caillí saor ó choir. Nuair a chonaic mise í ar dtús bhí sí chomh gránna is a bhí mise le seachtain ach nuair a bhuail an chailleach í leis an tslat, d'athraigh a cuma. Go dearfa, a athair, ní fhaca mé cailín ar bith riamh a bhí leath chomh dóighiúil.'

'Tá mo dheirfiúr ag insint na fírinne,' arsa an prionsa, 'agus tá mé cinnte, a athair, go gcuirfidh a scéal iontas ort. Níl baint ar bith ag an chailligh léi ach gur choinnigh sí í faoi dhraíocht ó bhí sí ina páiste. Ní chuirfidh sé iontas orm a chluinstin gur níon Rí atá inti agus níl sé ceart í a choinneáil i seomra dhorcha ar feadh na hoíche.'

'Is maith liom,' arsa an Rí, 'an tuairisc seo a fháil. Cluinfidh mé a scéal nuair a bheas an dinnéar thart.'

Ba mhór an lúcháir a bhí ar an bhanríon nuair a chonaic sí go dtáinig a cuid áilleachta ar ais chuig Úna. Nuair a bhí an dinnéar thart d'iarr an Rí ar an phrionsa an cailín coimhthíoch a thabhairt os a chomhair. Bhí lúcháir ar an phrionsa sin a dhéanamh de bhrí go raibh sé go trom i ngrá léi ón bhomaite a tháinig sí amach as an uaimh. Nuair a tháinig an cailín bocht i láthair an Rí chaoin sí go dúthrachtach. Bhí trua ag an Rí di agus chuir a cuid áilleachta iontas air. D'iarr Úna cead í a phógadh agus dúirt an Rí: 'Tá mo cheadsa agus cead na banríona agat í a phógadh agus a cuid deor a thriomú. Abair léi go bhfuil pardún aici siúd is nár chuala mé focal amháin den scéal atá le hinsint aici.'

B'álainn an radharc é an dá chailín a fheiceáil i lámha a chéile. Ní raibh ar thalamh na hÉireann beirt eile le cur i gcomórtas leo.

'Suigh ag a taobh anois, a Úna,' arsa an Rí, 'go gcluinimid a scéal.'

'Go raibh míle maith agat, a Rí uasail,' arsa an cailín álainn. 'Cluinfidh tú anois scéal atá chomh fíor is atá sé brónach. Is mian liom a rá ar dtús gur níon de chuid Rí na Spáinne mise gí nach bhfaca mé m'athair ná mo mháthair ó bhí mé ceithre bliana d'aois.'

'Sin an tuairisc is iontaí a fuair mé le linn mo shaoil,' arsa an Rí. 'Creidim an uile fhocal de do scéal de bhrí go bhfuil tú cosúil le do mháthair.'

'An féidir, a Rí uasail, go bhfaca tú mo mháthair? Inis domh, an bhfuil sí beo?'

'Cuirfidh sé iontas ort a chluinstin,' arsa an Rí, 'go dtáinig d'athair agus do mháthair ar cuairt go dtí an tír seo anuraidh agus gur chaith siad seachtain sa chaisleán seo. Agus anois nuair a smaoiním air d'inis siad domh gur goideadh páiste uathu seal blianta ó shin agus nach bhfuarthas riamh í.'

'Is mise an leanbh a goideadh,' arsa an cailín. 'An gcuideoidh tú liom pilleadh chun an bhaile?'

'Gheall d'athair agus do mháthair cuairt eile a thabhairt go hÉirinn i mbliana agus táimid ag dréim go mbeidh siad anseo i gceann míosa. Má fhanann tusa anseo,' arsa an Rí, 'cuirfidh mise an prionsa seo (mo mhac) go dtí an Spáinn le hinsint dóibh go bhfuil tú i gcúram Rí na hÉireann agus gur mhaith liom dá dtigeadh siad anseo chomh tapaidh is is féidir leo. Más fearr leat é, ar an taobh eile, a ghabháil abhaile ar dtús thig leat an aistear a dhéanamh i gcuideachta mo mhic.'

'Is é an réiteach deireanach an ceann is fearr,' arsa an cailín álainn. 'Ní bheidh suaimhneas intinne ar bith agam go bhfeice mé mo bhunadh. Agus ó tharla go bhfuil m'athair agus mo mháthair ag teacht anseo ar cuairt beidh mise leo nó go dearfa is é mian mo chroí a bheith i gcuideachta do níona, gan trácht ort féin agus an bhanríon agus do mhac uasal.'

'Tá mé sásta le do rún,' arsa an Rí. 'Beidh an prionsa réidh le a ghabháil leat ar maidin amárach. Beidh féasta againn in d'onóir anocht agus féasta i bhfad níos mó nuair a thiocfas tú ar ais ins an tsamhradh.'

Thug an cailín buíochas lánchroíoch don Rí agus thit deora an áthais go frasach óna súile.

'Tabhair ordú do na saighdiúirí Cailleach an Ardáin Ghlais a thabhairt anseo i mbomaite,' arsa an Rí leis an phrionsa.

'Dhéanfar sin go tapaidh,' arsa an prionsa.

Chuaigh an prionsa agus cuid de na saighdiúirí go dtí an seomra ina raibh an chailleach faoi ghlas agus eochair, ach nuair a d'fhoscail siad an doras fuair siad í ina luí marbh ar an urlár. Tháinig an prionsa ar ais agus d'inis don Rí cad é mar a tharla.

'An bhfuil tú cinnte go bhfuil sí marbh?' arsa an Rí.

'Tá, a athair,' arsa an prionsa.

'Maith go leor,' arsa an Rí, 'tabhair ordú í a chur sé troithe faoin talamh.'

Ba é sin deireadh na caillí.

Chaith níon Rí na Spáinne an oíche sa tseomra leapa ab fhearr sa chaisleán agus ar maidin lá arna mhárach chuir an prionsa agus í féin tús ar an aistear go tír na Spáinne.

Nuair a tháinig siad go geaftaí an chaisleáin chuir teachtaire an Rí ceist orthu cad é a thug ansin iad.

'Tháinig muid ó thír na hÉireann,' arsa an prionsa, 'agus is dóiche go mbeidh aithne ag an Rí orainn.'

'Má tháinig sibh as Éirinn,' arsa an teachtaire, 'beidh lúcháir ar an Rí sibh a fheiceáil. Fan anseo go dtige mise ar ais.'

Bhí an Rí an-mhór leis an phrionsa nuair a bhí sé in Éirinn ar a chuid laetha saoire agus d'aithin sé é ar an bhomaite.

'Tá fáilte roimh mhac Rí na hÉireann,' ar seisean. 'Inis domh cé hí an cailín álainn seo atá in do chuideachta.'

'Ba mhaith liom, a Rí uasail,' arsa an prionsa, 'bomaite a ligint thart gan freagar a thabhairt ar do cheist. Ní mian liom barraíocht iontais a chur ort i dtobainneacht. Amharc uirthi go cúramach agus b'fhéidir nach mbeadh sé riachtanach agam focal ar bith a rá.'

Leis sin, tháinig an cailín chun tosaigh agus chuir a dhá láimh thart fá mhuineál a hathara.

'Is mise Deirdre,' ar sise, 'do leanbh bán, agus is tusa m'athair dílis.'

Ní raibh an Rí ábalta focal a labhairt ach thug an prionsa tarrtháil air. I mbomaite eile tháinig a chuid cainte ar ais chuige agus dúirt sé leis an phrionsa: 'An bhfuil mé in mo chodladh,' ar seisean, 'agus an brionglóid é seo?'

'Ní brionglóid ar bith é,' arsa an prionsa, 'ach bhí an nuaíocht róthobann agat. Seo do níon a goideadh nuair a bhí sí ina páiste. Bhí sí faoi dhraíocht ar feadh blianta ach níl sí faoi dhraíocht ar bith anois.'

'Cá bhfuil mo mháthair?' arsa an cailín.

'Tá sí sa chaisleán fá láthair,' arsa an Rí, 'ach caithfimid a bheith faichilleach. Tá croí lag ag an bhanríon agus d'fhéadfadh scanradh tobann a bás a thabhairt. Tá dochtúir ins an chaisleán agus inseoimid an scéal iontach seo dósan ar dtús. Beidh sé comhgarach má bhíonn a chuid seirbhíse a dhíth orainn.'

Leathuair ina dhiaidh sin bhí an Rí, an prionsa agus Deirdre i láthair na banríona. D'inis an prionsa fá mar a casadh an cailín air in Éirinn. 'Beidh cuimhne agat,' ar seisean leis an bhanríon, 'gur inis tú do m'athair nuair a bhí tú in Éirinn, gur chaill tú féin agus an Rí girseach bheag seacht mbliana déag ó shin.'

'Tá sin fíor,' arsa an bhanríon, 'ach táimid cinnte nach bhfuil sí beo.'

Fhad is a bhí an comhrá seo ag gabháil chun tosaigh bhí an oiread sin áthais ar Dheirdre is gur líon a súile le deora. Bhí trua ag an bhanríon di. Phóg sí í agus ansin dúirt sí: 'An bhfuil ball beag breithe ar chúl do chluaise clí?'

'Níl a fhios agam,' arsa an cailín.

Leis sin, shonraigh an bhanríon an ball breithe agus ghlaoigh sí os ard: 'Mo níon, mo níon!'

Go díreach mar a bhí an Rí ag dréim, thit sí i laige agus le caochadh súile bhí an dochtúir ag a taobh. I ndiaidh braon beag brandaí a ól, tháinig sí chuici féin, dhá láimh na níona a bhí i bhfad caillte casta thart fána muineál.

Nuair a chuaigh an scéala ar fud na Spáinne go bhfuarthas níon an Rí, tháinig uaisle na tíre go dtí an caisleán. Thit fear uasal amháin i ngrá le Deirdre ach is beag a shíl sé go raibh grá a croí tugtha cheana féin do mhac Rí na hÉireann.

Fá dheireadh scab na huaisle agus maidin amháin bhí comhrá ag Deirdre lena hathair.

'Tá an samhradh anseo anois,' ar sise, 'agus ba chóir dúinn cuairt a thabhairt ar Rí na hÉireann. Ba mhaith leis an phrionsa a ghabháil abhaile agus ní mian liomsa scarúint leis.'

'Ach ab é an prionsa,' arsa an Rí, 'ní móide go bhfeicfeadh d'athair ná do mháthair go deo thú, agus má tá tú i ngrá leis, ní thig linn seasamh in do bhealach.'

'Tá sé chomh maith agam a insint duit, a athair, gur gheall mé é a phósadh sular fhág muid Éire agus tá súil agam go mbeidh tú sásta le mo rogha.'

'A níon mo chroí,' arsa an Rí, 'cad é an fáth a mbeinn ar a athrú de dhóigh? Níor casadh orm riamh aon fhear óg le cur i gcomórtas leis. Chead againn an nuaíocht a chur i bhfios don bhanríon.'

Le scéal fada a dhéanamh gairid pósadh Deirdre agus an prionsa lá arna mhárach ach caitheadh an bhainis in Éirinn. Ba é sin tús carantais fhada idir Éire agus an Spáinn.

NÓTA

1 *Derry People and Tirconaill News*, 30 January, 6, 13, 20, 27 February, 6, 13 March 1937.

Mac na Baintrí

Ins na laetha fadó bhí baintreach ina cónaí i gContae Thír Eoghain comhgarach ag an áit a bhfuil an Caisleán Dearg fá láthair. Ní raibh aici ach mac amháin agus fán am a thoisíos an scéal bhí sé fá thuairim cúig bliana déag d'aois. Bhí sé ar bhuachaill chomh breá is a tífeá i siúl lae agus bhí meas mór ag an uile dhuine air.

Maidin amháin chuaigh sé ag iascaireacht agus dúirt sé lena mháthair go mbeadh sé ar ais ag am dinnéara. 'Tá tuile san abhainn inniu,' arsa an mháthair, 'agus ba chóir duit a bheith faichilleach.'

'Ná bíodh eagla ar bith ort, a mháthair,' arsa an buachaill, 'bhéarfaidh mé aire mhaith domh féin.'

Tamall beag ina dhiaidh sin chuaigh an bhaintreach go dtí an tobar fá choinne canna uisce. Bhí carraig mhór in aice an tobair agus bhí cailín óg, dóighiúil ina suí ar an charraig.

'Shíl mé,' arsa an bhaintreach, 'go raibh aithne agam ar an uile ghirseach sa cheantar seo, ach caithfidh mé a aidmheáil nach bhfaca mé thusa riamh.'

'Ní raibh mé anseo riamh roimhe,' arsa an cailín, 'ach beidh mé anseo go deireadh na seachtaine. An bhfuil mac agat a bhfuil Pádraig mar ainm air?'

'Tá,' arsa an bhaintreach. 'Chuaigh sé amach ag iascaireacht ach beidh sé ar ais gan mhoill. Ar casadh ort riamh é?'

'Níor casadh,' arsa an cailín, 'ach chonaic mé é i mbrionglóid. Rugadh é féin agus mise an lá amháin. Tá tuile san abhainn,' ar sise.

'Tá go cinnte,' arsa an bhaintreach.

'Glac mo chomhairle,' arsa an cailín, 'agus tar liomsa go dtí an abhainn.'

D'fhág an bhaintreach an canna ag an tobar agus in am ghairid bhí an péire ar bhruach na habhna. Sheas siad tamall beag ag amharc ar an tuile agus fá dheireadh léim an cailín isteach san uisce. I mbomaite eile chonaic an bhaintreach Pádraig ag teacht anuas leis an tuile agus thoisigh sí ag béicfigh. Ní raibh cúis imní ar bith aici de bhrí go dtug an cailín Pádraig slán go dtí an bruach le caochadh súile.

'Thit mé san abhainn, a mháthair,' arsa Pádraig, 'agus is dóiche go mbáithfí mé ach ab é an cailín seo.'

'Ní raibh baol ar bith ort,' arsa an cailín.

'Tá eagla orm go raibh,' arsa an buachaill, 'ach níl dadaí contráilte anois ach gur chaill mé bradán agus mo shlat iascaireachta.'

'Níl siad caillte,' arsa an cailín, agus leis sin, tháinig sióg fhad leo, an tslat i láimh amháin agus bradán sa láimh eile. Thug Pádraig buíochas don tsióg agus chuir an bhaintreach an bradán ina haprún.

'Tabhair buíochas don chailín seo,' arsa an tsióg. 'Aon rud dá dtig leis an tslua sí a dhéanamh ar a son, dhéanfar i gcónaí é.'

Nuair a d'imigh an tsióg dúirt an bhaintreach leis an chailín nach raibh a fhios aici cad é an dóigh le buíochas a thabhairt di.

'Is é an dóigh is mian liomsa buíochas a thabhairt di,' arsa Pádraig, 'grá mo chroí a thairgint di.'

'Sin an buíochas is fearr,' arsa an cailín. 'Sin an fáth a thug anseo mé. Níon baird mé,' ar sise 'ach ní thig liom níos mó a rá fá láthair.'

'An dtiocfaidh tú abhaile linn?' arsa Pádraig.

'Tiocfaidh,' arsa an cailín. 'Níl dúil agam scarúint leat ach caithfidh mé a insint duit go bhfuil trioblóid romhainn. Beidh an bhuaidh linn má ghlacann tú mo chomhairle.'

'Sin an rún atá agam,' arsa Pádraig.

Tháinig siad abhaile go teach na baintrí agus i ndiaidh béile maith a chaitheamh d'inis an cailín a scéal mar a leanas. 'Tá m'athair ina bhard agus tá an posta is airde aige i gCúirt Rí na hÉireann. Níl níon ar bith aige ach mise agus tá Eibhlín mar ainm orm. Cupla mí ó shin thit namhaid de chuid m'athara i ngrá liom agus ní raibh suaimhneas ar bith againn ón lá sin go dtí an lá inniu. Fá thuairim seachtain ó shin bhí m'athair ó bhaile lá amháin agus fágadh mise liom féin. Ag uair an mheán lae chonaic mé scaifte fear ag teannadh leis an teach agus d'aithin mé go raibh siad ag teacht mar gheall ar mé a fhuadach. Ní raibh slí ar bith agam ach mé féin a ísliú le rópa ó fhuinneoig chúil agus a ghabháil i bhfolach i gcoill atá buailte leis an teach. Chaith mé an oíche sin in uaimh agus thit mé 'mo chodladh. Ag bánú an lae tháinig an tsióg a chonaic sibh inniu fhad liom agus chuir ceist orm an raibh mé ag brionglóidigh. Dúirt mé go raibh agus go raibh comhrá agam le buachaill arbh ainm dó Pádraig.'

'Sin mac baintrí i gContae Thír Eoghain,' arsa an tsióg. 'Ar mhaith leat é a fheiceáil?' ar seisean.

'Ba mhaith liom,' arsa mise.

'Maith go leor,' arsa an tsióg. 'Is fearr duit slán a fhágáil ag Teamhair go ceann tamaill. Inseoidh mise do d'athair,' ar seisean, 'go bhfuil tú slán agus go mb'éigean duit an baile a fhágáil. Ansin rachaidh mé leat go Tír Eoghain.'

'Choinnigh an tsióg a fhocal agus sin an fáth a bhfuil mé anseo.'

'Tá súil agam,' arsa Pádraig, 'go bhfanóidh tú anseo go brách. Ní thiocfaidh do namhaid an bealach seo.'

'Faraor,' arsa Eibhlín, 'ní mar sin atá an scéal. Tá siad ar mo lorg ar an bhomaite seo ach tá na siógaí á gcur ar seachrán. Ní mhairfidh sin ach tamall. Gheobhaidh siad amach an áit seo roimh dheireadh na míosa agus beidh do chuidiúsa a dhíth orm an t-am sin. Féadann sé go mbeimid ábalta an bhuaidh a fháil orthu ach ní gan trioblóid.'

'Thig leat taobhadh liomsa,' arsa Pádraig. 'Níl eagla orm mo bheatha a chur i gcontúirt ar do shonsa,' ar seisean.

'Tá do bheatha chomh dílis agamsa le mo bheatha féin,' arsa Eibhlín.

'Mo bheannacht oraibh araon,' arsa an bhaintreach.

Chuir Eibhlín a lámh ina póca agus tharraing amach slabhradh óir. 'Am ar bith,' ar sise, 'ar mian liom an tsióg a theacht chugam cuirim an slabhradh seo thart fá mo mhuineál.' Ansin chuir sí an slabhradh ar a muineál agus shiúil an tsióg isteach ar an doras. 'An bhfuair tú nuaíocht ar bith ó chonaic mé fá dheireadh thú?' arsa Eibhlín.

'Fuair,' arsa an tsióg. 'Tá do namhaid fá láthair i gContae Mhaigh Eo agus beidh go ceann seachtaine nó níos mó. Tá a fhios acu anois gur imir na siógaí cleas orthu agus tá siad ar buile. Ní bheimid ábalta iad a choinneáil ón chontae seo ach ní bheidh siad anseo go ceann míosa de réir mo bharúla. Is cuma cén uair a thiocfas siad beidh an slua sí anseo rompu. Beidh cuidiú Phádraig a dhíth orainn,' arsa an tsióg agus, leis sin, chuaigh sé as amharc.

Mhair an scéal mar seo ar feadh míosa ach sa deireadh tháinig an tsióg fhad le teach na baintrí le scéala go raibh ceithre mharcach ag cuartú ó theach go teach fá thuairim deich míle ar shiúl. 'Tá mé den bharúil,' ar seisean, 'go mbeidh siad anseo amárach.'

'Inis domh,' arsa Eibhlín, 'an mbeidh cuidiú le fáil againn ón tslua sí?'

'Beidh go cinnte,' arsa an tsióg, 'ach ní bheidh sé inár gcumhacht iad a chur chun báis. Cuirfimid an fraoch le thinidh agus bhéarfaidh an toit mórán trioblóide dóibh. Is fearr duitse agus do mháthair Phádraig,' ar seisean, 'a ghabháil isteach sa dún ina bhfuil na siógaí i bhfolach. Rachaidh mise agus seachtar eile fhad leis an choill atá ar bhruach na habhna agus beidh Pádraig linn. Caithfimid troid a chur orthu siúd is nach dtig leis na siógaí buille a bhualadh. Titfidh an chuid is mó den troid ar Phádraig ach fhad is a bheas an claíomh seo ina láimh beidh sé dofheicseanach. Má chailleann sé an claíomh beidh an bhuaidh ag na marcaigh.'

'Nach fearr domhsa a ghabháil leis?' arsa Eibhlín.

'Ní fearr,' arsa an tsióg. 'Ní bheidh faill againne aire a thabhairt duit gan neamart a dhéanamh inár gcuid oibre. Beidh na siógaí ag déanamh súgán de rútaí na gcrann le cur roimh a ngearráin mar gheall ar go dtitfidh siad faoi na marcaigh. Ní bheadh Pádraig ábalta acu ar dhóigh ar bith eile.'

'An síleann tú,' arsa Pádraig, 'go mbeidh sé riachtanach iad a mharbhadh?'

'Mura n-éirí leat iadsan a chur chun báis, muirfidh siadsan thusa,' arsa an tsióg. 'Ní greann ar bith seo ach cogadh dáiríre.'

'Más mar sin atá an scéal,' arsa Pádraig, 'titfidh na buillí go trom.'

Maidin lá arna mhárach roimh éirí na gréine chuaigh Eibhlín agus an bhaintreach go dún na sióg i ndiaidh slán a fhágáil ag Pádraig. Gan mhoill ina dhiaidh sin thug na siógaí agus Pádraig aghaidh ar an choill. Bhí cnoc beag in aice na coilleadh ar a raibh mórán fraoigh agus cuireadh an fraoch ar lasadh.

'Tá an ghaoth inár n-éadan,' arsa Pádraig.

'Thig linn an ghaoth a athrú,' arsa an tsióg, 'nuair a thiocfas an namhaid comhgarach. Caithfimid iad a mhealladh isteach sa choill agus cuideoidh na crainn leatsa thú féin a chosaint.'

Gan mhoill ina dhiaidh sin bhí na marcaigh ar amharc. Tháinig siad chun tosaigh ar cosa in airde. Thiontaigh an ghaoth agus thiomáin an toit isteach sa choill iad. Bhí an toit ag dalladh na marcach chomh maith leis na gearráin agus bhí siad ag rith ar fud na coilleadh gan a fhios acu cá raibh siad ag gabháil. Lean Pádraig agus na siógaí iad agus siúd is nach dtiocfadh leis na marcaigh é a fheiceáil bhí contúirt go dtitfeadh Pádraig faoi cheann de na gearráin. Thoisigh na siógaí ag déanamh rópaí agus á gcur trasna ó chrann go crann. In am ghairid thit ceann de na gearráin comhgarach don áit a raibh Pádraig ina sheasamh agus caitheadh an marcach go dtí an talamh. Sula raibh faill aige éirí sciob Pádraig an ceann de leis an chlaíomh. 'Níl ach triúr acu ann anois,' ar seisean leis an tsióg a bhí ag a thaobh.

'Is leor sin,' arsa an tsióg.

Tháinig duine eile de na marcaigh thart agus chonaic sé an gearrán a bhí gan mharcach. Thuirling sé mar gheall ar a chomrádaí a fháil ach chuir claíomh Phádraig deireadh leis.

'Níl ach beirt fágtha anois,' arsa Pádraig.

'Is leor sin,' arsa an tsióg.

D'fhág Pádraig an claíomh ar an talamh mar gheall ar a shúile a chumailt agus chonaic duine de na marcaigh é. Thug sé áladh ar an áit a raibh Pádraig ina sheasamh ach nuair a bhí sé fá thuairim seacht slat ar shiúl thit an gearrán trasna ar cheann de na rópaí a bhí leagtha ag na siógaí. Bhí an claíomh ag Pádraig ina láimh sula raibh an marcach ábalta éirí, agus bhain sé an ceann de leis an chéad bhuille.

'Ach ab é gur éirigh linn an gearrán a leagaint,' arsa an tsióg, 'bheadh mac na baintrí ar shlua na marbh.'

'Tá sin fíor,' arsa Pádraig. 'Bhí sé náireach agam an claíomh a fhágáil ar an talamh. Tá mé buíoch de na siógaí agus tá súil agam go mbeidh an bhuaidh againn in am ghairid.'

'Is maith an rud an misneach,' arsa an tsióg, 'ach tá trioblóid go leor romhainn go fóill. Seo na gearráin a chaill a gcuid marcach agus caithfear aire a thabhairt dóibh. Tá an fraoch dóite anois agus beidh an toit imithe i mbomaite eile. Tá marcach amháin fágtha agus ní baol dó titim ina chodladh. Fágfaidh sé an choill nuair a bheas deireadh leis an toit.'

'An é an ceannfort atá fágtha?' arsa Pádraig.

'Is é,' arsa an tsióg. 'An fear a bhfuil dúil aige Eibhlín a phósadh.'

'Tím,' arsa Pádraig. 'Beidh ár sáith le déanamh againn.'

Nuair a bhí an toit imithe tháinig siad amach as an choill agus thug siad na gearráin leo. Leis sin tháinig sióg nach bhfaca Pádraig riamh roimhe chucu le rása agus d'inis dóibh go raibh marcach ar a bhealach go dún na sióg.

'Sin an ceannfort,' arsa duine de na siógaí a bhí le Pádraig sa choill. 'Tá Eibhlín agus do mháthair i gcontúirt,' ar seisean.

'Cad é is fearr dúinn a dhéanamh?' arsa Pádraig.

'Caithfimid é a leanúint,' arsa an tsióg. 'Tabhair thusa leat an gearrán donn agus tabhair d'aghaidh ar an dún. Coinnigh an claíomh in do láimh agus má fhaigheann tú suas leis an namhaid ní fheicfidh sé ach gearrán gan mharcach. Is dóiche go ndéanfaidh sé moill leis an ghearrán a cheangal de chrann go dtige sé ar ais ón dún. Lig don ghearrán seasamh go dtí go bhfaighe sé greim air. Buail é ansin mar a bhuail tú an chuid eile agus nuair a bheas sé marbh tabhair an dá ghearrán leat go dtí an dún. Beidh sinne ansin chomh luath leat.'

Ba ghairid go raibh Pádraig sa diallait agus d'imigh an gearrán donn mar a bheadh séideán gaoithe ann. Go díreach mar a dúirt an tsióg chonaic an marcach gearrán ag teacht ina dhiaidh ar cosa in airde agus d'aithin sé é mar cheann de na gearráin a thug sé leis ón bhaile. Thuirling sé agus bhí lúcháir air nuair a chonaic sé gur sheas an gearrán go socair. Fuair sé greim ar an tsrian agus ar an bhomaite sin scoilt Pádraig a cheann le buille den chlaíomh. Thit sé marbh faoi cheann an ghearráin.

Thug Pádraig an dá ghearrán go dún na sióg agus bhí lúcháir mhór ar Eibhlín agus a mháthair é a fheiceáil beo. 'Ach ab é na sióga í,' ar seisean, 'chuirfeadh na marcaigh deireadh liom.'

'Féadann sin a bheith fíor,' arsa duine de na sióga í, 'ach rinne tú obair inmholta leis an chlaíomh.'

'An síleann tú,' arsa Eibhlín, 'go bhfuil deireadh lenár gcuid trioblóide anois?'

'Tá, go ceann bliana,' arsa an tsióg, 'ach bheadh sé dainséarach pilleadh chun an bhaile san am i láthair. Is fearr duit fanacht i dteach na baintrí go dtige mise ar ais go dtí an dún seo.'

'An bhfuil dúil agat an chontae seo a fhágáil?' arsa Pádraig.

'Tá,' arsa an tsióg. 'Tá sé riachtanach agam a ghabháil go Teamhair de bhrí go bhfuil eagla orm go mbeidh éirí amach in éadan an Rí agus athair an chailín seo. Fágfaidh na sióga í slán agaibh anocht agus rachaidh bliain agus lá thart sula raibh muid ar ais. Tabhair aire mhaith do na gearráin ar eagla go mbeadh siad a dhíth orainn san am atá le a theacht.'

Nuair a shroich na sióga í Teamhair bhí comhrá fada acu leis an Rí nó go dearfa bhí siad go han-mhór leis. D'inis siad d'athair Eibhlín go raibh a níon slán ach go raibh dúil aici bliain eile a chaitheamh i gContae Thír Eoghain.

'Sin mar is fearr é,' arsa an bard. 'Tá trioblóid ag briseadh amach sa taobh seo den tír agus tá arm an Rí ag déanamh réidh fá choinne cogaidh. Beidh cuidiú na sióg a dhíth orainn nuair a thoiseos an troid.'

'Beimid ar thaobh an Rí,' arsa na sióga í.

Cupla lá ina dhiaidh sin thoisigh an cogadh. Bhí saighdiúirí an Rí dílis dó agus throid siad go bríomhar.

Thoisigh an troid ar chnoc a bhí deich míle ón chaisleán agus ba deacair an méid fear a bhí ar thaobh an namhad a áireamh. Nuair a chuaigh mí thart bhí mórán marbh ar gach taobh agus shonraigh an Rí go raibh a chuid fear ag cailleadh talaimh. Bliain ina dhiaidh seo bhí an troid ag gabháil ar aghaidh go díreach mar a thoisigh sé agus ba deacair a rá cén taobh a thiocfadh amach as le buaidh. Bhí saighdiúirí an Rí ag titim ar gcúl lá ar lá agus fá dheireadh bhí an briseadh deireanach á throid i máigh a bhí in aice leis an chaisleán. Ní raibh ach fá thuairim dhá chéad fear fágtha ar gach taobh. Bhí arm an Rí gléasta i gcultacha glasa agus bhí cultacha dubha ar na saighdiúirí a bhí ina n-éadan. Bhí an Rí agus an bard ag amharc ar an troid ó fhuinneoig sa chaisleán.

Thoisigh an troid ag briseadh an lae agus tamall beag ina dhiaidh sin chonaic an Rí agus an bard fiche gearrán ag teannadh le máigh an áir ach ní raibh aon mharcach le feiceáil. Thug na gearráin áladh isteach i measc na bhfear a bhí ag marbhadh a chéile agus thoisigh na saighdiúirí dubha ag titim ar gach taobh de na gearráin. Chuir seo iontas ar an Rí agus an bard agus i gceann uaire ní raibh saighdiúir amháin fágtha ag an namhaid, siúd is go raibh céad go leith de shaighdiúirí an Rí beo slán. D'fhág an Rí an caisleán agus shiúil sé i gcuideachta an bhaird fhad leis an áit a raibh na gearráin ina seasamh. Leis sin chuala sé guth ag rá: 'Tá an t-am ag gach fear a chlaíomh a chaitheamh ar an talamh.'

Thit fiche claíomh ar an léana agus chonaic an Rí naoi gcloigne déag d'fheara breátha agus cailín óg amháin ina suí ins na diallaití. Ghlaoigh an bard os ard: 'Mo níon! Mo níon!'

'Tá mé anseo, a athair,' arsa Eibhlín, 'agus seo ag mo thaobh an fear a shábháil mé agus a shábháil arm an Rí inniu.'

Chuir an Rí agus an bard fáilte fhíor roimh Phádraig agus ansin d'inis Eibhlín an scéal a leanas: 'Chonaic mé

Pádraig i dtús i mbrionglóid agus ar siocair go raibh namhaid ar mo lorg, chuaigh mé, ar chomhairle sióige, go Contae Thír Eoghain. Lean ceathrar fear mé ach chuir Pádraig agus na siógaí deireadh leo. Fá thuairim bliain ó shin fuair muid le fios gur chuir namhaid an Rí cogadh air agus thoisigh Pádraig ag déanamh réidh fá choinne na hoibre a rinneadh anseo inniu. B'éigean dó iomlán Chontae Thír Eoghain a shiúl mar gheall ar na fir seo a fháil isteach san arm bheag. Ní raibh acu ach ceithre ghearrán a bhain siad ó na marcaigh a marbhadh agus b'éigean dóibh sé cinn déag eile a fháil. Nuair a bhí seo uilig déanta thug na siógaí fiche claíomh dóibh. Bheadh duine ar bith a mbeadh ceann de na claímheacha seo ina láimh dofheicseanach agus sin an fáth nach bhfaca sibh aon duine againn go dtí gur fhág muid na claímheacha síos. Ansin chaith siad mí ag cleachtadh úsáid a dhéanamh de na claímheacha agus maidin amháin tháinig sióg fhad leo agus dúirt go raibh an namhaid ag fáil na buaidhe ar arm an Rí, agus go raibh ár gcuidiú a dhíth go cruaidh. Chuir muid tús ar an aistear go Teamhair agus bhí muid go díreach in am leis an choróin a shábháil do Rí na hÉireann.'

'Ní hé an choróin amháin a shábháil sibh,' arsa an Rí, 'ach mo bheatha fosta. Tá an cogadh seo ag gabháil ar aghaidh le corradh le bliain agus ba bheag mo chuid codlata ar feadh an ama sin. Tá mé ag éirí sean,' ar seisean, 'agus ní fada a bheas mo réim. Ní thig liom níos lú a dhéanamh anois ná an choróin a thabhairt don fhear bhreá seo agus beidh sé ina Rí ón lá seo amach.'

'A Rí uasail,' arsa Pádraig, 'ní raibh mise ag dréim leis an onóir seo. Is fíor go dtáinig muid anseo le cuidiú leat agus Eibhlín a thabhairt abhaile chuig a hathair. Féadaim a rá fosta gurb é mian mo chroí Eibhlín a phósadh má tá a hathair sásta.'

'Tá bród orm,' arsa an bard, 'fear mar thú a fheiceáil lena taobh.'

'Maith go leor,' arsa an Rí, 'beidh Rí agus Banríon nua againn nuair a bheas an pósadh thart.'

Fuair na buachaillí ó Thír Eoghain a bhí le Pádraig an lá sin postaí arda san arm úr a toghadh gan mhoill ina dhiaidh sin agus tháinig an bhaintreach a chónaí go Teamhair.

Chead againn slán fada a fhágáil acu!

NÓTA

1 *Derry People and Tirconaill News*, 20, 27 March, 3, 10, 17, 24 April 1937.

Aguisín I

Gadaí Dubh na Slóna

Bhí Rí ina chónaí in Éirinn fada ó shin agus bhí triúr mac aige. Bhí a bhean (an bhanríon) ina bean chaíúil, dóighiúil faoi mheas ag gach duine ach go háirithe ag an Rí é féin. Lá amháin tháinig an bás uirthi agus scairt sí ar an Rí go colbha na leapa. 'Faraor,' ar sí, 'tá mo laethasa ar bhealach a bheith caite agus is mian liom anois achainí a iarraidh ort sula bhfágaim an saol seo agus is é sin: go dtabharfaidh tú gealltanas domh, mar gheall orm féin agus ar mo pháistí, go ndéanfaidh tú teach ar an oileán uaigneach atá amuigh san fharraige agus go bhfágfaidh tú ann iad nó go raibh an fear is óige acu bliain is fiche d'aois. Cuir máistir scoile ina gcuideachta agus oiread bídh agus dí is a bheas a dhíth orthu ar feadh an ama sin, agus ná bíodh fios ná tuairisc ag aon duine cá bhfuil siad.'

Gheall an Rí sin a dhéanamh agus é ag gol go brónach. Ansin d'fhág an bhanríon slán aige féin agus ag na páistí agus dhruid a súile le gan a bhfoscailt níos mó ar an tsaol seo. Chuir a bás chomh trom sin ar an Rí nár amharc sé fá dhadaí go ceann míosa, agus ag smaoineamh ansin ar an ghealltanas a thug sé don bhanríon nuair a bhí sí ar leabaidh an bháis, chonacthas dó go raibh an t-am aige é a choimhlíonadh. Chruinnigh sé mórán cuidithe agus lucht ceirde agus ba ghairid go raibh caisleán breá tógtha aige ar an oileán. Thug sé leis ansin na páistí agus máistir scoile, bia agus deoch den uile chineál, agus i ndiaidh deireadh a fhágáil ar an oileán, tháinig sé abhaile go huaigneach, cráite.

I gceann bliana nó mar sin tháinig dhá phrionsa a bhí ina gcónaí sa chúige ba chomhgaraí dó ar cuairt chuige. Ba mhór an fear seilge an Rí é féin agus fhad is a d'fhan na prionsaí aige is ag seilg a chaith siad an chuid is mó den am.

Aon oíche amháin dá raibh siad ag caint is ag comhrá dúirt fear de na prionsaí gur mhór an t-iontas gur fhan an Rí a fhad gan pósadh arís.

'Faraor,' arsa an Rí, 'chuir bás na banríona chomh trom sin orm gur deacair liom pósadh go brách.'

'Ná géill dó sin,' arsa an prionsa, 'ní féidir leat a bheith beo mar atá tú. Má thig tú linne ar maidin amárach ní bheidh tú i bhfad gan bean chéile.'

'Bíodh sé mar sin,' arsa an Rí.

Ar maidin lá arna mhárach d'fhág an triúr an caisleán agus shiúil leo go titim na hoíche. Chuaigh siad isteach i dteach bheag ar thaobh an bhóthair agus d'fhiafraigh fear de na prionsaí cá raibh teach a leithéid seo d'fhear uasal.

'Tá coill fá leathmhíle den áit seo,' arsa fear an tí, 'agus níl agaibh le déanamh ach an bealach a bhfuil sibh air a leanúint agus tífidh sibh teach an fhir sin in imeall na coilleadh.'

Thug siad buíochas don tseanduine agus shiúil leo go dtáinig siad go dtí an caisleán ina raibh an cailín a bhí siad a iarraidh ina cónaí. Thaitin sí go maith leis an Rí agus rinneadh cleamhnas eatarthu an oíche sin. Pósadh iad lá arna mhárach agus tháinig siad abhaile go cúirt an Rí.

Chuaigh dhá bhliain déag thart i ndiaidh a bpósta agus ar feadh an ama sin chónaigh an Rí agus an bhanríon óg go sásta, suaimhneach i gcuideachta a chéile. Lá amháin chuaigh an bhanríon chun cainte le Cailleach na gCearc agus nuair a bhí sí ag gabháil isteach ar an doras, bhuail sí a cos ar chloich agus thit sí.

'Go mbrise an diabhal do mhuineál,' arsa an Chailleach.

'Cad é a bheir ort a leithéid d'achainí a thabhairt ormsa,' arsa an bhanríon, 'agus gur tú an seirbhíseach is lú meas dá bhfuil fúm?'

'Tá, bhal,' arsa Cailleach na gCearc, 'má bheir tú trí ní domhsa a iarrfas mé ort inseoidh mé duit cad é an fáth a dtug mé an achainí.'

'Inis domh,' arsa an bhanríon, 'na trí ní atá a dhíth ort agus gheobhaidh tú iad má tá sé in mo chumhacht.'

'An chéad ní atá a dhíth orm,' arsa an Chailleach, 'lán mála de mhin choirce.'

'Cad é an méid a choinníos an mála?' arsa an bhanríon.

'Seacht scór cloch d'arbhar agus an méid a d'fhásfadh orthu go ceann seacht mbliana.'

'Maith go leor,' arsa an bhanríon, 'gheobhaidh tú sin. Ainmnigh an dara ní.'

'Tá,' arsa an Chailleach, 'lán mála d'olann agus coinneoidh an mála an méid olla a d'fhásfadh ar sheacht scór caorach go ceann seacht mbliana.'

'Gheobhaidh tú sin,' arsa an bhanríon. 'Cad é an rud an tríú ní?'

'Lán méadair d'im,' arsa an Chailleach, 'agus coinneoidh an meadar ime seacht mbó ar feadh seacht mbliana.'

'Dheánfar sin uilig,' arsa an bhanríon.

Rinneadh, agus i gceann seachtaine tháinig an bhanríon fhad le Cailleach na gCearc arís agus d'fhiafraigh di ábhar an achainí.

'Tá,' arsa an Chailleach, 'go bhfeicim go mb'fhearr dhuit marbh ná an dóigh a bheas ort i ndeireadh do shaoil. Tá tú pósta anois le dhá bhliain déag agus níor inis an Rí dhuit ar feadh an ama sin go bhfuil triúr mac aige ar oileán amuigh san fharraige, agus máistir scoile á dteagasc. Is gairid anois go raibh an fear is óige acu bliain agus fiche d'aois agus bhéarfar abhaile ansin iad, roinnfear an saibhreas eatarthu agus díbreofar thusa. Tá sé d'fhiacha ort, ar an ábhar sin, an chomhairle a bhéarfas mise dhuit a dhéanamh. Gabh abhaile anois agus faigh éan coiligh (coileach óg) marbh. Tug leat an fhuil i soitheach, gabh a luí agus lig ort go bhfuil tú tinn. Cuir fá choinne an Rí ansin agus, nuair a mhothós tú ag teacht é, ól bolgam den fhuil. Nuair a thiocfas seisean isteach sa tseomra, bí thusa ag caitheamh amach fola. Fiafróidh an Rí cad é a tháinig ort agus abair gur chuala tú go bhfuil tú pósta ar fhear atá chomh cruaidh sin i gcroí agus go mbeadh sé dhá bhliain déag gan éileamh a chur ar a thriúr clainne atá go huaigneach ar oileán amuigh san fharraige, agus a shéan i rith an ama sin ortsa go raibh a leithéidí ann. Mar gheall ar do shásamh cuirfidh seisean fána gcoinne ansin. Lig thusa ort go bhfuil lúcháir in do chroí iad a fheiceáil agus, i ndiaidh am dinnéara, cuir cuireadh ar na prionsaí cluiche cártaí a imirt. Bhéarfaidh mise paca dhuit agus ní bheidh moill ort baint leo. Cuir ansin de gheasa orthu a ghabháil go dtí an Domhan Íochtarach agus an Gearrán Óir a ghoid ó Ridire Ghlas an Ghleanna. Ní baol duit ina dhiaidh sin iad a fheiceáil go brách.'

D'imigh an bhanríon léi abhaile agus rinne an méid a d'iarr an Chailleach uirthi. Chuir an Rí fá choinne na bprionsaí agus chruinnigh uaisleacht na tíre go dtí an chúirt le fáilte a chur rompu.

I ndiaidh am dinnéara chuir an bhanríon cuireadh ar an mhac ba sine cluiche cártaí a imirt. Níor chuir an Rí suim ar bith sa mhéid seo agus shíl na prionsaí mar an gcéanna nach raibh ann ach greann.

Ní raibh siad i bhfad ag imirt gur bhain an bhanríon an cluiche.

'Cuir do gheasa,' arsa an prionsa.

'Fan go fóill,' ar sise. 'Is maith liom cluiche a imirt leis an dara fear ar dtús.'

Thoisigh an dara fear ar imirt agus níorbh fhada gur éirigh dó mar a d'éirigh dá dheartháir.

'B'fhéidir go n-imreofá thusa cluiche fosta,' ar sise leis an fhear ab óige.

'Ní fhearr liom 'mo thost,' arsa an prionsa.

Thoisigh an imirt ach, má thoisigh, chuaigh an cluiche ar an bhanrín an iarracht seo.

Thug sí ansin aghaidh ar an dá phrionsa a d'imir ar dtús agus dúirt: 'Cuirimse faoi gheasa troma draíochta bhur gcinn agus bhur gcosa agus bhur gcoimeád beatha a bhaint díbh mura dtuga sibh chugam an Gearrán Óir atá ag Ridire Glas an Ghleanna sa Domhan Íochtarach.'

Ar chluinstin na bhfocla seo don Rí agus na huaisle a bhí i láthair, líon a gcroí suas le buaireamh agus iontas.

'Anois,' arsa an bhanríon (ag tabhairt a haghaidh ar an mhac ab óige), 'cuir thusa do gheasa tharla gur bhain tú an cluiche.'

'Tím,' arsa an prionsa óg (ag éirí ina sheasamh), 'gur fá choinne deireadh a chur liom féin agus le mo dheartháireacha a thug tú anseo sinn, agus tá tú buartha anois gan mise a bheith faoi gheasa mar iadsan, ach ní fhéadann tú imní ar bith a bheith ort fá sin nó an áit a mbeidh siadsan, beidh mise, agus an áit a gcaillfear iadsan, caillfear mise. Cuirim de bhreithiúnas ort anois go mbeidh tú 'do shuí ar mhullach chaisleán m'athara gan bia gan deoch go dtige sinne ar ais, bíodh sin fada nó gairid.'

Nuair a chuala an bhanríon seo is beag nár thit sí i laige, ach bhí na focla ráite agus ní raibh tabhairt ar ais orthu.

Ar maidin lá arna mhárach bhí an bhanríon ina suí ar mhullach an chaisleáin ag éirí na gréine, agus d'fhág na prionsaí slán ag a n-athair agus shiúil leo béal a gcinn ag tarraingt ar an Domhan Íochtarach.

Ní theachaigh siad an-fhada gur casadh seanduine orthu ar an bhealach. Bheannaigh sé dóibh go carthanach agus chuir tuairisc orthu cá raibh siad ag gabháil.

'Táimid ag tarraingt ar an Domhan Íochtarach,' arsa fear de na prionsaí, 'agus tá sé de gheasa orainn an Gearrán Óir atá ag Ridire Glas an Ghleanna a ghoid.'

'Is trua liom bhur gcás,' arsa an seanduine, 'mar tá a fhios agam gur cailleadh gach duine dá dtug iarracht riamh an Gearrán Óir a ghoid. Ach tharla gur casadh orm sibh, agus gur trua liom bhur leithéidí a fheiceáil ag tarraingt ar an bhás, rachaidh mise libh agus má tá duine ar dhroim an domhain a ghoidfeadh an Gearrán Óir, is mise an duine sin.'

'Táimid fíorbhuíoch duit,' arsa an fear ba sine de na prionsaí, 'agus ba mhaith linn fios a bheith againn cé thú féin nó arbh fhéidir linn díolaíocht ar bith a thabhairt duit ar son an charthanais seo.'

'Is mise,' arsa an seanduine, 'Gadaí Dubh na Slóna agus níl a dhíth orm ar son mo sheirbhíse ach a bheith in bhur gcuideachta.'

Thug na prionsaí sárbhuíochas a gcroí dó agus shiúil an ceathrar leo go dtáinig siad go dtí an Domhan Íochtarach. Bhí an ghrian ina luí nuair a tháinig siad ar amharc chaisleán an Ridire Ghlais agus chuaigh siad isteach i seanmhuileann a bhí i gceann amháin den ghleann leis an oíche a chaitheamh. Ní raibh siad i bhfad sa mhuileann gur thit na prionsaí ina gcodladh.

Tamall beag i ndiaidh an mheán oíche mhuscail an Gadaí Dubh iad agus d'inis dóibh nach rabh am ar bith ab fhusa an Gearrán a ghoid ná nuair a bhí muintir an chaisleáin ina gcodladh. Thug na prionsaí isteach go raibh an ceart aige, agus tharraing an ceathrar ar an chaisleán, ach nuair a tháinig siad céad slat den áit a raibh an Gearrán, chroith sé é féin agus mar bhí cloigeanna [cloigíní] ag crochadh leis, mhuscail an tormán na saighdiúirí a bhí ag coimheád an chaisleáin. Theith an Gadaí agus na prionsaí ach ní theachaigh siad i bhfad gur beireadh orthu agus sáitheadh isteach i bpríosún iad.

Lá arna mhárach cuireadh scéala chuig an Rí (an Ridire Glas) gur beireadh ar cheathrar fear ag goid an Ghearráin Óir, agus d'ordaigh sé tinidh a lasadh ar ardán a bhí in aice an chaisleáin le iad a dhódh. Rinneadh sin i mbomaite, agus tháinig an Rí é féin le breith bháis a thabhairt orthu. Bhí mórán uaisle cruinnithe agus déarfá go raibh buaireamh ar gach duine ag amharc ar na trí prionsaí óga, dóighiúla a bhí le cur chun báis.

'Is trua liom,' arsa an Rí (ag tabhairt aghaidh ar an Ghadaí), 'go mbeidh agam le breith bháis a thabhairt ort féin agus ar na prionsaí óga seo atá in do chuideachta. Is dóigh liom nach mbeadh siadsan anseo ar chor ar bith ach ab é thusa agus ar an ábhar sin dóifear iadsan ar dtús mar gheall ar an phionós is mó a thabhairt duitse ag amharc orthu.'

Ceangladh an prionsa ba sine ansin agus nuair a bhíthear ag gabháil a chaitheamh sa tinidh, d'éirigh an Gadaí ina sheasamh agus labhair mar a leanas:

'A Ridire Ghlais an Ghleanna, is mian liom sula gcuirtear an prionsa seo chun báis a rá leat go raibh mé féin níos comhgaraí don bhás in mo shaol ná atá seisean go fóill.'

'Dá mbeifeá chomh comhgarach sin don bhás,' arsa an Rí, 'ní bheifeá anseo inniu, ach inis do scéal agus má mheasaimse go bhfuil an fhírinne agat, bhéarfaidh mé maithiúnas don phrionsa.'

'Bhal,' arsa an Gadaí, 'is cuimhneach liom nuair a bhí mé ag fás suas 'mo shomachán gasúir gur fhág mé m'athair agus mo mháthair agus d'imigh liom béal mo chinn mar gheall ar saibhreas a chruinniú. Aon oíche amháin dá raibh mé ag siúl fríd choillte móra, fada, d'éirigh mé chomh tuirseach sin is gurbh éigean domh suí ag bun crainn ar acht fanacht ann go maidin. Ní raibh mé i bhfad 'mo shuí go bhfaca mé solas giota uaim is d'éirigh mé is tharraing air. Shíl mé ar dtús gur teach nó áit chónaithe de chineál inteacht a bhí ann, ach nuair a tháinig mé comhgarach fuair mé amach nach raibh dadaí ann ach tinidh a bhí lasta ar éadan na léana. D'aithin mé gur duine saolta ab éigean an tinidh a lasadh is chuaigh mé suas i gcrann go bhfeicinn an dtiocfadh duine ar bith á cóir. Níorbh fhada go bhfaca mé seanchailleach ag teacht is mála léi ar a droim. Ar ball tháinig beirt eile a bhí chomh críonta, gránna leis an chéad cheann is shuigh an triúr thart fán tinidh is thoisigh ag cuntas is ag roinnt a gcuid airgid.

'Dá dtigeadh Gadaí Dubh na Slóna orainn anois,' arsa bean acu, 'nár thrua sinn!'

Ba é sin an chéad uair a fuair mé amach go raibh mé fógraiste a bheith 'mo ghadaí ar fud an tsaoil. In am ghairid thit na cailleacha ina gcodladh, a mála féin d'ór is airgead ag gach duine acu faoina ceann.

D'fhan mé féin sa chrann gur bhreathnaigh mé go raibh siad i dtromchodladh is ansin tháinig mé anuas go faichilleach agus sciob liom na málaí. Ní raibh ann ach go raibh siad ar mo dhroim i gceart agus mé ag baint chugam nuair a mhuscail na cailleacha is siúd ar shiúl iad féin is mise mar a bheadh séideán gaoithe ann. Mhair an rása nó go raibh an lá ag glanadh is fá dheireadh nuair a bhí siad ag cur géar orm chuaigh mé suas i gcrann mór fuinseoige. Tháinig an triúr go bun an chrainn ach bhí siad chomh sáraithe sin nach raibh siad ábalta dreapaireacht ar bith a dhéanamh.

'Glóir do Dhia,' arsa mise liom féin agus mo theangaidh amuigh fad bata, 'b'fhéidir go bhfuil mé réidh libh.'

'Ach, a thiarcais, ní raibh na cailleacha réidh liomsa, nó in oiread bomaití rinne bean amháin acu tua di féin is thoisigh bean eile acu ag gearradh an chrainn léi.

'Maise, go ngearra tú na cosa caola díot féin,' arsa mise nuair a fuair mé m'anál liom. Chas an Rí go raibh ramhú maith sa chrann ach, mar sin féin, níorbh fhada gur thoisigh sé ag croitheadh fúm. San am chéanna bhris an géag ar a raibh mé 'mo shuí is siúd anuas mé i measc na gcailleach. Leis sin, rinne an coileach scairt agus b'éigean do na cailleacha baint chucu mar a bheadh splanc soilsí ann.

'Fágaim agat féin anois é, a Ridire Ghlais an Ghleanna, nach raibh mé níos comhgaraí don bhás ná atá an prionsa de bhrí go raibh an tua tógtha leis an cheann a bhaint díom?'

'Is ró-iontach do scéal,' arsa an Rí, 'agus bheirim maithiúnas don phrionsa mar a gheall mé. Séid suas an tinidh go ndóitear an dara fear.'

NÓTA

Seo a leanas an leagan den scéal 'Gadaí Dubh na Slóna' ag Brian Ó Cianaigh a foilsíodh ar *ACS* (1/8/1903, 1–3; 23/8/1903, 2–3; 29/8/1903, 2). Níor foilsíodh an chuid deiridh den scéal ar *An Claidheamh Soluis*. Níl iomlán an scéil ann ar an drochuair agus tá difríochtaí idir an leagan seo agus an leagan a foilsíodh ina dhiaidh sin ar an *Derry People*.

Aguisín II

Dónall Ó Ceallaigh agus a Chlann

Bhí Dónall Ó Ceallaigh agus a bhean (go ndéana Dia trócaire ar anamna na marbh) ina gcónaí fá thuairim deich mbliana fichead ó shin i dteach bheag ceann tuí fá leathmhíle de na Cealla Beaga. Ní raibh acu de mhuirín ach dhá ghirseach agus gasúr. Niall ab ainm don ghasúr agus ba é an duine ab óige den triúr é.

Fán am a thoisíos an scéal bhí aois a bpósta go maith ag an dá chailín. B'fhada le Dónall fá dheireadh a bhí Máire (an níon ba sine) ar a láimh aige agus mar nach raibh na buachaillí ag teacht ag amharc uirthi, d'inis sé do dhuine thall is abhus go dtabharfadh sé cúig phunta is fiche mar spré d'fhear ar bith a phósfadh í. Tharraing seo mórán de bhuachaillí na paróiste fán teach, agus siúd is go raibh fonn pósta ar mhórán acu, ní theachaigh aon duine acu i gceann cleamhnais le Máire. Ach, go dearfa, leis an fhírinne a dhéanamh thógfadh a mbunús uilig an dara bean dá bhfaigheadh siad í.

Mhair an chúis mar seo ar feadh ráithe an gheimhridh agus, fá dheireadh, i dtrátha na Féile Bríde, tháinig gliúcach mór, cromshlinneánach, camchosach go teach Dhónaill ag iarraidh Máire agus na cúig phunta is fiche. B'fhearr le Máire í féin táilliúir beag, ramhar, cúraíolta a bhí ina chónaí sna Cealla ach chonacthas di nuair nach dtáinig an táilliúir ar ais a shuirí léi ón am a rinne sé na brístí do Dhónall (bliain go leith roimhe sin) nach raibh mórán gar a bheith ag dréim leis agus thug sí isteach don ghliúcach a phósadh. Níor mhair an cleamhnas i bhfad á dhéanamh agus rinneadh réiteach leis an bhainis a chaitheamh i gceann cupla lá ina dhiaidh sin. Tugadh cuireadh chun bainise do mhórán de na comharsanaigh agus fuarthas dhá ghalún déag den phoitín ab fhearr ó Sheán na Cruite a bhí ina chónaí ar an Bhall Bhán. Ní bréag a rá gur caitheadh bainis phléisiúrtha i dteach Dhónaill.

Anonn tamall san oíche nuair a fuair Dónall é féin cupla gloine le hól, gheall sé cúig phunta is fiche eile don dara níon agus ó sin go maidin ní raibh buachaill sa teach nach raibh ar theann a dhíchill ag iarraidh Síle a mhealladh. Ach is cosúil gur chuir Síle spéis mhór sa táilliúir nuair a bhí sé ag déanamh brístí Dhónaill agus gí nach raibh an táilliúir ag an bhainis ar chor ar bith ní thearn Síle dearmad air le linn na buachaillí a bheith ag blandaireacht léi. Ba é an deireadh a bhí air gur pósadh Síle agus an táilliúir an Domhnach ina dhiaidh sin.

Dhíol Dónall síos spré na beirte nuair a bhí siad á fhágáil. Chaith sé oíche ag gach lánúin acu ina dtithe féin agus gí go raibh an t-am ann ansin tús a chur ar obair an earraigh, ba mhór ab fhearr le Dónall a mhac a fháil pósta mar bhí a fhios aige go raibh a bhean féin ag éirí sean.

'Cad é do bharúil de níon Éamainn Bhig?' ar seisean le Niall nuair a tháinig sé abhaile.

'Diabhal mórán ar bith a shílim di,' arsa Niall. 'Ach má mheasann tú go bhfóirfeadh níon Uí Chaiside domh, rachaidh mé féin agus m'uncal ag amharc uirthi anocht.'

'Tá an cailín maith go leor,' arsa Dónall, 'ach tá a fhios agat nach bhfuil airgead ar bith ag a hathair.'

'Airgead aige nó uaidh,' arsa Niall, 'b'fhearr liomsa a níon ná Anna Éamainn Bhig agus leathscór bológ.'

'Maith go leor,' arsa an t-athair, 'sásaigh thú féin agus sásóidh tú mise.'

Rinneadh cleamhnas an oíche sin idir Niall agus Nóra Ní Chaiside. B'fhada roimhe sin ó bhí bainis ar bith ar an bhaile seo, agus níor fhan créatúir ar thóin tí i dteach ar bith dá bhfuair cuireadh. Nuair a bhí an bhainis thart tháinig an lánúin óg abhaile go teach Dhónaill.

Chuaigh bliain nó beirt thart agus ní raibh an saol ag éirí go rómhaith le Dónall ná lena mhac. D'fhág spré na níonach an-lom ar fad iad agus fá dheireadh ní raibh beathach ceathairchosach ar an tsaol acu (amach ó chat agus madadh), ach seanbhó amháin. Ba ghnách le Dónall seachtain a chaitheamh ag Máire agus seachtain ag Síle anois agus arís, agus siúd is go raibh an bheirt ina gcónaí go te, téagartha, níorbh fhada go raibh siad ag éirí tuirseach leis. D'iarr siad air sa deireadh gan a theacht á gcóir níos mó.

Ghoill seo go han-trom ar Dhónall agus mar ba bhocht leis a bheith ina ualach ar a mhac i dtólamh, d'imigh sé lá amháin go Meiriceá ina sheanduine mar a bhí sé. Tharraing sé ar dheartháir dá chuid a bhí i Nua-Eabhrac agus cad é a tharla ach go raibh an deartháir ar leabaidh an bháis nuair a chuaigh sé ansin. D'fhan Dónall aige, ag tabhairt aire dó, go bhfuair sé bás, agus ba bheag an dochar dó de bhrí go dtearn an deartháir tiomna agus d'fhág cúig chéad punta ag Dónall.

'Tá mo sháith agam go brách anois,' ar seisean leis féin nuair a fuair sé an deartháir curtha, 'agus, in ainm Dé, tarraingeoidh mé ar Éirinn arís.'

Sé seachtainí ón lá a d'fhág Dónall na Cealla bhí sé sa bhaile arís. Chuaigh sé ar ruaig go teach Mháire ar dtús go bhfeiceadh sé an mbeadh fáilte ar bith roimhe.

'Go mbeannaí Dia anseo,' ar seisean ag cur a chinn isteach ar an doras.

'Tá tú ar ais, mhaige,' arsa Máire go gruama.

'Tá, gan amhras,' arsa Dónall. 'Creidim nach bhfuil bealach ar bith agat mé a choinneáil go maidin?'

'Ní go rómhaith é,' arsa Máire. 'Tá mórán oibre idir lámha agam.'

'Bhail, fágaimse mo bheannacht agaibh,' arsa Dónall. 'Ní dóiche go bhfeicfidh sibh i dtobainneacht arís mé.'

Shiúil sé leis ansin go dtáinig sé go teach an táilliúra agus bheannaigh sé dóibh mar an gcéanna.

'D'aithin mise,' arsa Síle (ag tabhairt freagair air), 'nach bhfanófá i bhfad i Meiriceá.'

'Suigh síos,' arsa an táilliúir, 'go bhfaighe tú braon tae ar aon chor.'

'Níl tart ná ocras orm,' arsa Dónall, 'agus dá mbeadh féin ní chaithfinn an rud nach bhfaighinn ó chroí mhaith. Fágaim anois mo bheannacht agaibh agus b'fhéidir go dtiocfaidh an lá go fóill a mbeadh fáilte romham dá dtiginn ar cuairt chugaibh.'

Leis an fhírinne a chur ar an táilliúir bhocht bhí croí maith aige ach, go dearfa, níorbh é sin do dhá níon Dhónaill.

Bhí sé ag teannadh leis an oíche nuair a tháinig Dónall fhad le teach a mhic agus nuair a chonaic Nóra ag teacht é rith sí ina araicis agus chuir céad míle fáilte roimhe. Croíúil mar a bhí fáilte Nóra níor lú ná sin fáilte Néill agus ba ghairid go raibh gearrbhéile taitneamhach réidh fá choinne Dhónaill. Bhuail Séamas Ó Caiside isteach chucu nuair a bhí sé ag éirí dorcha agus pionta biotáilte leis. Cuireadh thart an oíche go pléisiúrtha ag éisteacht le Dónall ag cur síos go dúthrachtach ar na hiontasa a chonaic sé san Oileán Úr.

Tharla sé go raibh aonach san Cealla lá arna mhárach. D'iarr Dónall ar Niall is ar Nóra a theacht leis go bhfeiceadh siad cad é an cineál aonaigh a bheadh ann. Tháinig agus thug siad an chéad ruaig go margadh na mbó. Nuair a bhí siad tamall beag ag siúl thart chuir Dónall ceist ar fhear a bhí ag díol mothasáin cad é an luach a bhí aige uirthi.

'Ceithre phunta dhéag,' arsa an fear.

'Bhéarfaidh mé dhá phunta dhéag duit,' arsa Dónall. Nuair a chonaic Niall gur thairg Dónall (a shíl sé a bhí gan pingin rua) dhá phunta dhéag ar bhó, tháinig iontas an domhain air. In oiread bomaití scoilt fear eile a bhí ina sheasamh ann an difear agus críochnaíodh an margadh.

Ach le scéal fada a dhéanamh gairid, cheannaigh Dónall na trí ba ab fhearr a bhí ar an aonach an lá sin fá choinne Néill.

Nuair a chuala Síle agus Máire go raibh fairsingeacht airgid abhaile le Dónall, bhí siad ag ithe na méar díobh féin. Níor lú orthu an diabhal ná Niall a bheith ag éirí sa tsaol mar a bhí sé ach d'aithin siad go maith nár thuill a gcuid gníomhartha mórán díolaíochta.

D'fhág Dónall iomlán a chuid saibhris ag Niall is ag Nóra agus chaith sé féin agus a bhean saol fada suaimhneach acu.

NÓTA

ACS 29 Lúnasa, 5, 12, 19, 26 Meán Fómhair, 1903. Is leagan gearr é seo den scéal 'Athair agus a Chuid Níonach.'

FILÍOCHT

Gleann Domhain

[Fonn: 'Cailín Deas Crúite na mBó']

Tá baile beag ró-dheas in m'eolas
Is cuireann sé bród ar mo chroí
Tá ardán deas álainn ina aice
'Gus tobar deas fíoruisce faoi.
Is aoibhinn don té atá ina chónaí
In áit a bhfuil lúcháir is greann
Is is cinnte gurb é sin don áit seo,
An baile beag deas ag an ghleann.

Is ansin atá an cailín is deise
Dá bhfaca mo shúile riamh,
Is ní bheinnse gan foscadh ná dídean
Dá bhfanfainn go fóill lena taobh.
Gheobhainn céad míle fáilte ón mháthair
Is in airgead níl sise gann,
Is thiocfadh liom deireadh mo laetha
A chaitheamh ró-chomhgarach don ghleann.

An féidir go bhfuil mé 'mo dheoraí
Is gur fhág mé amach cairde mo chléibh,
Nó an féidir nach molfainn choíche
Mo sheanchónaí dílis ar sliabh.
Ach pillfidh mé ar ais ins an tsamhradh
I measc seinm na n-éan ar gach crann
Go gcaithe mé deireadh mo laetha
Sa bhaile bheag, dheas ag an ghleann.

Nóta: Brian Ó Cianaigh, Strabane, 9 September 1901. *ACS* (21/9/1901, 439).

Solas ar an Bhealach

'Éist le mo scéal, a dhuine chóir,
Gí tá mé fós gan chiall,
Ná triall an bóthar sin anocht,
Mar tá sé ag éirí mall.'

Mar seo a labhair páiste beag seacht mblian'
Oíche Nollag i bhfad ár gcúl,
Bhí solas geal na bhFlaitheas thuas
Ag lasadh ina súil.

'Tar liom,' ar sí, 'don áit a bhfuil
Mo mháthair léithi féin,
Abair gur deas mo dhuilliúr glas
'Gus beidh sí sásta ansin.'

Bhí an oíche 'titim air go tiubh,
Is lean sé an cailín beag,
Ba mhaith dó féin go dtearn sé sin
De bhrí go raibh sé lag.

Ó, cé a bhí ann ach fear an tí
A bhí caillte orthu le fad'.
Cá bhfuil anois aon teach mar é,
Tá lúcháir ann gan stad.

'Go mbeannaí Dia thú, 'níon mo chroí,
Tá grá an Rí in d'ucht,
Chaill mé mo bhealach ach bhí tú
Lem' thabhairt anseo anocht.'

Nóta: Supplement to *Dundalk Democrat* (21/12/1901, 10).

SLIABH NA MBAN

Ó, tá mé liom féin ar an tráigh go fóill,
Liom féin i measc an tslua;
Is aoibhinn an áit, ach mo léan is mo chreach,
Ní anseo atá mo chroí inniu.
Níl oíche ná lá ó d'fhág mé mo ghrá
Nach mbím faoi thuirse is brón,
Is smaoiním go deo ar an spéirbhean óg.
Ins an ghleanntán ag Sliabh na mBan.

Ba deise a súil ná an réalt san oíche
Is bhí a gruag chomh buí le hór,
Bhí a haghaidh chomh deas le bláth an róis,
Ach, faraor, gan mé le mo stór.
Ach tá néaltaí dubha ag cruinniú go tiubh,
'Gus ag méadú ar sliabh agus gleann,
Is sílim in mo chroí nach mbím feasta choíche
Le mo stóirín ar Shliabh na mBan.

Is brónach an saol in gach áit a mbím
Ó d'fhág mé mo thír bhocht féin,
Is is tír bhocht í óir tá an glas ina luí
'Gus a saoirse go fóill i gcéin.
Ach tiocfaidh an lá, le lúcháir is ádh,
Má tá suaimhneas domh i ndán,
A scabfar an ceo is beidh mé go deo
Le mo stóirín ar Shliabh na mBan.

NÓTA: *The above translation of 'Slievenamon' is from the pen of Mr B. O'Keeney, and will soon be published to the music of that charming Munster air. Dundalk Democrat* (23/11/1901, 5). Foilsíodh é fosta ar an *Irish Emerald* ar 7 Nollaig 1901.

SMAOINTE AN DEORAÍ

A Éire, a mhuirnín, is mé atá go cráite
Ag smaoineamh inniu ar na laetha fadó,
Nuair a bhí mé go séanmhar i measc do chuid sléibhte,
Chomh sómhar le aon duine i gContae Mhaigh Eo.

Níl dadaí lem' shaoradh ó bhrón ná ó bhuaireamh –
Tá neart le mo dhaoradh san áit seo, faraor!
Ach cuirim mo bheannacht 'dtí an té atá ag fanacht
Is ag oibriú le dánacht ar do shonas, mo thír!

A Éire, a ghrá, nuair nach féidir liom pilleadh,
Ó, caoinfidh mé tuilleadh in uaigneas anseo,
Agus bheirim mo mhallacht don dlí a rinne an Ghalltacht
Is é a thug orm scarúint le Contae Mhaigh Eo.

I suaimhneas nó i gcogadh ba doiligh liom bogadh
Ón áit inar rugadh an teaghlach go léir
Atá anois díbrithe ó shléibhte na hÉireann
Ón tír sin ró-aoibhinn gan sárú faoin spéir.

A Éire, mo ghairm, tá na laetha ag gabháil tharam
Is ní fada go mbeidh mé san uaigh 'mo luí
Ach beannaím gach duine atá ag troid fá do choinne
Is do theangaidh bhinn, mhilis amach ó mo chroí.

Agus guím choíche gach lá agus oíche
Go gcuideoidh Dia leo in Éirinn na féil',
An Sasanach a dhíbirt a tháinig le mallacht
A thit go ró-chinnte ar fhíorchlainn na nGael.

Ba bheag é do mhisneach le blianta, a Éire!
Do chláirseach faoi shuan is do chliú ag gabháil síos,
Gan duine ná deoraí ag teacht do do chóirse
Mura dtigeadh an tiarna ag tógáil an chíos'.

Do chlann féin do d'fhágáil faoi thrócaire namhad
Is ag teitheadh le crá uait i gceartlár a mbláith;
An talamh á bhánú 'gus beagán á dhéanamh
Le saorsacht a fháil duit, a Éire, a ghrá!

Ach tháinig an t-athrú a thógfas ó náire
Cruit cheolmhar na Teamhra 'gus brat glas ár dtír'
Is beidh Éire go séanmhar, go rafar is tréanmhar
Faoi chúram ag tréinfhir, fíor-Ghaelach is saor.

Beidh an tseamróg ag fás ann is ní bheidh sí gan meas ann
Beidh saorsacht ann freisin ag soilsiú le grá,
Ó mhaidin go hoíche ar chnoca mo thíre –
Mo bheannacht leat, a Éire, anois is go brách.

NÓTA: *The following poem, from the pen of Mr B. O'Keeney was awarded second place at last year's Oireachtas in Dublin. No words of ours are necessary to commend it as suitable for recitation at Gaelic League entertainments. Ulster Herald* (14/2/1903, 7).

A Bhuachaillín mo Chroí
[Fonn: 'Péarla an Bhrollaigh Bháin']

A bhuachaillín mo chroí,
Ná scar uaim feasta choích'
Má tá tú féin ar tí go mbeadsa beo 'bhfad.
Is fada mé faoi bhrón
Is tusa 'siúl an domhain,
Ach is anois a chuirim romhat an fháilte ró-mhaith.
Ó d'fhág tú mé ár dtús
Tá athrú ar do ghnúis,
Mo chrá go deo! an chúis a thug ar shiúl thú;
Agus míle, míle glóir
Don Ardrí mar is cóir,
A threoraigh thú, a stór, go taobh do rúinse.

Is iomaí lá is oích'
A chaith mé ag gol is ag caoi
Ó scar tú liom faraor le a ghabháil thar sáile;
Agus smaoineas in mo chrá
Go leanfainn féin mo ghrá
Ach níor éirigh liom aon tráth mo chairde a fháil.
Níor bhinn liom ceol na n-éan
Is níor iarras só ná séan.
Ach scabtha anois tá an néal a bhreoigh mo shaolsa,
Nuair a tím thú le mo thaobh,
A chuisle gheal mo chléibh!
Ó, ná scaraimis choíche – 'sé sin mo ghuíse.

NÓTA: *An Claidheamh Soluis* (21/3/1903, 3).

Teangaidh na hÉireann

A theangaidh bhinn, mhilis, fhíordhílis na hÉireann,
A theangaidh na naomh, na laoch is na saoi,
Céad fáilte arís romhat go tír ghlas na féile,
Céad, céad míle fáilte amach ó mo chroí.
Le blianta ba doiligh do bhinnghuth a chluinstin,
In áitibh ar dhual duit a bheith labhartha go deo
Ach d'fhill tú go bródúil mar sholas na maidine
'Cur aoibhnis ar shléibhte is ag scabadh an cheo.

Ó Dhoire go Corcaigh is ó sin go Port Láirge
Ó chathair na hÉireann go Baile an Átha
Ó Ghleannta na hAontrom' go coillte Chill Airne
Tá muintir na tíre ag éirí gach lá
Chun teangaidh Naomh Pádraig a choimheád is a shábháil
Is an Béarla a dhíbirt go tapaidh is go tréan.
Buaidh, buaidh libh, a chairde – an brat glas in airde!
Suas, suas leis an Ghaeilig, ár seanteangaidh féin!

Tá An Craoibhín – mo chroí é – ag oibriú go bríomhar,
Ag brostú chun tosaigh na cúise gach lá,
Tá an tAthair Ó Laoghaire ag déanamh mar an gcéanna
An méid atá ina chumas is ní beag sin le rá.
In Ardscoil Naomh Pádraig tá an tAthair Ó hÍcí
Ag spreagadh an eolais a theastaíos go mór
Is tá an tAthair Ó Duinnín fíorghnoitheach i gcónaí
'Tabhairt misnigh is cuidiú do gach Gaeilgeoir.

Ní féidir liom tráchtadh ar iomlán na ndaoine
Atá ag oibriú go bródúil i gcúis Chlann na nGael
Is tá Éire ag ardú a cinn, ní nach ionadh
Nuair a tí sí na tréanfhir atá i mbearna an bhaoil.
Fad saoil do gach duine ar éadan na cruinne
Ar mian leis ár dteangaidh fhíorársa a bheith beo
Agus nárbh é sin don té sin nach mian leis ár gcineadh
Is ar mhaith leis ár nGaeilig a bheith caillte go deo.

Is trua gur chaill sinn an tAthair Ó Gramhna –
Go maire a chuimhne in Éirinn go brách –
Is é Dia a thug dúinn é, is é Dia a thóg uainn é
Go moltar A thoilsean gach oíche agus lá.
Ach gí go bhfuil uaigneas inár gcroíthe ina dhiaidhsean
Tá toradh na hoibre a rinne sé gan dua
Le feiceáil go frasach ag Gaela na tíre
I ngach uile chontae in Éirinn inniu.

Is aoibhneach an radharc é gach maidin is tráthnóna,
Na páistí a fheiceáil i gceann a gcuid leabhar
Le lúcháir ina gcroíthe – mar sin dóibh i gcónaí –
Ag foghlaim na teanga – á léamh is á labhairt.
Níorbh fhearr leo mar an gcéanna an chláirseach á seinm
Ná ceol na bpíob Gaelach dá bhinneas a nglór
Ná ag éisteacht le seanscéaltaí deasa cois tineadh,
Le dánta is amhráin a rinneadh fadó.

A Ghaela mo chléibhe, síos, síos leis an Bhéarla
Is é a thug go hÉirinn an mí-ádh ar dtús,
A dhíbir ár muintir thar sáile le géarchrá
Is ní hé sin an teangaidh is cóir a bheith thuas.
Chun tosaigh le misneach, a chairde is uaisle,
Is do Chonradh na Gaeilge atá sé i ndán
Ár dtír bhocht a shaoradh – is glórmhar an chúis í,
A theangaidh ár sinsear, go maire tú slán!

NÓTA: *Derry People and Tirconaill News* (20/6/1903, 7). Ní hionann amach is amach an leagan seo agus an leagan a foilsíodh ar *The Gaelic American.*

CILL AIRNE

Ar Chill Airne bíonn go deo
Cuimhne ag freastal dúinn go deo;
Áilleacht ársaigh Inse Fáil
Níl tú scartha uainn go fóill!
Gráíonn nádúr gach aon tír
Ní sé i gcónaí aithne Dé,
Siúlann áilleacht leis go fíor
Ach is ansiúd a chónaíonn sí.

Cúrfa
Fanann aingle ann gach lá
'Dearcadh ar na mílte bláth' –
Tír ár gcroí, Cill Airne
Seinn achoích', Cill Airne.
Níl sa domhan go léir le fáil
Áit chomh saibhir leis i mbláth,
Imíonn buaireamh agus brón
Leis an mhaidin ann gach lá.
Sméara 'crochadh ar gach craobh
'Measc na n-úll is na sabharcán buí
Cumhracht shláintiúil ar an aer
Chuirfeadh aoibhneas ar aon chroí.
Cúrfa
Síleann aingle nach bhfuil faoi
Spéir nó grian aon áit mar í
Tír ár ngrá, Cill Airne!
Seinn go brách, Cill Airne.

NÓTA: B. O'Keeney. Foilsithe in 'The Tyrconnell Series' *Easy Lessons in Modern Irish,* Part 1: B. O'Keeney (Dublin, Sealy, Bryers and Walker, 1902), 24.

Machnamh an Deoraí ar a Bhaile Dúchais

Tá an samhradh anseo is tá éanlaith na coilleadh
Ag seinm go fonnmhar i measc duilliúr na gcrann,
Tá gatha na gréine ag soilsiú ar bhántaí
Tá cumhracht na mbláth ar gach sliabh agus gleann.
Ach b'fhearr liom ar ais in mo sheanbhaile dúchais
Ná aoibhneas na cruinne ar fheabhas a bhfuil ann
Ar ais le mo chairde anois ins an tsamhradh
Is mo chnámha a shíneadh ar an tseanardán donn.

Le blianta b'annamh, ró-annamh mo gháire
Ba mhinic, ró-mhinic mo shíorghol is mo bhrón,
Ón lá sin a thréig mé mo bhaile beag dílis,
Le saibhreas a chruinniú ag siúl 'fud an domhain.
Tá an saibhreas gan chruinniú, tá léan ar gach taobh díom,
Níl suaimhneas le fáil agam, oíche ná lá;
Is is doiligh liom pilleadh go saothraí mé tuilleadh
Is í an díbirt mo mhilleadh is mo léan géar go brách.

A bhaile mo chléibhe, bhí siamsa i ndán duit
'Gus beannacht ó neamh ar do bhrollach ina luí,
Bhí mil ar na blátha a d'fhás ar do bhántaí
Is ba chliúúil do mhuintir i gcarantas croí.
An sabharcán san earrach, an rós ins an tsamhradh
Is na húllaí go hálainn san fhómhar ag fás.
Faoi spéir níl do shárú, a bhaile fhíorghrámhair,
Is go bhfeice mé arís thú, is trua mo chás.

Níor bhinne an smólach i nduilliúr an chaorthainn
Ag scabadh a ceol binn go sáimh ar an aer,
Ná binnghuth mo stóirín is í ag seinm go glórmhar,
Is ag siúl i measc na mbólacht le bánú an lae.
Ach is iomaí tráthnóna a shuigh muid ag comhrá
Ar bhruach na habhna ag luí na gréine;
Is is minic a dúirt sí is gan aon duine comhgarach
'Fan agam go deo in do bhaile bheag féin.'

Is cráite mo chroí, 'rá go bhfuil mé mo dheoraí,
Is mé ag caoineadh go brónach i measc coimhthígh i gcéin,
Ach fágfaidh mé slán ag an áit seo amárach
Is teannfad chun siúil chun mo thír álainn féin.
I mí mheán an tsamhraidh beidh blátha go líonmhar
Beidh súile mo Mháirín mar dhealramh na gréine'
Nuair a chluinfidh sí an deoraí ag rá lena stóirín
'Ní scarfad go deo le mo bhaile bheag féin.'

NÓTA: *Derry People and Tirconaill News* (28/9/1929, 9).

Éire Mo Ghrá

[Fonn: 'Eibhlín a Rún' nó 'Erin the Tear' etc.]

Muscail do mhisneach, a Éire, a stór!
Tóg do cheann uasal arís mar is cóir;
Is álainn do ghnúis go fóill,
Brónach ró-fhad' do cheol
Ardaigh go binn do ghlór,
Éire mo ghrá.

'Éire, go fóill tá do bhinnteangaidh beo,
'Éire, ní chaillfear an Ghaeilig go deo.
Beidh sí faoi mheas is cáil
Fhad is tá Gael le fáil
Is namhaid le cur faoi sháil
Oíche nó lá.

NÓTA: Brian Ó Cianaigh, Nollaig 1930. *Derry People and Tirconaill News* (27/12/1930, 6).

Slán le Deoraíocht
[Fonn: 'Skibbereen']

Mo mhíle slán le deoraíocht, le buaireamh agus brón,
Is iomaí lá, mo léan is mo chrá, a chaith mé ag siúl an domhain.
Go deo arís ní luífead síos i measc coimhthígh abhus ná thall,
Tá anois mo chairde le mo thaobh arís i nDún na nGall.

An lá a d'fhág mé Dún na nGall bhí uaigneas in mo chroí,
Is beag a shíl mo Mháirín Bhán go scarfainn léi achoíche.
Is é a dúirt sí liom, 'A rún mo chléibh', tar comhgarach chugam anall,
An dtréigfidh tú do ghrá inniu agus bántaí Dhún na nGall?'

'A Mháirín ghlégheal, álainn, óg, tabhair domhsa cead mo chinn
Beidh maoin i láimh agam go fóill agus aoibhneas lena linn.
Beidh lásaí óir ort mar is cóir go moch agus go mall
Is caisleán agam fá do dhéin i gceartlár Dhún na nGall.'

Na mílte míle ó thír mo bhreith' bhí saibhreas domh i ndán
Is é grásta Dé a threoraigh mé is a thug mé abhaile slán,
I measc na mbláth faoi shéan is ádh is i bhfad ón tír mhór thall
Is suairc mo shaol gan bhuairt gan bhaol ar shléibhte Dhún na nGall.

Seo sláinte fhíor do chlainn na nGael atá scabtha i bhfad i gcéin
Abhaile arís go bpille siad is gur fada a bheas a réim!
Bíodh grá ár dtíre ina n-ucht nuair a thiocfaidh siad anall
Mo bheannacht leo go léir anocht ó ardchnoic Dhún na nGall.

NÓTA: *Derry People and Tirconaill News* (27/6/1931, 10). *The above poem by Mr Brian O'Keeney, Loughros Point, Ardara, was awarded 2nd prize in the literary competition, Tirconaill Feis, 1930. [In publishing the poem in last week's issue other matter got mixed up with the copy and, unfortunately, appeared in print. We regret the mistake. – Ed]*

Tóg do Cheann, a Mháthair Éire!

[Fonn: 'The Wearing of the Green']

Tóg do cheann, a mháthair Éire, tá na néaltaí dubh' ar shiúl,
Triomaigh suas, a rún, na deora a bhí le blianta in do shúil;
Tá do chlann ag teacht thar sáile, laochraí cróga, calma, fíor'
Cluinfidh an domhan a ngártha bríomhar' nuair a shroichfeas siad an tír.
Fáilte romhaibh ar ais chun an bhaile, b'fhada, righin bhur spás i gcéin
Ní raibh aon áit riamh thar sáile mar ár dtír bhreá, álainn féin.
Os ár gcionn tá grian na saorsacht', inár gcroíthe grása Dé,
Séan is ádh ar gach taobh dínn, is é seo bánú geal an lae.
Is iomaí lá is oíche a bhí ár máthair bhocht faoi bhrón
Nuair a díbríodh a cuid clainne thall is abhus ar fud an domhain

B'éigean dóibh an baile a fhágáil nuair a bhí siad ina mbláth
Agus na cairde ba dílse a bheith scartha leo go brách.
Glóir don Rí tá an t-athrú mór ann, tá ár dtír arís faoi cháil
Tá an Gael inniu ar uachtar – brat an tSasanaigh ar lár;
Tá an chruit go fóill le cluinstin, tá na mílte laochraí réidh
Lenár dtír a thógáil suas arís ag bánú geal an lae.

Tá do theangaidh féin, a Éire, ag teacht chun cinn gach uile lá
Is beag nach raibh a binnghuth múchta nuair a bhí síolrach Gael faoi sháil
D'fhan sí beo i measc na sléibhte mar a bheadh ceolta na mná sí.
Thug sí buaidh ar lucht an Bhéarla is beidh sin léi feasta choíche.
Tóg do chroí, a mhuirnín dílis, tá do chlann inniu ag dréim
Go mbeidh sonas ort choíche is gur ag méadú a bheas do réim.
Slán go raibh an cineadh Gaelach agus slán go raibh an té
Atá ag freastal ort, a Éire bhocht, ag bánú geal an lae.

Dónall na Gealaí (ainm cleite Bhriain don chomórtas). *Derry People and Tirconaill News* (22/8/1931, 6). *The above poem by Mr. Brian O'Keeney, LoughrosPoint, Ardara won first prize in the literary competitions at the recent Tirconaill Feis.*

Brat na hÉireann

[Fonn: 'God Save Ireland']

Tá an taca thart go deo
Nuair a bhí ár dtír faoi cheo
Brat ár namhad os ár gcionn go moch is go mall.
Tógaigí anois bhur nglór,
Bíodh an glas, an bán is an t-ór
Thar gach sliabh is gleann ó Chóbh go Dún na nGall.

Cúrfa
Buaidh go deo le tír na hÉireann!
Tabhair di onóir agus grá,
Síos le brat an tSasanaigh!
Scaoil in airde ar an ghaoith
Brat na bhfear a mbeidh a gcuimhne beo go brách.

Éire dhílis, níl go fóill,
Deireadh leis an ghreann is an ceol,
A thug cliú is cáil duit ins an am fadó.
Tá do chruit arís faoi mheas,
Thoir is thiar, aduaidh is aneas
'Gus do theangaidh bhinn go bríomhar, ceolmhar.

Cúrfa
Buaidh go deo le tír na hÉireann!
Tabhair di onóir agus grá,
Síos le brat an tSasanaigh!
Scaoil in airde ar an ghaoith
Brat na bhfear a mbeidh a gcuimhne beo go brách.

Ní le traochlag, fann nó feall,
D'éirigh laochraí Dhún na nGall
Nuair a bhí síolrach Gael faoi sclábhaíocht is brón
Ach le dóchas i ngach croí
Go mbeidh Éire beo choích'
Is go mbeadh sí fós faoi cháil ar fud an domhain.

Cúrfa
Buaidh go deo le tír na hÉireann!
Tabhair di onóir agus grá,
Síos le brat an tSasanaigh!
Scaoil in airde ar an ghaoith
Brat na bhfear a mbeidh a gcuimhne beo go brách.

NÓTA: 'File an Ghleanna,' Bealtaine 1932. (Sin ainm cleite Bhriain don chomórtas seo). *Strabane Chronicle* (27/8/1932, 8). Bhain an dán seo duais ag Feis Thír Chonaill. Síleann an t-údar gur cheart do Ghaeil na hÉireann amhrán fíorGhaelach a bheith acu feasta (mar a deir an Béarla, *Rallying Song*) agus níl ceann ar bith againn chomh fóirsteanach fána choinne seo le fonn 'God Save Ireland.'

Áilleacht Thír Chonaill

[Fonn: 'Cailín Deas Crúite na mBó.']

Is iomaí ball aoibhinn in Éirinn
Atá cliúúil i ndánta sárbhinn',
Is is iomaí sin file san uaigh
A chuimhnítear fós lena linn.
Ach seinnfidh mé 'Áilleacht Thír Chonaill'
Anois nuair atá an sceach ina bláth
Agus aoibhneas inmholta an tsamhraidh
Ag teannadh liom oíche 'gus lá.
Bhreathnaigh mé locha Chill Airne
Is na maolchnoic i gContae an Chláir
Chonaic mé an Deisceart go hiomlán
Is an tIarthar atá molta i stair.
Shiúil mé thar shléibhte agus gleanntáin
I measc áilleacht na dtíortha i bhfad i gcéin,
Ach phill mé agus phóg mé an driúchta
Ar bhántaí mo sheanchontae féin.

Is glas iad na coillte fá láthair,
Fíorbheo le síorchantan na n-éan,
Tá cumhra na neoinín sna bóithrí
Ag gealladh dúinn sláinte is séan.
Fán tráigh tá na faoileáin ar eiteoig,
Ag seoladh anall is anonn;
Ní mian leofu scarúint achoíche
Le cuanta Thír Chonaill na dTonn.

Is aoibhinn do bhánchnoic, a Thír Chonaill,
Donnghléasta i gcótaí deas' fraoigh,
Tá binnghlór na sruthán le cluinstin
Ag manrán mar cheoltaí na sí.
Na sabharcáin go flúirseach san earrach
Na rósa i mbláth ag Féil' Eoin,
A Thír Chonaill, a ghrá, níl do shárú
Ar áilleacht in éadan an domhain.

Nóta

Derry People and Tírchonaill News (30/10/1937, 5). *The following is the winning poem at Feis Tirchonaill, held at Letterkenny in June last for the* Derry People *prize of £2 2s, which was won by Mr Brian O'Keeney, Ardara, the well-known Donegal author and playwright ... Mr. O'Keeney's composition was unanimously awarded the premier prize.*

Fáilte don Uachtarán

Céad fáilte romhat, a Chraoibhhín Ó,
Mar uachtarán ár dtíre;
Gur fada, flaithiúil a bheas do réim
Mar threoraí is mar aoire.
Is maith linn thú i mbearna an bhaoil
Le ár dteangaidh bhinn a shábháil
Is tá an Gael inniu ag guí go tiubh
Go n-éireoidh leat go hádhúil.

Réab tú téad an ghalldachais
Nuair a bhí ár dtír bhocht cráite.
Thóg tú suas an cineadh Gael
Nuair a bhí siad beagnach báite.
Thug tú grá d'Inis Fáil
Ó fháinne an lae go hoíche
Is an brat a scaoil tú ar an ghaoith
Ní ísleofar é go brách.

Go bhfeicimid le linn do shaoil
Gach ball d'Éirinn álainn,
Mar a bhí an scéal san am fadó
Saor, saor ó Chóbh go Málainn.
Ár dtír go huile faoi do réim
An fharraige ar gach taobh di
Ár nGaeilig cheolmhar i ngach béal
Mar a labhair tú féin riamh í.

A Éire dhílis, tóg do cheann,
Agus mol do Chraoibhín Aoibhinn.
Tá ar do bhántaí bánú an lae
An saorsacht taobh ar taobh linn.
Beidh Aontroim, Dún agus Ard Mhacha
Is Doire Cholm Cille,
Fear Manach agus sean-Tír Eoghain
In d'ucht gan mórán moille.

Nóta: *The Derry Journal*, 15 July, 1938, 14.

"Kitty Ní Ġáḋra"

1.

Is fada mé 'g m'teaċt fá ṁullaċ na n-
árdán dom,
Mar i ndúil 's go bfeicfinn mo leanḃ na
sceáfl a cinn;
A cúl trom, triopallaċ, fairsinge, fáinneaċ,
fionn
Seo mo ṫriall ċugaiḃ is níl Kitty Ní Ġárḋa
liom.

2.

Tá 'n Éirne 'r buile 'san tSionainn go léir
faoi bruċt,
Fá ṫeag na bruinneal' ḃí somanta, lán
de'n stuaim;
A leiṫéid ní faca mé ó Ċorcaiġ go Clár na
bóinn',
'Sé mo léan gur imṫiġ mo Kitty Ní Ġárḋa
uaim.

3.

Da bfeicfeaḋ siḃ 'réir í i ndiaiḋ an
bás í 'ċlaoḋ,
A cuid ribíní óir anuas fá ċionn uirṫí;
Gaċ ribeóg da gruaig mar cuaċa de
ṫrilsiġe buiḋe
'Sé mo sgéal truaġ naċ bfuair mé an
ċainnt aici.

Aṁarc anonn

4

A ḋeárḃraṫair ḋílis ḋa ḃfeicfeá san
teámpoill í,
'S a cónáir¹ déanta réiḋ i lár an tiġe
A cúm seang, séiṁ 'gus í gan smál
na luiḋe,
Sínte 'gcré sé mo léan gur fágaḋ í.

5

Go dtigiḋ an Ċáisg i lár an Ḟóġmair
buiḋe
'S go dtigiḋ 'n Ḟéil Pádraig seaċtṁain
na dó na diaiḋ
Go bfásaiḋ bláṫ bán ṫríḋ ċlár mo
cónra² níos
Cuiṁaiḋ mo ġráḋ 's go bráṫ ní ċuirfiḋ
mé díom.

1 Cónáir (= cónra) coffin
2 Cónra gen. of Cónáir (Donegal usage.)

Kitty Ní Ghadhra

Is fada mé ag imeacht fá mhullach na n-ardán donn
Mar i ndúil is go bhfeicfinn mo leanbh nó scáil a cinn;
A cúl trom, triopallach, fairsing, fáinneach, fionn,
Seo mo thriall chugaibh is níl Kitty Ní Ghadhra liom.

Tá an Éirne ar buile is an tSionainn go léir faoi bhrúcht
Fá éag na bruinneal' a bhí soineanta, lán den stuaim.
A leithéid ní fhaca mé ó Chorcaigh go Clár na Bóinn'
Is é mo léan gur imigh mo Kitty Ní Ghadhra uaim.

Dá bhfeicfeadh sibh aréir í i ndiaidh an bás í a chloí,
A cuid ribíní óir anuas fá cheann uirthi;
Gach ribeog dá gruaig mar cuacha de thrilsí buí
Is é mo scéal trua nach bhfuair mé an chaint aici.

A dheartháir dhílis, dá bhfeicfeá sa teampall í,
Is a cónair déanta réidh i lár an tí,
A com seang, séimh agus í gan smál ina luí,
Sínte i gcré is é mo léan gur fágadh í.

Go dtigidh an Cháisc i lár an fhómhair bhuí
Is go dtigidh an Fhéil' Pádraig seachtain nó dhó ina diaidh,
Go bhfásaidh bláth bán fríd chlár mo chónra aníos
Cumhaidh mo ghrá is go brách ní chuirfidh mé díom.

Nóta: Ní amhrán é seo a chum Brian ach ceann a chuala sé óna mhuintir ina óige. Tá sé le fáil i litir a chuir Brian chuig Fionán Mac Coluim ar 28/3/1930. Deir sé an méid seo a leanas faoin amhrán: 'Fuair mé ó mo mháthair [é]. D'fhoghlaim sí an t-amhrán seo óna máthair níos mó ná ceithre scór bliain ó shin.' Bhí sé ag súil go gcuirfí i gcló é ar *Béaloideas*. Tá leagan den amhrán seo 'Cití Ní Ghadhra' i gcló in *Dúchas*, 1733, 318–20. Bhreac Seán Ó Caiside an leagan seo síos ó Chonn Mac an Ghoill in Ard an Rátha.

POETIC TRIBUTE TO THE PRESIDENT

We are privileged to publish in to-day's issue a delightful tribute to President Hyde from the pen of Mr. Brian O'Keeney, teacher of Irish under Co. Donegal Vocational Education Committee.

Mr. O'Keeney was the winner of the two principal literary prizes (prose and poetry) at the recent Tirconaill Feis. A former Gaelic League Organiser, he had the distinction of receiving the all-Ireland prize for best poem in Gaelic, from the hands of Dr. Hyde at an Oireachtas held in the Rotunda in Dublin. He is a steady Gaelic contributor to many newspapers and periodicals.

FÁILTE DO'N UACHTARÁN

Céaḋ fáilte roṁat, a Ċraoiḃín Ó!
Mar Uaċtarán ar dtíre;
Gur fada flaiṫeaṁail 'ḃéar do réim
Mar ṫreóraiḋe a's mar aoḋaire.
Is maiṫ linn ṫú i "mBearna 'n Ḃaoġail"
Le'r dteanga ḃinn a fáġail,
'S tá'n Gaeḋeal indiu ag guiḋe go tuit
Go n-éireoċaiḋ leat go h-áḋṁail.

Do réab tú téad an Ġallḋaċair
Nuair 'ḃí ar dtír boċt ċráiḋte
Do ṫóg tú suas an ċineaḋ Gaeḋeal
Nuair 'ḃí siad deaġnaċ báiḋte
Do ṫug tú gráḋ do Inis Fáil
Ó fáinne 'n lae go h-oiḋċe
'S an ḃláṫ a ṡgaoil tú ar an gaoiṫ
Ní ṡileoċar é a ċoiḋċe.

Go bfeicimíd le linn do ṡaoġail
Gaċ ball de Éirinn álainn,
Mar 'ḃí an sgéal fán am fad ó:
Banḃ, saor ó Ċoḃ go Málainn:
Ar dtír go h-uile faoi do réim;
An ḟairrge ar gaċ taoḃ di.
Ar nGaeḋilg ċeólṁar i ngaċ béal
Mar laḃair tú-féin ariaṁ.

A Éire ṗilir, tóg do ċeann
Gur ṁol do "Ċraoiḃín Aoiḃinn"
Tá ar do ḃántaiḃ bánú 'n lae
An saorsaċt taoḃ ar taoḃ linn.
Béiḋ Aontrom Dún agus Árḋ Ṁaċ'
A's Doire Ċolm Cille,
Fir Monaċ agus sean Tír Eoġain
In d'uċt gan mórán moille.

BRIAN Ó CIANAIG, O.S.

1938

Saothar Cruthaitheach::
Scéalta agus Dráma

GNÍOMHARTHA LAE

Lá tirim, gaothach a bhí ann i ndeireadh mhí na Lúnasa, an cineál lae a bhí a dhíth go cruaidh ar na daoine a raibh a gcuid féir ina luí ar feadh seachtaine roimhe sin agus an fhearthainn ag titim anuas air oíche agus lá. Bhí Tomás Mór Ó Gallchóir agus a mhac Peadar ina suí roimh éirí na gréine agus ábhar ceithre choca féir croite amach acu sular mhuscail aon duine i mBaile na Gaoithe ach iad féin. Fear cneasta, diaganta, caoinbhéasach ab ea Tomás agus más rud é go raibh aon locht air ar dhroim an tsaoil, ba é sin díobháil na foighde. Chuirfeadh an taisme ba lú ar an domhan fearg air, go háirithe lá fómhair, agus nuair a thigeadh an fhearg, b'fhusa mionna mór a chluinstin uaidh ná Fáilte an Aingil. Am ar bith a mbíodh deifir air níor ghnách leis focal ar bith a labhairt agus dhéanfadh sé níos mó oibre i lá ná a dhéanfadh beirt fhear ar bith sa chomharsanacht. Dá dtéadh aon rud chun siobarnaí, chluinfí é i Mín na gCuiseog, dhá mhíle ar shiúl. Nuair a bheadh sé neamhghnoitheach níorbh fhearr leis ag ithe aráin agus ime ná ag déanamh gar inteacht do na comharsanaigh, ach ná taradh siad á chóir nuair a bheadh sé i gceann oibre.

Donnchadh Ó Ceallaigh ab ainm don chomharsa ba chomhgaraí do theach Thomáis ach b'fhada ó Dhonnchadh a bheith ina fhear tí le cur i gcosúlacht le Tomás. Bhí dhá níon ag Donnchadh, Síle agus Anna, ach ní raibh mac ar bith riamh aige. Bhí sé féin tugtha don fhalsacht agus ach ab é go n-éiríodh Síle in am mheasartha ar maidin leis an bhricfeasta a dhéanamh réidh is ag an Rí atá a fhios cén uair a d'éireodh Donnchadh nó a bhean nó Anna. Ba mhór le Tomás an méid ama a chaitheadh a mhac i dteach Dhonnchaidh mar bhí eagla a sháith air go meallfadh bean de na níonacha Peadar uaidh. Bhí Síle agus Bríd (bean Thomáis) go han-mhór lena chéile mar an gcéanna agus níor thaitin sin leis ach oiread.

Bíodh na nithe seo mar atá siad is le gníomhartha lae i lár an fhómhair bhuí a bhaineas an scéal seo.

Nuair a bhí iomlán an fhéir croite tháinig Tomás agus Peadar chun tí lena mbricfeasta a chaitheamh agus bhí sin réidh ag bean chéile Thomáis Mhóir. Ní raibh siad ach i lár an bhéile nuair a bhuail Síle Ní Cheallaigh isteach chucu.

'Bígí go subhach,' ar sise nuair a chonaic sí na fir ag ithe.

'Bail ó Dhia ort ar maidin,' arsa Tomás.

'Tá do bheannacht agam i gcomhair an lae i gcás ar bith,' arsa Síle, ag caochadh ar Bhríd.

Las aghaidh Pheadair suas mar a bheadh rós i ngarraí ach níor thug Tomás fá dear é. Is dóiche gur shonraigh Bríd é ach bhí ciall aici a bheith ina tost.

'An bhfuil d'athair i gceann an fhéir inniu?' arsa Tomás.

'Níl go fóill,' arsa Síle. 'Tá sé ina chodladh.'

'Codladh traonaigh chuige,' arsa Tomás. 'Shílfeadh duine agus an méid féir atá ar láimh aige nach mbéarfadh an ghrian air ina luí maidin mar seo.'

'Níl sé i bhfad uilig ó chuaigh sé a luí,' arsa Síle. 'Chaith sé bunús na hoíche i dteach Éamainn Róise. Nár chuala sibh go dtáinig Micheál abhaile tráthnóna inné as Meiriceá?'

'An ndeir tú sin linn?' arsa Bríd. 'Is maith an tamall ó d'imigh sé. Nach bhfuil cuimhne agatsa air, a Thomáis?'

'Tá, mo sháith,' arsa Tomás. 'Sin an boc a dhíol liom an gamhain a bhí ar leathshúil an tseachtain sular imigh sé.'

'Níl gnoithe a bheith ag trácht ar a leithéid sin anois,' arsa Bríd. 'Bíodh geall air, a Shíle, go bhfuil sé ina fhear uasal.'

'Deir m'athair gur fear breá atá ann. Ach ní dhéanfaidh seo cúis domhsa. Bhí cearc againn ar fáir le coicís agus d'fhág sí na huibheacha ar maidin chomh luath is a d'fhoscail mé doras an sciobóil. Ní féidir linn í a fháil isteach ó shin agus tá eagla orm go rachaidh na huibheacha amú. An bhfuil cearc ar bith ar gor agatsa, a Bhríd?'

'Ní cearc amháin atá ar gor agamsa, a rún, ach leathdhuisín. Thig leat do rogha acu a thabhairt abhaile leat. A Shíle, a stór, nach deas atá do ghruaig cóirithe agat? Cuireann tú in mo chuimhne cailín a bhí ar aon scoil liomsa.'

'Cad é a d'éirigh di ó shin?' arsa Síle.

'Tá, a rún, go bhfuil sí féin agus go leor eile a bhí óg an t-am sin thuas ins na flaithis.'

'Ní fearr abhus a mbunús,' arsa Tomás ag éirí ón tábla.

'Ná tabhair aird ar an bhreallán sin, a Shíle,' arsa Bríd, agus d'imigh Síle ar lorg na circe.

Thóg Tomás aibhleog as an tinidh lena phíopa a dheargadh agus, leis sin, bhuail fear bocht a bhí ag cruinniú a choda isteach chucu. Niall Rua an t-ainm ba ghnách a thabhairt air. Duine gan choir gan urchóid ab ea Niall agus ar siocair go raibh sé leathshimplí bhíodh níos mó trua agus fáilte roimhe ná dá mbeadh sé ar a athrú de dhóigh. Is cosúil go bhfuair sé beagán léann Béarla i dtús a shaoil agus chleacht sé an dá theangaidh a mheascadh fríd a chéile sa chruth gurbh iomaí tamall grinn a bhíodh ag an aos óg ag éisteacht leis ag caint.

'*It's good day to you*, a Thomáis Mhóir,' ar seisean, ag suí síos, 'agus *fine harvest weather* lena chois sin.'

'Fáilte romhat, a dhuine,' arsa Tomás. 'An bhfuil scéal úr nó seanscéal leat?'

'*No, sir,*' arsa Niall, 'ach an trioblóid a bhí ar an bhaile mhór inné.'

'Cad é a tharla ansin?' arsa Tomás.

'Tá, a Thomáis, rud nár mhaith liom,' arsa Niall. '*Nothing ever went to* mo chroí i gceart ach *to see* an dá *policemen stuck in* sceadamán mo dhearthár.'

'Cad é ba chiontach leis sin?'

'Thit sé amach le baicle *tramps*, lucht siúil, tá a fhios agat, agus bhuail sé duine nó beirt acu.'

'Ní raibh a fhios agam go dtí sin,' arsa Tomás, 'go raibh deartháir ar bith agat.'

'Tá, maise,' arsa Niall. 'Tá sé ina shórt *retired beggarman* mar a déarfá. Bíonn sé ag díol éadaigh anois ó theach go teach.'

Thug Bríd arán agus tae do Niall agus thug Tomás trí pingine dó in airgead rua. Bhí mála folamh leis, mar ba ghnách, faoina ascaill ach ní ghlacfadh sé rud ar bith le cur sa mhála ach buidéil fholmha agus uibheacha. Ba chuma cad é a déarfaí leis chuirfeadh sé an dá chuid sa mhála i gcuideachta a chéile agus nuair a thiocfadh an tráthnóna is ró-annamh a bhíodh aon ubh slán sa mhála. Ar an ábhar sin stad na daoine ag tabhairt na n-uibheach dó. Shásódh pingin i gceart é.

Shiúil Tomás isteach sa scioból agus tháinig amach i mbomaite agus an ráca briste ina láimh leis. Nuair a d'amharc sé thart chonaic sé girseach le baintrigh a bhí ina cónaí ar an cheann eile den bhaile ag teacht anuas an cabhsa agus seanráca eile léise.

'Diúc, diúc,' arsa Bríd, ag scabadh bídh na gcearc ar an tsráid.

'Fiú, fiú, fiú,' arsa Tomás, ag amharc ar an ráca a bhí i láimh na girsí. Ní raibh ann ach an dá fhiacal.

'D'iarr mo mháthair ort,' arsa an ghirseach, 'caoi bheag a chur ar an ráca seo le do thoil. Níl aon cheann eile ar an tsaol againn.'

'An síleann do mháthair,' arsa Tomás, 'nach bhfuil dadaí agamsa le déanamh lá fómhair ach ag cur caoi ar sheanrácaí? Tá an ráca sin cosúil léi féin, fiacal thall is fiacal abhus.'

'Níl an triomú ach ag toisiú,' arsa Bríd ag iarraidh an dochar a bhaint as an rud a dúirt Tomás.

Le scéal fada a dhéanamh gairid cuireadh caoi ar an ráca agus d'imigh an ghirseach abhaile.

'Tabhair amach deoch bhainne ionsorm,' arsa Tomás le Bríd, 'nó sílfidh Peadar go dteachaigh mé a luí.'

Tugadh an deoch dó ach ní mó go raibh sí ólta aige nuair a bhí níon eile de chuid na baintrí ina seasamh ag a thaobh. Chuir Bríd fáilte roimpi ach focal amháin níor labhair Tomás.

'Rinne Nóra dearmad,' arsa an cailín, 'a rá libh nuair a bhí sí anseo leis an ráca, go bhfuil Úna Ní Dhochartaigh le cur tráthnóna inniu. Shíl mo mháthair nuair nach raibh duine ar bith as an bhaile seo ag an fhaire aréir go mb'fhéidir nár chuala sibh go raibh sí marbh. Chuala muid go minic le bliain fána bás ach níor imigh sí dáiríribh go dtí seo.'

'Slán turais di,' arsa Tomás, 'cá bith áit a bhfuil sí. Ní thiocfadh léi bás a fháil mar a dhéanfadh duine eile. Bhí an t-iomrá Dé hAoine go raibh sí marbh agus chuir mé paidir léi an lá sin mar shíl mé go mbeadh sí glan, scríobtha, sciúrtha le a bheith soir linn ar maidin Dé Domhnaigh agus gan a bheith ag cur lá den tseachtain amú léi. Nach bhfuil a fhios ag do mháthair go bhfuil ceithre choca mhóra le déanamh agam féin agus ag Peadar roimh an oíche?'

'Tá a fhios aici,' arsa an cailín, 'ach shíl sí más rud é go bhfuil tórramh ort i mBaile an Chaorthháin gur mhaith leat scéala a fháil ina thaobh.'

'Nach bhfuil a fhios agat go maith go bhfuil tórramh orm sa bhaile sin. Bhí an t-iomlán acu ag tórramh m'athara ach go raibh ciall aigesean bás a fháil i ndeireadh na bliana.'

'Níl ach amaidí sa chineál sin cainte,' arsa Bríd. 'Tá fhios agat go maith go gcaithfidh tú a ghabháil chun tórraimh.'

Thiontaigh Tomás thart le freagar a thabhairt ar Bhríd agus leis sin tháinig séideán de ghaoith thuathail a thóg an hata dá cheann agus siúd in airde é sa spéir chomh díreach le bata.

'Ag tórramh an diabhail go raibh tú,' ar seisean, ag féachaint suas ar an áit a raibh an hata ag gabháil as amharc. Ba leis an tséideán a chuir sé an phaidir.

'Seo mac Phaidí Aindí ag teacht trasna na páirce ar cosa in airde,' arsa Bríd.

'Tórramh eile, bíodh geall air, i Mín an Bhradáin,' arsa Tomás.

Ba ghairid go raibh an diúlach in aice leo agus é i mbarr a anála.

'Cad é atá cur cur bhuartha ortsa?' arsa Tomás. D'aithin sé go maith go raibh rud inteacht contráilte.

'Tá bearach le Donnchadh Ó Ceallaigh i bpoll mónadh sa Lag Dubh,' ar seisean.

'Is trua nach bhfuil Donnchadh é féin i bpoll eile lena thaobh,' arsa Tomás. 'Codlaíonn sé san earrach nuair ba cheart dó a bheith ag déanamh claíocha agus síleann sé ansin go bhfuil sé beag go leor ag na comharsanaigh a chuid eallaigh a tharraingt amach as na poill lá fómhair. Is deas an saol atá ann! Úna Ní Dhochartaigh le cur síos i bpoll agus bearach Pheadair Uí Cheallaigh le tarraingt amach as poll eile an lá is fearr a tháinig ó thús an fhómhair.'

'Thiocfadh leis a bheith níos measa,' arsa Bríd. 'Rachaidh mise chun tórraimh in d'áit agus chead agatsa cuidiú leo an bearach a shábháil. Tá Dia láidir agus beidh an féar tógtha roimh an oíche go fóill.'

'Éireoidh sé féin in airde, dálta an hata,' arsa Tomás. 'Tabhair amach an rópa cnáibe atá faoin *dresser*.'

Fuarthas an rópa agus d'imigh Tomás agus mac Phaidí trasna an chnoic. Bhí an t-allas go talamh leo nuair a tháinig siad go bruach an phoill.

'Ghlac tú d'am ag teacht,' arsa Donnchadh agus é go dtína bhásta sa pholl ag taobh an bhearaigh.

'Ghlac tusa d'am ag déanamh na gclaíoch san earrach,' arsa Tomás.

Ní raibh an dara focal eatarthu nó gur léim Tomás isteach sa pholl, rópa cnáibe ina láimh aige. D'oibir sé féin agus Peadar go cumasach nó go raibh na rópaí trasna faoi chorp an bhearaigh agus gur tarraingeadh amach í slán, folláin ar an bhruach. Bhí Donnchadh fliuch, salach go dtína bhásta ach ní mó go raibh snáithe tirim ar Thomás óna mhuineál síos. Bhain sé an baile amach gan oiread is focal amháin a labhairt agus níorbh é a chuid paidreach a bhí ag cur bhuartha air ar theacht trasna an chnoic dó.

'Tá mé caillte go brách,' ar seisean, ag cur a chinn isteach ar an doras.

'Níl tú i bhfad uaidh,' arsa Bríd. 'Steall díot na bróga salacha agus athraigh do chuid éadaigh. Ar chuala tú scéal iontach ar bith ó d'imigh tú?'

'Tá scéal iontach a dhíth ort, nach bhfuil?' arsa Tomás.

'Níl, maise,' arsa Bríd. 'Tá mo sháith scéala agam go dtí an oíche. Tomhais cá bhfuil do mhac.'

'Ina luí, creidim.'

'Níl a shaothar air,' arsa Bríd. 'Tá sé féin agus Síle Ní Cheallaigh ar shiúl á bpósadh.'

'Níl do chuid magaidh in easbhaidh orm san am atá i láthair,' arsa Tomás.

'Magadh, an ea? Nach bog a luíos an craiceann ort?'

'Luífeadh sé chomh bog ortsa dá mbeifeá ar maos i bpoll mónadh le dhá uair an chloig.'

'Tá a fhios agam,' arsa Bríd, 'gur deacair leat an scéal a chreidbheáil ach tá mé ag insint na fírinne. Toil Dé go raibh déanta.'

D'aithin Tomás ar an bhomaite go raibh an scéal rófhíor agus bhris an gol air.

'Peadar bocht,' ar seisean. 'Peadar bocht! Tá muid gan mhac anocht.'

Gí gur theip sé ar Bhríd na deora a choinneail ar gcúl (óir bhí a croí báite ina haonmhac), bhrostaigh sí suas í féin go tapaidh.

'Ná hamharc mar sin ar an chás, a Thomáis,' ar sise. 'Níl dadaí chomh holc sin nach dtiocfadh leis a bheith níos measa. Beidh mac againn anocht mar a bhí i gcónaí agus, an rud atá a dhíth orainn feasta, níon chomh maith le mac. Tá aithne againn ar Shíle ó bhí sí ina páiste agus níl aon chailín eile sa pharóiste ab fhearr liomsa ar m'urlár ná Síle Ní Cheallaigh. Tá eagla ar Pheadar nach ligfear isteach anseo iad agus níl againn le déanamh anois ach umhlú do thoil Dé agus fearadh na fáilte a chur roimh an phéire.'

'Aidmhím go bhfuil an ceart agat,' arsa Tomás, 'agus leis an fhírinne a dhéanamh ní thig drochfhocal a rá i dtaobh Shíle. Dá dtéadh ag Anna é a mhealladh bheadh ábhar imní againn. Ach, faoin Rí, cad é a éireos don fhéar atá croite?'

'Siúil amach go binn an tí agus tífidh tú sin,' arsa Bríd.

Shiúil an bheirt amach agus d'amharc Tomás síos ar an pháirc. Bhí trí choca mhóra críochnaithe agus an ceathrú ceann leath bealaigh. Bhí leathdhuisín de bhuachaillí óga ag tógáil an fhéir.

'Cumhdach an Rí orainn,' arsa Tomás, 'cá has a dtáinig na fir sin?'

'Buachaillí as na bailte sin thall a fuair cuireadh chun bainise,' arsa Bríd. 'Níl leis an lánúin óig ach Aodh Maguidhir agus Anna. D'iarr Peadar ar an chuid eile an féar a thógáil.'

'Dhéanfaidh sé fear maith tí go fóill,' arsa Tomás. 'Seo chugainn Donnchadh agus caithfimid gan míshásamh ar bith a thaispeáint dó.'

B'fhíor dó. Léim Donnchadh trasna an chlaí agus thug Tomás coiscéim ina araicis agus rinne croitheadh láimhe leis.

'Níl mé ag gabháil a rá leat nach bhfuil iontas orm fán scéal a chluinim,' arsa Tomás, 'ach umhlaím do thoil Dé. Go gcuire Dia an t-ádh ar an phéire óg agus go dtuga Sé grása agus sláinte dúinn uilig.'

'Tá mé fíorbhuíoch duit, a Thomáis Mhóir, ar son na cainte sin. Bhí a fhios agam le tamall go raibh an bheirt mór lena chéile ach focal amháin níor chuala mé fán phósadh go dtáinig mé abhaile ón Lag Dubh. Agus cuireann sin in mo cheann gur chóir domh buíochas a thabhairt duit anois féin ar son do chuidithe. Ach ab é thú, bheadh an bearach sa pholl go fóill.'

'Dhéanfaimid dearmad den méid atá thart,' arsa Tomás. 'Tá bainis ar láimh againn agus caithfimid ár ndícheall a dhéanamh.'

'Is ormsa atá an t-ádh uilig,' arsa Bríd. 'Tá a fhios ag an uile dhuine an meas a bhí agam i dtólamh ar Shíle.'

'Bhí sí mar sin leat,' arsa Donnchadh. 'Ach beidh níos mó ná sin le socrú againn ar ball. Tá mise ag fágáil na feirme glan balach ag Síle mar spré bainise. Tá spré Anna sa bhanc agam, corradh le dhá chéad punta. Tá mo theachtaireacht déanta anois ach amháin cuireadh chun bainise a thabhairt daoibh.'

'Go raibh míle maith agat,' arsa Tomás.

'Beimid agat roimh luí na gréine,' arsa Bríd. 'Gheall Nóra Bhán fanacht anseo go maidin inár n-áit. Is dóigh liom go mbeidh an lánúin óg [ag teacht] abhaile gan mhoill.'

'Fan ort bomaite,' arsa Tomás. 'Ba mhaith liom, a Dhonnchaidh, dá gcuirfeá duine de na buachaillí go dtí an baile mór agus gluaisteán a fháil fá mo choinnese. Tá eagla ar Pheadar go bhfuil fearg ormsa leis mar gheall ar gur phós sé i ngan fhios domh. Níl fearg ná imní ormsa agus tá mé ag gabháil chun an bhaile mhóir le mo bheannacht a thabhairt don phéire. Is leo an méid is fiú mise.'

'Rath Dé ort, a Thomáis Mhóir,' arsa Donnchadh, 'is agat a bhí an chiall is an stuaim i gcónaí. Beidh an gluaisteán anseo gan mhoill, mise i mbannaí ort.'

Bhí leatheagla ar Dhonnchadh nuair a tháinig sé ar an teachtaireacht go mbeadh fearg ar Thomás fán phósadh ach nuair a chonaic sé an fháilte a bhí roimhe agus an réiteach a rinneadh tháinig áthas an domhain air. Ba ghairid gur cuireadh lorg ar an ghluaisteán agus go raibh Tomás ar an bhealach go dtí an baile mór.

Bhí Peadar agus Síle ina seasamh ag Oifig an Phoist nuair a tháinig Tomás amach as an ghluaisteán, agus nuair a chonaic siad nach raibh cosúlacht ar bith feirge air thit deora an áthais go frasach ó shúile an phéire. B'aoibhinn, fíorchroíoch, lánlúcháireach an comhghairdeachas a rinne Tomás leo.

'Bhí mac agam ar maidin,' ar seisean, 'beidh mac agus níon agam ón oíche anocht amach.'

Fuair Tomás greim láimhe ar Shíle athuair agus dúirt: 'Tá cuimhne agam gur dhúirt tú ar maidin go raibh mo bheannacht agat i gcomhair an lae. Tá mo sheacht mbeannacht agaibh araon anois i gcomhair an tsaoil nua.'

Bhí mórán de lucht na bainise cruinnithe nuair a tháinig Tomás agus an lánúin óg go teach Dhonnchaidh ag titim na hoíche, agus bhí an ghrian go hard sa spéir ar maidin lá arna mhárach nuair a cuireadh deireadh leis an bhainis ab fhearr a bhí acu riamh i mBaile na Gaoithe.

NÓTA: *Derry Journal* (22/7/1931). Tá an t-ainm cleite 'Eamonn an Chruic' leis.

Scéal an tSeanduine

Shiúil mé síos an bealach mór oíche amháin nuair a bhí mé fá thuairim deich mbliana nó mar sin mar gheall ar canna uisce a thabhairt abhaile. Deireadh fómhair a bhí ann agus bhí solas na gealaí chomh geal sin is nach raibh gnoithe ar bith le lóchrann. Nuair a tháinig mé go bruach an tobair chonaic mé seanduine aosta ina shuí ar charraig cupla slat uaim. Shíl mé ar dtús gur taibhse a bhí ann nó teachtaire inteacht ón domhan eile ar lorg duine saolta a bhéarfadh éisteacht don scéal a bhí le hinsint aige. Tháinig eagla orm ach mar sin féin bhí leisc orm a theacht abhaile le canna folamh. Sheas mé ag amharc air ar feadh bomaite gan a fhios agam cad é ab fhearr domh a dhéanamh agus, fá dheireadh, labhair sé.

'Ná bíodh aon eagla ort, a bhuachaill bhig,' ar seisean. 'Ní taibhse ar bith mise ach fear a tógadh fá mhíle den áit a bhfuil tú 'do sheasamh.'

Bhí an eagla imithe agus shiúil mé suas go dtí an charraig ar a raibh sé ina shuí.

'Má tá tú 'do chónaí sa teach is comhgaraí,' ar seisean, 'bhí aithne mhaith agam ar d'athair mhór. Is dóigh liom go bhfuil sé ar shlua na marbh.'

'Fuair sé bás sular rugadh mise,' a dúirt mé.

'Go raibh a anam fá shuaimhneas,' ar seisean. 'Ba chineálta an comharsa é.'

'Is iontach liom,' arsa mise, 'nár chuala mé m'athair ag caint ort má tá tú 'do chónaí fá mhíle den áit seo.'

'Faraor,' ar seisean, 'níl cónaí ar bith agam sa tsaol seo. Chuaigh leathchéad bliain thart ó chodail mé faoi mo scraith féin. Chaith mé na cúig bliana fichead deireanacha i gCúige Chonnacht agus rinne mé suas m'intinn fá thuairim mí ó shin go dtabharfainn an ruaig dheireanach ar an áit a rugadh mé. Beidh mé ceithre scór agus deich mbliana má bhím beo go Domhnach agus níl mórán ama idir mé féin agus an uaigh. A mhic mo chroí,' ar seisean, 'is brónach mo scéal ach ní maith liom thú a choinneáil níos faide.'

Bhí a ghuth binn, milis agus chuaigh na focla a dúirt sé go dtí mo chroí. Bhí mo shúile líonta le deora i mbomaite agus d'fhéach mé i nguth bhrónach é a mhealladh chun an oíche a chaitheamh againn. D'aithin sé go raibh trua agam dó agus thug sé isteach a theacht liom.

Nuair a tháinig muid fhad leis an teach bhí m'athair ina sheasamh ag an doras.

'Seo fear bocht,' arsa mise, 'nach bhfuil áit aige lena cheann a leagaint. Casadh orm ag an tobar é agus thug mé abhaile liom é.'

'Is maith a rinne tú sin,' arsa m'athair. 'Tar isteach, a dhuine bhoicht, agus síl go bhfuil tú sa bhaile. Is mór an trua fear chomh sean leat a fheiceáil ar lorg déirce agus foscadh na hoíche.'

'Sin mar atá an scéal agamsa,' arsa an seanduine. D'fhág sé síos an mála a bhí sé a iompar agus bhain de a hata. Choisreac sé é féin agus dúirt an phaidir a leanas: 'Guím go mbeidh beannacht Dé agus beannacht seanduine atá ar bhruach na huaighe ort féin agus ar do chúram anocht agus go brách.' Shiúil sé isteach agus shuigh ar an chathaoir a bhí cóirithe ag mo mháthair dó ag cois na tineadh agus fhad is a bhí a shuipéar á dhéanamh réidh bhí mé ag fanacht go himníoch le scéal a bheatha a chluinstin.

In am ghairid bhí an suipéar thart agus bhí muid uilig inár suí thart fán tinidh.

'Is dóigh liom,' arsa m'athair leis an tseanduine, 'go raibh aithne agat in d'oige ar an cheantar seo.'

'Bhí na seacht n-aithne agam ar an áit seo nuair a bhí mé óg,' arsa an seanduine. 'Tógadh mé sa ghleann sin thíos ach níor chuir mé mo chos ann le leathchéad bliain. Níl mé ag dréim,' ar seisean, 'go dtuigfidh daoine mar sibhse an cineál scéil atá le hinsint agamsa agus ní dóiche go gcluinfidh cluasa an duine bheo é go deo arís. Is gairid an spás atá idir mé féin agus an uaigh ach beidh fáilte agam roimh an bhás nuair a thiocfas sé. Tá mo mhuirínse, beannacht orthu, cruinnithe thart fán tinidh seo anocht. Go mba fada a bheas an scéal sin le hinsint acu! Rugadh mise sa bhliain 1800 agus fiche bliain ina dhiaidh sin pósadh mé ar chailín chomh breá is a tógadh riamh i gContae Dhún na nGall. Phronn Dia dhá mhac orainn agus ní raibh néal ar an tsaol go dtí go raibh an buachaill ba sine fiche bliain d'aois. Oíche amháin tháinig an buachaill ab óige abhaile ag am codlata agus ní raibh an buachaill eile leis. Ba ghnách leis an phéire a ghabháil a chuartaíocht cupla oíche sa tseachtain ach thigeadh siad abhaile i gcónaí i gcuideachta a chéile.'

'Cá bhfuil Seán?' arsa mo bhean. 'An dtáinig tubaiste air?'

Ní bhfuair sí freagar ar bith ó Dhónall (an buachaill ab óige) agus d'aithin mé go raibh rud inteacht contráilte.

'Inis an fhírinne dúinn,' arsa mise, 'cad é a tháinig ar Sheán?'

Thoisigh Dónall ag caoineadh ach níor dhúirt sé focal. Ar an bhomaite sin tháinig Seán anuas an tsráid agus thit sé in éadan doras na cisteanaí. Léim mé 'mo shuí agus d'fhoscail an doras. Thóg mé féin agus Dónall é agus chuir ina shuí é ar chathaoir ag an tinidh. Bhí a fhios agam go raibh sé ar meisce ach thug mé buíochas do Dhia go dtáinig sé abhaile slán. Thairg a mháthair braon bainne te dó ach ní raibh sé ábalta é a ól. Chuir muid a luí é agus ansin dúirt muid an

Paidrín Páirteach. Ní theachaigh aon duine againn a luí an oíche sin ach Seán bocht. Bhí barraíocht imní orainn.

Ag bánú an lae tháinig cóiste fhad leis an doras agus shiúil oifigeach de chuid arm na Sasana isteach.

'An bhfuil Seán Ó Baoill ina chónaí anseo?' ar seisean.

'Sin ainm mo mhic,' arsa mise, 'ach tá sé ina chodladh fá láthair.'

Tharraing an t-oifigeach amach piostal.

'Abair leis,'' ar seisean, 'go dtabharfaidh mé cúig bhomaite dó lena chuid éadaigh a chur air. Ghlac sé an scilling aréir agus chuir síos a ainm mar shaighdiúir d'arm na Sasana.'

B'éigean do Sheán a chuid éadaigh a chur air fá dheifir agus a ghabháil leis an oifigeach. Thit mo bhean i laige agus chaoin Dónall an oiread sin is gur shíl mé go mbrisfeadh sé a chroí. D'fhéach mé go cruaidh mo mhisneach a choinneáil suas ach sháraigh sé orm. Bhí solas ár mbeatha imithe agus fágadh muid i ndorchadas.

Ón lá a d'imigh Seán uainn ní theachaigh Dónall isteach in aon teach sa chomharsanacht. Ba ghnách leis suí mórán den am ag cois na tineadh agus níor mhinic a labhair sé. D'aithin muid fá dheireadh go raibh sé ag titim isteach i ndrochshláinte agus níor lig muid dó aon chineál oibre a dhéanamh. Bhí sé ag éirí níos laige agus níos laige lá ar lá go dtí go dtáinig an bás fána choinne. D'fhág muid ina luí é sa reilig bheag atá i lár an ghleanna agus tháinig muid abhaile go brónach.

Dhá bhliain ina dhiaidh sin bhí muid inár suí oíche amháin ag cois na tineadh nuair a tháinig fear bocht isteach agus é crom leath bealaigh síos go dtí an talamh. Bhí comhartha an bháis ar a aghaidh agus bhí sé gléasta i mbratógaí. Níor labhair sé focal ach shuigh sé ar chathaoir a bhí comhgarach ag an tinidh. Bhí sé chomh lag sin is go raibh leisc orainn é a cheistniú. Fá dheireadh shiúil mo bhean suas fhad leis agus leag a lámh ar a ghualainn.

'Inis domh,' ar sise, 'an tú mo mhac?'

'Is mé, a mháthair,' ar seisean. 'Is mise Seán.'

D'aithin muid a ghuth chomh luath is a labhair sé. Tháinig sé ar ais abhaile le bás a fháil.

Tamall beag ina dhiaidh sin d'ól sé braon beag bainne agus chuir muid a luí é. Bhí sé rólag le mórán cainte a dhéanamh agus d'inis muid dó go mbeadh sé níos láidre ar maidin.

'Níl ionam ach scáile,' a dúirt sé nuair a luigh sé síos.

'Beidh tú ag bisiú an uile lá,' arsa a mháthair.

'B'fhéidir,' ar seisean, 'b'fhéidir.'

Maidin lá arna mhárach bhí a ghuth ní ba láidre agus d'inis sé dúinn gur chaill sé a shláinte san Afraic agus gur cuireadh abhaile é. 'Thairg siad pinsean cúig scillinge sa tseachtain domh,' ar seisean, 'ach chead acu é a choinneáil. Beidh ár sáith againn uilig sa tsaol atá le a theacht.'

Mí nó mar sin ón oíche a tháinig Seán abhaile bhí sé ar shlua na marbh agus cuireadh é le taobh Dhónaill. Fágadh muid gan mhac agus féadaim a rá, gan chara.'

Chumail an seanduine na deora óna shúile agus dúirt: 'Tá mo shaol ar bhealach a bheith críochnaithe. Fuair mo bhean bás an t-earrach ina dhiaidh sin agus ní raibh suaimhneas ar bith le fáil agam sa bhothán inar tógadh mé. D'fhág mé slán ag an ghleann agus chuaigh amach sa tsaol fhuar, uaigneach. Níl níos mó le hinsint.'

Chóirigh mo mháthair leabaidh dó agus chodail sé go maith an oíche sin. Lá arna mhárach nuair a bhí an bricfeasta thart, thug sé cuairt ar an reilig ina raibh a bhean agus a dhá mhac ag fanacht le scairt an aingil. Nuair nach raibh sé ar ais ag an mheán lae, mar a gheall sé, chuaigh m'athair á chuartú. Fuair sé ina luí marbh é sa reilig, a dhá láimh ina luí ar a ucht agus a phaidrín casta thart orthu.

Cuireadh é lá arna mhárach agus sin deireadh an scéil.

NÓTA: *The Derry People and Tirconaill News*, 3, 10, 17 October, 1936.

Oíche Shamhna

Oíche Shamhna a bhí ann. Bhí Diarmaid Ó Dónaill ina shuí ag an tinidh ag insint scéaltaí fá na sióga. Thaitin seo go mór leis na páistí. Tháinig fear arbh ainm dó Dónall Mac Pháidín isteach. Bhí fáilte mhór roimhe ar siocair go raibh sé muintearach ag Diarmaid.

'Is fada anois ó thug tú cuairt orainn,' arsa Diarmaid.

'Dhá bhliain go díreach,' arsa Dónall. 'Tá an ghealach lán anocht, ar seisean, 'agus is fada an t-am ó bhí gealach lán againn Oíche Shamhna.'

'Níl bréag agat,' arsa Diarmaid. 'Beidh na sióga ag an dún ag an mheán oíche agus ó tharla go bhfuil an aimsir ciúin rachaimid ag amharc orthu.'

'Tá mé sásta,' arsa Dónall.

'Tím,' ar seisean, 'go bhfuil na páistí uilig go maith. Cá bhfuil an buachaill is sine?'

'Chuaigh Diarmaid Óg go hAlbain ag tús an fhómhair. Bhí muid ag dréim le litir uaidh inniu agus táimid imníoch gan cluinstin uaidh.'

'Tá eagla orainn,' arsa bean an tí, 'go dtáinig taisme de chineál inteacht air nuair nár scríobh sé.'

'Coinnigh suas do chroí,' arsa Dónall. 'Tá Dia chomh láidir is a bhí Sé riamh agus b'fhéidir go mbeadh sé sa bhaile roimh an am seo amárach.'

'Tá súil agam,' arsa Diarmaid, 'go dtiocfaidh do scéal isteach fíor. Má tá sé beo, slán tá sé fiche bliain anocht.'

'Nach bhfuil cuimhne go maith agam ar an oíche sin,' arsa Dónall, 'agus sin an fáth a bhfuil mé anseo. Tháinig mé le hinsint dó go bhfuil dúil agam an fheirm a thabhairt dó. Is mise a athair baiste.'

'Ní raibh muid ag dréim le nuaíocht chomh maith sin,' arsa Diarmaid, 'agus dá mbeadh do mhac – féadaim do mhac a thabhairt air ó tharla gur tú a athair baiste – dá mbeadh sé anseo anocht, tá mé cinnte go dtabharfadh sé buíochas lánchroíoch duit. Gí go bhfuil Oíche Shamhna ann bheadh sinn uaigneach anocht ach ab é go dtug tú an chuairt seo orainn.'

'Níl mé ag dréim leis anocht,' arsa Dónall, 'ach tá mé fíorchinnte go bhfuil sé ar a bhealach abhaile.'

Thoisigh na páistí eile ag imirt cleasannaí agus bhí Dónall ina measc.

'Tá a fhios agamsa an cleas is fearr den iomlán,' arsa Síle, an cailín ba sine.

'Téigh ar aghaidh leis,' arsa Dónall.

'Caithfidh mé a ghabháil thart fá chruach choirce trí huaire,' arsa Síle, 'agus ansin trí shifín a tharraingt. Inseoidh na gráinníneacha ar na sifíní na blianta a rachas thart sula bpóstar mé.'

'Sin seanchleas maith,' arsa Dónall, 'ach caithfidh tú a ghabháil leat féin.'

'Dhéanfaidh mé sin,' arsa Síle. 'Níl eagla orm roimh na siógaí.'

Chuaigh Síle amach leis na sifíní a tharraingt. Tháinig sí ar ais gan iad.

'Tá buachaill ag an gheata, a athair,' ar sise, 'agus deir sé go dtiocfaidh sé isteach má tá fáilte roimhe.'

'An strainséir é?' arsa Diarmaid.

'Ní hea,' arsa Síle. 'Tá aithne mhaith agamsa air.'

'Abair leis teacht isteach,' arsa Diarmaid.

D'fhoscail Síle an doras agus shiúil Diarmaid Óg isteach. Bhí dhá láimh a mháthara thart fána mhuineál sular shroich sé lár an urláir.

'Is liomsa an chéad phóg,' arsa Síle. 'Is mise a fuair é.'

Níor lú ná sin an lúcháir a bhí ar gach duine den mhuirín – Dónall chomh maith leo. Bhí Oíche Shamhna phléisiúrtha i dteach Dhiarmaid Uí Dhónaill.

NÓTA: *Derry People and Tirconaill News,* 31 October, 1936.

Scéal Chois Tineadh

Oíche Dhomhnaigh a bhí ann seal mór blianta ó shin agus go díreach fá thuairim mí roimh an Nollaig. Bhí mé 'mo shuí ag cois na tineadh, m'intinn leathdhéanta suas agam fán dóigh a gcuirfinn an t-am isteach go ham codlata. Leis sin bhuail duine inteacht ag an doras agus nuair a d'oscail mé é shiúil mo chomharsa Cathal Mac Giolla Easpaig isteach.

'Céad fáilte,' arsa mise. 'Tá lúcháir orm thú a fheiceáil.'

'Tá a fhios agam sin,' arsa Cathal. 'Tá na hoícheanna fada agus ní maith le duine a bheith leis féin. Nár chóir don phéire againn a ghabháil go teach Shéamais Uí Ghallchóir agus oíche mhaith scéalaíochta a bheith againn?'

'Tá mé sásta,' arsa mise. Thug mé braon bainne don chat, chuir an glas ar an doras agus bhí muid araon ag teach Shéamais deich mbomaite ina dhiaidh sin.

Ní raibh duine ar bith sa teach nuair a chuaigh muid isteach ach Séamas agus a bhean agus seanbhean ó chúl an chnoic arbh ainm di Nóra Rua. Bhí eagla ar Nóra roimh thaibhsí agus chuir sé iontas orainn í a fheiceáil taobh amuigh dena teach féin i ndiaidh luí na gréine. D'inis bean Shéamais dúinn go dtáinig sí trasna an chnoic le solas lae agus nach raibh sí ag gabháil abhaile go maidin.

'Tá sin fíor,' arsa Nóra. 'Ní rachainn ó seo go dtí an scioból sa dorchadas dá bhfaighinn cathair Dhoire mar phronntanas.'

'Is fada anois,' arsa Cathal, 'ó chuala Donncha agus mé féin seanscéal uait. Ní féidir, a Shéamais, go dtearn tú dearmad orthu.'

'Tá cuimhne agam ar an uile seanscéal dár chuala mé riamh,' arsa Séamas, 'ach d'inis mé chomh minic sin iad is go bhfuil eagla orm go bhfuil sibh tuirseach leo.'

'Ní mar sin atá an scéal,' arsa Cathal. 'Ba mhaith liom geall a chur,' ar seisean, 'go bhfuil scéaltaí agat nár chuala ceachtar againn riamh.'

'Tá scéal amháin agam a bhaineas liom féin,' arsa Séamas, 'agus ní cuimhneach liom gur inis mé é le fiche bliain. Ní maith liom dearmad a dhéanamh air agus ar an ábhar sin inseoidh mé é anocht leis an am a chur thart.'

'Má tá baint ar bith ag an scéal le taibhsí,' arsa Nóra, 'tá mise 'mo shuí ró-chomhgarach ag an doras. Suífidh mé sa choirnéal ag cois na tineadh.'

'A bhean chroí,' arsa Séamas, 'ná bíodh aon eagla ort. Caithfidh mé a rá go bhfuil baint ag an scéal le taibhsí, agus an chuid is measa acu, ach ní thiocfaidh siad anseo anocht.'

'Féadann sin a bheith fíor,' arsa Nóra, 'ach níl siad intaofa.'

Shuigh muid uilig thart fán tinidh agus chuir Séamas tús ar an scéal mar a leanas.

'Fán am a thoisíos mo scéal bhí mé fá thuairim seacht mbliana déag d'aois. Cheannaigh m'athair scaifte caorach agus chuaigh siad ar seachrán i measc na gcnoc.

'A Shéamais,' ar seisean, 'caithfidh tú a ghabháil ar lorg na gcaorach agus ná tar ar ais gan iad.'

'Bhí sé ag éirí mall tráthnóna nuair a d'fhág mé an baile. Ní raibh mé ach míle nó mar sin ar thaobh chúl an chnoic atá le feiceáil ón doras seo nuair a tháinig ceo trom isteach ón fharraige. Ní fhaca mé ceo le linn mo shaoil le cur i gcomórtas leis. Bhí sé chomh trom sin is gurbh fhéidir tairne a thiomáint ann agus fuair mé le fios in am ghairid go raibh mé caillte ar fad. Tháinig dorchadas na hoíche fá dheireadh agus shuigh mé tamall ar charraig.'

'A dhuine bhoicht,' arsa Nóra.

'Fan go gcluine tú,' arsa Séamas. 'Bhí poll faoin charraig agus rinne mé suas m'intinn a ghabháil ar foscadh. Ar an bhomaite sin chonaic mé solas ag teacht comhgarach agus phreab mo chroí le lúcháir. Bhí fear ag iompar an tsolais agus nuair a tháinig sé fhad leis an áit a raibh mé 'mo sheasamh shonraigh mé go raibh ceann asail air agus corp ar dhéanamh bairille.'

'A Rí na Glóire,' arsa Nóra, 'tá mé ar crith ó mo cheann go dtí mo chois. Is trua nár fhan mé sa bhaile.'

'Tá an chuid is fearr den scéal le a theacht go fóill,' arsa Séamas.

'Lean leat,' arsa Cathal.

'Féadann tú a bheith cinnte,' arsa Séamas, 'go raibh drochdhóigh orm.'

'Siúil leat,' arsa an taibhse agus caith an oíche in mo theachsa.'

'D'aithin mé go maith nach dtiocfadh liom imeacht uaidh agus b'éigean domh é a leanúint. Tháinig muid fhad le teach nach raibh fuinneogaí ar bith air agus nuair a chuaigh muid isteach dhruid an taibhse an doras ina dhiaidh.'

'An bhfuil aithne agat orm?' arsa an taibhse.

'Níl,' arsa mise, 'agus tá súil agam nach mbíonn.'

'Cé leis a bhfuil mé cosúil?' ar seisean.

'Tá tú cosúil leis an diabhal,' arsa mise.

'Bhí mé ag fanacht leis sin,' arsa Nóra. 'Is é an diabhal a bhí ann go cinnte.'

'Tá seachrán ort,' arsa Séamas.

'Tá iontas orm,' arsa Cathal, 'nach dteachaigh tú as do mheabhair.'

'Ní theachaigh, maise,' arsa Séamas. 'Chaith mé díom mo chóta agus chuir mé troid ar an taibhse. Bhí bata maith ramhar agam in mo láimh agus thug mé buille dó ar mhullach an chinn. Thit ceann an asail ag a chosa.'

'Beidh sin go leor, a Shéamais,' ar seisean, 'go dtí go bhfaighe mé amach as an bhairille seo.'

'Cé a bhí ann ach mac Bhriain Uí Dhónaill, an fear a fuair bás ins an Oileán Úr fán am seo anuraidh.'

'Sin scéal iontach,' arsa Cathal, 'agus is dóigh liom go bhfuil an chuid is mó de fíor.'

'Tá sé uilig fíor,' arsa Séamas. 'Ní chreideann tú go dtiocfadh le fear ceann asail a chur air féin. An é sin do thrioblóid?'

'Go díreach,' arsa Cathal.

'Thig liomsa an cás a shocrú i mbomaite,' arsa Séamas. 'Fuair asal tincéara bás ins an chomharsanacht agus bhain mac Bhriain an craiceann den cheann agus líon é le féar. Ní raibh moill air rud mar sin a dhéanamh.'

'Creidim thú anois,' arsa Cathal.

'An fear a d'imreodh cleas den chineál sin,' arsa Nóra, 'ba cheart é a bháitheadh. Ní chodlóidh mé néal go maidin,' ar sise.

'Níl taibhsí ar bith sa tír seo le seal blianta,' arsa Séamas. 'Nuair a bhí mise óg,' ar seisean, 'bhí siad chomh fairsing le préacháin. Chuala mé m'athair ag rá gur throid siad briseadh eatarthu féin sa tseandún atá ar chúl theach Nóra agus nach bhfacthas mórán taibhsí in Éirinn ón lá sin go dtí an lá inniu.'

'Más mar sin atá an cás,' arsa Nóra, 'díolfaidh mé an teach agus an giota talaimh roimh an Nollaig. Gheobhaidh mé luach maith ar an áit agus beidh mé beo mar bhean uasal.'

'Cá bith fá na taibhsí,' arsa Séamas, 'ba mhaith le do dheirfiúr tú a theacht a chónaí chuici. Cad é an luach atá tú a iarraidh?'

'An fiú dhá chéad punta é?' arsa Nóra.

'Ní fiú,' arsa Séamas. 'Níl agat ach seacht n-acra de thalamh.'

'Cá bhfuil do níon?' ar sise le Séamas.

'Chuaigh sí go hurnaithe an tráthnóna,' arsa Séamas, 'agus is gairid go mbeidh sí ar ais.'

'Maith go leor,' arsa Nóra. 'Má ligeann Eilís domhsa fear a phiocadh di, bhéarfaidh mé an teach agus an talamh di. Ní iarrfaidh mise ach áit sa choirnéal agus ní dóiche go mbeidh mé mórán blianta sa chasán.'

Chuir comhrá Nóra iontas ar an iomlán againn agus ar an bhomaite sin shiúil Eilís isteach. Bhí lúcháir ar Nóra í a fheiceáil agus dúirt sí: 'Tá mise ag déanamh cleamhnais fá do choinne, a Eilís, agus má tá tú sásta is leat mo theach agus talamh.'

'B'fhéidir nach mbeadh an fear atá in d'intinn sásta,' arsa Eilís.

'Is furast sin a fháil amach,' arsa Nóra. 'Tá an fear atá in m'intinn ina shuí ag cois na tineadh.'

Ní raibh fear díomhaoin ar bith sa teach ach mé féin agus is beag nár thit mé den chathaoir.

Sin críoch an scéil ach amháin a rá gur pósadh Eilís agus mé féin cupla lá ina dhiaidh sin. Agus bhí Nóra ag an bhainis.

NÓTA: *The Derry People and Tirconaill News*, 7, 14, 21 November 1936.

TARNGAIREACHT AN BHACAIGH MHÓIR

Mura bhfuil aon rud agat le tabhairt domh, ná stróc mo mhála (seanrá)

An té ar ghnách leis a bheith ag siúl ar na bóithre i gContae Dhún na nGall seal mór blianta ó shin, is dóiche go gcasfaí air go minic seanduine mór, ard a raibh aithne ag sean agus óg air mar 'An Bacach Mór.' Fear fíorchroíoch, diaganta ab ea an seanduine céanna agus má bhí an duine bocht aimhleasta, lagintinneach ní raibh falsacht ná mí-ionraiceas ag baint leis ar feadh a shaoil. Lean mírath den uile chineál é ón lá a rugadh é go dtí go bhfuair sé bás ina sheanduine chrom, chreapalta maidin amháin ar thaobh an bhealaigh mhóir. Más rud é nach raibh mórán buíochais ag an tsaol ar an Bhacach Mhór an lá a d'éag sé, is dóiche go raibh chomh beag de bhuíochas aigesean ar an tsaol gí go raibh gach duine go maith dó. Deirtear gurbh é an Bacach an chéad duine agus an duine deireanach a rugadh riamh i mBaile na mBroc agus má tá sé fíor nach bhfuil cloch ar chloich sa bhaile sin inniu, ní ar an Bhacach bhocht ba cheart an milleán a chur de bhrí go raibh sé ag cruinniú a choda ar fud na contae ó bhí sé naoi mbliana d'aois. D'fhéach sé go minic a bheatha a shaothrú i gceann oibre ach d'éirigh leis go dona an uile am. Bhí sé seal ar aimsir ag Donnchadh na Cruite agus má bhris an seanghearrán a mhuineál lá amháin ag teacht abhaile ón phortach, ní ar an Bhacach Mhór a bhí an locht. Lean Donnchadh é le gabhal féir míle ón teach agus ba é sin an tuarastal a fuair sé. Agus an t-am a raibh sé ar aimsir ag an mhuilleoir, má chuaigh an muileann le thinidh oíche amháin nuair a bhí sé ina chodladh i gcoirnéal de nó gurbh éigean dó léimint amach ar chúlfhuinneoig agus isteach san abhainn, cé a déarfadh go raibh baint ar bith ag an Bhacach leis an dódh? Féach, mar an gcéanna, an t-am a bhain sé lán bascóide de luibheanna le cearca Mháire Rua a leigheas ón ghalar agus unsa tobaca a shaothrú dó féin. Cé a bheadh ina dhiaidh ar an duine bhocht má fuair an ceann deireanach de na cearca bás lá arna mhárach? Níl duine!

Ba ghnách le bacaigh na seanaimsire teach amháin a phiocadh amach i ngach paróiste leis an oíche a chaitheamh ann nuair a thigeadh siad thart cupla uair sa bhliain. Bhí an cleachtadh céanna ag an Bhacach Mhór agus nuair a thigeadh sé go híochtar na contae bhí fáilte agus fiche ag fanacht leis i dteach Éamainn Uí Dhónaill. Dá dtigeadh sé seacht n-uaire chomh minic bheadh an fháilte sin roimhe de bhrí gur dhearc Éamann agus a bhean ar gach duine a bhíodh ag cruinniú a choda mar theachtaire ó Dhia.

Bhí dhá pháiste ag an phéire seo agus fán am a thoisíos an scéal bhí an duine ba sine acu, Caitlín, ag teannadh le dhá bhliain déag agus an gasúr, Peadar, bliain go leith ní b'óige. Bhí croí an bhacaigh Mhóir báite ins na páistí, ní nach ionadh, agus níor fhág sé riamh slán acu gan deora ina shúile. Bhí na páistí mar an gcéanna leis-sean agus ní bréag a rá go raibh carantas neamhdha eatarthu.

Fágfaimid slán ag an Bhacach Mhór go ceann tamaill ach amháin faill a thabhairt dó a bheannacht a thabhairt do Chaitlín agus Peadar ar an ócáid ar a bhfuil mé ag trácht. Leanfaimid é go dtí an geafta mar gheall ar na focla atá le rá aige le hÉamann a chluinstin nó, mar a deir an seanfhocal: 'is iomaí cor a chuireas an saol de féin' agus is iomaí contúirt roimh an té a bhíos amuigh go moch is go mall i ngach cineál aimsire, ag taobhú leis an ghréin a chuid bratógaí a thriomú agus gan áit aige lena cheann a leagaint san oíche ach an áit a thairgtear dó ar ghrá Dé. B'fhéidir go dearfa gurb í seo cuairt dheireanach an Bhacaigh uasail agus chead againn éisteacht leis an méid atá le rá aige.

‘A Éamainn,’ ar seisean, ‘tá mé i ndiaidh slán a fhágáil ag do mhnaoi agus do chuid páistí dílse. Guím beannacht Dé ort féin agus orthusan agus cuirim faoi chúram Mhuire sibh. Níl tú gann i maoin an tsaoil seo agus go mba fada a bheas an scéal sin le hinsint agat. Tá aingle Dé ag fanacht ar an bhomaite seo le paidreacha na mbocht ar do shon féin agus ar son do chúraim a iompar go cosa an tSlánaitheora, agus tá dhá aingeal eile ag fanacht ort ag doras do thí nó is cinnte gur aingle do bheirt pháistí. Níl mé tugtha do tharngaireacht ach tá ceann le déanamh agam anois. Bhaist mé Peadar an Chinn Óir ar do ghasúr ar siocair a chuid gruaige órbhuí. Creid mé, a Éamainn, beidh Peadar ina shagart agus is cuma cé acu a bheas mise beo nó marbh an lá sin, coinnigh na focla seo in do chroí agus abair leis cuimhne a dhéanamh ina chéad Aifreann ar an Bhacach Mhór. Abair leis féin agus Caitlín paidir a rá ar mo shon anocht sula dté siad a luí nó an té a shiúlas mórán tógann sé dusta an bhealaigh mhóir. Slán agus beannacht leat, a chroí na féile.’

Fuair Éamann greim láimhe ar an fhear bhocht agus d’fhéach sé buíochas a thabhairt dó ach sháraigh sé air focal amháin a rá ar feadh bomaite. Fá dheireadh tháinig sé chuige féin agus dúirt: ‘Go dtuga Dia luach na bhfocal sin duit, a dhuine bhoicht! Tá eagla orm nach bhfuil mé fiúntach an lá lúcháireach beannaithe ar thrácht tú air a fheiceáil ach tá Dia láidir. Ná bíodh eagla ort go ndéanfaidh mé dearmad ar do tharngaireacht.’

D'imigh an bacach síos an bealach mór agus phill Éamann ar ais ar a theach féin.

'Cá bhfuil na páistí?' ar seisean lena mhnaoi.

'Is dóigh liom,' arsa an bhean, ‘go dteachaigh siad síos go páirc na heorna mar gheall ar bhlátha a chruinniú le cur ins na fuinneogaí anocht in onóir na Maighdine Muire. Beidh an chéad lá den Bhealtaine ann amárach.'

'Glóir do Dhia,' arsa Éamann. 'Caithfidh mé cuidiú leo,' ar seisean, 'agus nuair a thiocfas mé ar ais tá dúil agam tarngaireacht an Bhacaigh Mhóir a insint duit.'

Níor dhúirt an Bacach Mór focal amháin i dtaobh na bpáistí nach raibh fíor. B'fhéidir go siúlfá talamh na hÉireann gan péire eile a fheiceáil le cur i gcomórtas leo. Bhí an bheirt neamhscarthach ón lá a bhí Caitlín ábalta Peadar a thabhairt léi ar ghreim láimhe. Thóg siad níos mó tithe thart fá chois na gclaíoch ná aon saor cloiche in Éirinn. Lá amháin rinne siad teach beag de chlocha geala, bána. Ní raibh an teach níos mó ná hata fir agus chuir giota de scláta ceann air. Sheas an péire tamall ag amharc air nuair a bhí sé críochnaithe.

'Sin teach pobail,' arsa Caitlín.

'An ea?' arsa Peadar.

'Sea go cinnte,' arsa Caitlín, 'agus tá tusa 'do shagart.'

'Dá mbeinn 'mo shagart,' arsa Peadar, 'nach mbeinn ag léamh Aifrinn?'

'An dtearn tú dearmad,' arsa Caitlín, 'go bhfuil tú ag foghlaim Laidine ón mháistir scoile mar gheall ar a bheith ag freastal ar an altóir?'

'Ní dhéanfaidh sin sagart díom,' arsa Peadar. 'Bhí Séimín Phaidí Bhig ina chléireach ar an altóir le dhá bhliain agus anois tá sé ag tiomáint asail.'

Chuir sin deireadh leis an scéal agus leag Peadar 'teach an phobail' lá arna mhárach. Is aoibhinn saol na bpáistí a théitear le dea-shampla agus grá ach tigeann an t-am thart nuair a chaithfear an nead a scabadh. Cuireadh Caitlín fhad le clochar i nDoire agus chaoin Peadar ina diaidh ar feadh dhá lá. Thréig codladh na hoíche é agus bhíodh sé tostach mórán den am sa lá. Scríobh sé litir chuig Caitlín agus d'iarr ar a athair í a chur fríd an phosta. Gheall an t-athair sin a dhéanamh ach nuair a d'fhoscail sé an litir agus léigh sé: 'Más mian leat do dhearthair a fheiceáil beo, tar abhaile anocht.' Ní theachaigh an litir níos faide.

Ón am sin amach ní theachaigh Éamann aon áit gan Peadar a bheith leis mar gheall ar go ndéanfadh sé dearmad ar Chaitlín. 'Is gairid,' a deireadh an t-athair, 'go mbeidh

Caitlín sa bhaile ar a cuid laetha saoire agus nuair a bheas sí ag imeacht athuair, beidh tusa léi.'

Shásaigh seo Peadar agus d'fhan sé go foighdeach ar theacht abhaile Chaitlín.

Seachtain roimh an Nollaig thug an sagart paróiste cuairt ar theach Éamainn agus dúirt go raibh sé ag gabháil go Doire lá arna mhárach agus go mbeadh Caitlín abhaile leis. Thug Éamann buíochas dó agus bhí an oiread sin áthais ar Pheadar is go raibh obair aige é féin a choinneáil ó léimint thar na cathaoireacha sa chisteanach.

Ag titim na hoíche lá arna mhárach bhí Éamann Ó Dónaill agus a bhean chéile ina seasamh ag an gheafta ag fanacht le Caitlín. Bhí siad ag caint eatarthu féin fán Nollaig agus na daoine a raibh dúil acu cuireadh a thabhairt dóibh i gcomhair na Féile. Sheas Peadar tamall beag ag éisteacht leo agus fá dheireadh chuir sé ina cheann go raibh dearmad á dhéanamh airsean agus siúd isteach ar an doras é agus suas na staighrí. Chuaigh sé fhad lena leabaidh féin agus léim sé isteach, bróga is uile, agus tharraing na héadaí amach thar mhullach a chinn.

Nuair a shroich Caitlín an geafta, phóg sí a hathair agus a máthair go dúthrachtach. 'Cá bhfuil Peadar?' ar sise.

'Bhí sé anseo bomaite ó shin,' arsa an t-athair.

Chuaigh siad isteach sa chisteanach ach ní raibh Peadar le feiceáil. Le hintleacht mná rith Caitlín suas na staighrí agus isteach i seomra Pheadair. Thóg sí na héadaí a bhí ar a aghaidh agus shonraigh sí go raibh sé ag caoineadh.

Chuir sí a dhá láimh thart fána mhuineál agus phóg sí é gan focal a labhairt. Idir an lúcháir a bhí uirthi a bheith sa bhaile agus an brón a chuir sé uirthi Peadar a fheiceáil ag caoineadh, bhris an gol uirthi. Fá dheireadh tháinig na focla chuici.

'A Pheadair, mo chroí,' ar sise, 'inis domh cad é a tháinig ort.'

'D'fhág tusa mé agus chuaigh tú go Doire. Anois tá mé tinn agus má fhaighim bás, cad é a dhéanfas tú?'

'Ná habair sin, a Pheadair dhílis,' arsa Caitlín. 'Má fhaigheann tusa bás, gheobhaidh mise bás fosta.'

Bhí glór na caointe ina guth agus chuaigh seo go croí Pheadair. Tháinig aithreachas air fán chineál fáilte a chuir sé roimh a dheirfiúr agus an bhréag a d'inis sé di. D'iarr sé cead uirthi í a phógadh agus i mbomaite eile bhí an bheirt chomh lánlúcháireach is a bhí siad an lá a rinne siad an teach pobail.

'An bhfuil tú ag gabháil a fhanacht sa bhaile feasta, a Chaitlín?' arsa Peadar.

'Is fearr dúinn gan labhairt ar an am atá le a theacht,' arsa Caitlín. 'Níor chuir tú ceist orm cad é a thug mé abhaile ionsort ins an mhála atá liom.'

'Úllaí bíodh geall air!' arsa Peadar.

'Ceart,' arsa Caitlín. 'Tomhais cad é eile.'

'Slat iascaireachta, b'fhéidir.'

Thoisigh Caitlín ag gáirí. 'Cad é an dóigh,' ar sise, 'a dtiocfadh liom slat iascaireachta a chur isteach i mála? Cogar,' ar sise, 'seo trí scillinge a shábháil mé as an airgead a chuir m'athair chugam agus cuirfimid i dtaiscidh é go dtí go dtige an samhradh agus ansin ceannóimid an tslat ins an bhaile mhór.'

'Coinnigh thusa an t-airgead,' arsa Peadar. 'Is tú is sine.'

'Maith go leor,' arsa Caitlín. 'Cuir ort do bhróga anois agus rachaimid síos chun na cisteanaí leis na húllaí a fháil.'

'Tá na bróga ar mo chosa,' arsa Peadar, agus tháinig an péire anuas na staighrí ag gáirí.

'Tím,' arsa Éamann, 'go dtáinig an Mac Aimhleasta ar ais.' Bhí a shúil aige ar Pheadar.

'Ní raibh sé i bhfad i gcéin,' arsa Caitlín, 'agus ar an ábhar sin ní bheidh sé riachtanach an 'gamhain ramhar' a mharbhadh.'

Thug an freagar cliste seo le fios d'Éamann agus a bhean nach raibh Caitlín ag cur a cuid ama amú sa chlochar agus mhol siad a cuid intleachta. Chrom Peadar bocht a cheann le náire ach thug Caitlín tarrtháil air.

'Tar anseo,' ar sise, 'go bhfeicimid cad é atá sa mhála.' D'fhoscail sí é agus thug amach páipéar a bhí lán d'úllaí móra, dearga. Thug sí an t-iomlán acu do Pheadar agus dúirt leis iad a roinnt mar ba mhian leis. Ansin tharraing sí amach spideog adhmaid a bhí daite chomh deas sin is go dtabharfá mionna go rachadh sí ar eiteoig i mbomaite. 'Is leatsa sin fosta,' ar sise le Peadar agus thug Peadar a mhíle buíochas di. Thíos in íochtar an mhála bhí bocsa beag agus fuair an mháthair an bocsa. 'Gráinnín beag de shnaoisín Dhoire i gcomhair na Nollag,' arsa Caitlín. 'Ní thearn mé dearmad ortsa ach oiread,' ar sise lena hathair. 'Seo bocsa beag atá lán de thobaca ghearrtha agus ní dóigh liom go bhfuil a leithéid le fáil ins na siopaí thart fán áit seo.'

'Tá sin fíor,' arsa Éamann. 'Cuideoidh sé an Nollaig a dhéanamh pléisiúrtha. Ach, a Chaitlín, a chroí, cad é mar a d'éirigh leat na nithe seo uilig a cheannach ar na pingneacha beaga a chuir mé chugat?'

'Ná habair sin, a athair,' arsa Caitlín. 'Chuir tú mórán airgid chugam agus tá cuid de agam go fóill.'

'Ná hinis barraíocht,' arsa Peadar, ag smaoineamh ar an tslat iascaireachta.

Bhuail cuid de na comharsanaigh isteach le fáilte chun an bhaile a chur roimh Chaitlín. Ní bréag a rá go raibh bród orthu aisti agus go raibh oiread lúcháire orthu í a fheiceáil is dá mba leo féin í. Caitheadh Nollaig phléisiúrtha i dteach Éamainn an bhliain sin.

Téann na blianta thart agus ní fhanann an t-am ná an taoide le duine ar bith. Lean dhá Nollaig déag eile an Nollaig seo agus chead againn dearmad a dhéanamh orthu fá láthair. Níl baint acu leis an scéal seo ach seo chugainn an samhradh aoibhinn, álainn a tháinig an bhliain i ndiaidh an ama seo. Maidin Lá Fhéile Peadair agus Póil a bhí ann. D'éirigh an ghrian agus í chomh dearg leis na rósanna a bhí ag crochadh anuas leis na toim. Bhí cumhracht na mbláth ins an aer agus bhí aoibhneas na bhflaitheas ar shléibhte agus bántaí. Bhí an teach pobail a bhí suite fá thuairim leathmhíle ó theach Éamainn foscailte uair nó mar sin roimh an am ar ghnách leis, agus thoisigh na daoine, óg agus sean, ag cruinniú isteach ón uile thaobh de bhrí go bhfuair siad scéala an oíche roimhe go raibh sagart óg lena chéad Aifreann a rá an mhaidin sin ag an seacht a chlog.

Nuair a bhí an teampall beannaithe beagnach lán go doras chuaigh an sagart suas ar an altóir. Ní nach ionadh, bhí aghaidh gach duine air nó, go dearfa, bhéarfadh amharc amháin ar a ghnúis álainn suáilce don té a bheadh ar leabaidh an bháis. B'aoibhinn do na daoine a bhí láithreach agus chuaigh siad ar a nglúine go cráifeach le moladh agus buíochas a thabhairt do Dhia.

Nuair a tháinig am Comaoine d'éirigh spéirbhean óg ón chéad suíochán agus chuaigh sí go cois na haltóra. Lean fear agus bean í, agus chuaigh an triúr ar a nglúine i gcuideachta a chéile. Ba chóir go mbeadh na seacht n-aithne againn orthu: Éamann Ó Dónaill, a bhean agus Caitlín, agus níl moill orainn a fheiceáil anois gur ó láimh an bhuachalla a raibh aithne againn air mar Pheadar an Chinn Óir atá siad ag fáil Chorp agus Fuil an tSlánaitheora.

Nuair a bhí an tAifreann thart thug an sagart a bheannacht do gach duine a bhí láithreach. Ba é an duine deireanach a fuair a bheannacht an mhaidin sin seanduine a bhí crom leath bealaigh go dtí an talamh.

'An bhfuil aithne agat orm, a athair?' ar seisean nuair a d'éirigh sé óna ghlúine.

'Fan go bhfeice mé,' arsa an sagart. 'An féidir gur tú an Bacach Mór?'

'Is mé, a athair,' ar seisean. 'Glór is moladh is buíochas do Dhia. Tháinig mo tharngaireacht isteach fíor!'

NÓTA: *The Derry Journal*, 26/8/1938, 8, 2/9/1938.

FÓGRA NA MNÁ SÍ

Bhí Áras na Gréine suite i ngleanntán aoibhinn, álainn in imeall na Gaeltachta i dTír Chonaill. Teach den tseandéanamh ab ea é (teach a thóg tiarna talaimh ins na laetha fadó, ar dhá chéad acra den talamh ab fhearr sa chontae). Nuair a díbreadh na tiarnaí (slán turais dóibh) cheannaigh Éamann Ó Dónaill an teach agus an fheirm agus ar siocair a bháis, bliain roimh an am a thoisíos ár scéal, bhí a bhaintreach Úna Uí Dhónaill i seilbh na háite.

Lá amháin i ndiaidh am dinnéara bhí Úna ina suí sa tseomra ba mhó sa teach, litir ina láimh aici agus í ag machnamh go dícheallach nuair a shiúil an sagart paróiste isteach. Chuir sí fáilte chineálta roimhe agus bomaite ina dhiaidh sin thug sí dó an litir a bhí sí a léamh, ag rá san am chéanna, gur mhaith léi a chomhairle a fháil. Léigh an sagart an litir go cúramach sular labhair sé.

'Ar inis tú don dlíodóir,' ar seisean, 'go bhfuair d'fhear bás gan tiomna a dhéanamh?'

'D'inis go cinnte, a Athair,' arsa Úna. 'Ní dóigh liom gur fiú domh m'ainm féin a chur síos ar son na háite, agus tá rún déanta agam ainm Pheadair a chur síos agus an t-airgead atá sa bhanc a choinneáil in m'ainm féin.'

'Má ghlacann tú comhairle uaimse,' arsa an sagart, 'ní bheidh deifir ar bith ort seilbh go hiomlán a thabhairt do Pheadar ar an teach agus ar an talamh. Níl feirm ar bith eile ins an chontae le cur i gcomórtas leis an cheann seo agus ní féidir nach bhfuil a fhios agat go bhfuil do mhac aimhleasta, agus go bhfuil sé ag ól go trom le corradh le bliain. Thóg sé suas le droch-chuideachta agus is ró-annamh a intinn ar aon chineál oibre.'

'Caithfidh mé a aidmheáil, a Athair, go bhfuil sé tugtha don ól ar uairibh,' arsa Úna.

'Ar uairibh, an ea?' arsa an sagart. 'Tá mé den bharúil go mbíonn tú in do chodladh go minic ar theacht abhaile dó san oíche.'

'Is fíor é,' arsa Úna, 'go mbíonn sé amuigh go mall ach nach dóiche gur minice é ag cearrbhachas ná i dtigh an óil?'

'Ná creid a leithéid,' arsa an sagart. 'Tá eagla mo sháith orm go gcuirfidh sé an áit bhreá seo amú. An bhfuil na páipéir i lámha an dlíodóra?'

'Níl go fóill,' arsa Úna, 'ach tá mé ag dréim le cuairt uaidh in am inteacht inniu.'

'Tá mé ag iarraidh ort a bheith faichilleach agus gan an t-athrú seo a dhéanamh le barraíocht deifre,' arsa an sagart.

'Cá bhfuil Eibhlín inniu?' ar seisean.

'Chuaigh sí go hOifig an Phoist, a Athair,' arsa Úna, 'agus tá mé cinnte go mbeidh sí ar ais i mbomaite. Bhí an t-ádh amach go barr orm an lá a tháinig Eibhlín chugam.'

'Féadann tú sin a rá,' arsa an sagart. 'Fuair mé litir inné ón tsagart i gContae Liatroma a mhol domh áit fhóirsteanach a fháil fána coinne agus tá lúcháir orm a insint duit gur scríobh sí litir chuige ag rá gurbh aici a bhí an mháistreás ab fhearr in Éirinn.'

'Is maith liom na focla sin a chluinstin,' arsa Úna. 'Tá a fhios agat, a Athair, go gcoinním cailín i gcomhair obair an tí ach dúirt an dochtúir liom go raibh mé ag fáil bháis ón uaigneas agus go mba cheart domh cailín maith, ciallmhar a fháil le cuideachta a choinneáil liom go moch agus go mall. Ní cailín maith a fuair mé ach aingeal. Aingeal gan amhras is ea Eibhlín.'

'Tá lúcháir orm an cuntas sin a fháil,' arsa an sagart, 'de bhrí go bhfuil eagla orm nach bhfuil aingle ar bith le spáráil againn maidir leis an pharóiste seo i láthair na huaire.'

'Seo chugainn ceann acu anois,' arsa Úna le mionghháire nuair a chuala sí coiscéim Eibhlín ar leic an dorais.

'Do phardún, a Athair,' arsa Eibhlín ar theacht isteach di. 'Ní raibh a fhios agam go raibh tú anseo.'

'Bím mar na héanacha fiáine, a Eibhlín, tamall ansiúd agus tamall anseo,' arsa an sagart.

'Tá an cóimheas sin fóirsteanach,' arsa Eibhlín. 'Bíonn fáilte ag gach duine roimh na héanacha beaga, fiáine agus is cinnte go mbíonn fáilte ag gach duine roimh an Athair Ó Ceallaigh.'

'Cuirfidh sí dhá cheann orm, a bhean an tí, má fhanaim anseo níos faide,' arsa an sagart.

'Is é mar ata an scéal, a Athair,' arsa Úna, 'go n-aontaímse le gach rud a deireann Úna agus tá sise mar an gcéanna liom.'

'Is deas an péire sibh,' arsa an sagart go haoibhinn, 'ach thiocfadh leis an scéal a bheith níos measa. Tá dúil agam,' ar seisean, 'a theacht ar ais roimh thitim na hoíche mar gheall ar chomhairle an fhir uasail ar thrácht tú air a chluinstin.'

'Go raibh míle maith agat,' arsa Úna.

'Níl moill labhairt leis an Athair Ó Ceallaigh,' arsa Eibhlín nuair a bhí an sagart imithe.

'Tá sin fíor,' arsa Úna. 'Ní rachaidh an té a ghlacfas a chomhairle i bhfad ar seachrán. Tá mise, a Eibhlín, i gcruachás ar an bhomaite agus ní mór go bhfuil a fhios agam cé acu ceart nó contráilte an réiteach atá dúil agam a dhéanamh.'

'Go gcuire Dia ar do leas thú,' arsa Eibhlín.

'Tá mé ag fanacht leis an dlíodóir,' arsa Úna. 'Tá sé ag iarraidh orm ainm Pheadair a chur síos ar son na háite seo.'

'Ní gá duit a bheith ag fanacht leis,' arsa Eibhlín. 'Nuair a bhí mise ag teacht isteach lig cailín na cisteanaí isteach sa leabharlann é ar siocair go raibh an sagart ins an tseomra seo.'

'Más mar sin atá an cás,' arsa Úna, 'tá an t-am agam a ghabháil chun cainte leis. Beidh faill agatsa litir nó beirt a scríobh sula dtige mise ar ais.'

Thaitin an réiteach seo go maith le hEibhlín, agus nuair a thug a máistreás a haghaidh ar an leabharlann ba é an chéad rud ar smaoinigh Eibhlín air litir a chur abhaile chuig a máthair. Ní raibh sí i bhfad i gceann na hoibre seo go dtí gur fhoscail an doras ag a cúl agus shiúil buachaill óg isteach sa tseomra. Bhí cuma air mar dhuine nár chodail néal le seachtain agus ní raibh moill a aithne go raibh braon ólta aige.

'Cá bhfuil mo mháthair?' ar seisean.

'Tá do mháthair gnoitheach ar feadh bomaite,' arsa Eibhlín, 'ach nár inis tú di ar maidin go raibh tú ag gabháil go Doire?'

'D'inis go cinnte,' arsa an buachaill, 'ach bhí mé mall ag an traein. Tá mé ag fanacht anois le traein an tráthnóna.'

'Más mar sin atá an scéal,' arsa Eibhlín, 'is dóigh liom go dteastaíonn greim bídh uait.'

'Níl bia ag cur lá imní orm,' arsa an buachaill, 'agus b'fhearr liom mar an gcéanna gan mo mháthair mé a fheiceáil go dtige mé ar ais.'

'Ní chreidim,' arsa Eibhlín, 'go dtáinig tú anseo gan réasún inteacht. Inis domh, a Pheadair, cad é atá ar d'intinn?'

'Níl moill mo chuid trioblóide a chur i bhfocla,' arsa an buachaill. 'Tá dúil agam, a Eibhlín, tusa a phósadh nuair a thiocfas mé ar ais ó Dhoire agus ansin beidh tú in do mháistreás ar an teach seo in ionad a bheith in do sheirbhíseach.'

'Tá mise sásta leis an phosta atá agam anseo,' arsa Eibhlín, 'agus bheadh sé amaideach an scéal a leanúint níos faide. Ní thig liomsa tú a phósadh, a Pheadair, agus ní fhéadann tú a bheith ag cur do chuid ama amú.'

'Ní chreideann tú,' arsa an fear óg, 'go bhfuil mé ag caint dáiríribh ach glac m'fhocal air go bhfuil. Is liomsa,' ar seisean, 'an áit seo ó bhun go barr agus ní cheannódh trí mhíle punta é ar maidin amárach.'

'Níl baint ar bith agamsa leis an áit agus ní bheidh baint agam leatsa,' arsa Eibhlín. 'Tá rud amháin a thig leat a dhéanamh agus is é sin mise a dhíbirt ó Áras na Gréine más toil leat é. Tabhair gealltanas domh anois go bhfuil deireadh leis an amaidí seo, sin nó ní bheidh mise anseo ar theacht ar ais duit.'

'Shíl mé, a Eibhlín,' arsa an buachaill, 'go raibh meas mór agat ar mo mháthair, agus insím duit anois gurb é mian a croí go bpósfaidh tú mise dá luaithe dá luas.'

'Tá mé ag fanacht leis an ghealltanas a d'iarr mé ort,' arsa Eibhlín.

'Inis domh ar dtús an bhfuil réasún ar bith agat mé a dhiúltú?' arsa an buachaill.

'Tá,' arsa Eibhlín, 'más mian leat a chluinstin. Ní phósfaidh mé fear go deo ach an té a dtig liom grá mo chroí a thabhairt dó, agus ní hé sin Peadar Ó Dónaill.'

'Cuireann tú iontas orm,' arsa an buachaill. 'An bhfuil aon rud agat in m'aghaidh?' ar seisean.

'Ar dhóigh amháin, níl.'

'Agus ar dhóigh eile?'

'B'fhearr liom gan níos mó a rá,' arsa Eibhlín. 'Níl aon rud le gnóthan ar dhíospóireacht den chineál seo.'

'Níor dhúirt tú go hiomlán,' arsa an buachaill, 'nach raibh dadaí agat in m'aghaidh.'

'Níor dhúirt,' arsa Eibhlín, 'agus níl dúil agam é a rá.'

'Tá mé ag éisteacht,' arsa an buachaill.

'Agus tá mise ag caint,' arsa Eibhlín. 'Tá dhá mhí caite,' ar sise, 'ó tháinig mise chun an tí seo, agus ar feadh an ama sin ní raibh tusa ag an Phaidrín Pháirteach ach aon oíche amháin. An oíche sin féin bhí comhartha ólacháin ort agus níor dhúirt tú paidir ná cré.'

'Is trom do bhuille,' arsa an buachaill, 'ach is dóiche go bhfuil sé tuillte agam.'

'Is mar mhaithe leat féin a dúirt mé an oiread sin agus mar mhaithe leis an mháthair a thóg thú,' arsa Eibhlín.

'Focal amháin agus beidh mé ag imeacht,' arsa an buachaill. 'Ní fearg atá orm ach buaireamh, agus an rud nach bhfuil neart air, caithfear cur suas leis. Abair liom anois go mbeidh comhrá agat le mo mháthair i dtaobh na ceiste seo agus ní iarraim níos mó.'

'Geallaim,' arsa Eibhlín, 'go socróidh do mháthair agus mé féin an cás sula dtige an meán oíche.'

'Go raibh míle maith agat,' arsa an buachaill. 'Ní bhíonn athrú intinne i bhfad ag teacht agus níl mé gan dóchas.'

Ba le croí cráite a shuigh Eibhlín síos le críoch a chur ar an litir nuair a d'imigh an buachaill. Bhí a fhios aici le hintleacht mná go raibh néal dubh sa spéir os cionn Áras na Gréine. Sula raibh an litir sa chlúdach aici shiúil fear óg isteach i ngan fhios di. Sheas sé ag an tábla a bhí ar chúl Eibhlín agus thoisigh sé ag léamh na litre a d'fhág an sagart as a láimh tamall beag roimhe sin. Nuair a shonraigh Eibhlín fá dheireadh é, ní raibh ann ach nár thit sí i laige. Bhí os a coinne fear óg chomh breá is a leag sí súil riamh air agus é gléasta go cuibheasach mar oifigeach ins na hÓglaigh.

'Ná bíodh imní ort, a chailín chaoin,' arsa an t-oifigeach.

'Cad é an fáth nach mbeadh imní orm?' arsa Eibhlín. 'Níl aithne ar bith agam ort agus ní raibh mo mháistreás ag dréim le cuairteoir.'

'Tá sé sin uilig fíor,' arsa an t-oifigeach, 'agus iarraim do phardún. Bhí réasún agam a theacht isteach mar a tháinig mé agus ní éireoidh grian an lae amáraigh go dtí go gcluinfidh tú an réasún sin. Ná hiarr orm, le do thoil, níos mó tuairisce a thabhairt duit san am atá i láthair.'

'Is cuma liom fán dóigh a dtáinig tú isteach,' arsa Eibhlín, 'ach má chluineann mo mháistreás go raibh tú anseo, go raibh tú ag léamh a cuid litreach, agus nach dtug mise aon iarracht na nithe seo a chur i bhfios di, cad é an dóigh a dtiocfaidh liom an scéal a mhíniú?'

'Ní bheidh míniú ar bith riachtanach,' arsa an t-oifigeach. 'Níl ach beirt,' ar seisean, 'ar thalamh na hÉireann a dtig leo an tuairisc ar thrácht tú uirthi a thabhairt di.'

'Agus is iad sin?'

'Oifigeach de chuid na nÓglach agus Eibhlín Ní Néill.'

Má bhí iontas ar Eibhlín ar dtús, bhí a sheacht n-oiread uirthi anois.

'Ó tharla go bhfuil m'ainm agus mo shloinneadh agat, an mbeadh sé iomarcach agam an cheist a chur cé leis a bhfuil mé ag caint?'

'Glac m'fhocal air,' arsa an t-oifigeach, 'go mbeidh an tuairisc sin in do sheilbh sula mbeidh faill ag an oíche anocht críoch a chur ar uaigh an lae.'

'Níl aon leisc orm d'fhocal a ghlacadh de bhrí go sílim go bhfuil mé i gceann cainte le fear uasal, ach is olc a d'fhóirfeadh sé domh mo phosta a chailleadh, go ceann tamaill eile i gcás ar bith,' arsa Eibhlín.

'Ní chaillfidh tú do phosta ar mhaithe liomsa,' arsa an t-oifigeach.

'Sin mar is fearr é,' arsa an spéirbhean álainn. 'Tá mo mháthair bocht,' ar sise, 'agus níl duine ar bith eile den mhuirín ag saothrú pingne ó thoisigh an trioblóid atá sa tír fá láthair.'

Ní raibh aon seachrán ar an oifigeach uasal go raibh Eibhlín ag insint na fírinne, agus bhí chomh beag de sheachrán air go raibh sé ar an bhomaite sin i láthair an chailín ab áille dá bhfaca sé le linn a shaoil. Shonraigh sé go raibh na deora ag cruinniú ina cuid súl agus ba é mian a chroí istigh a cuid misnigh a neartú.

'Beidh lúcháir ort a chluinstin,' ar seisean, 'go bhfuil do mháthair go han-mhaith. 'Chaith mé tús na seachtaine seo sa teach inar tógadh thú.'

Ar chluinstin na bhfocal seo d'Eibhlín las a haghaidh mar a bheadh rós na maidine. 'An féidir,' ar sise, 'go bhfuil aithne agat ar mo mháthair?'

'Fuair mé aithne uirthi tá cupla lá ó shin,' arsa an t-oifigeach. 'Is é do dheartháir Éamann a thug chun an tí mé. Ní raibh dhá chomrádaí eile sna hÓglaigh ba dílse dá chéile ná Éamann Ó Néill agus mise. Is iomaí oíche a chaith muid araon ar shléibhte Liatroma agus na Dúchrónaigh ag tairgint breabanna mar gheall ar eolas a fháil ar ár n-ionad ceilte; agus is iomaí sin casán achrannach, aimhréiteach a shiúil muid ag taobh leis an fhraoch agus an fhásach, dídean á thabhairt dúinn mar gheall ar néal codlata a sciobadh roimh éirí gréine. Tá, a Eibhlín, na seacht n-aithne agam ar do dheartháir dhílis, an cara ionúin a d'inis domh fán dóigh ar chaill tusa an scoil sula raibh tú bliain ag teagasc.'

'Tá lúcháir orm a insint duit gur thóg tú lód de mo chroí,' arsa Eibhlín. 'Ní fhaca mé Éamann le corradh le bliain,' ar sise.

'Tá a fhios agam sin,' arsa an t-oifigeach. 'Tháinig sé abhaile Dé Domhnaigh agus mise ina chuideachta. Tífidh tú é Dé Domhnaigh seo chugainn le cuidiú Dé. Beidh áthas ort a chluinstin,' ar seisean, 'go bhfuil na Dúchrónaigh buailte agus iad ag fágáil na tíre.'

'Míle buíochas do Dhia,' arsa Eibhlín. 'Lig domh anois,' ar sise, 'buíochas a thabhairt duitse agus fáilte a chur romhat in ainm Éamainn.'

'Agus in ainm Eibhlín fosta,' arsa an t-oifigeach go haoibhinn.

'Bíodh ina mhargadh,' arsa Eibhlín ag síneadh a láimhe chuige.

'Rinne tú dearmad ar feadh bomaite,' arsa an t-oifigeach, 'ar an chruachás a raibh tú ann sular bhuail mise isteach sa tseomra seo. Tá imní ort agus is é Peadar Ó Dónaill is ciontaí leis.'

'Tím go bhfuil aithne agat ar Pheadar fosta,' arsa Eibhlín.

'Aidmhím go bhfuil,' arsa an t-oifigeach, 'ach glac m'fhocal air go bhfuil an trioblóid sin thart. Tá caoi ormsa deirfiúr Éamainn Uí Néill a chosnadh ó seo amach agus ná bíodh aon chineál eagla ort feasta.'

'Go dtuga Dia luach na bhfocal sin duit,' arsa Eibhlín. 'Bhí Peadar anseo sula dtáinig tusa isteach.'

'Ní raibh sé anseo romhamsa,' arsa an t-oifigeach. 'Chonaic mé é ag teannadh leis an teach agus mar bhí an doras foscailte, tháinig mé isteach go tobann agus chuaigh mé i bhfolach ar chúl na gcótaí atá crochta sa halla. Bhí a fhios agam go raibh sé ag ól agus bhí eagla orm go raibh sé ar lorg trioblóide. Níor dhruid sé an doras sin ina dhiaidh agus chuala mé an uile fhocal a dúirt sé. Tá sin uilig thart anois; tá saoirse na hÉireann cinnte agus tá súil agam go bhfuil an t-am ag teannadh linn nuair a bheas tusa agus mise i seilbh ár gcuid ranna de thoradh na síochána.'

'Déarfaidh mé áiméan leis an phaidir sin,' arsa Eibhlín.

'Maith go leor,' arsa an t-oifigeach. 'Tá cuairt agam le tabhairt ar theach an tsagairt,' ar seisean, 'agus ansin tiocfaidh mé ar ais mar gheall ar comhrá a bheith agam le do mháistreás. Má bheireann sí iarracht roimh an am sin an cleamhnas idir tú féin agus Peadar a chríochnú, tabhair le fios di go mbeidh faill a dhíth ort le d'intinn a dhéanamh suas.'

'Dhéanfar sin uilig ach beidh mise i ndeacracht dáiríribh nuair a thiocfas Peadar abhaile,' arsa Eibhlín.

'Ní bheidh, a Eibhlín,' arsa an t-oifigeach. 'Fág an cás agamsa le socrú.'

'Go raibh míle maith agat,' arsa Eibhlín. 'Is trua liom,' ar sise, 'nach dtig liom mo lánbhuíochas a chur i bhfocla.'

'Thig leat, a Eibhlín,' arsa an t-oifigeach. 'Tabhair gealltanas pósta domh óir, go deimhin, is iad sin na focla a chuirfeas an phunann chinn ar aoibhneas mo bheatha. Beidh cead agat an gealltanas a bhriseadh mura mbeidh Éamann sásta leis an chleamhnas.'

'Tá an gealltanas le fáil agat ó mo chroí amach,' arsa Eibhlín.

'Cuireann sin críoch ar shocrú bheag eile,' arsa an t-oifigeach le miongháire. 'Bí ag dréim ar ais liom roimh luí na gréine,' ar seisean.

'Beidh mé ag cuntas na nóiméad,' arsa Eibhlín.

Ní raibh ann ach go raibh an t-oifigeach imithe go dtí go dtáinig Úna ar ais ón leabharlann.

'Fuair mé réite leis an dlíodóir fá dheireadh,' ar sise, 'agus tá súil agam go mbeidh níos mó suaimhneas intinne agam ó seo amach.'

'Is maith liom sin, a mháistreás,' arsa Eibhlín.

'Is mian liom a insint duit,' arsa Úna, 'go mbeidh seilbh iomlán ag Peadar ó thús na míosa seo chugainn ar gach aon rud a bhí i seilbh a athara taobh amuigh den airgead atá sa bhanc. Bhí dúil agam go minic, a Eibhlín,' ar sise, 'tuairisc a thabhairt duit fá na nithe seo go léir, ach d'fhan mé go dtí go mbeadh comhrá agam leis an dlíodóir. Fuair m'fhear bás tá bliain ó shin agus fuair an chéad bhean a bhí aige bás dhá bhliain sular pósadh mise air. Is mise an dara bean. Bhí mac amháin aige leis an chéad phósadh. Séamas ab ainm dó. Bhí sé bliain go leith d'aois nuair a d'éag a mháthair. Nuair a rugadh Peadar thug a uncal Séamas leis mar gheall ar go mbeadh sé comhgarach ag an scoil, agus nuair a bhí sé fá thuairim dhá bhliain déag, phill sé go hÁras na Gréine. Bhí sé ag obair ar an fheirm go dtí gur bhris an trioblóid mhallaithe amach ar fud na tíre agus, in ainneoin chomhairle a athara, chuaigh sé faoi sheirbhís na nÓglach. B'éigean dó an baile a fhágáil agus tamall beag sula bhfuair a athair bás, chuaigh sé go hAlbain.'

'An bhfuil sé in Albain anois?' arsa Eibhlín.

'Níl, faraor,' arsa Úna. 'Báitheadh é ráithe nó mar sin sula dtáinig tusa anseo. Bhí sé ag baint faoi i dteach uncail eile dá chuid agus bhí sé san uaigh sula bhfuair muid cuntas ar a bhás. Bhí buachaill as an áit seo ag a thórramh.'

'Ní fhágann sin duine ar bith fá choinne na háite seo ach Peadar,' arsa Eibhlín.

'Ní fhágann,' arsa Úna. 'Beidh sé ina fhear shaibhir má bheireann sé aire dó féin.'

'Níl ceart ar bith agamsa,' arsa Eibhlín, 'aon bharúil a thabhairt ar an réiteach a rinne tú leis an dlíodóir. Tá mise mar na héanacha fiáine ar labhair an sagart orthu, anseo inniu agus ar shiúl amárach.'

'Níl mé ag dréim, a Eibhlín, gur mar sin a bheas an scéal,' arsa Úna. 'Tá rún agam le hinsint duit agus tá súil agam go gcuirfidh sé áthas ort. Ní fhágfainn an áit seo ag Peadar ach amháin go bhfuil dúil agam cleamhnas a dhéanamh idir tusa agus é féin. Tá an buachaill bocht óg, amaideach agus teastaíonn comhairle agus cuidiú mná mar thusa air lena choinneáil ar bhealach a leasa.'

'Tá eagla orm, a mháistreás,' arsa Eibhlín, 'nach féidir liom aontú leis an réiteach sin. Ní bheidh moill ar Pheadar bean lena mhian a fháil.'

'Caithfidh sé comhairle a ghlacadh uaimse,' arsa Úna, 'sula dtig leis bean lena mhian a phósadh. Níl aithne agam ar aon chailín atá inchurtha leatsa agus tá mé lánchinnte go mbeadh saol aoibhinn againn ár dtriúr in Áras na Gréine. Níl sé riachtanach agam Peadar a chomhairliú i dtaobh na ceiste seo mar tá a fhios agam gur tusa aoibhneas a chroí. Ná habair liom, a Eibhlín, go ndiúltóidh tú mé. Tá do chuidiú a dhíth orm le m'aonmhac a choinneáil ó shlí na haimhleasa.'

'Tuigim do chás,' arsa Eibhlín, 'ach is fearr dúinn gan an scéal a chur níos faide ar an bhomaite.'

'Bíodh ina mhargadh,' arsa Úna. 'Toil Dé go raibh déanta,' ar sise.

'Má tá scríbhneoireacht ar bith le déanamh,' arsa Eibhlín, 'rachaidh mise i gceann oibre.'

'B'fhearr liom,' arsa Úna, 'port a chluinstin ar an chruit fhad is a bheas muid ag fanacht le cuairt an tsagairt.'

'Rinne mé dearmad,' arsa Eibhlín, 'gur dhúirt sé go raibh dúil aige a theacht ar ais.'

'Tá mé ag dréim leis bomaite ar bith,' arsa Úna.

Tharraing Eibhlín uirthi an gléas ceoil agus thoisigh ag seinm. Leis sin buaileadh buille ar dhoras an tseomra.

'Seo an sagart anois,' arsa Úna. 'Fan mar atá tú, a Eibhlín, agus fosclóidh mise an doras.'

Rinne sí sin ach ba é an t-oifigeach óg a thug grá a chroí d'Eibhlín a shiúil isteach. Níor luaithe a leag Úna súil air ná thit sí i laige ag a chosa. Thug Eibhlín tarrtháil ar a máistreás agus thóg an t-oifigeach a ceann ón urlár.

'Faigh braon beag branda,' arsa an t-oifigeach le hEibhlín, 'má tá a leithéid le fáil.'

Rith Eibhlín fá choinne an bhranda agus nuair a phill sí cuireadh Úna ina suí ar chathaoir uilleann agus tugadh di lán spanóige den bhiotáilte. Gan mhoill ina dhiaidh sin d'fhoscail sí a súile agus chonaic sí an t-oifigeach athuair.

'An dtabharfaidh tú do lámh domh, a Shéamais,' ar sise, 'más rud é nach ag éirí as an uaigh atá tú?'

'Ní raibh mé san uaigh go fóill,' arsa an t-oifigeach, ag síneadh a láimhe chuig Úna.

'Agus an bréag é,' ar sise, 'gur báitheadh thú cúig mhí ó shin agus go raibh mac Antoin Uí Dhochartaigh ag do thórramh?'

'Níor báitheadh mé cúig mhí ó shin,' arsa an t-oifigeach, 'agus más rud é,' ar seisean, 'go raibh mac Antoin ag mo thórramh ní fhaca mise é.'

Bhain na focla seo miongháire as Eibhlín agus thaitin seo leis an oifigeach. Ní raibh fonn ar bith grinn ar Úna Ní Dhónaill.

'Anois, a Eibhlín,' arsa an t-oifigeach, 'tá an t-am agat mo scéalsa a chluinstin. Thig leis an bhean seo mé a cheartú má théim ar seachrán. Rugadh mise ins an teach seo agus fuair mo mháthair bás sula raibh mé dhá bhliain d'aois. Phós m'athair athuair agus is í seo an bhean a phós sé: mo leasmháthair. Tamall ina dhiaidh sin cuireadh mise fhad le teach m'uncail, míle ón áit a bhfuil mé in mo shuí, agus chaith mé níos mó ná deich mbliana faoina chúram. Lá amháin tháinig m'athair (go ndéana Dia trócaire air) fá mo choinne agus tháinig mé abhaile leis. D'oibir mé ar an fheirm go moch agus go mall go dtí gur chuir na Sasanaigh cogadh orainn, agus ansin tógadh mé mar shaighdiúir ins na hÓglaigh. Domhnach amháin ag bánú lae maraíodh beirt de na saighdiúirí dubha ins an chomharsanacht seo agus b'éigean domhsa m'aghaidh a thabhairt ar na sléibhte. Nuair a tógadh mé mar oifigeach cuireadh go Contae Liatroma mé agus sin mar a fuair mé aithne ar do dheartháir Éamann. Bhí seisean ar a dhíbirt freisin. Tháinig mé abhaile aon oíche amháin agus lig mo leasmháthair isteach mé. Bhí m'athair ina chodladh agus ní fhaca mé é an t-am sin ná ó shin. Is cosúil gur dhíol sé scaifte caorach an lá roimhe sin agus bhí an t-airgead a fuair sé orthu i mbocsa sa tseomra inar chodail sé. Ní raibh mise ins an tseomra sin ó tháinig mé chun an tí ag an mheán oíche go dtí gur fhág mé slán ag mo leasmháthair tamall roimh éirí gréine.'

'Tá sin uilig fíor, a Shéamais,' arsa Úna.

'Maith go leor,' arsa an t-oifigeach. 'Nuair a d'éirigh m'athair,' ar seisean, 'chuntais sé an t-airgead mar gheall ar é a chur sa bhanc agus bhí sé cúig phunta gann. Bhí mise imithe agus b'fhurast an ghadaíocht a chur síos domh. Cá bith duine a d'inis do m'athair go raibh mise sa bhaile tamall den oíche ba é sin an duine a chuir ina cheann go raibh ganntanas airgid orm agus gur dóiche gur ghoid mé na cúig phunta. Chuaigh an scéal ó bhéal go béal go dtí gur ghlac na hÓglaigh a raibh aithne acu orm orthu féin an cás a mhionscrúdú. Fuair siad amach in am ghairid cé a thug leis an t-airgead agus an áit inar caitheadh é ar ólachán. Níl gnoithe domh,' arsa an t-oifigeach, 'an scéal a leanúint mórán níos faide. Cuireadh mise agus cúigear eile go hAlbain mar gheall ar airgead agus gunnaí a sholáthar. Bhuail taom tinnis mé agus bhí mé faoi chúram dochtúra i dteach uncail de mo chuid nuair a fuair m'athair bás. Bhí mé rólag le a theacht abhaile.'

'Ní raibh do sheoladh agamsa, a Shéamais,' arsa Úna, 'agus níor fhéad mé scéala a chur chugat. Nuair a fuair mé le fios cad é mar a goideadh an t-airgead, d'inis mé do d'athair ar leabaidh an bháis nach raibh tusa ciontach.'

'Ní raibh sin riachtanach,' arsa an t-oifigeach. 'D'inis na hÓglaigh dó an scéal go hiomlán.'

Chuir seo críoch ar scéal an oifigigh agus ar an bhomaite sin tháinig an sagart paróiste isteach.

'Tá lúcháir orm, a Shéamais,' ar seisean, 'do lámh a chroitheadh agus fáilte a chur romhat go hÁras na Gréine arís.'

'Go raibh céad míle maith agat, a Athair,' arsa an t-oifigeach. 'Thug mé cuairt ar theach an tsagairt ach ní raibh tú sa bhaile.'

'Ní raibh, ach níor chuir sé iontas ar bith orm nuair a chuala mé go dtáinig tú isteach ar thraein na maidine. D'inis mo chroí domh an Domhnach a chuir mé guí an phobail le d'anam nach raibh an scéal inchreidte,' arsa an sagart.

'Is furasta é a mhíniú, a Athair,' arsa an t-oifigeach. 'Báitheadh buachaill a raibh an t-ainm céanna air agus bhí seisean ina oifigeach fosta. De réir an chuntais a bhí sna páipéir nuaíochta shíl muintir na paróiste seo gur mise a báitheadh agus ní raibh sin iontach. Bhí an t-ainm Séamas Ó Dónaill ceart go leor ach níor dhúirt an cuntas gur ó Chontae Ard Mhacha an t-oifigeach a cailleadh. Cuireadh óglach ón áit seo trasna na farraige leis an fhírinne a fháil amach agus chinn muid gan an cuntas a cheartú go dtí go mbeadh an cogadh leis na Dúchrónaigh thart.'

'Bhí siad go cruaidh ar do lorg an t-am sin, a Shéamais,' arsa an sagart. 'Lig domh anois,' ar seisean, 'comhbhrón a dhéanamh leat fá bhás d'athara. Bhí mé lena thaobh nuair a d'éag sé.'

'Tá a fhios agam sin, a Athair,' arsa an t-oifigeach, 'agus ní thig liom go leor buíochais a thabhairt duit. Ní dhéanfaidh mé dearmad ar an oíche sin cá bith fad a bheas mé beo. Bhí mé in mo luí tinn i dteach m'uncail agus ag uair an mheán oíche chuala mé an ceol ba bhrónaí agus ba truacánta dár chuala cluas riamh. D'aithin mé go maith cá has a dtáinig an ceol sin. Fógra na Mná Sí, a Athair, Fógra na Mná Sí! Mí nó mar sin ina dhiaidh sin, chuala mé an bhean sí arís agus lá arna mhárach fuair m'uncal bás tobann. Bhí sé ina fhear shaibhir agus beidh lúcháir ort a chluinstin gur fhág sé iomlán an mhéid ab fhiú é agamsa.'

'Bhí tú ádhúil,' arsa an sagart. 'Fuair d'athair bás gan tiomna ar bith a dhéanamh.'

'Ní bhfuair, a Athair,' arsa an t-Oifigeach. 'Tamall sula bhfuair sé bás chuaigh beirt d'Óglaigh na háite seo chun cainte leis maidir le hairgead a chaill sé, agus nuair a chuala sé an fhírinne chuaigh sé fhad le dlíodóir agus d'fhág an áit seo agamsa. Tá an tiomna in mo sheilbh.'

'Is cuma fán tiomna, a Athair,' arsa Úna. 'Is é Séamas an mac is sine agus is leis an áit.'

'Tá caoi orm feirm eile a cheannach i gcomhair Pheadair agus beidh tamall cainte agam leis amárach,' arsa an t-oifigeach.

'Agus cuideoidh mise leat,' arsa an sagart. 'Níor cailleadh riamh leath dá raibh i gcontúirt.'

'Tá críoch anois ar obair an lae seo, a Athair,' arsa an t-oifigeach, 'ach amháin cuireadh chun bainise a thabhairt duit. Sílim go bhfuil cead Eibhlín agam a rá go bhfuil muid araon le pósadh an tseachtain seo chugainn.'

'Sin an nuaíocht is fearr den iomlán,' arsa an sagart.

'Ba mhaith liomsa, a Shéamais, focal a rá nuair atá an tAthair Ó Ceallaigh láithreach,' arsa Eibhlín. 'Ba é mian mo chroí é dá ndéanfadh mo leasmháthair suas a hintinn deireadh a saoil a chaitheamh in Áras na Gréine.'

'Beidh a háit anseo, a Eibhlín, fhad is a bheas tusa agus mise beo,' arsa Séamas. 'Ní abrann sin ach oiread nach bhfuil dúil agam teach a thógáil fá choinne Pheadair a bheas inchurtha leis an teach seo.'

'Go raibh míle maith agaibh araon,' arsa Úna. 'Thig linn na rudaí seo go léir a shocrú nuair a bheas an bhainis thart.'

'Is maith an tús é sin ar an tsaol nua,' arsa an sagart. 'Fágaim mo bheannacht agaibh anois agus tá súil agam, a Shéamais, gur fada uainn an lá sula gcluinfidh tú arís Fógra na Mná Sí.'

NÓTA: *The Derry Journal,* 22/1/1941. Feis Tirconaill. *The outstanding success was that of Mr Brian O'Keeney O.G., Loughros Point, who won first prize for the best original unpublished Irish story. The Derry Journal,* 5/7/1940, *Derry People and Tirconaill News,* 6/7/1940, 3.

Gníomhartha Lae sa Ghaeltacht

[Dráma nuachumtha in aon ghníomh a fuair an chéad duais ag Feis Bhéal Feirste. Glacann sé cúig bhomaite dhéag agus fiche an dráma seo a léiriú].

[Tabhair fá dear:

Tá Tomás ina fhear mhórchroíoch, dhiaganta ach gur furast fearg a chur air nuair a bhíonn sé gnoitheach. Ar chluinstin dó fá phósadh Pheadair, éiríonn sé brónach ach imíonn an fhearg agus an brón nuair a thigeas an lánúin óg abhaile (a gcuid éadaigh Domhnaigh orthu).

Bacach bocht, neamhurchóideach agus ar bheagán céille is ea Niall Rua. Is gnách leis Béarla agus Gaeilig a mheascadh fríd a chéile ina chuid cainte. An t-údar.]

Tomás Ó Gallchóir	Feirmeoir i nGaeltacht Thír Chonaill
Bríd Ní Ghallchóir	Bean Thomáis
Peadar Ó Gallchóir	Mac Thomáis
Diarmaid Ó Dónaill	Comharsa
Síle Ní Dhónaill	Níon Dhiarmada
Niall Rua	Bacach bocht, leathshimplí a bhíos ag cruinniú a choda
Eilís Ní Cheallaigh	Níon baintrí sa chomharsanacht
Donnchadh Phaidí Bhig	Buachaill óg ó chúl an chnoic

Éadaí oibre na tuaithe.
Radharc: an chisteanach i dteach Thomáis.

[Tá BRÍD *le feiceáil ag an tábla ag gearradh builín aráin nuair a éiríonn an brat. Tá gach aon ní i gcomhair bhricfeasta na bhfear ar an tábla. Tigeann* TOMÁS *agus* PEADAR *isteach ar an doras cúil. Crochann* TOMÁS *a hata ar thairne agus fágann* PEADAR *a bhearád ar an stól. Suíonn an bheirt acu ag an tábla].*

TOMÁS (*ag suí síos*): Mo chroí thú, a Bhríd! Tím go bhfuil an bricfeasta réidh agat. Shíl mé nach raibh tú 'do shuí go fóill.

BRÍD: Is fada 'mo shuí mé ach níor éirigh mé chomh luath libhse.

(Cuireann sí an tae sna cupaí agus toisíonn na fir ag ithe).

TOMÁS: D'fhág muid an teach le breacadh an lae agus níl aon ghas féir in íochtar na páirce nach bhfuil croite amach againn. Ní fhaca mé lá fómhair i bhfiche bliain inchurtha leis.

[Tigeann Síle Ní Dhónaill isteach ar an doras cúil.]

SÍLE: Bail ó Dhia ar an obair.

TOMÁS: Bail ó Dhia ort féin ar maidin.

SÍLE (*ag suí ar an stól*): Is maith liom, a Thomáis, go bhfuil do bheannacht agam i gcomhair an lae i gcás ar bith.

[Tá bearád PHEADAIR *ag* SÍLE *ina láimh agus í ag amharc air].*

PEADAR: An bhfuil scéal ar bith leat, a Shíle?

SÍLE: Ní chluinim dadaí iontach.

BRÍD: Nach maith an scéal an aimsir bhreá atá againn?

SÍLE: Féadann tú sin a rá.

TOMÁS: An bhfuil d'athair i gceann an fhéir inniu, a Shíle?

SÍLE: Níl go fóill. Is gairid ó d'éirigh muid. Tá m'athair go dearfa ina luí go fóill.

TOMÁS: Codladh traonach chuige! Nach síleann tú go mba cheart dó bheith amuigh leis an fhuiseoig maidin mar seo?

SÍLE: Is dóiche nach bhfuil a fhios agat go raibh muid inár suí ó oíche.

BRÍD: An bhfuil rud ar bith contráilte, a Shíle?

SÍLE: Níl ar chor ar bith. Nár chuala sibh go dtáinig Dónall Éamainn Óig abhaile as Meiriceá aréir?

BRÍD: Gheall ar an Rí, an bhfuil Dónall sa bhaile? Nach bhfuil cuimhne agat air, a Thomáis?

TOMÁS: Tá, maise, mo sháith. Sin an boc a dhíol an gamhain liom a bhí ar leathshúil an tseachtain sular imigh sé.

[Gáire ón iomlán].

PEADAR (*ag éirí ón tábla*): Más rud é gur chaill d'athair a chuid codlata aréir, ní bheidh mórán fonn oibre air inniu.

[Téann sé isteach sa tseomra ar chúl na tineadh].

[*Ar feadh an ama seo ó thús an dráma bíonn* BRÍD *ag freastal ar an tábla, ag cur mónadh ar an tinidh, ag glanadh sceana srl. Nuair a théann* PEADAR *isteach sa tseomra éiríonn* TOMÁS *ina sheasamh agus toisíonn sé ag cur tobaca sa phíopa*].

SÍLE (*ag éirí ina seasamh*): Ní dhéanfaidh seo cúis domhsa.

TOMÁS: Cad é an deifir atá ort?

SÍLE: Tá mé ar theachtaireacht. Cad é do bharúil, a Bhríd, nár éirigh an chearc ghorm de na huibheacha go luath ar maidin agus ní féidir linn í a fháil isteach ó shin. Shíl mo mháthair go mb'fhéidir go mbeadh cearc ghoir agatsa agus, mura bhfuil, rachaidh na huibheacha amú.

BRÍD: Níl moill ar bith ort cearc ghoir a fháil anseo. Seas san áit a bhfuil tú go bhfaighimid greim ar cheann.

[*Toisíonn* BRÍD *ag scabadh giotaí beaga aráin ag an chúldoras, agus ag scairtigh: 'Diúc, diúc, diúc.' Ba chóir cearc a bheith ag duine éigin taobh amuigh den doras agus í a shíneadh chuig* BRÍD *go híseal. Bheireann sí an chearc do* SHÍLE].

SÍLE: Sonas ar do láimh, a Bhríd, agus go bhfága Dia an síneadh inti.

[Nuair atá an píopa lasta ag TOMÁS, *suíonn sé ar an chathaoir arís, a chúl leis an doras cúil. Tigeann* BRÍD *ón doras go dtí an tábla agus nuair atá* SÍLE *ag gabháil amach ar an doras tigeann*

PEADAR *amach as an tseomra agus tugann sé beart di i ngan fhios do* BHRÍD *agus* TOMÁS. *Imíonn* SÍLE, *an chearc faoi ascaill amháin agus an bheart faoin ascaill eile].*

PEADAR: Ná bíodh deifir ar bith ortsa, a athair. Tá an lá ag gabháil i bhfeabhas agus tiontóidh mise an féar.

TOMÁS: Maith go leor, a Pheadair. Rachaidh mise síos ar ball.

[Imíonn PEADAR, *toisíonn* BRÍD *ar obair an tí agus tigeann* NIALL RUA *isteach, mála ina bhfuil buidéil fholmha ar a ghualainn leis.]*

TOMÁS: Céad fáilte romhat, a dhuine. Is fada anois ó chonaic mé thú.

NIALL: Go raibh maith agat, *my good sir,* a Thomáis an chroí mhóir.

BRÍD: Fág síos do mhála, a Néill. Beidh braon tae agat.

NIALL: Ní bheidh, *my good lady,* le do thoil. *I thank you kindly*. Tá mé i ndiaidh tae a fháil i dteach Dhiarmada. *Nice people,* bhur ndálta féin.

TOMÁS: An bhfuil scéal úr nó seanscéal leat inniu?

NIALL: Níl, maise, ach amháin an trioblóid a bhí sa bhaile mhór inné. *Bad work,* a Thomáis, *bad work*.

TOMÁS: Cad é a bhí contráilte fán bhaile mhór, a Néill?

NIALL: Obair náireach, a Thomáis. *Nothing ever went to* mo chroí i gceart ach *to see* an dá *policemen stuck* i sceadamán mo dhearthár.

TOMÁS: Ní raibh a fhios agam go dtí sin go raibh deartháir ar bith agat.

NIALL: Tá, maise. Tá sé ina *retired beggarman* mar a déarfá. Bíonn sé ag díol éadaigh ó theach go teach agus thit sé amach le baicle *tramps* inné. Sin tús agus deireadh an scéil, *my good man*.

TOMÁS: Dona go leor. Agus anois, a Néill, cad é a thig liom a dhéanamh ar do shon inniu?

NIALL: Rud ar bith is mian leat féin, a Thomáis. Tá *splendid sale* ar bhuidéil fholmha agus uibheacha.

TOMÁS: Tá sin ceart go leor ach cuireann tú an dá chuid sa mhála i gcuideachta a chéile agus cluinim nach mbíonn aon ubh slán leat ar theacht chun an bhaile mhóir duit.

NIALL: *Bad habit, sir,* ach níl aon neart air. Sin mar a chleacht mé i dtús mo shaoil.

TOMÁS: Tím, tím. Seo dhuit cupla pingin rua. Ní bhrisfidh tú na pingneacha.

NIALL (*ag tógáil an mhála*): Go raibh beannacht Dé is Mhuire anuas ort féin agus do chúram. *And you also, my good woman*. Go bhfeice mé slán thú, a Thomáis uasail, *and may your days be long in the land*.

TOMÁS: Áiméan, a Néill, agus go gcuire Dia slán thú.

[Imíonn NIALL *agus tigeann* EILÍS *NÍ CHEALLAIGH isteach, seanráca briste léi ina láimh. Níl sa ráca ach dhá fhiacal. Cuireann* BRÍD *fáilte roimh* EILÍS *ach tá a shúil ag Tomás ar an ráca.*

TOMÁS: B'fhéidir, a Eilís, go bhfuil tú ag gabháil ag cuidiú linn an féar a thógáil?

EILÍS: Cuideoidh mé leat tamall tráthnóna ach d'iarr mo mháthair ort, más é do thoil é, caoi bheag a chur ar an ráca seo. Níl aon cheann eile ar an tsaol againn.

TOMÁS (*ag breith ar an ráca*): An síleann do mháthair nach bhfuil dadaí le déanamh agamsa lá fómhair ach caoi a chur ar sheanrácaí? Tá an ráca seo cosúil léi féin, fiacal thall is abhus.

BRÍD: Ná bí róchruaidh ar an ghirsigh, a Thomáis.

TOMÁS: Ghlacfadh sé leath lae an rud seo a chóiriú. Ach fan bomaite. Tá ráca sa scioból agus féadann tú é a thabhairt leat. Ní bheidh sé a dhíth orainne go dtí an cúig a chlog.

EILÍS: Go raibh maith agat. Beidh mé féin agus an ráca anseo roimh an cúig.

(*Imíonn* EILÍS*).*

[*Toisíonn* TOMÁS *ag deargadh a phíopa arís agus i gceann bomaite tigeann* EILÍS *isteach athuair.*]

EILÍS: hObair go ndéanfainn dearmad. D'iarr mo mháthair orm a insint duit, a Thomáis, go bhfuil Nóra Ní Dhochartaigh le cur tráthnóna inniu.

TOMÁS: Slán turais di cá bith áit a dteachaigh sí. Ní thiocfadh léi bás a fháil mar a dhéanfadh duine eile. Bhí an t-iomrá go raibh sí marbh Dé hAoine agus shíl mé go mbeadh sí scríobtha, sciúrtha le bheith soir linn Dé Domhnaigh seo tharainn, agus gan a bheith ag cur lá den tseachtain amú léi.

BRÍD: Is cosúil nach raibh a háit cóirithe ag Dia go dtí seo.

TOMÁS: Maise, ba bheag an áit a dhéanfadh cúis di, an lá is mó a bhí sí.

EILÍS: Bhí mo mháthair ag smaoineamh go raibh tórramh ort agus go mbeifeá imníoch gan scéala a fháil.

TOMÁS: Nach bhfuil a fhios agat go raibh muintir an bhaile sin ag tórramh m'athara ach go raibh ciall aigesean bás a fháil i ndeireadh na bliana. Cad é an dóigh is féidir liom tórramh Nóra a fhreastal agus ábhar ceithre choca mhóra croite amach againn?

BRÍD: Tá Dia chomh láidir is a bhí sé riamh.

EILÍS: Is fíor sin, a Bhríd. Caithfidh mise a bheith ar shiúl.

[Imíonn EILÍS. *Suíonn* TOMÁS *síos go himníoch].*

TOMÁS: Cluinfidh muintir Bhaile na mBradán go bhfuair muid scéala fán tórramh agus bheadh sé náireach agam gan a ghabháil.

BRÍD: Is fada go dtí an dó a chlog agus má thig géar orainn, rachaidh mé féin chun an tórraimh.

Téann BRÍD *go dtí an fhuinneog agus amharcann sí amach].*

Caithfidh sé go bhfuil an saol uilig ag gabháil ar seachrán. Seo Donnchadh Phaidí Bhig ag teacht trasna na páirce agus é ar cosa in airde.

TOMÁS: Tórramh eile ar chúl an chnoic, bíodh geall air. Cuirfidh siad amach as mo mheabhair mé.

[*Tigeann* DONNCHADH *isteach agus é i mbarr a anála*].

TOMÁS: Tá mé cinnte, a Dhonnchaidh, nach bhfuil dea-scéal ar bith leat ach cuir chugainn é i gcás ar bith.

DONNCHADH: Níl mo scéal rómhaith, a Thomáis, ach níl neart air. Tá bearach le Diarmaid Ó Dónaill i bpoll mónadh amuigh san Lag Dubh.

TOMÁS: Cumhdach an Rí orainn! Is trua nach bhfuil Diarmaid i bpoll eile le taobh an bhearaigh. Bíonn sé ina luí ar a leabaidh san earrach nuair ba cheart dó bheith ag cóiriú na gclaíoch. Is deas an saol atá ann: Nóra Ní Dhochartaigh le cur síos i bpoll agus bearach Dhiarmada le tarraingt amach as poll eile an lá fómhair is fearr a tháinig le linn mo chuimhne.

BRÍD: Ná lig don fhearg buaidh a fháil ort, a Thomáis. Tá an t-iomlán níos fearr ná drochphósadh. Cuidigh leo an bearach a shábháil agus cuir do dhóchas i nDia.

TOMÁS: Glacfaidh mé do chomhairle, a Bhríd. Is ag Dia is fearr a fhios.

[*Imíonn sé féin agus* DONNCHADH. *Suíonn* BRÍD *ag an tábla agus tigeann* PEADAR *isteach. Tá a chuid éadaigh Domhnaigh air*].

BRÍD: In ainm an Rí, a Pheadair, cá has a dtáinig tú?

PEADAR: Tá iontas ort, a mháthair, mo chulaith Dhomhnaigh a fheiceáil orm. Thug mé an chulaith do Shíle nuair a bhí sí ag fágáil an tí seo ar maidin. Tá sí féin agus mise le pósadh ag an trí a chlog inniu, sin nó táimid ag imeacht go Meiriceá ar maidin amárach. Ná bíodh fearg ort liom, a mháthair. Thug mé grá mo chroí do Shíle nuair a bhí muid araon ar scoil agus ní féidir cur eadrainn anois. [*Ag cur a láimhe ar ghualainn a mháthara*]. Iarraim anois, a mháthair, do chomhairle agus do bheannacht.

BRÍD: Tá an dá chuid le fáil agat, a mhic mo chroí. Má tá réiteach déanta agat le haghaidh do phósta, ná bris d'fhocal. Ní thabharfainn an chomhairle sin duit ach ab é go síleann d'athair nach bhfuil cailín ar bith eile sa pharóiste le cur i gcomórtas le Síle Ní Dhónaill agus tá mé féin ar an intinn chéanna. Tífidh mise go dtitfidh an buille seo chomh héadrom ar d'athair is is féidir é, agus beidh sinn anseo ag fanacht libh ag titim na hoíche.

PEADAR: A mháthair dhílis, thóg tú lód de mo chroí agus má tá deora in mo shúile níl iontu ach deora na háthaise. Anois, a mháthair, do bheannacht.

BRÍD (*á phógadh*): Mo sheacht mbeannacht agus beannacht Dé ar mo leanbh bhán agus ar an chailín chaoin a thug grá a croí dó.

[Imíonn PEADAR, *ag triomú a shúl, agus i ndiaidh osna a tharraingt suíonn* BRÍD *síos arís go brónach. Ceol íseal ón orchestra ar feadh leathbhomaite. Tigeann* TOMÁS *isteach ar an doras cúil].*

TOMÁS *(ag suí ar an stól)*: Tá mé ar bhealach a bheith caillte.

BRÍD: Tá, a Thomáis. Beidh cuimhne againn go deo ar ghníomhartha an lae seo. [*Glacann sí misneach úr.*] Nár dhúirt tú liom go raibh tú ag brionglóidigh aréir?

TOMÁS: Dúirt mé sin, a Bhríd. Shíl mé go raibh mé ag bainis.

BRÍD (*ag éirí agus ag teacht comhgarach do* THOMÁS): Caithfidh tú tú féin a bhrostú suas, tá nuaíocht le cluinstin agat, a Thomáis, a chroí.

TOMÁS: Ná habair, a Bhríd, go bhfuil tubaiste ar bith eile i ndán domh anocht nó amárach.

BRÍD: Má ghlacann tú mar is cóir é, ní drochscéal ar bith atá le hinsint agamsa.

TOMÁS: Umhlaím do thoil Dé; inis domh cad é atá ag cur imní ort.

BRÍD: Ní cúis imní ar bith mo scéal. Tá Peadar agus Síle Ní Dhónaill ar shiúl á bpósadh.

TOMÁS (*ag éirí ina sheasamh*): A Rí na glóire síoraí, cuidigh linn! [*Suíonn sé síos ag an tábla, glór caointe ina ghuth, agus deireann sé:*] Peadar bocht, Peadar bocht. Bhí mac againn ar maidin ach táimid gan mhac anocht.

[*Tigeann an brat anuas go fadálach go dtí an talamh agus suas arís go fadálach. Glacann seo bomaite amháin agus ar feadh an ama seo ba cheart don orchestra an fonn 'Has sorrow thy young days shaded?' a sheinm go híseal, truacánta. Fhad is atá an brat ag éirí tá* BRÍD *ag cuimilt súile agus éadan Thomáis le héadach póca*].

BRÍD (*nuair atá an brat thuas go hiomlán*): Ná habair, a Thomáis, go mbeimid gan mhac anocht. Beidh mac againn anocht go díreach mar a bhí aréir agus beidh níon againn fosta.

TOMÁS: Tá an ceart agat, a Bhríd. Cuirfidh mise fearadh na fáilte roimh an phéire.

BRÍD: Ar ndóiche. Nach dtearn tú féin an rud céanna atá Peadar a dhéanamh nuair a bhí tú ar aon aois leis-sean? Ní raibh tú bliain agus fiche an lá a pósadh sinn.

TOMÁS: Agus ní raibh imní ar bith orm ó shin i dtaobh an phósta sin.

BRÍD: Agus beidh chomh beag imní ar Pheadar.

TOMÁS: Sin mo bharúil féin, a Bhríd. Níl cailín i gContae Dhún na nGall inchurtha le Síle Ní Dhónaill.

[*Téann* BRÍD *go dtí an fhuinneog agus amharcann sí amach*].

BRÍD: Seo Diarmaid ag teacht go dtí an doras.

TOMÁS: Tá fáilte roimhe.

[*Tigeann* DIARMAID *isteach agus ní an bheirt croitheadh láimhe leis*].

TOMÁS: Tá fáilte agus fiche romhat anseo agus ná síl go bhfuil míshásamh ar bith orainn.

DIARMAID: Go raibh maith agat, a chroí na féile. Ach ba mhaith liom a rá leat, a Thomáis, nár chuala mé aon fhocal i dtaobh an phósta seo go dtáinig mé abhaile ón Lag Dubh. Agus is cóir domh buíochas a thabhairt duit anois féin ar son do chuidithe. Ach ab é thú bheadh an bearach sa pholl go fóill.

TOMÁS: Ná habair é, a Dhiarmaid. Tá gnoithe na bainise le socrú againn agus dhéanfaimid dearmad ar gach rud eile anocht. Níl an aimsir ag briseadh agus gheobhaimid an féar tógtha amárach.

DIARMAID: Tá an féar ar bhealach a bheith tógtha anois. Amharc síos an pháirc.

[Téann TOMÁS *fhad leis an fhuinneoig].*

TOMÁS: Cá has a dtáinig na fir sin, a Dhiarmaid? Tá siad ag cur críoch ar an choca dheireanach.

DIARMAID: Sin buachaillí ó chúl an chnoic a fuair cuireadh chun na bainise anocht agus d'iarr Peadar orthu an féar a thógáil go dtige seisean agus Síle ar ais ó theach an phobail.

TOMÁS: Dhéanfaidh sé fear maith tí go fóill.

DIARMAID: Peadar an ea? Níl buachaill eile ó seo go Corcaigh le cur i gcomórtas leis.

BRÍD: Ná cailín chomh maith le Síle.

TOMÁS: Aingeal atá inti.

DIARMAID (*ag fáil greim láimhe ar* THOMÁS): Go dtuga Dia luach na bhfocal sin don phéire agaibh. Cuireann an chaint sin áthas ar mo chroí. Ní fear saibhir mise, a Thomáis, ach buíochas le Dia thig liom dhá chéad punta a chur síos le Síle maidin amárach.

TOMÁS: A Dhiarmaid, a rún, an comharsa is fearr ar thalamh na hÉireann, ní raibh mise ag dréim lena leithéid sin.

BRÍD: An fear a mbeidh Síle mar bhean chéile aige bheadh sé saibhir gan pingin rua.

DIARMAID: Tabhair domh do lámh, a Bhríd. Bhí tú mar mháthair ag Síle ó bhí sí ina páiste. Beidh sí mar níon agat anocht agus rachaidh a hainm agus ainm Pheadair síos ins an bhanc amárach ar son an airgid a dúirt mé. Caithfidh sibh araon a theacht ionsar an bhainis.

TOMÁS: Beimid ansin le cuidiú Dé. Fágfaimid Máire Mhór i mbun an tí go maidin. Deir Bríd liom go bhfuil an lánúin óg ag teacht anseo ar dtús agus féadann tú a bheith ag dréim linn gan mhoill i ndiaidh luí na gréine.

DIARMAID: Maith go leor, a Thomáis. Beannacht agaibh anois.

TOMÁS *agus* BRÍD: Beannacht Dé is Muire leat.

[*Imíonn* DIARMAID. *Níl ann ach go bhfuil Tomás agus* BRÍD *ina suí ag an tábla arís i ndiaidh* DIARMAID *a fhágáil ag an doras nuair a thigeann* PEADAR *agus Síle isteach. Éiríonn* TOMÁS *agus* BRÍD *agus cuireann siad fáilte fhíorchroíoch roimh an lánúin óg*].

TOMÁS (*ag fáil greim láimhe athuair ar Shíle*): Is cuimhneach liom, a Shíle, gur dhúirt tú ar maidin inniu go raibh mo bheannacht agat i gcomhair an lae. Tá mo bheannacht agaibh araon anois i gcomhair an tsaoil nua.

PEADAR (*ag síneadh a láimhe chuig a athair*): Bheirim buíochas duit, a athair, ar son na cainte sin. Bhí eagla orm go mbeadh fearg ort.

TOMÁS: Níl fearg ar bith orm, a mhic mo chroí. Bród atá orm.

[*Seasann* SÍLE *le taobh Bhríde agus labhrann siad leo féin go híseal].*

TOMÁS (*ag amharc ar* SHÍLE): Bhí d'athair anseo bomaite ó shin agus gheall muid a ghabháil libhse go teach na bainise. Cuirfidh an bhainis críoch ar ghníomhartha an lae seo ach, a pháistí dílse, is cóir dúinn ar dtús Dia a altú agus buíochas a thabhairt Dó go moch is go mall. Go moltar A ainm naofa anois agus go brách.

[*Titeann an brat*].

CRÍOCH

NÓTA: *An tUltach,* Iml. 10 Uimh. 4, Mí na Féil' Eoin 1933, 6–8, Iml. 10 Uimh. 5, Mí na Lúnasna, 8.

SCÉALTA GEARRA

Bean na Mine Buí

Bhí bean ina cónaí i gContae Dhún na nGall fada ó shin agus bhí mac aici arbh ainm dó Antoine. Bhí siad anbhocht agus nuair a bhí Antoine bliain is fiche d'aois d'fhostaigh sé le feirmeoir i gContae Thír Eoghain. Chuireadh sé beagán airgid chuig a mháthair ó am go ham agus sa deireadh phós sé bean a bhí an-saibhir. Bhí lúcháir mhór ar mháthair Antoine nuair a chuala sí fán ádh mhór a tháinig i mbealach a mic.

Bliain amháin nuair a bhí an Nollaig ag teacht comhgarach tháinig Antoine abhaile chuig a mháthair. Bhí sí ag ól brachán mine buí nuair a tháinig sé isteach.

'Céad fáilte romhat, a mhic mo chroí,' ar sise. 'Shíl mé go dtearn tú dearmad díom.'

'Ní baol domh sin,' arsa Antoine. 'Caithfidh tú a theacht liom go Contae Thír Eoghain leis an Nollaig a chaitheamh. Sin an rud a thug anseo mé.'

'Ní raibh mise cúig mhíle ón teach seo ón lá a rugadh mé,' arsa an mháthair, 'agus cad é an dóigh a dtig liom a ghabháil chomh fada sin ó bhaile? Ní bhfaighidh mé ar ais choíche.'

D'inis Antoine di go dtiocfadh sé ar ais léi go luath sa Bhliain Úr agus, fá dheireadh, thug sí isteach a ghabháil leis. Maidin lá arna mhárach chuaigh siad ar ais ar thraein luath agus nuair a tháinig siad go dtí an Srath Bán shíl an bhean bhocht go raibh sí i Nua-Eabhrac. Bhí carr Antoine ag fanacht leo ag an stáisiún agus bhí corradh le fiche míle le a ghabháil acu sula dtáinig siad ar amharc na háite ina raibh Antoine ina chónaí.

'Tá mé caillte go deo,' ar sise nuair a stad an carr ag an doras.

Le scéal fada a dhéanamh gairid chaith sí mí i dTír Eoghain agus bhí bean Antoine go han-mhaith di. Bhí sí ag ithe agus ag ól den chuid is fearr ar feadh an ama seo.

D'fhág Antoine sa bhaile í fá dheireadh ach ní raibh bomaite aige le fanacht. Chruinnigh na comharsanaigh isteach le fáilte a chur roimpi agus d'fhiafraigh siad cad é mar a chaith sí an t-am agus cad é na hiontais a chonaic sí.

'Ná bí ag caint,' ar sise. 'Ní fhaca mé gráinnín mine buí ón lá a d'fhág mé Éire go dtí an lá a tháinig mé ar ais.'

NÓTA: *Derry People and Tirconaill News* (6/1/1934, 8).

Scéal Fá Ólachán

Bhí Sasanach ar laetha saoire seal ó shin i mBun Dobhráin agus oíche amháin bhí sé féin agus fear an tí ósta ag caint fá ólachán.

'Bhí aithne agam,' arsa an Sasanach, 'ar fhear agus thiocfadh leis leathghalún a ól in aon deoch.'

'Tá buachaill aimsire agamsa,' arsa fear an tí ósta, 'agus thig leis galún a ól in aon deoch.'

'Cuirfidh mé geall,' arsa an Sasanach, 'nach dtig leis rud ar bith den tsórt a dhéanamh.'

'Maith go leor,' arsa an fear eile.

Chuir siad fá choinne an bhuachalla agus galún leanna.

'An dtig leat,' arsa fear an tí ósta, 'an galún leanna sin a ól in aon deoch amháin?'

'Beidh mé ar ais i mbomaite,' arsa an buachaill, 'agus bhéarfaidh mé mo bharúil duit.'

Gan mhoill ina dhiaidh sin tháinig an buachaill ar ais.

'Thig liom an galún a ól ar an bhomaite seo,' ar seisean.

'Cad chuige,' arsa an máistir, 'nár dhúirt tú sin nuair a chuir mé an cheist ort?'

'Ní raibh mé cinnte san am sin go dtiocfadh liom é a dhéanamh,' arsa an buachaill.

'Agus cad é an fáth a bhfuil tú cinnte de anois?' arsa an Sasanach.

'B'éigean domh a ghabháil fhad le teach tábhairne agus féacháil leis,' arsa an buachaill.

Nóta: *Derry People and Tirconaill News* (13/1/1934, 8).

An Fidléir

Bhí Proinsias Mac Lochlainn, fidléir, ag bainis i Mín an Bhradáin am amháin agus bhí sé ag teacht abhaile ag bánú an lae. Tháinig se trasna na páirce atá in aice an droichid agus chonaic sé tarbh ag teannadh leis ar cosa in airde. Bhí a fhios aige nach mbeadh faill aige an sconsa a bhaint amach agus bhí drochdhóigh ar an duine bhocht. Thoisigh sé ag seinm ar an fhideal agus nuair a chuala an tarbh an seanphort breá sin 'Ruaigeanna an Chonnachtaigh' sheas sé chomh socair le huan. Lean Proinsias den cheol agus fá dheireadh thoisigh an tarbh ag damhsa. Bhí an talamh anbhog agus mhair an damhsa go dtí nach raibh le feiceáil ach ceann agus droim an tairbh. Bhí Proinsias sábháilte.

NÓTA: *Derry People and Tirconaill News* (20/1/1934, 6).

Athair ag Santú Airgid

Bhí triúr againn ag coinneáil cuideachta le Máire agus aon oíche amháin tharla sé go raibh muid uilig i dteach a hathar. Bhí gach duine againn ag dréim Máire a phósadh agus bhí a fhios ag a hathair cad é mar a bhí agus rinne sé margadh linn.

'Cá bith duine agaibh is mó a mbeidh airgead aige bliain ón oíche anocht, thig leis Máire a phósadh,' ar seisean.

Nuair a bhí an bhliain thuas tháinig an triúr againn go dtí an teach.

'Cuir an t-airgead ar an tábla,' arsa athair Mháire.

Chuir Dónall Mac Pháidín síos naoi scillinge agus chuir mise síos an uile phingin a bhí agam – ocht bpingin déag in airgead rua. Cuireadh amach sinn ar an doras cúil agus hinseadh dúinn a ghabháil abhaile. Chuala mé ina dhiaidh sin go bhfuair Art Ó Ceallaigh iasacht deich bpunta agus nuair a chonaic athair na girsí an méid sin d'airgead d'iarr sé ar Art an cailín a phósadh.

NÓTA: *Derry People and Tirconaill News* (27/1/1934, 6).

Ag Teacht Abhaile

Nuair a bhí muid ag fágáil an tí thug Peadar seanlóchrann dúinn ar siocair go raibh an oíche dorcha. Ní raibh muid leath bealaigh go dtí go dteachaigh an solas as.

'Féadann Peadar a bheith ina fhear dheas,' arsa Éamann, 'ach coinníonn sé drochlóchrann.'

'Tá teach baintrí ar thaobh an bhealaigh mhóir,' arsa Tomás, 'agus más rud é nach bhfuil an bhean ina codladh, bhéarfaidh sí coinneal dúinn. Fág an cás agamsa agus tífidh tú greann.'

'An bhfuil aithne aici ort?' arsa Éamann.

'Ní go rómhaith é,' arsa Tomás.

Nuair a tháinig muid fhad leis an teach ní raibh solas ar bith le feiceáil.

'Tá sí ina luí,' arsa Éamann.

'Ní bheidh sí i bhfad mar sin,' arsa Tomás. 'Fan san áit a bhfuil tú agus buailfidh mise ag an doras.'

Bhuail, agus i mbomaite chuala muid guth na baintrí ag scairtigh: 'Cé atá ansin?'

'Tá fear tinn ar thaobh an bhealaigh mhóir agus bheadh deoch bhainne a dhíth air,' arsa Tomás.

Nuair a chuala an bhaintreach seo chuir sí uirthi a cuid éadaigh agus ba ghairid go raibh sí ag an doras, crúiscín bainne ina láimh.

'Cá bhfuil an fear tinn?' ar sise.

'Sin rud nach bhfuil a fhios agam,' arsa Tomás agus leis sin d'ól sé an deor dheireanach den bhainne os a coinne. Shín sé an crúiscín chuici ag rá: 'An mbeadh faill agat cearc a mharbhadh agus a bhruith domh?'

Tháinig fearg dáiríre ar an bhaintreach agus dúirt sí: 'Is ábhar rógaire thú cá bith thú féin.'

Rinne Éamann gáire agus chonaic an bhaintreach go raibh cleas á imirt uirthi agus dhruid sí an doras go tapaidh. B'éigean dúinn teacht abhaile gan solas.

NÓTA: *Derry People and Tirconaill News* (3/2/1934, 8).

An Bheoir Lochlannach

Tháinig beirt Lochlannach go hÉirinn fada ó shin mar gheall ar rún déanta beorach ón fhraoch a fháil. Chaith siad an chéad oíche i nDoire agus chuir siad tuairisc ar fhear an tí ina raibh siad ar lóistín fán rún.

'Níl ach beirt fhear in Éirinn,' arsa an fear, 'a bhfuil an rún sin acu – athair agus a mhac, agus tá siad ina gcónaí i gContae Dhún na nGall. Níl beoir ar bith sa domhan le cur i gcomórtas léi agus más mian libh cuairt a thabhairt ar na fir seo rachaidh mise libh amárach agus thig libh bhur ndícheall a dhéanamh an rún a fháil uathu.'

Thug na Lochlannaigh buíochas don Éireannach agus tháinig an triúr go teach na bhfear a raibh an rún acu an lá ina dhiaidh sin. Cuireadh fáilte rompu agus fuair siad deoch den bheoir a rinneadh ón fhraoch.

'Sin an bheoir is fearr a bhlais mé riamh,' arsa fear de na Lochlannaigh. 'Má tá sibh sásta an rún a dhíol,' ar seisean, 'níl agaibh ach an luach a ainmniú.'

D'amharc an t-athair ar an mhac agus ansin thug sé freagar ar an Lochlannach.

'Níl oiread óir agus airgid i dtír na Lochlannach,' ar seisean, 'is a cheannódh an rún. Ach ó tharla go dtearn sibh an turas seo ba mhaith linn dá bhfanódh sibh seachtain san áit seo.'

Bhí na Lochlannaigh sásta leis an chuireadh seo agus ar feadh na seachtaine bhí comhrá acu leis an athair nuair a bhí sé leis féin. D'inis an t-athair dóibh fá dheireadh go dtabharfadh sé an rún dóibh ar choinníoll amháin.

'Cad é do choinníoll?' ar siadsan.

'Caithfidh sibh mo mhac a mharbhadh ar dtús,' arsa an t-athair.

'Ní maith linn dúnmharbhadh,' arsa na Lochlannaigh, 'ach más rud é nach dtig linn an rún a fháil ar dhóigh ar bith eile, níl teacht as againn.'

'Níl dóigh ar bith eile,' arsa an t-athair.

Bhí comhrá fada ag na Lochlannaigh an oíche sin. 'Má chuireann muid an mac chun báis,' arsa fear acu, 'thig leis an athair diúltú aon chineál tuairisce a thabhairt dúinn.'

'Tá sin fíor,' arsa an fear eile. 'Chead againn a insint don mhac an rud a dúirt an t-athair.'

Nuair a chuala an mac cad é mar a bhí thug sé isteach an rún a dhíol ar mhála óir agus mála airgid. Bhí sé ina fhear shaibhir go brách ina dhiaidh ach thit an t-athair marbh nuair a chuala sé go raibh an rún ag na Lochlannaigh.

NÓTA: *Derry People and Tirconaill News* (28/7/1934, 6).

An Rí agus Éirí na Gréine

Ins an am fada ó shin bhí Rí in Éirinn a raibh aird mhór aige ar bhánú an lae. Ba é mian a chroí a bheith ina shuí gach maidin leis an ghrian a fheiceáil ag éirí. Bhí an cleachtadh seo maith go leor ach ab é gur doiligh leis an Rí a bheith ina shuí in am, is é sin le rá, ba deacair é a mhuscailt. Bhí sé d'fhiacha ar dhuine de na searbhóntaí bualadh ar dhoras an tseomra inar chodail an Rí gach maidin go moch agus is minic a d'iarr sé ar an tsearbhónta imeacht go tapaidh nó go mbrisfeadh sé a mhuineál. Corrmhaidin bheadh sé ag éirí agus é ag rá leis an bhuachaill 'baint chuige' ach, dá dtitfeadh sé ina chodladh athuair agus a bheith mall ag éirí na gréine, bheadh an oiread sin feirge air nach dtiocfadh le duine ar bith labhairt leis ar feadh an lae.

Mhair an scéal mar seo ar feadh cupla bliain agus b'fhada ón Rí a bheith sásta lena bheatha. Lá amháin tháinig buachaill beag fhad le caisleán an Rí agus chuir tuairisc an dtiocfadh leis an Rí a fheiceáil.

'Ní thig leat an Rí a fheiceáil,' arsa an giolla a d'fhoscail an doras. 'Má tá achainí ar bith agat le déanamh, inis domhsa é agus cuirfidh mé é os comhair an Rí.'

'Má tá tú chomh garach sin,' arsa an buachaill, 'inis don Rí go gcaithfidh mé é a fheiceáil.'

Leis sin chuala siad fuaim charráiste an Rí.

'Bhí an Rí amuigh ag seilg,' arsa an giolla, 'agus seo é ag teacht anois.'

Nuair a tháinig an Rí amach as an charráiste shiúil an buachaill suas fhad leis.

'A Rí uasail,' ar seisean, 'is mac baintrí mé agus ba mhaith liom a bheith 'mo shearbhónta agat.'

'An dtiocfadh leat mé a mhuscailt an uile mhaidin ag bánú an lae,' arsa an Rí, 'agus a bheith cinnte go mbeidh mé as mo leabaidh sula bhfága tú doras sheomra an chodlata?'

'Geallfaidh mé sin, a Rí.'

Maidin lá arna mhárach ag an bhreacadh liath bhuail an buachaill ag an doras.

'Bain chugat,' arsa an Rí agus gan é ach leathmhuscailte, 'nó brisfidh mé an uile chnámh in do chorp.'

'Ní thig leat sin a dhéanamh gan an doras a fhoscailt,' arsa an buachaill.

Léim an Rí amach as an leabaidh go feargach agus d'fhoscail an doras. Nuair a chonaic sé cé a bhí ann chuir sé a lámh ar cheann an bhuachalla agus dúirt: 'Is tú an buachaill is fearr a bhí agam riamh. Gheobhaidh tú ardú páighe ón bhomaite seo.'

NÓTA: *Derry People and Tirconaill News* (1/9/1934, 6).

Beirt Chairde

Bhí beirt fhear i mbaile cois farraige i nDún na nGall fada ó shin agus ar feadh mórán blianta bhí siad go han-mhór lena chéile. Éamann Ó Gallchóir a bhí ar fhear acu agus Tomás Ó Dochartaigh a bhí ar an fhear eile. Lá amháin tháinig bean déirce go dtí an baile. Bhuail sí isteach i dteach Thomáis ar dtús agus ansin chuaigh sí fhad le teach Éamainn. Is cosúil gur inis sí d'Éamann go dtug Tomás drochainm dó agus chuir sin deireadh leis an charantas a bhí idir an dá chomharsa ab fhearr a bhí sa chontae. Nuair a tífeadh duine acu an fear eile ag teacht, thiontódh sé an bealach eile ar eagla go gcasfaí ar a chéile iad. Mhair an scéal mar seo ar feadh dhá bhliain. Tharla sé go raibh an péire ag aonach fómhair na nGleanntach agus rinne Tomás suas a intinn labhairt le hÉamann agus an seancharantas a athbheoú. Fá dheireadh chonaic sé Éamann giota beag ón áit a raibh sé ina sheasamh. Bhí cúl Éamainn leis agus ní fhaca sé Tomás go dtí go dtáinig sé comhgarach aige.

'Bhí eagla orm le dhá bhliain gur namhaid de mo chuid a bhí ionat,' arsa Tomás, 'ach tím anois nach namhaid de do chuidse mise.'

'Cad chuige sin?' arsa Éamann.

'Tá,' arsa Tomás, 'níor chualathas riamh ar thalamh na hÉireann gur thiontaigh fear de na Gallchóraigh a chúl le namhaid.'

'Tabhair domh do lámh,' arsa Éamann.

Ón lá sin go dtí go bhfuair siad bás níor bhaol go gcuirfeadh scéal mná déirce eatarthu.

Nóta: *Derry People and Tirconaill News* (8/9/1934, 6).

An Fear Gránna

Bhí Rí in Éirinn fada ó shin agus lá amháin nuair a bhí sé amuigh ag seilg chonaic sé fear a bhí ag cruinniú sméara dubha. D'amharc an Rí ar an fhear ar feadh bomaite agus ansin thoisigh sé ag gáirí.

'Cad é an t-ábhar gáirí atá agat?' arsa an fear.

'Inseoidh mé sin duit,' arsa an Rí. 'Chonaic mé mórán daoine le linn mo shaoil ach ní fhaca mé duine ar bith riamh a bhí leath chomh gránna leatsa. An bhfeiceann tú an gunna seo?' arsa an Rí.

'Tím,' arsa an fear.

'Maith go leor,' arsa an Rí. 'Seo dhuit an gunna agus tabhair leat é. Má chuireann duine ar bith ceist ort cá bhfuair tú é, abair gurbh é an Rí a thug duit é agus go bhfuil a chead agat duine ar bith a scaoileadh a shíleas tú atá níos gráice ná thú féin.'

Rinne an fear mar a hiarradh air agus shiúil sé leis ar feadh lá agus bliain. Fá dheireadh casadh fear air a bhí ag tiomáint asail.

'Stad!' ar seisean le fear an asail. 'Tá cead agam tú a scaoileadh.'

'An bhfuil dadaí agat in m'éadan?' arsa an fear eile.

'Níl,' arsa fear an ghunna, 'ach fuair mé cead ón Rí fear ar bith a scaoileadh a bheadh níos gráice ná mé féin.'

'Agus an bhfuil mise níos gráice ná thusa?' arsa fear an asail.

'Tá go cinnte,' arsa an fear a raibh an gunna aige.

'Scaoil leat,' arsa an fear eile. 'B'fhearr liom go mór a bheith marbh.'

NÓTA: *Derry People and Tirconaill News* (15/9/1934, 6).

An Feirmeoir agua an Dlítheoir

Bhí feirmeoir ina chónaí sna Rosa fada ó shin agus bhí cuid de na comharsanaigh ag tabhairt trioblóide dó. Fá dheireadh rinne sé suas a intinn go rachadh sé chun dlí. Bhí dlítheoir i Leitir Ceanainn a raibh cliú mór aige agus bhuail an feirmeoir isteach san oifig maidin amháin go luath agus chuir a chás roimh an dlítheoir.

'Caithfidh tú punta a chur síos.'

Rinne an feirmeoir mar a hiarradh air agus ansin chríochnaigh sé a scéal.

'Tím,' arsa an dlítheoir, 'go bhfuil na comharsanaigh ag cur imní ort ach níor bhris siad an dlí. Má ghlacann tú mo chomhairle ní rachaidh tú níos faide leis an chás.'

'Agus cad é fán phunta a thug mé duit?' arsa an feirmeoir.

'Bainimse amach punta ar son comhairle,' arsa an dlítheoir. 'Féadann tú slán a fhágáil ag an phunta sin.'

Las an feirmeoir a phíopa agus shonraigh an dlítheoir nach raibh aon dúil aige imeacht.

'Caithfidh mise a ghabháil go Teach na Cúirte anois,' arsa an dlítheoir, 'agus nuair a bheas tú réidh thig leat doras na hoifige a dhruid 'do dhiaidh.'

Chonaic an feirmeoir go raibh an punta caillte go brách nuair a chuaigh an dlítheoir amach. Leis sin, shiúil bean isteach san oifig.

'An tusa an dlítheoir?' ar sise leis an fheirmeoir.

'Is mé go cinnte,' a dúirt sé.

'Tá bean ina cónaí sa bhaile s'againne,' ar sise, 'agus caithfidh mé í a thabhairt chun dlí.'

'Tá sin furast go leor,' arsa an feirmeoir, 'ach má tá mise ag gabháil a ghlacaint an cháis, caithfidh tú punta a dhíol anois.'

Dhíol an bhean an punta.

'Anois,' arsa an feirmeoir, 'caithfidh mise a ghabháil go Teach na Cúirte agus thig leatsa fanacht anseo go dtige mé ar ais. Beidh mé anseo i gceann leathuaire.'

Tháinig an feirmeoir abhaile go tapaidh agus níor chuala sé ón lá sin go dtí an lá inniu cad é mar a socraíodh cás na mná.

NÓTA: *Derry People and Tirconaill News* (22/9/1934, 6).

Coigilt na Tineadh

Is iomaí nós a chleacht ár sinsir a bhfuil dearmad déanta orthu fá láthair agus tá coigilt na tineadh ar cheann acu. Cuirtear braon ola ar fhód mónadh anois agus tá deireadh leis an tseanchleachtadh.

Bhí táilliúir agus bean ina gcónaí sa tsean-am comhgarach ag baile Ard an Rátha. Ní raibh siad mar a déarfá saibhir ach bhí an oiread sin de mhaoin an tsaoil acu nach raibh mórán le himní a chur orthu. Oíche amháin ag am codlata thit siad amach fá choigilt na tineadh. Sa deireadh, rinne siad margadh: go gcaithfeadh an té a labharfadh ar dtús, i ndiaidh éirí na gréine lá arna mhárach, an tinidh a choigilt go ceann bliana.

D'éirigh an péire ar maidin; chuaigh siad i gceann oibre go tostach agus, anonn tamall sa lá, bhuail fear isteach chucu a bhí ar lorg caorach.

'Chonacthas domh,' ar seisean (a aghaidh ar an táilliúir), 'go raibh tusa 'do shuí go moch agus go mb'fhéidir go bhfaca tú na caoirigh a chaill mé aréir ag teacht an bealach seo.'

Thoisigh an táilliúir ag feadalaigh.

Rinne an fear amach nach raibh éisteacht rómhaith ag an táilliúir agus labhair sé ní b'airde ach sin a raibh ar a shon aige. Cheistnigh sé an bhean ansin agus thoisigh sise ag portaíocht.

'Is deas an péire sibh,' arsa an fear nuair a bhí sé ag imeacht.

Níl ann ach go raibh fear na gcaorach imithe go dtáinig fear a bhí ag díol éisc isteach.

'Go mbeannaí Dia anseo,' ar seisean.

Ní bhfuair sé freagar ar bith agus shíl sé go mb'fhéidir nár labhair sé ard go leor.

'Tá na scadáin úra is fearr agam inniu,' ar seisean, 'a dhíol mé le fiche bliain. Tá préataí fairsing agus thiocfadh libh níos measa a dhéanamh ná cupla duisín acu a cheannach.'

Thoisigh an fheadalach arís.

'An bhfuil an fear seo bodhar?' arsa fear an éisc leis an mhnaoi.

Chuir an bhean suas fonn 'Cailín Deas Crúite na mBó' ach focal amháin níor labhair sí.

'Níl ionaibh ach stocairí,' arsa an fear go feargach. 'Ní ligfeadh cruas croí daoibh pingin a chaitheamh. Tá sibh gan mhúineadh, gan chreideamh agus beidh sibh gan iasc.'

Nuair a thiontaigh fear an éisc thart leis an teach a fhágáil casadh fear air i lár an dorais agus ábhar péire brístí leis faoina ascaill.

'Féadann tú a ghabháil abhaile,' arsa fear an éisc. 'Mura bhfuil an lánúin seo bodhar tá seachrán intinne orthu.'

Níor thuig fear na mbrístí cad é a bhí contráilte agus shiúil sé suas fhad leis an tábla a raibh an táilliúir ina shuí air.

'Tá bó agam,' ar seisean leis an táilliúir, 'agus sílim go bhfuil an spiorad istigh inti. D'ith sí mo chuid brístí Domhnaigh inné agus b'éigean domh ábhar péire eile a cheannach. An dtiocfadh leat iad a dhéanamh anocht nó amárach?'

Níor lig an táilliúir air gur chuala sé é. Sheas an fear tamall ag fanacht le freagar agus ansin labhair sé le bean an tí.

'Cad é a tháinig ar an fhear seo?' ar seisean.

Ní raibh freagar ar bith le fáil agus chonacthas don fhear go raibh an péire ag magadh air. Rinne sé suas a intinn go mbeadh sásamh inteacht aige.

'Tá giota éadaigh liom,' ar seisean leis an táilliúir, 'ach ní chuirfidh tusa aon ghreim ann choíche. Tháinig mé le hinsint duit go dtearn tú péire brístí fá choinne mo dhearthár agus gur thit siad de sula raibh sé leath bealaigh sa bhaile.'

'Tá tú bréagach,' arsa an táilliúir ag léimint anuas ón tábla.

Rith an fear amach go tapaidh agus ar siocair nach raibh bróga ar bith ar an táilliúir ní raibh sé ábalta é a leanúint.

'Cá has a dtáinig an boc sin?' ar seisean lena mhnaoi.

'Níl a fhios agam,' ar sise, 'ach tá ort an tinidh a choigilt an uile oíche go ceann bliana.'

'Níl bréag agat,' arsa an táilliúir.

Is fada an táilliúir agus a bhean ar shlua na marbh ach instear an scéal seo i dTír Chonaill go fóill agus is iomaí duine a dúirt le linn é a chluinstin gurbh aoibhinn do na daoine a tháinig romhainn agus an bheatha shimplí a chleacht siad.

NÓTA: *Derry People and Tirconaill News* (17/11/1934, 6 agus 24/11/1934, 6).

An Solas Nua-Aimseartha

Bhí baintreach ina cónaí i gContae Dhoire seal blianta ó shin agus bhí mac aici arbh ainm dó Séamas. Bhí deartháir aici ina dhochtúir i mBaile Átha Cliath agus ba ghnách leis seachtain dá chuid laetha saoire a chaitheamh an uile shamhradh i dteach na baintrí. Bhí aird mhór ag an dochtúir ar Shéamas agus bliain amháin, nuair a bhí sé ag pilleadh go Baile Átha Cliath, d'iarr sé ar an bhaintreach cead a thabhairt do Shéamas a theacht leis.

'Díolfaidh mé a bhealach ar ais go dtí an doras,' ar seisean.

Shásaigh an réiteach seo an bhaintreach go mór agus níor lú ná sin an lúcháir a bhí ar Shéamas cead a fháil cuairt a thabhairt ar phríomhchathair na hÉireann. Ní raibh Séamas taobh amuigh den pharóiste inar tógadh é riamh agus, ar ndóiche, ní raibh aon rud dá bhfaca sé nár chuir iontas air. Bhí sé ag ceistniú an dochtúra, an uile bhomaite beagnach, fá gach aon rud nár thuig sé, agus ba mhór sin. Rinne an dochtúir a dhícheall gach rud a mhíniú.

An chéad oíche a chaith Séamas ins an chathair ní theachaigh sé a luí go dtí an meán oíche. Bí solas tintreach i dteach an dochtúra agus sin rud nach bhfaca Séamas le linn a shaoil go dtí an oíche sin. Sula dteachaigh sé a chodladh chaith sé tamall maith ag scrúdú an lampa thintrigh a bhí i seomra na leapa agus, fá dheireadh, d'fhéach sé an solas a chur as. Níor éirigh leis agus bhí an solas sa tseomra go maidin.

Ag deireadh na seachtaine tháinig Séamas abhaile agus ní raibh buachaill óg fá chúig mhíle de theach na baintrí nach raibh láithreach le fáilte a chur roimhe agus cuntas a fháil ar na hiontais a bhí le feiceáil sa phríomhchathair. Ní raibh an bhaintreach féin i mBaile Átha Cliath riamh agus chuir sí níos mó ceisteanna ar Shéamas ná duine ar bith de na buachaillí.

'hObair domh dearmad a dhéanamh,' arsa Séamas fá dheireadh, 'trácht a dhéanamh ar an chineál solais atá acu.'

'An bhfuil sé an-mhaith nó an-olc?' arsa fear de na stócaigh.

'Bhí an solas maith go leor,' arsa Séamas, 'ach ní chuirfeadh an diabhal é féin as é. Bhí sé ag dódh go maidin agus féadaim a rá nár chodail mé uair amháin ó d'fhág mé an baile.'

'A Shéamais, a stór,' arsa an bhaintreach, 'cad chuige nár shéid tú as é?'

'Cad é an dóigh a dtiocfadh liom é a shéideadh amach,' arsa Séamas, 'nuair a bhí sé istigh i mbuidéal acu?'

NÓTA: *Derry People and Tirconaill News* (1/12/1934, 8).

AN STILEOIR AGUS AN SÁIRSINT

Fá thuairim ceithre scór bliain ó shin, nó mar sin, bhí fear ina chónaí i mBaile na Mónadh arbh ainm dó Diarmaid Ó Baoill. Bhí feirm bheag talaimh aige ach chaith sé mórán dá chuid ama ag déanamh poitín. Fán am a thoisíos an scéal foscladh beairic in Ard an Rátha agus tháinig seachtar de na saighdiúirí dubha chun na beairice, sáirsint os a gcionn. Fear breá, macánta a bhí sa tsáirsint ach bhí sé anuas go trom ar lucht déanta poitín. Ba ghairid, ar ndóiche, go bhfuair sé aithne ar Dhiarmaid agus gí go raibh sé go hanmhór leis bhí a intinn déanta suas aige deireadh a chur le déanamh poitín sa pharóiste. Bhí a sháith tuairisce aige go raibh Diarmaid i bhfostó go trom leis an obair seo agus, oíche amháin, tamall i ndiaidh an mheán oíche, thug sé féin agus fear de na *peelers* ruaig go teach Dhiarmada. Nuair a chonaic siad solas ins an teach chomh mall sin san oíche bhí siad cinnte go raibh an stileoir i gceann oibre. Oíche shamhraidh a bhí ann agus mar bhí doras na cisteanaí foscailte shiúil siad isteach go faichilleach. Bhí Diarmaid ina shuí ag cois na tineadh ag caitheamh a phíopa.

'Céad fáilte romhaibh,' ar seisean. 'Nach mall atá sibh amuigh?'

'Níl neart air,' arsa an sáirsint. 'An dtig leat braon a thabhairt dúinn?'

'Ní minic a bhím gan é,' arsa Diarmaid, 'ach ní bheidh sé réidh go deireadh na seachtaine.'

Thoisigh an triúr ag gáirí.

Lá arna mhárach bhí Diarmaid ins an bhaile mhór agus casadh an sáirsint air.

'Ba mhaith liom a rá leat,' arsa an sáirsint, 'nach bhfuil dúil ar bith agamsa cineál ar bith trioblóide a thabhairt duit ach tá sé chomh maith agat gnoithe an phoitín a thabhairt suas ó seo amach. Ní bheidh tú ábalta aon deor de a dhíol ar an bhaile seo feasta, agus, má bheirtear ort, beidh an cháin chomh trom is go gcuirfidh sí ó theach is ó thinidh thú.'

'Cuirfidh mé geall leat,' arsa Diarmaid, 'má gheallann tú cothrom na Féinne a thabhairt domh.'

'Cad é do gheall?' arsa an sáirsint.

'Cuirfidh mé punta leat go dtabharfaidh mé bairille poitín fríd an bhaile mhór seo agus thart ag doras na beairice, ar sholas lae, seachtain ó inniu.'

'Bíodh ina mhargadh,' arsa an sáirsint. 'Má éiríonn leat ní bheidh bris ar bith ort lena linn.'

Tháinig Diarmaid abhaile ach ní raibh a fhios aige cad é an dóigh faoin ghréin a dtiocfadh leis an geall a bhaint. D'aithin sé go maith go raibh an sáirsint ina fhear uasal agus go dtiocfadh leis taobhú lena fhocal, agus bhí a fhios aige mar an gcéanna go scabfadh na *peelers* an uile lód mónadh a thiocfadh isteach go hArd an Rátha an tseachtain sin ar siocair gur chuala siad gurbh iomaí braon a thug Diarmaid isteach ar an nós sin.

Tharla go raibh seanbhean tinn i mBaile na Mónadh fán am seo agus fuair an créatúir bocht bás cupla lá ina dhiaidh sin. Bhí intinn Dhiarmada déanta suas i mbomaite. Chuaigh sé fhad le mac na mná a bhí marbh agus d'inis an scéal go hiomlán. D'fhág an péire teach na faire agus tháinig siad go teach Dhiarmada. D'ól siad leathphionta poitín eatarthu agus rinne siad réiteach an bairille a chur sa chónair ag an deich a chlog maidin lá arna mhárach agus é a thabhairt go dtí an reilig in Ard an Rátha. Cuireadh scéala amach go mbeadh an tórramh ag an trí a chlog tráthnóna mar gheall ar na daoine a choinneáil ar shiúl go dtí an t-am sin.

Bhí go maith agus ní raibh go holc.

Maidin lá an tórraimh fuarthas seanghearrán agus trucail. Cuireadh an chónair, bairille beag poitín istigh inti, ar an trucail agus shiúil Diarmaid agus mac na mná éagtha i dtoiseach, duisín nó mar sin de bhuachaillí óga na háite ag siúl ina ndiaidh. Nuair a tháinig siad go ceann an bhaile mhóir bhí an sáirsint ina sheasamh ar an tsráid. Nuair a tháinig an tórramh comhgarach, bhain sé de a bhearád agus dúirt paidir mar is gnách agus ansin shiúil sé le lucht an tórraimh go dtí an reilig ag an cheann eile den bhaile. Bhí an uaigh déanta agus fágadh síos an chónair ar an bhruach.

'Caithfimid fanacht leis an tsagart,' arsa Diarmaid, agus, leis sin, shiúil sé anuas agus rinne croitheadh láimhe leis an tsáirsint.

'Tá eagla orm,' arsa an sáirsint, 'go bhfuil do gheall caillte agat. Seo an lá deireanach agus ní bheidh mórán ama agat nuair a bheas an t-adhlacadh seo thart.'

Bhí a fhios ag na buachaillí cad é a bhí sa chónair agus scab siad thall agus abhus.

'Rachaimid suas fhad leis an uaigh,' arsa Diarmaid leis an tsáirsint. 'Tím,' ar seisean go dteachaigh mac na mná atá le hadhlacadh ar lorg an tsagairt agus táimid linn féin.'

'Cluinim go raibh aois mhór ag an mhnaoi seo,' arsa an sáirsint.

'Thig leat í a fheiceáil má tá dúil agat ann,' arsa Diarmaid ag tógáil chlár na cónaire.

'Is tú an rógaire is mó ar thalamh na hÉireann,' arsa an sáirsint nuair a chonaic sé an bairille sa chónair. 'Ach bhain tú do gheall.'

Cuireadh an chónair ar an trucail arís agus tháinig lucht an tórraimh abhaile go Baile na Mónadh. Cuireadh an bhean ag an trí a chlog tráthnóna agus tháinig an sáirsint leis féin go teach Dhiarmada an oíche sin. Dhiúltaigh Diarmaid an punta a ghlacadh ach d'ól an péire buidéal poitín agus, sular scar siad, gheall Diarmaid nach ndéanfadh sé deor eile poitín le linn a shaoil.

Agus choinnigh sé a fhocal.

NÓTA: *Derry People and Tirconaill News* (8/12/1934, 8 agus 15/12/1934, 8).

Scéilíní

An tAsal

Tráthnóna Dé Sathairn seo a chuaigh thart thug mé turas go hArdachadh (Ómeith) agus chaith mé tamall pléisiúrtha ag mo dhuine muintearach Pádraig Mac an Bhaird. Bhí sé d'fhiacha orm a theacht go hIúr Cinn Trá ar an traein an oíche sin agus d'fhág mé slán ag Pádraig agus shiúil mé liom go tapaidh ag tarraingt ar an stáisiún. Bhí seanbhean ag tiomáint asail agus ag teacht go dtí an stáisiún fosta. Dar ndóigh labhair mé léi agus ní bréag é bhí Gaeilig bhreá bhlasta aici.

'Nach fliuch an tráthnóna é?' ar sí.

'Sea, go deimhin,' arsa mise.

'Buíochas le Dia,' ar sí, 'bhí aimsir bhreá againn le seachtain – *Go on,*' ar sise leis an asal.

'An i mBéarla is gnách leat an t-asal a thiomáint?' arsa mise.

'Sea, maise,' ar sí, 'de bhrí nár fhoghlaim sé an Ghaeilig nuair a bhí sé óg & ní shiúlfadh sé coiscéim amháin anois mura gcluinfeadh sé an '*Go on*' sin.'

'Dona go leor,' arsa mise & mé ag gáirí.

'Cé acu is fearr leat labhairt i nGaeilig nó i mBéarla?' ar sí.

'Is fearr liom labhairt i nGaeilig,' arsa mise.

'Och, faraor,' ar sí ag tabhairt buille de bhata ar an asal, 'tá barraíocht de na daoine ar chiall an asail anois; níl meas ná aird acu ar an Ghaeilig siúd is go bhfuil na daoine óga thart fá seo ag fáil sampla maith ón tsagart agus óna dteagascóirí.'

'Tá a fhios agam go bhfuil,' arsa mise, 'agus ní féidir go mbeidh siad ar chiall an asail i gcónaí. Beannacht Dé leat.'

'Beannacht Dé is Mhuire leat,' ar sí, 'agus go dté tú slán abhaile.'

ACS, 9/8/1902, 369.

Beirt Fhear ag Tarraingt ar an Fheis in Ard an Rátha Lá Fhéile Muire

SÉAMAS: Céad fáilte romhat, a Bhriain. Cad é mar atá tú?

BRIAN: Níl éagaoint agam, buíochas do Dhia.

S: Nach moch ar maidin atá tú ar do chois, beannú ort?

B: Sea, mhaise, go dearfa agus tím nach bhfuil tusa tú féin 'do chodladh.

S: Chan fhuilim, a Bhriain. Tá mé ag gabháil ar aistear inniu a thaitineas liom go maith. Creidim gur chuala tú go raibh feis le bheith in Ard an Rátha inniu, agus nuair a bheas an tAifreann thart tá mé ag dréim, le cuidiú Dé, an chuid eile den lá a chaitheamh ansin.

B: Tá mé amhlaidh, a Shéamais, má bhím beo, slán agus tá lúcháir orm go bhfuil muid ag fáil lá mar seo fána choinne. Nuair a d'éirigh mé ag a cúig a chlog agus d'amharc mé amach, chuirfeadh aoibhneas na maidine áthas ar do chroí. Bhí spéir ghormdhearg os cionn na gCealla Beaga agus shílfeá go raibh Cnoc na Binne Báine le thinidh, bhí sé chomh dearg sin le lonradh na gréine. Dearbhaim duit nach bhfuil cuimhne agam ar aon mhaidin dá bhfaca mé riamh a bhí níos áille ná maidin inniu.

S: Char éirigh mise chomh luath sin. Is cuimhin liom go raibh mé ag cur mo bhróga orm nuair a bhuail sé an sé. Ach, i dtaobh na feise, is dóigh liom go mbeidh cruinniú iontach againn inniu.

B: Is cinnte go mbeidh de bhrí go bhfuil muintir na Carraige agus Ghleann Cholm Cille ag teacht ina gcéadtaí agus chuala mé fosta –.

S: Gabhaim pardún agat, a Bhriain, ach nach breá an mhuc í sin atá ag feirm Pháidí Bháin i mbliana?

B: Is breá, maise, rathúnas uirthi. Tá cosúlacht uirthi go bhfuair sí a cuid.

S: Inis leat, a Bhriain.

B: Bhí mé ag rá go raibh go leor daoine ag teacht ó na Gleanntaí agus thart timpeall Íochtar Tíre gí go bhfuil a lán seoiníneachta agus Galldachais ansin go fóill.

S: Ná bac leis, a Bhriain. Is gairid go dté lasair na Gaeilge fhad leo.

B: B'fhurast le Dia sin. Chan fhuil blas ná meas ar ár dtír ó thoisigh an Ghaeilig ag fáil bháis agus ní bheidh nó go raibh sí le cluinstin arís ar fud na tíre.

S: Tá tú ceart ansin agus, ar an ábhar sin is mian liomsa – 'mo sheanduine mar atá mé – mo dhícheall a dhéanamh inniu le misneach agus buíochas a thabhairt do lucht stiúrtha na feise.

B: Is trua liom nach bhfuil go leor de do chineál sa tír, a Shéamais, ach níl eagla orm nach bhfosclóidh an lá inniu súile na ndaoine a thiocfas go hArd an Rátha. An bhfuil tú istigh ar cheann ar bith de na comórtais?

S: Tá. Is é mo bharúil gur cuireadh síos m'ainm ar son scéalaíochta.

B: Is maith liom sin agus, leoga, beidh lúcháir ar na buachaillí go huile tú a fheiceáil ansin.

ACS, 6/9/1902, 440.

Más iarracht a bhí anseo le canúint Thír Chonaill a thaispeáint, bheadh na léitheoirí meallta go mór óir ní raibh blas Ghaeilge Thír Chonaill ar an phíosa. Tharla sin go minic sna chéad bhlianta den Athbheochan le saothar na gConallach, bíodh an locht ar na húdair féin nó ar na heagarthóirí. Tá leasú Conallach déanta agam ar an téacs.

Idir Lifear agus an Srath Bán

Níl lá le ráithe nár smaoinigh mé ar litir bheag a scríobh chugat i dtaobh na hoibre atá á dhéanamh san áit seo ar son na teanga; ach go dearfa ní i gcónaí is féidir liom mórán tuairisce a thabhairt do dhuine ar bith taobh amuigh den cheantar ina bhfuil mé ag obair san am i láthair. Ach ceapaim go bhfuil tú ag fáil cuntais go coitianta as páipéir Dhoire & go mba cheart domh gan mórán de do chuid ama a thógáil á léamh athuair. Is dóigh liom ina dhiaidh sin nár chuala tú go raibh cuid de na cailíní thart fá seo ábalta litreacha grá a scríobh i nGaeilig siúd is nach bhfuil siad bliain go leith ag foghlaim na teanga go fóill. Tráthnóna Dé Sathairn seo a chuaigh tharainn casadh buachaill orm ar an bhealach atá idir Lifear agus an Srath Bán.

'Maise,' ar seisean i mBéarla, 'tá lúcháir orm do chastáil orm mar fuair mé litir maidin inniu atá scríofa i nGaeilig & níl a fhios agam faoin ghréin cad é atá inti.'

Shín sé litir ionsorm & léigh mé í go lúcháireach mar a leanas:

'A Shéamais, a ghrá, cad é a tháinig ort le gur fhan tú ón choirm cheoil aréir? Bhí mé ag dréim ar tú a fheiceáil. Ba mhaith le mo mháthair dá dtiocfá anuas Dé Domhnaigh chun tí s'againne ar cuairt agus tae a bheith agat anseo ag a sé a chlog tráthnóna. Bíodh an fhidil leat & beidh damhsa againn i ndiaidh na hoíche. Go deimhin is fada liom go bhfeicfidh mé thú. Mise, do chara fíor, Máire.'

Nuair a chuir mé Béarla ar an litir do Shéamas bhí sé chomh sásta le páiste a gheobhadh brúitín.

'Coinnigh do rún,' ar sé, 'agus is gairid go gcluinfidh tú tuilleadh.'

Agus chuala mé ó shin go raibh Séamas & an fhidil i dteach Bhriain an oíche sin, agus go bhfuil sé féin & Máire le pósadh i gceann seachtaine. Go dtuga Dia saol fada sona don bheirt.

Mise, Brian Ó Cianaigh

Tuilleadh – Féadann tú an litir seo a chur isteach sa *Claidheamh* & b'fhéidir go bhfeicfeadh Máire inteacht eile í & go ndéanfadh sí mar an gcéanna. Is iomaí Séamas díomhaoin inniu a bheadh pósta le fada dá bhfaigheadh sé cuireadh tráthnóna a chaitheamh ag ól tae ó mhná a bhfuil níonacha le spáráil acu. B. Ó C.

ACS, 31/1/1903, 782.

An Fhidil

Chuaigh Éamann Ó Caiside a chuartaíocht go teach Pheadair Mhóir oíche amháin. Bhí Peadar ina shuí cois na tineadh ag seinm ar fhidil nuair a chuaigh sé isteach & bhí Máire (bean Pheadair) ag sníomh go dithniseach.

'Ná bac liomsa,' arsa Éamann, 'lean den fhidil nó go dearfa is maith liom í a chluinstin.'

Sheinn Peadar leis go ceann leathuaire nó mar sin agus fá dheireadh labhair Máire amach.

'Cad é do bharúil de Pheadar,' ar sise ag tabhairt a haghaidh ar Éamann, 'a rinne an fhidil sin amach as a cheann féin?'

Éamann (ag amharc ar Pheadar): 'Níl iontas ar bith liom ann, a Mháire, & tím gur fhág sé go leor ina dhiaidh le ceann eile a dhéanamh.

ACS, 14/2/1903, 10.

DHÁ SHEANDUINE I DTÍR CHONAILL
COMHRÁ AR CHÚIS NA TALÚN

(Buaileann SEÁN Ó BRÓGÁIN trasna na sráide mar gheall ar tamall cainte a dhéanamh le PÁDRAIG MAC AODHA. Tá PÁDRAIG ina shuí ar bhairille taobh amuigh den doras agus é ag léamh páipéir).

PÁDRAIG: Bhail, a Sheáin, cad é mar atá do chorpán inniu?

SEÁN: Go measartha, buíochas do Dhia.

PÁDRAIG: Is mór an gar an mheasarthacht féin. Is iomaí fear níos óige ná ceachtar againn ina luí san uaigh.

SEÁN: Och, och, is fíor do phort, a mhic. Inné féin go díreach bhí mé ag smaoineamh ar an ármhach atá déanta ag an bhás ar an bhaile seo le sé nó seacht de bhlianta.

PÁDRAIG (*ag éirí greannmhar*): B'fhéidir nárbh fhearr beo a leath.

SEÁN: Ó bubú, a Phádraig, ná habair sin. Tá na páipéir seo do do chur chun siobarnaí. Ach cad é fán Bhille Úr?

PÁDRAIG: Dhiabhal a fhios ag duine cad é is cóir a rá ina thaobh. Is é mo bharúil go rachaidh sé chun tosaigh ach ar siocair go bhfuilthear ag cur leis agus ag baint de, is deacair a rá go fóill cad é an mhaitheas a bheas ann don tír.

SEÁN: Ba mhaith liom féin deireadh a bheith leis na tiarnaí nó is minic a bhí –.

PÁDRAIG: Fan go fóill, a Sheáin. Dearc ar an cheist mar seo. Má thógtar an Bille an iarracht seo féin, nach bhfuil a fhios agat go mbeidh tú ag díol cíosa mar atá tú anois go dtí ag an Rí atá a fhios cén uair?

SEÁN: Tá a fhios agam sin ach nach mbeidh na tiarnaí díbrithe i gcás ar bith?

PÁDRAIG: Beidh gan amhras ach nárbh fhearr go mór bliain nó beirt eile a chur suas leo (na tiarnaí) nó go bhfaighfí margadh níos fearr a dhéanamh agus ansin iad a dhíbirt? Síleann daoine nach bhfuil acu le déanamh sa tír seo ach deireadh a chur le tiarnaí agus go mbeidh siad ar dhroim na muice go brách. Ach deirimse go bhfuil muid ag cailleadh níos mó ar dhóigheanna eile. Dearc ar an aos óg ag gabháil chun Aifrinn Dé Domhnaigh. Níl snáithe ar a gcraiceann nach bhfuil déanta i dtíortha eile nuair ba cheart iad a bheith déanta sa bhaile. Rinneadh na bróga atá ortsa i Sasain.

SEÁN: Tá tú bréagach.

PÁDRAIG: Gabhaim pardún agat más ea. Shíl mé gurbh iad do bhróga Domhnaigh a bhí ort.

SEÁN: Ná cuir aird ar mo bhróga, le do thoil, ach léigh giota domh fán Bhille.

(Léann PÁDRAIG óráid de chuid SHEÁIN RÉAMANN ansin agus gan mhoill ina dhiaidh téann SEÁN abhaile go sásta suaimhneach).

ACS, 30/5/1903, 1.

Brian Ó Cianaigh, Lifear, Co. Dhún na nGall.

I bPurgadóir ar an tSaol Seo

Cuireadh cumann conspóide ar bun i mbaile bheag ghallda in íochtar Chontae Dhún na nGall geimhreadh amháin fá thuairim deich mbliana ó shin. Ba ghnách le gach comhalta tamall cainte a dhéanamh ar an uile cheist a bhíodh ceaptha le pléideáil agus gí go raibh lán níos mó fear sa Chumann ná a bhí de mhná, ba rómhinic a buaileadh na fir bhochta san iomarbhá. Aon oíche amháin bhí bean ag caint go cumasach ar an anás a chaithfeadh a bheith i dteach ar bith a bhí gan mhnaoi. 'Má ta aon fhear i láthair,' ar sí, 'a chaithfeas éirí ar maidin agus tinidh a chur síos agus a bhfuil aige lena bhricfeasta féin a chomóradh, éiríodh sé anois agus abradh sé nach bhfuil sé i bpurgadóir ar an tsaol seo.' Le linn na cainte seo d'éirigh fear caol, ard ina sheasamh i gcoirnéal amháin den teach ach, má d'éirigh, ní tháinig focal as a bhéal. Shuigh an bhean síos agus dhearc gach duine ar an té a bhí ina sheasamh. Ba é fear na mná a bhí ag caint a d'éirigh.

ACS, 6/6/1903, 3.

Tá an scéilín seo sa cholún sin a bhfuil Giotaí mar theideal air.

Dóigh Úr le Breith ar Ghadaí

Bhí fear ina chónaí i mBaile an Droichid fá thuairim fiche bliain ó shin agus ní raibh aige ach mac amháin. Gasúr simplí gan urchóid a bhí sa mhac agus bhíodh eagla mhór air roimh an tsagart paróiste. Tharla sé go raibh an sagart ag teacht ag éisteacht (faoistin) lá go teach a athara agus nuair a chonaic an gasúr ag teacht é chuaigh sé i bhfolach faoi leabaidh i gceann de na seomraí. Thoisigh an sagart ag éisteacht ag taobh na leapa seo. Nuair a bhí deireadh thart chonaic an t-athair an mac sa chisteanach agus d'fhiafraigh sé de cá raibh sé ó mhaidin.

'Ná lig ort, a athair,' ar seisean, 'is í Máire Mhór atá ag goid na n-uibheach uainn.'

ACS, 29/8/1903, 3.

Tá an scéilín seo sa cholún sin a bhfuil *Giotaí* mar theideal air.

An Comhrá Deireanach

Bhí buachaill agus cailín ag suirí le chéile fada ó shin. Thigeadh an buachaill an uile oíche ag amharc uirthi. B'fhearr leis an chailín buachaill eile nach dtigeadh ach go hannamh. Oíche amháin nuair a tháinig an fear a thigeadh go minic, dúirt sí:

Céad fáilte romhat, a mhinic a thig,
Is mairg nach é an mhinic nach dtig
A thigeas chomh minic le minic a thig.

Dúirt an buachaill:

Cuir fáilte roimh an mhinic nach dtig,
Mar is cinnte nach bhfilleann an mhinic a thig –
Taradh nó fanadh an mhinic nach dtig!

D'imigh sé ansin agus níor tháinig sé ar ais ní ba mhó.

ACS, 5/9/1903, 3.
Tá an scéilín seo sa cholún sin a bhfuil *Giotaí* mar theideal air.

In Loving Memory
Of
BRIAN O'KEENEY, Loughros Point.
Died 16th March 1943
His Wife JOSEPHINE
Died 9th June 1978
Their Son VINCENT
Died 21st April 1930
Their Daughters
MAUREEN
Died 18th June 1940
BRIDIE
Died 3rd February 2015
KATHLEEN
Died 21st December 2019

Rest In Peace

O'KEENEY

We hold you all within
our hearts
And there you shall remain
To walk with us throughout
our lives
Until we meet again